Computer Software: Legal Protection in the United Kingdom
Second Edition

AUSTRALIA
The Law Book Company Ltd
Sydney : Brisbane : Melbourne : Perth

CANADA
The Carswell Company Ltd
Agincourt, Ontario

INDIA
N.M. Tripathi Private Ltd
Calcutta and Delhi
and
M.P.P. House
Bangalore
and
Universal Book Traders
New Delhi

ISRAEL
Steimatzky's Agency Ltd
Jerusalem : Tel Aviv : Haifa

PAKISTAN
Pakistan Law House
Karachi

Computer Software: Legal Protection in the United Kingdom

Second Edition

Henry Carr

Richard Arnold

Barristers

Sweet & Maxwell

1992

Published in 1992 by
Sweet & Maxwell of
183 Marsh Wall, London E14 9FT
Typeset by Advance Typesetting Ltd, Oxford
Printed in Great Britain by Short Run Press, Exeter

ISBN 0 421 44380 4

Contents

8 Contracts

9 Remedies

Preface to the Second Edition

Although it is only five years since the first edition of this book, such has been the quantity of new legislation and, to a lesser extent, judicial decisions, that the new edition has had to be substantially rewritten.

Principal among the changes is the enactment of Part I of the Copyright, Designs and Patents Act 1988 as successor to the Copyright Act 1956. The 1956 Act, which was passed at the beginning of the computer era, made no reference to computers or computer programs whatsoever. Not until the passage of the Copyright (Computer Software) Amendment Act 1985 was specific statutory provision made, and then only by a limited amendment to the 1956 Act. The 1988 Act, on the other hand, is the first attempt in the United Kingdom to draft a copyright statute for the computer age. Specific reference to computers is made at numerous points in the Act, and some significant changes in the law have been made. In consequence Chapters 4 and 5 have been completely revised. In addition to a detailed consideration of the new statutory provisions, the implications of such important decisions of the courts as *Interlego, Johnstone Safety* and *M. S. Associates* to the protection of computer software are considered. Particular attention has been paid to the question of non-textual copying of software ('structure, sequence and organisation' and 'look and feel').

At the time that the first edition was written the semiconductor topography right was only a gleam in the European Commission's eye. Since then this *sui generis* right has come and gone, to be replaced with a modified version of the new design right created by Part III of the 1988 Act. Chapter 6 now concentrates upon a discussion of this new form of protection which is likely to be of increasing importance with the trend towards hardwiring of software. In addition there is a revised treatment of the subject of copyright in screen displays, as distinct from copyright in the underlying program.

The other principal legislative change is the arrival of the Computer Misuse Act 1990. Although this is primarily aimed at curtailing activities which affect the operation of computer systems, it does also afford useful protection to computer software. Although this is slightly tangential to the main thrust of the book, we feel that it is of sufficient importance to merit inclusion as a new Chapter 10.

Judicial decisions affecting computer software are in many fields surprising by their absence. Furthermore, such decisions as are handed down are frequently unreported or are not reported in the mainstream law reports. Nevertheless, the question of the patentability of computer programs has received significant attention both from the European Patent Office (EPO), in cases such as *VICOM/Computer-related invention* and a number of decisions concerning applications by IBM, and from the Court of Appeal, in *Merrill Lynch's Application* and *Gale's Application*. In consequence Chapter 7 has been entirely rewritten.

Another area that has been the subject of extensive judicial attention is that of confidential information, although few of the many recent cases on this topic have been concerned with computer software. The *Spycatcher* case in particular, although arguably a case on its own special facts, is the first recent case on confidential information to reach the House of Lords, and contains discussion of some fundamental issues. This has caused extensive revision of Chapter 3. In addition, in the light of the many recent cases concerning the confidentiality obligations of ex-employees, and in particular the decision of the Court of Appeal in *Faccenda Chicken Ltd v Fowler*, the discussion of this topic has been expanded and moved from Chapter 8 to Chapter 3.

The area of contractual protection has received relatively little attention from either the legislature or the courts, despite the fact that litigation over computer contracts has been a growth area over the last four years. There has been increasing academic debate in this area, however, notably over the vexed question of whether the supply of computer software constitutes a supply of goods or a supply of services, although the decision of the Court of Appeal in *Saphena v Allied Collection Agencies* has perhaps reduced the practical importance of the distinction. Chapter 8 has been both revised and significantly expanded to provide coverage of software supply, maintenance and escrow agreements in addition to software licences.

Although the primary focus of the book is on domestic law, the impact of European law and institutions on the protection of software has greatly increased. In addition to the stream of authority on patentability from the EPO, European Community competition law has steadily grown in importance and so is given an expanded treatment. Most significantly, the Council of the European Community has, after intense lobbying by interested parties and debate among commentators, issued a Directive on the protection of computer software. This will require amendments to United Kingdom law by 1 January 1993. It remains to be seen how these will be implemented, and exactly how far the amendments will go. The authors express the hope that, to avoid confusion, the Government will effect the necessary changes to the 1988 Act by an amending Act, and not (as has been done with semiconductor topography design rights) by statutory instrument. In the meantime, a brief commentary on the Directive has been included in Chapter 2.

A consequence of all these changes is that this edition is the work of two pairs of hands rather than one. Richard Arnold has contributed Chapters 3, 6, 7, 8 and 10 of the new edition, but both of us take responsibility for the entire text. A further consequence is that the text is, regrettably, considerably longer than that of the first edition. In order to keep the book to a manageable length, we have reluctantly taken the decision to confine the appendices to the statutory material which we believe that readers will find most useful.

Given the changes in authorship and content, we feel that is worth briefly restating the objective of the book. That is to provide an introduction to the principal legal mechanisms by which computer software may be protected from unauthorised use, plagiarism and damage in the United Kingdom. This is not a book on 'computer law', an interdisciplinary subject which has been created by academics and is perhaps starting to become a recognised professional specialisation. Texts on computer law necessarily contain a rather wider coverage than just the means of protecting computer software. Nor is this book a treatise on each and every legal mechanism that may conceivably be employed in a case involving computer software. In a case of software 'piracy' (the counterfeiting of published software), many different rights may be infringed. For example, the copyright in the packaging of the artwork or the trade marks under which the software is marketed may be infringed. These raise no issues which are peculiar to computers or computer software, however. Instead the book concentrates upon the legal issues which are specific to the protection of software, such as literary copyright in computer programs, semiconductor topographies, the patentability of software and so on. The authors' aim is to assist producers of computer software and their legal advisers in safeguarding the substantial investment in time, effort and money that software represents.

We have endeavoured to state the law as at 1 October 1991.

We would both like to express our gratitude to our publishers for tolerating our delays; to Amanda Tipples for checking the proofs; and above all, to our wives, Jan Dawson and Mary Elford, for their support.

Henry Carr
Richard Arnold
Gray's Inn
London
May 1992

Table of United Kingdom Cases

Table of Cases from Other Jurisdictions

Table of Cases in the European Court of Justice, Court of First Instance and Commission

Table of European Patent Office Decisions

Table of United Kingdom Statutes

Table of United Kingdom Statutory Instruments

Table of Statutory Material from Other Jurisdictions

Table of EEC Regulations, Directives and Notices

Table of Treaties and Conventions

1 The Nature of a Computer Program

1.1 DEFINITION

A program has been described in a variety of ways, as a particular expression of an idea set out in the flow chart, as an instruction manual for humans in machine readable form, as a process for controlling a result in a computer, as the completion of an incomplete machine, and as an accessory used in computing or data processing systems. The *Penguin Computing Book*[1] offers a definition which lays stress on the human element of skill and discretion which is required in the development of computer software. A computer program is stated to be:[2] 'Man's interpretation of the actual or potential activities of a computer system, in terms of arithmetic logic and control operations (or combinations of these in a higher level).'

The Australian Federal Court in the case of *Apple Computer Inc. & Another v Computer Edge Pty Ltd & Suss*[3] preferred a more functional description:[4] 'A program is a concise set of instructions that directs the computer to do the tasks required of it step by step and to produce the desired result.'

The accuracy of these definitions may be assessed against a technical description of the operation and development of a computer program.[5]

1.2 OPERATION

A program is executed by the central processing unit (CPU) of the computer, which is the centre of control for arithmetical and logic operations within the microprocessor. The CPU consists of an arrangement of electronic circuits which are activated by impulses of electric

---

1 Susan Curran and Ray Curnow. Published simultaneously by Allen Lane and Penguin Books 1983.
2 *Ibid.* at 139.
3 [1984] FSR 481.
4 *Ibid. per* Lockhart J at 509.
5 For other useful descriptions of computer programs see 11 Hofstra LR 329 (1982); 96 Harvard LR 1723 (1983).

current. A logic gate within the CPU is either turned on or off depending on the presence or absence of such pulses.

The presence or absence of pulses of current is represented by binary digits ('bits'). The CPU recognises '1' as indicative of the presence of a pulse, and '0' as indicative of its absence.

A computer program is a series of bits, each bit representing the presence or absence of a pulse. The program operates within the CPU as a series of pulses in a prearranged sequence in accordance with the order of bits devised by the computer programmer. Accordingly, the 'instructions' of a computer program represent a series of impulses which operate within the computer to make the machine perform certain predefined functions.

Each instruction is held in a memory location within the computer, which has an address, by which the location may be identified. The addresses of the memory locations in which program instructions are to be found are held in the program counter. The CPU locates the address of each instruction of the program, accesses it from the memory location, from where it is reproduced and executed in the instructions register. The program counter may contain a 'jump' instruction, which makes the CPU jump beyond the next instruction in sequential order in the software, to access and execute a subroutine.

1.3 DEVELOPMENT

In order to write a program, it is necessary to define the sequence of logic which it is intended that the machine should execute. The programmer develops a skeleton of such sequential logic operations, bearing in mind the problem to be solved, the requirements of the language in which the program is to be written, and the capabilities of the hardware in which the program is intended to operate. This skeleton is known as the 'algorithm', and is the plan or concept of the program.

A more developed form of the logic of the program may then be produced, known as a 'flow chart'. A flow chart is a schematic representation of the problem to be solved, graphically presenting the steps involved in its solution.

It would then be possible to write a program in accordance with the algorithm and flow charts as a series of binary digits, which would be machine readable. Such a series of bits is known as 'object code'. However, since each program instruction represents a large number of bits, it would be a laborious and time-consuming process to write directly in object code. Accordingly a variety of languages has been devised, the expressions of which represent a predefined sequence of bits. These languages, which are essentially 'shorthand' for object code, are human readable, as opposed to machine readable. Programming languages are said to be low level if they are machine readable, or close to machine readable. The nearer a language is to ordinary English, the higher its level.

One method of shortening binary expressions is by employing a numerical system with a base of 16. This is known as hexadecimal notation, and consists of letters and numbers which represent a series of bits. Frequently a program may be written in hexadecimal code, which is regarded as low level machine readable language.

A higher level of computer languages, where bits are represented in a predetermined pattern by a series of mnemonic codes, is known as assembly language. The highest level languages are known as source code, where command words may represent a lengthy sequence of bits. For example, the expression 'GO TO' in BASIC is directly translatable into a series of binary digits, but in its command form is comprehensible to human beings.

High level assembly and source code cannot be understood by the CPU. Accordingly, they must be translated from high level to low level language – from source to object code. This process of translation is performed automatically by a program known as an assembler or compiler, which is normally stored within the CPU and which converts human readable language to a series of binary digits. Object code assembled from source code therefore contains the same sequence of binary digits that were expressed by the programmer in 'shorthand', high level language. That sequence is transliterated into a different medium, and operates within the CPU as a stream of pulses.

1.4 CLASSIFICATION OF SOFTWARE

Programs are loosely classified within the computer industry as 'applications' programs or 'operating' programs.[6] An applications program is the most familiar form of computer software, which makes a microprocessor perform a specific task. For example, an applications program such as *Wordstar* turns a computer into a word processor. *Pac Man* makes it into an audio-visual game. By contrast, an operating program performs a function within the computer as part of the operation of the machine, for example by the execution of an applications program. A compiler program is part of an operating system in that it converts source code to object code.

1.5 STORAGE OF COMPUTER SOFTWARE

In order to be executed within the CPU the program instructions must be loaded into the memory of the computer. Memory media on which

---

6 This distinction has been described as 'rather too arbitrary and not very useful' for copyright purposes. *Apple Computer Inc. & Another v Computer Edge Pty Ltd & Suss* [1984] FSR 481 *per* Fox J at 491. The distinction is not a rigid one since a single program may answer both descriptions.

software is stored may be broadly divided into two categories – read/write memory and read only memory.

As its name implies, a read/write memory has a general purpose in that data and instructions may be written into it and read from it. Data and instructions are not permanently stored in read/write memory, and will be wiped from the memory each time power is turned off from the circuit.

A computer may be used for a variety of applications, depending on the particular program which is loaded into its memory. Accordingly it would frequently be a waste of memory space permanently to retain applications programs in the internal memory of the computer, unless the computer is specifically designed to perform a sole task. Therefore, programs may be stored on external storage media, such as floppy disks, magnetic tape and punched cards. Each external storage device contains object code which may be loaded into the available space in the read/write memory of the computer when it is desired to use the machine for that purpose. Data input by the user when operating the machine in accordance with the specific application is also held in the read/write memory, and may be saved on a separate floppy disk. Such read/write memory is normally referred to as a Random Access Memory (RAM).

By contrast, read only memory (ROM) is a form of memory which cannot be written into by the user, and in which data and instructions are permanently retained for the performance of a specific task. A ROM contains an unchanging sequence of bits which are fixed in the memory during the course of its manufacture and which remain even when the power is turned off in the circuit. Accordingly the data contained in the ROM is not changeable – cannot be written into – and the ROM is usually built into the hardware of the computer. For that reason a computer program held in a ROM is sometimes referred to as 'firmware'.

It is particularly useful to retain certain operating programs in ROMs, since they may be used as part of the operation of the computer in relation to any applications program.

All computers have internal memory capacity. Frequently this is divided up between RAM and ROM memory space. Memory capacity is measured in terms of memory locations. Memory locations are arranged in multiples of 2^{10} (1,024). This number is expressed in computer jargon by the letter 'k'. Accordingly it is common to see memory capacity of a small microprocessor expressed as 48K RAM and 16K ROM. This means that it has an internal read/write memory capacity of $48 \times 1,024$ memory locations, and a read only memory capacity of $16 \times 1,024$ memory locations.

However, the distinction between read/write and read only memories becomes blurred in relation to storage devices known as Programmable Read Only Memory (PROM) and Erasable Programmable Read Only Memory (EPROM). In a PROM, the pattern of memory locations and addresses is fixed during manufacture, but the instructions to be held in those locations are programmed in by the computer user. Similarly, in an EPROM, the user may program data into fixed memory locations, which may be subsequently erased and replaced by other data input.

2 The Ideal Protection – Competing Policy Considerations

2.1 GENERAL AIMS OF LEGAL PROTECTION

The obvious growth potential of the industry means that ideas, rather than capital, are at a premium. And yet at the same time, the misappropriation of ideas in a free competitive market is simple, and inevitable. Just as with all intellectual property, software may be misappropriated in a variety of circumstances. An employee researcher in a software house changes jobs, taking his knowledge of his former employer's projects with him. A company grants another access to its programs in the hope of a joint venture. A software house improves on existing techniques, and wishes to recoup its research and development costs from widespread sales. In all these situations the misappropriation of ideas is considerably cheaper than their independent development.

So the same general aims apply to the legal protection of software as to all intellectual property. Such protection is intended to provide the economic incentive necessary for creativity, and the encouragement necessary for the dissemination of results of such creativity. The point was well put in the American case of *Structural Dynamics v Engineering Mechanics*:

> One is aware of the need that useful knowledge should be disclosed. It may be that in controlled societies, one reason for the apparent lack of development of technology is the restriction on disclosure. But it is also true that some protection favours innovation and that encouragement of a discoverer or developer enhances a basic human motivation for inventiveness.[1]

2.2 SPECIFIC AIMS OF PROTECTION FOR COMPUTER PROGRAMS

These general aims become more specific when considered against opposed interests within the software industry. The multinational producer of hardware and software stands to lose large amounts of profits in

---

1   401 F. Supp 1102 (1975).

the absence of legal remedies, but also has the volume of production to take full advantage of monopoly protection. The small software house needs an economic return on its development costs, but also the opportunity to research without legal restraint. It is in the interest of customers for the costs of software to fall while the industry continues to expand at its present rate.

The tension between competing interests in the software industry is well illustrated by the dispute between Acorn-Soft Computers Limited and the magazine *Personal Computer World*.[2] Acorn-Soft obtained an *ex parte* injunction to restrain sales of an edition of the magazine in which an article described methods of transferring Acorn programs from tape to disk. Acorn alleged that this article amounted to an incitement to infringe copyright. Acorn's policy in commencing the litigation was strongly criticised in an editorial of *Practical Computing* which suggested that software owners should be entitled to make back-up copies for their own use:

> If software is intellectual property then you are buying the right to run it, and therefore to take as many back-up copies as you need, transfer it from tape to disc and, if necessary, from floppy disc to hard disc . . . Of course, you must not sell copies to anyone else: that would be piracy.[3]

Acorn-Soft responded by letter, in which they put the manufacturer's viewpoint. Commenting on the fact that they provided a free replacement service for damaged cassettes, so that the honest user would not normally need to make unauthorised copies, they pointed out that locking devices were regarded as the only practical protection to prevent widespread copying:

> We consider it worth spending money to develop such locking procedures in order to protect the substantial investment we make to develop software, and also to protect the rights of our authors.
> However, these attempts are rendered useless by the publication of an article which describes in detail how to by-pass such locking procedures.[4]

The problem posed by the Acorn-Soft case is now specifically considered in section 296 of the Copyright, Designs and Patents Act 1988. The section applies where copies of a copyright work are issued to the public in an electronic form which is copy-protected. The person issuing the copies to the public is given the same rights as a copyright owner in respect of infringement of copyright against a person who, knowing or having reason to believe that it will be used to make infringing copies:

> (a) makes or commits specified acts of dealing in any device or means specifically designed or adapted to circumvent the form of copy-protection employed or
> (b) publishes information intended to enable or assist persons to circumvent that form of copy-protection.

---

2 (Unreported). See *Practical Computing*, Volume 2, Issue 3, March 1984. See also the Irish case of *Lotus Development Corp. v Clissmann* discussed in *Magill*, June 1984, at 43.
3 *Practical Computing*, Volume 2, Issue 3, March 1984, at 5.
4 *Practical Computing*, Volume 2, Issue 3, May 1984.

The difficulty in the application of this section to a case like Acorn-Soft would be to establish that the person who published the information knew or had reason to believe that it would be used to make infringing copies.[5]

The illustration points to a variety of goals that legal protection should seek to achieve. First, that adequate economic return should result from software development. Secondly, this economic goal must be balanced by the need to encourage dissemination of ideas and to allow a customer to use software without undue interference. Finally, legal protection must have administrative workability. The cost of maintenance of protection and litigation should not be reflected in increased charges to the customer. The suitability of legal solutions may be judged against the background of these criteria.

2.3 THE SOFTWARE INDUSTRY WITHOUT LEGAL PROTECTION

It should be emphasised that the need for any legal protection at all is by no means unchallenged. If it were shown that legal protection provided no benefits to the software industry, then it would seem clear that such protection should be removed, and the industry left to regulate itself in a free market. In that event, the intervention of the law would be positively detrimental, as it would only serve to create monopolies in software and thereby stifle independent research.

The rationale behind the laws of intellectual property is that they provide the economic incentive necessary for creativity. Without proprietorial rights, an innovator would not make public his ideas since they would become common property on such publication. Even if advances were made in a given area, the incentive for dissemination would therefore be absent. New developments would stagnate.

To see if this thesis is applicable to the software industry it is necessary to ask whether the rapid advances in computers would still have been made over the last 20 years in the absence of legal protection. It may be that the theft of ideas is an illusory fear with regard to computer programs. If the economic aspirations of a software company were fulfilled by the mere production of programs it would be absurd to extend their interest over these programs to a term of years.

2.4 CATEGORIES OF COMPUTER SOFTWARE

It is possible to divide computer programs into three broad categories:[6]

(1) specialist applications programs, produced to the order of a single customer or group of customers, for a specific purpose;

---

5   See, by way of comparative illustration, *CBS Songs Ltd and others v Amstrad Consumer Electronics plc* [1988] AC 1013.

6   These are commercial distinctions relating to the market at which the software is aimed, as opposed to the function which it is intended to perform. For further analysis see Staines, [1983] 6 EIPR 142.

(2) general commercial programs, which achieve widespread sales throughout the business world. Examples are the many word processor programs which are at present available;

(3) mass market programs, which include computer games for home computers.

2.4.1   Specialist applications programs

It would appear that the absence of legal protection would be unlikely to deter production and dissemination of the first program type mentioned above. Specialist applications programs are frequently device specific so that they may only be used in a particular type of hardware. Generally, there would be less incentive to copy a program of specific application, which is by definition individually tailored to a customer's needs. In any event the economic return for research and development is likely to have been recovered by the software house on initial sale.

2.4.2   General commercial programs

In the case of general commercial programs, there is no doubt that copying of disks for use by a particular customer is widespread, and is an enormous drain on the anticipated profit of developers. Copy disks are not used merely as replacements. For example, a customer who acquires five machines from a manufacturer may choose to purchase one software package and make four unauthorised copies.

Included in the category of general commercial programs are programs which may be produced not for a specific customer, but speculatively in the belief that such a program has a market because of some improvement it makes on existing material. The importance to the computer industry of such general commercial programs is obvious. Frequently, their whole value lies in the fact that they improve on existing software. In the absence of legal protection, two alternatives would present themselves to a software company for recovery of their investment in such a general commercial program. First, they could attempt to recover all of their costs plus a fair profit on the first sale of the program. This solution would lead to an astronomical increase in cost and a consequent reduction in demand for software. Alternatively, speculative development, in the belief that a program would find a market, would cease. It would be necessary to bargain with potential buyers as a group, for example, subscribers to a database, before development of any program. This would effectively eliminate general commercial programs and restrict the industry to the production of specific applications programs, or to low budget, high volume computer games.

2.4.3   Mass market programs

In the case of programs for mass marketing, developers of such software face precisely the same problems as have been experienced by film and music producers in relation to video and audio piracy. It is essential to achieve mass dissemination and widespread availability of such programs to the public at a low cost. Profits are made on high volume, as opposed to high price, sales. The opportunity and incentive to copy successful products is apparent. The observations of Lord Denning in *Rank Film Ltd v Video Information Centre* seem equally appropriate to the software industry as to cinematograph films:

> 'It is, it is a glorious thing, to be a pirate king', said W. S. Gilbert: he was speaking of ship pirates. Today we speak of film pirates. It is not a glorious thing to be, but it is a good thing to be in for making money. Film pirates plunder the best and most recent cinema films. They transpose them onto magnetic tapes: and then sell video cassettes on the black market.[7]

2.5 THE EFFECT OF UNAUTHORISED COPYING

Having stated that unauthorised copying is capable, in varying degrees, of affecting each type of computer software, the real question to be answered is whether such copying actually deters production and dissemination of a program. Various commentators have challenged this assumption.[8] It has been suggested[9] that software protection would continue to thrive even if present legal remedies were removed. A program is generally sold as a package, including documentation manuals, 'debugging' and updating guarantees, and adjustments for hardware. The need for the copier independently to develop the know-how to make his copy a viable product would give the developer sufficient lead time to recover his investment cost.

This argument would, of course, have most relevance to specialist applications programs. However, even in respect of such programs, it is submitted that this assertion is no longer accurate. For example, in the American case of *Synercom Technology v University Computing Co.*[10] the plaintiff alleged copyright infringement of input formats for its stress analysis software (STRAN). In developing STRAN, Synercom had made major advances in the solution of structural engineering problems in that its superior input formats enhanced the analytical capacity of its programs and decreased training time. The defendants developed a competitive software package compatible with the STRAN formats. They were therefore able to improve their software while avoiding the substantial investment which would have been required to develop their own input formats: 'EDI [the defendant] was in a position to simply pluck the fruits of Synercom's labour and risks.'[11] Synercom's estimated investment loss was over half a million dollars.

---

7   [1982] AC 380 at 403.
8   See Breyer, 84 Harvard LR 281 (1970); Melville, [1980] 2 EIPR 354.
9   Breyer, 82 Harvard LR 281.
10   199 USPQ 537 (1978).
11   *Ibid.* at 540.

It has been estimated by a major international software company producing programs for commercial application that for every authorised copy of its software available on the market there are between three and eight unauthorised copies. The scale of copying is alleged to have resulted in lost sales and royalties of over £600 million.

Nonetheless, commentators have suggested that general purpose programs would continue to be produced without legal protection.[12] Hardware companies would continue to develop software even if they would lose their investment because of the promotional value in increasing computer demand. Educational institutions, receiving government support, would produce general programs serving other than commercial purposes.

It is submitted that these analyses fail to give adequate consideration to the importance of lead time in respect of programs which are intended to achieve widespread sales. In particular, general commercial programs and computer games depend largely on their innovative appeal for return on investment.

Lead time results from the research and development invested by a manufacturer to yield the particular advantage which renders his product attractive over its immediate competitors. The costs of the launch campaign alone for the successful Lotus 1-2-3 microcomputer software are estimated at about $3 million.[13] If competitors are effectively allowed to erode such lead time and to avoid the necessary research and development by unauthorised copying, then the incentive to produce and disseminate such material disappears.

An essential cause of the rapid advance of computer technology has been the unconcentrated state of the industry. The paramount importance of technical innovation over large capital investment has permitted the growth of small independent software houses. The major developments in the software industry have been produced against a background of intense competition.[14] While it may well be that major manufacturers of hardware would continue to invest in software on a promotional basis, the small software house would have no way of recovering its investment cost on a particular product without adequate legal protection of its work. The software industry would then become more concentrated and less competitive.

It is therefore concluded that only by granting the author some protection in his work over a limited period can the software industry continue to expand and disseminate its product.

In considering the various protective laws which may be available in relation to software, an essential consideration is purely pragmatic. Is there any area of law within whose principles the subject-matter of computer

---

12 Breyer, Note 8 above.
13 Gonenc, *OECD Observer*, No. 131, November 1985, at 21.
14 *Ibid.* at 20. While acknowledging the major contributions of hardware products, Gonenc lists certain of the considerable advances in computer languages, computer-assisted software engineering, fourth generation integrated software, and systems and packages for microcomputers achieved by specialised software firms.

software may be included? Most of this book will be devoted to answering that question. But in such discussion, one must not lose sight of the important policy considerations behind the law. An attempt will therefore be made to evaluate each area of law from a policy standpoint against the aims which have been defined above[15] – economic returns, social dissemination and administrative workability.

2.6 CONFIDENTIALITY

Figures provided in 1980 for the World Intellectual Property Organization[16] indicated that 78 per cent of software firms relied on trade secrets law for protection, 15 to 17 per cent on copyright protection and 5 per cent on patent protection. While there has now been a shift in favour of copyright law, in the light of legislative amendment in the United Kingdom and the United States, and decisions in the United States,[17] it is clear that up to the early 1980s the bulk of the industry relied on confidentiality as protection for software.

It is not, however, a necessary conclusion that trade secrets protection provides the optimum remedies for computer software. It may well be that the software industry has flourished over the relevant period because of *some* legal protection, but in spite of the particular type of protection that has been available.

The attractions of trade secrecy are obvious. In the United States in the past, whereas courts periodically denied copyright[18] and patent[19] protection for software, it was clearly affirmed that the law of trade secrets was applicable to computer software provided that sufficient secrecy could be shown.[20]

Furthermore, as the very essence of this form of protection is secrecy, it has inherently appealed to the industry to seek protection which is on the one hand relatively certain, and on the other hand minimises the possibilities of infringement by non-disclosure of the information sought to be protected.

An obligation of confidence is essentially an equitable duty of good faith which may be implied by law from the circumstances surrounding its

---

15   For further analysis of the goals of legal protection see Pope, 30 Alabama L Rev. 527 (1979).
16   Braubach, [1980] 2 EIPR 225.
17   United States Copyright Act 1976, 17 USC 101 *et seq.* amended by Computer Software Copyright Act 1980; *Tandy Corp. v Personal Micro Computers Inc.* 524 F.Supp 171 (1981); *Midway Manufacturing Co. v Artic International Inc.* 547 F.Supp 999 (CWD 111, 1982) aff'd 685 F.2d 870 (3d Cir. 1982); *Apple Computer Inc. v Franklin Computer Corporation,* 545 F.Supp 812 (ED Pa. 1982) cert. dismissed 104 SCt 690 (1984); *Whelan Inc. v Jaslow Dental Laboratory Inc.* [1987] FSR 1 (3d Cir.); *Broderbund Software Inc. v Unison World Inc.* 648 F.Supp 1127; *Lotus Development Corp. v Paperback Software International* 740 F.Supp 37 (D.Mass. 1990). In the United Kingdom see the Copyright, Designs and Patents Act 1988.
18   *Synercom Technology Inc. v University Computing Co.* 199 USPQ 537 (1978), *Data Cash Systems Inc. v JS & A Group Inc.* 203 USPQ 735 (1980).
19   For example *Gottschalk v Benson* 409 US 252 (1972), *Parker v Flook* 437 US 584 (1978).
20   *Cybertec Computer Products Inc. v Whitfield & Others* 203 USPQ 1020 (1977).

disclosure.[21] Whilst any information may be protected by an obligation of confidence, it is essential to show that that information is secret.[22] The requirement of secrecy may be judged by a consideration of the following factors:

(1) the extent to which the information is known outside the owner's business;

(2) the extent to which employees involved in his business appreciate that the information is confidential;

(3) the extent of measures taken by the owner to guard the secrecy of the information.[23]

A consideration of the secrecy requirement immediately shows that confidentiality does not provide ideal economic protection for all types of software. Obligations of confidence may protect a specialist applications program or a program which is sold as part of a package with hardware. But even in these cases, it would be essential to show that those parts of the software alleged to have been misappropriated are not generally known in the industry.

In the case of programs intended for mass distribution, widespread disclosure erodes the degree of protection which may be obtained through secrecy. While there are certain circumstances in which confidentiality is not immediately destroyed by mass marketing there is no doubt that the secrecy of a product on the market is a wasting asset, and that on widespread sales such secrecy is eroded into common knowledge.[24]

From a practical point of view, the difficulties in bringing a successful action for breach of confidence are enormous.[25] On the one hand it is essential to show that the program or parts of it possess relative novelty in that they are not widely known, or not known for that purpose in the industry. It is then necessary to show that those parts which have been identified as secret have in fact been taken by the alleged infringer. The difficulties of identifying with sufficient particularity the precise nature of a complaint of breach of confidence have been well illustrated by the case law.

It seems anomalous that a program whose value lies in its innovation should be denied legal protection by reason of its widespread popularity.

Furthermore, the requirement of secrecy prevents dissemination of ideas within the industry. Confidentiality, if a requirement for legal protection, therefore hinders development and leads to duplication of research.

It may finally be added that precautions intended to maintain secrecy are an additional expense to the industry, which is reflected in the price of software paid by the consumer.

21   *Coco v A. N. Clark (Engineers) Ltd* [1969] RPC 41.
22   *Saltman Engineering Co. Ltd v Campbell Engineering Ltd* (1948) 65 RPC 203.
23   *Coco v A. N. Clark*, Note 21 above.
24   See Chapter 3 generally.
25   See Chapter 3 paragraph 3.6.

2.7   CONTRACT

It is perfectly possible to bind a party to a contract, for example a software licence agreement, by a term of non-disclosure.[26] Such a term, while having the same effect as an obligation of confidence, need not be founded on confidentiality. In the event of an unauthorised disclosure, the software developer would, of course, have his remedies in contract against the other contracting party assuming that that party was capable of paying damages. He would not, however, be able to prevent persons who were not parties to the contract from continuing to use or disclose information learnt by them. The extent of contractual remedies, which are essentially personal, cannot, therefore, prevent widescale industrial copying.[27]

2.8   PATENT LAW

In the United States in the mid-1960s, the courts had come down in favour of patent protection for computer software.[28] And yet out of 10,000 patent applications in 1965, only 450 were in respect of computer programs.[29] The reason for the reluctance of the industry to claim patent protection may be as a result of the increased risk of infringement due to mandatory disclosure. Patent applications are published by the Patent Office with sufficient detail for the invention to be performed by a person skilled in the art.[30] Therefore a description of the software is disclosed to the world. The risk of misappropriation may be judged to be greater than if the development is kept secret.[31]

It cannot be overstressed that an enormous problem in software litigation is detection and proof of infringement. A program may be copied for private use on a machine in any of its stages, and external evidence of such copying destroyed. A program may even be stolen over telephone lines.[32] On the other hand the economic advantages of patent protection as compared, for example, with copyright protection are apparent. A monopoly is given over the 'industrial application'[33] as opposed to 'expression of the idea'.[34] It is an infringement not just to copy, but to use or keep anything falling within the claimed monopoly even if the infringement has been independently developed.[35] This means that where a program is novel, non-obvious and

---

26   *Ibid.*

27   For incorporation of conditions in retail sales of software see Chapter 8 at paragraph 8.1.7.

28   See for example *In Re Prater* 415 F.2d 1393 (1969).

29   See Gemignani, 7 *Rutgers Journal of Computers and Law* 275 note 30 (1980).

30   Patents Act 1977 section 14(3).

31   Detection and proof of infringement is a significant problem in software protection. See Chapter 9 at paragraphs 9.1.2 to 9.1.3.

32   Roddy, 7 *Rutgers Journal of Computers and Law* 232 (1980). (This type of act is classed as an infringement of copyright by section 24(2) of the Copyright, Designs and Patents Act 1988.)

33   Patents Act 1977 section 1(1)(c).

34   As under copyright law: *L.B. (Plastics) Ltd v Swish Products Ltd* [1979] RPC 551.

35   For infringing acts see Patents Act 1977 section 60.

of commercial importance, patent protection is unquestionably of great advantage. For example, in the United States, following the grant of a patent for a data processing system for cash account management, the patentees Merrill Lynch announced that licences were available to users at a rate of $10 per account per year.[36] Because of the volume of accounts handled, it was estimated that licensing fees in the United States could amount to between $20 and $40 million a year.[37]

However, the evidence suggests that because of the difficulties of detection and proof of infringement, smaller companies may hesitate to apply for protection requiring public disclosure. If faced with the alternatives of disclosure or absence of legal remedy it would appear that the industry might choose to strengthen secrecy precautions. Therefore, it would appear that disadvantages which result from a lack of dissemination would in some degree continue to occur if patents were the sole protection available for software.

Administrative problems in relation to the patentability of software were the principal reasons for recommendation by the President's Commission on the Patent System against program inclusion.[38] It was pointed out that reliable searches would be beyond the scope of the Patent Office because of the volume and technical nature of the prior art.

As to costs, patent litigation is extremely expensive.[39] The validity of a granted patent can always be challenged in an infringement action, which frequently necessitates costly experiments by both parties.

2.9   COPYRIGHT LAW

In jurisdictions throughout the world, copyright statutes have been enacted or amended specifically to include computer software. In the United Kingdom, the Copyright, Designs and Patents Act 1988 should serve to dispel certain doubts about the suitability of copyright law to provide adequate protection for computer software.

Previously, concern had been expressed that any protection which permitted the unauthorised use of computer programs was unsuitable; and that the law of copyright prevented reproduction as opposed to use. However, it is submitted that the 1988 Act has clearly included the act of storage of a computer program within its definition of copying, and has thereby rendered unauthorised use actionable as an infringement.[40]

36   US Patent No. 4,346,442; *Financial Times*, 30 September 1982.
37   *Financial Times*, Note 36 above. But as to patentability in the United Kingdom see *Merrill Lynch's Application* [1988] RPC 1 discussed at Chapter 7 paragraph 7.1.5.
38   United States Report of the President's Commission on the Patent System 12 (1966).
39   The Patents County Court has been established in the UK as an alternative forum for patent actions. It is intended to provide quicker and cheaper resolution of disputes.
40   Section 17; discussed in detail in Chapter 5 below.

An undesirable feature of copyright law prior to the new Act was the availability of conversion damages in respect of infringements. Essentially, the copyright owner was treated as the owner of all infringing copies, and was deemed to be entitled to their entire value. This meant that damages in copyright actions operated as a windfall to plaintiffs. Instead of recovering their actual loss, or a reasonable royalty, successful plaintiffs recovered excessive sums amounting to the defendant's entire turnover in the infringing articles. Actions of dubious merit were settled on favourable terms to the plaintiff, because of the fear of conversion damages.

This unjust remedy has now been removed by the 1988 Act in actions commenced after 1 August 1989.[41]

A separate, and illusory, concern as to the suitability of copyright law was the fear that infringement could be avoided by minor textual variations. This is not the attitude that courts in the United Kingdom and the Commonwealth have taken to such unauthorised copying. Time and again it has been asserted that an author who avails himself of the labour of a copyright work, instead of taking the pains of his own research, is making illegitimate use of that work and thereby infringing copyright.[42] This is true even if he attempts to disguise copying by immaterial alteration of the form in which the work is expressed. The point is made in the case of *Ravenscroft v Herbert*:

> Copying protects the skill and labour employed by the Plaintiff in the production of his work. That skill and labour embrace not only language orginated and used by the Plaintiff, but also such skill and labour as he has employed in selection and compilation. . . . An author is not entitled, under the guise of producing an original work, to reproduce the arguments and illustrations of another author so as to appropriate to himself the literary labours of that author.[43]

In fact, the possibility that copyright law may be interpreted in a manner which provides too extensive protection for software, and thereby inhibits future developments, is of far more concern. Courts in the United States have been prepared to conclude that a program constituted an infringement of copyright on the basis of similarities in the 'total concept and feel' of the programs in issue.[44] In other words resemblances in screens and user inter-faces, as opposed to similarities in code, whether textual or structural, have led to a finding of infringement. There is a danger in the look and feel cases that two quite separate works may be confused, namely, the audio-visual work comprised in the output screens, and the literary work comprised in the underlying code. It is submitted that this departure from the traditional copyright analysis, which analysis looks to the form of expression rather than the results of a work, is a most undesirable development. It is capable of

---

41   See Chapter 9 at paragraph 9.6 for a full consideration.
42   *Jarrold v Houlston* (1857) 3 K & J 708; *Corelli v Gray* (1913) 29 TLR 570.
43   [1980] RPC 193 at 204, 206. For a more detailed discussion, see Chapter 5 below.
44   *Broderbund Software Inc. v Unison World Inc.* 648 F.Supp 1127 (W.D.Ca. 1986); *Lotus Development Corp. v Paperback Software International* 740 F.Supp 37 (D.Mass. 1990). These decisions are discussed further in Chapter 5 paragraph 5.1.1.5; and in Chapter 6 paragraph 6.7.1.

being used by copyright owners to inhibit legitimate competition by their rivals in the same field.

There is no reason to believe that in the absence of such protection, software development would in any way be impeded or discouraged. In the authors' view, the very wide 'look and feel' tests are unlikely to be adopted by the Court in the United Kingdom.[45]

2.9.1 The EC Directive[46]

On 14 May 1991 Council Directive 91/250/EEC on the Legal Protection of Computer Programs came into force. Pursuant to Article 10 of the Directive Member States are required to bring into force the laws, regulations and administrative provisions necessary to comply with the Directive before 1 January 1993. In the circumstances, while the provisions of the Directive may not yet represent the law of the United Kingdom they are an important indication of legislative amendments which will be made in the near future.

The recitals to the Directive contain an inclusionary definition of the term 'computer program'. It is specified that the term shall include programs in any form, including those which are incorporated into hardware. This should settle any lingering doubts as to whether microcode is capable of protection by the Laws of Copyright. It is further provided that the term also includes preparatory design work leading to the development of a computer program provided that the nature of the preparatory work is such that a computer program can result from it at a later stage. This part of the recital is somewhat obscure since it suggests that a line must be drawn between different stages of preparatory work. It would be an unenviable task to attempt to translate this general aim into specific legislation.

From the point of view of the United Kingdom the EC Directive is most significant in its exceptions to the acts restricted by copyright. These exceptions may be divided into three parts:

(1) Interfaces;
(2) Maintenance;
(3) Decompilation.

2.9.1.1 *Interfaces*

Article 1(2) provides *inter alia* that: 'Ideas and principles which underlie any element of the computer program including those which underlie its interfaces

---

45 It is important to emphasise that there is a distinction between copying the structure sequence and organisation of the code of a computer program; and the 'look and feel' of the program. It is submitted that the former is actionable in the United Kingdom; the latter does not prove infringement of copyright in the underlying code, although it may possibly involve infringement of other works.

46 OJ 12 April 1989 C91/4. Useful discussions of the Directive are contained in Reed, [1991] EIPR 47 and Hart, [1991] EIPR 111.

are not protected by copyright under this Directive'. The exclusion of ideas and principles, in contrast with the expression of those ideas, is a familiar principle in both United Kingdom and United States law. It is a proposition which is easy to state but has led to great difficulties in its application. These difficulties are discussed in detail in Chapter 5. Even in the most extreme 'look and feel' cases in the United States, the courts purport to exclude ideas and principles from copyright protection.

The most significant aspect of Article 1(2) lies in its reference to interfaces. This term is potentially obscure, but is somewhat clarified by an explanatory recital: 'Whereas the parts of the program which provide for such inter-connection and interaction between the elements of software and hardware are generally known as "interfaces" . . .'. Accordingly, the Directive appears to be aimed at low level interfaces which link programs, hardware and other programs rather than user interfaces.

It is important to note that the Directive does not exclude interfaces from copyright protection. It only excludes the ideas and principles which underlie the interfaces. It is noteworthy that in the case of *Total Information Processing Systems Ltd v Daman Ltd*,[47] the only authority in which the United Kingdom courts have considered the problems of interface programs, Judge Paul Baker QC expressly referred to the distinction between ideas and their expression in declining to treat an interface file as a separate copyright work.

Accordingly, it is submitted that the Directive does not exclude interfaces, but it highlights the fact that the distinction between ideas and their expression is of particular application to such programs.

2.9.1.2 Maintenance

Pursuant to Article 5(1) of the Directive the lawful acquirer of a computer program does not require authorisation of the rights holder to perform acts which are necessary for the use of the computer program in accordance with its intended purpose, including error correction. However, this exception only applies 'in the absence of specific contractual provisions'. The inclusion of an exception for error correction is welcome. An attempt to enforce copyright protection to prevent error correction would already be contrary to United Kingdom law, as representing a derogation from grant by the copyright owner to the user of the software.[48] However, since the exception can be overridden by contractual provisions it is open to any software developer to reserve such right to itself.

It is to be noted that Article 5(1) does not refer to enhancements or upgrading, the performance of which constitute adaptations, arrangements or other alterations of a computer program and are restricted acts pursuant

---

47 [1992] FSR 171.
48 *Saphena Computing Ltd v Allied Collection Agencies Ltd* (unreported, Mr Recorder Havery QC, 22 July 1988). There is no obligation, either in the existing law or in the EC Directive, for the software house to facilitate the correction of errors by the user by the provision of source code.

to Article 4(b). It seems difficult to say that such acts are necessary for the use of the computer program; by definition, they are improvements rather than repairs.

Article 5(2) provides that: 'The making of a backup copy by a person having a right to use the computer program may not be prevented by contract insofar as it is necessary for that use.' Again, it is arguable that this already represents United Kingdom law, as an attempt to prevent the making of necessary back up copies would constitute a derogation from grant. The fact that it is expressly stated in the Directive as an exception should settle any doubts on this issue.

In contrast to Article 5(1) this right cannot be excluded by contract. It is noted that the right does not extend to the making of a stock of back up copies for sale to third party users.

Article 5(3) entitles the lawful user of a copy of a computer program to observe, study or test the functioning of a program in order to determine the ideas and principles which underlie any element of the program. Such right only applies if he does so while performing any of the acts of loading, displaying, running, transmitting or storing a program which he is entitled to do. This Article does not give a general right to the user to 'reverse engineer' the program. In particular no right is given to the user to reproduce or adapt any part of the program, and the exception purely relates to the determination of underlying ideas and principles. The exception is a necessary addition to the exclusion of ideas and principles from the scope of protection contained in Article 1(2).

2.9.1.3   Decompilation

Article 6 gives to the lawful user of a computer program a limited right to decompile the software. Article 6(1) provides as follows:

> The authorisation of the right holder shall not be required where reproduction of the code and translation of its form within the meaning of Article 4(a) and (b) are *indispensable* to obtain the information necessary to obtain the interoperability of an independently created computer program with other programs . . . (emphasis added)

The right only applies to the obtaining of information necessary to achieve interoperability, and further only applies where reproduction and translation are indispensable. This may prove to be a difficult test to satisfy. Further specific limitations on the scope of the decompilation right are contained in the remainder of Article 6(1) and in Article 6(2). In particular, the decompiler must show that the information necessary to achieve interoperability has not previously be readily available; and that the acts of reproduction and translation are confined to the parts of the original program which are necessary to achieve interoperability.

The information obtained cannot be used for goals other than to achieve the interoperability of the independently created computer program; cannot be given to others except where necessary for the interoperability of such a program; and cannot be used for the development, production or marketing of a computer program substantially similar in its expression, or for any other act which infringes copyright.

In summary the limitations on the scope of the decompilation exception would appear to exclude any possibility of a general right to reverse engineer computer software. On the other hand, this exception will permit acts which under current United Kingdom law would constitute infringements of copyright.

2.9.2 Published and unpublished works

The test of whether a work has been published differs in trade secrets, patents and copyright law. In the present discussion, a published work refers to a literary work of which reproductions have been 'issued to the public'.

The Whitford Committee[49] and the Green Paper[50] regarded computer programs as essentially unpublished works. In the Whitford Committee Report it was stated that: 'It is difficult to envisage a situation in which such works will become best sellers.'[51]

This view may no longer be accurate in the light of the development of computer programs which have been disseminated to a mass market. Several actions have already been brought precisely to protect rights in best-selling software.[52]

On the other hand, many programs which may be copied are works which are not on general release to the public – specialist applications programs which are essentially unpublished works.

It has been suggested[53] that whether confidentiality or disclosure is a prerequisite of legal protection, the effect on the industry is the same – secrecy. Since computer programs may be either published or unpublished works, dissemination can only be encouraged where a programmer is offered the choice of publishing his work with legal remedies against misappropriation. Copyright law in the United Kingdom offers this choice, since protection is given to both published and unpublished works – provided that certain preconditions set down in the statute are satisfied.[54]

---

49 Whitford Committee Report 1977 (Cmnd 6732).
50 Government Green Paper on Copyright Reform (1981) (Cmnd 8302).
51 Note 49 above at page 129 paragraph 495.
52 See for example in the United States, *Apple Computer Inc. v Franklin Computer Corporation*, 545 F.Supp 812 (ED Pa. 1982) cert. dismissed 104 SCt 690 (1984); in Australia, *Apple Computer Inc. & Another v Computer Edge Pty Ltd & Suss* [1984] FSR 481; in France, Paris Appeal Court, 4 June 1984, *Atari Ireland Valados & Others*; in Italy, Tribunal of Turin, 17 October 1983, *Atari Inc. & Bertolino v Sidam Srl*; in the United Kingdom, *Sega Enterprises v Richards* [1983] FSR 73.
53 See above, sections 2.6 and 2.7.
54 Copyright Act 1956 section 2(1) and (2); Copyright, Designs and Patents Act 1988 sections 153 to 155.

2.9.3   Formalities

In contrast to the measures necessary for trade secrecy or patent protection, copyright is obtained and maintained in the United Kingdom without formality and expense. Protection arises automatically, without the need for deposit, registration or marking.[55] Reduction in the cost of measures for legal protection could be reflected in the price of software paid by the consumer.

2.10   UNFAIR COMPETITION

The doctrine of unfair competition, as developed in the United States, would seem at first glance to provide a degree of flexibility sufficient to cater for both economic interest in protection and social interest in dissemination. The doctrine of misappropriation of ideas, as developed in the case of *International News Services v Associated Press*[56] suggested several bases for the tort, including the protection of property rights and the prevention of unjust enrichment. The principle adopted in subsequent cases is that the misappropriation of the fruits of another's labour, whether tangible or intangible, will be enjoined if the public interest so demands.

The doctrine leaves an enormous amount to the discretion of the particular tribunal hearing the case. The question of whether a development is or is not unfair may be entirely subjective.[57] In practice, courts have experienced difficulty in software litigation in sufficiently comprehending the precise method by which two similar results have been arrived at to say that one has been an unfair misappropriation of the other.[58] While in theory a plaintiff could obtain legal redress, unless the purpose of the appropriation was justifiable in the interest of free competition or research, it may be thought unlikely that in practice such a nebulous doctrine would be sufficiently precise to provide clear legal answers.[59]

2.11   CONCLUSION

It would appear that from a policy standpoint, no existing legal solution is ideal. Much depends on the precise nature of the program sought to be protected. Where such a program constitutes a major departure from the prior art, patent protection may be desirable and appropriate. Where a specialist applications program is developed for a particular customer, the

---

55   United States Copyright Act 1976 sections 410, 411. Even in the United States, compliance with formalities is inexpensive.
56   248 US 215 (1918).
57   For example *Pittsburgh Athletic Co. v K.Q.V. Broadcasting Co.* 24 F.Supp 490 (1938).
58   For example *Data Cash Systems*, Note 18 above.
59   In any event, the existence of a comparable doctrine in the United Kingdom and the Commonwealth is unarguable since the decision of the Privy Council in *Cadbury Schweppes Pty Ltd v The Pub Squash Co. Ltd* [1981] RPC 429.

recipient of such information may well be bound by obligations of confidence. It is concluded, however, that the application of copyright protection to computer programs has clear advantages for developers and users of software, which may be summarised as follows:

(1) The Copyright Acts in the common law jurisdictions are, broadly speaking, similar in the nature and extent of protection that they provide. International protection is obtained in many countries under international treaties and conventions.[60]

(2) Copyright may subsist in both published and unpublished works, and is available in the United Kingdom and Commonwealth without formal application.

(3) The requirement that a substantial part of a work must have been *copied* in order to show infringement of copyright allows a degree of independent research and development to be undertaken. Amendments to the legislation as a result of the EC Directive are likely to provide additional freedom in this respect.

At the present time, it is perhaps most important for the computer industry to be fully aware of the extent of all possible methods of legal protection against misappropriation. The rest of this book will therefore be devoted to a consideration of the scope of legal remedies in their application to computer programs.

---

60 For example under the Berne Convention and the Universal Copyright Convention.

3 Confidential Information

3.0 INTRODUCTION

One of the most important means of protection relied upon by the software industry in the United Kingdom and the Commonwealth is secrecy or confidentiality. It is common practice, for example, for software to be supplied in the form of object code only, with the source code being retained by the supplier or perhaps held in escrow. Since it is difficult for the user to understand or decompile the object code, this effectively prevents him from copying or modifying the program (other than by pure duplication of the object code).This approach to protecting software has the great advantage of simplicity: it is easy for a software supplier to implement, and hard for the user to circumvent. Furthermore the physical control that the software supplier has over the source code in this way is often such as to put him in a very strong position in the event of dispute. Physical control is only part of the protection available, however, for it is also possible legally to prevent use of the information that the software constitutes or contains if it is secret and subject to an obligation to keep it so. This is the province of the law of confidential information.

Unlike the copyright, design right and patent laws, the law of confidential information is entirely judge-made law which has developed through the accidents of litigation. This means that there is no single source of the law, and it is difficult to state the law with certainty. In 1981 the Law Commission concluded in its Report on Breach of Confidence[1] that:

> The survey of the present law and of its many uncertainties and inadequacies, which we have given in this report, shows that there are many problem areas which it would be most unsatisfactory, both in the interests of the individual and of the law, to leave to be resolved (if at all) by piecemeal litigation.

Accordingly, the Commission recommended that the law ought to be put on a statutory basis. Since 1981 there has been a flood of cases on confidential information, most notoriously the *Spycatcher* case. As a result the basic principles have become reasonably well settled. Some of the

---

1 Law Commission Report 110 (1981) Cmnd 8388.

uncertainties identified by the Commission remain, however, yet legislation seems as far away as ever.

In this chapter the basic principles of the law of confidential information are stated and their application to computer software discussed. In addition, there is a section on the allied topic of confidentiality in court proceedings.

3.1 PROTECTION OF INFORMATION AND IDEAS

It is worth stating at the outset that the beauty of the law of confidence so far as the software industry is concerned is that the law was expressly evolved to protect information. Information is the very subject-matter of the law, whereas other forms of protection such as copyright, design rights and patents only protect information incidentally if at all. Furthermore, it is clear that the law protects fundamental ideas or concepts as well as more detailed information. Thus in *Fraser v Thames Television Ltd*,[2] the basic idea for a television series was held to be confidential information; by contrast, in *Green v Broadcasting Corporation of New Zealand*,[3] the 'format' of the television programme *Opportunity Knocks* (which was public knowledge at the relevant time) was held not to be a copyright work. In the New Zealand case of *Talbot v General Television Corp Pty Ltd*,[4] Harris J expressly rejected the proposition that an obligation of confidence could not extend to an idea or concept, holding that since the idea in question was confidential it was suitable subject-matter for protection:

> I am satisfied that what was called the 'commercial twist', or the particular slant of the plaintiff's concept (or idea) does give it a quality which takes it out of the realm of public knowledge.[5]

So unauthorised use of an idea, as well as reproduction of its expression, may be restrained as a breach of confidence.

This means that computer programs, whether in high or low level language, may be protected by obligations of confidence and so may their underlying concepts and algorithms where appropriate. This question is discussed further in paragraph 3.3.1.

3.2 THE CONCEPTUAL BASIS OF CONFIDENTIALITY

Various theories have been advanced by courts and academics as to the conceptual basis of the law of confidence including contract, property, trust,

---

2 [1984] QB 44.
3 [1989] RPC 700.
4 [1981] RPC 1.
5 *Ibid.* at 9.

fiduciary relationships, unjust enrichment and good faith.[6] The most important basis, at least so far as software suppliers are concerned, is probably that of contract. In many contractual situations (for example, licensor and licensee, employer and employee, principal and agent) there may be an express or implied term in the contract which imposes an obligation of confidence. It is clear, however, that although an obligation of confidence may be imposed by contract, contract cannot account for all the situations in which such an obligation has been held to exist. For example, obligations of confidence have been found in non-contractual situations such as in pre-licence negotiations which prove abortive,[7] or in relation to third parties who took no part in the original transaction.[8] The suggestion that the law of confidence is based wholly on contract was refuted by Lord Greene MR in the seminal case of *Saltman Engineering Ltd v Campbell Engineering Ltd*:[9] 'The obligation to respect confidence is not limited to cases where parties are in a contractual relationship.'

In its most general aspect, it is now settled that the law is in fact founded on the equitable duty of good faith. Megarry J observed in *Coco v A.N. Clark (Engineers) Ltd*:

> The equitable jurisdiction in cases of breach of confidence is ancient; confidence is the cousin of trust. The Statute of Uses 1535 is framed in terms of use, confidence or trust; and a couplet attributed to Sir Thomas More Lord Chancellor avers that:
>
> > Three things are to be helpt in Conscience;
> > Fraud, Accident and Things of Confidence.[10]

The Court of Appeal in the case of *Seager v Copydex Ltd* held that:

> The law on this subject does not depend on any implied contract. It depends on the broad principle of equity that he who has received information in confidence shall not take unfair advantage of it. He must not make use of it to the prejudice of him who gave it without obtaining his consent.[11]

Similarly Lord Denning MR stated in *Frazer v Evans*[12] that the jurisdiction was based: '. . . not so much on property or on contract as on the duty to be of good faith'. These statements of principle now have the endorsement of the House of Lords in the *Spycatcher* case:

> The obligation [of confidence] may be imposed by an express or implied term in a contract but it may also exist independently of any contract on the basis of an independent equitable principle of confidence.[13]

---

6   See for example *Duchess of Argyll v Duke of Argyll* [1967] Ch. 302 at 318; *Frazer v Evans* [1969] 1 QB 349; Ricketson, 'Confidential Information – A New Proprietary Interest?' [1978] 11 Melbourne ULR 223 and 289; *Copinger & Skone James on Copyright*, Sweet & Maxwell, 1991 (13th edn), Chapter 21; Gurry, *Breach of Confidence*, Oxford, 1984, Chapter 2.
7   *Seager v Copydex Ltd* [1967] 1 WLR 923; *Fraser v Thames Television Ltd* [1984] QB 44.
8   *Stevenson Jordan & Harrison Ltd v MacDonald & Evans* (1952) 69 RPC 10.
9   (1948) 65 RPC 203 at 211.
10   [1969] RPC 41 at 46.
11   [1967] 1 WLR 923 at 931 *per* Lord Denning MR.
12   [1969] 1 QB 349 at 361.
13   *Attorney-General v Guardian Newspapers Ltd (No. 3)* [1989] 2 FSR 181 at 306 *per* Lord Keith of Kinkel.

Although the terms of a contract may impose a duty of confidence the remedy is not dependent on contract and exists as an equitable principle.[14]

> . . . in the vast majority of cases . . . the duty of confidence will arise from a transaction or relationship between the parties – often a contract, in which event the duty may arise by reason of either an express or an implied term of that contract . . . But it is well settled that a duty of confidence may arise in equity independently of such cases . . .[15]

So the obligation of confidence is an equitable one, originating in equity's jurisdiction over fiduciary relationships. But fiduciary relationships are now only one class of confidential relationship. Equity imposes obligations of confidence on fiduciaries and non-fiduciaries alike.[16]

An important limitation on the scope of confidentality emerges from the above analysis. Information does not become entitled to protection merely because it is sensitive. It is a necessary prerequisite that any disclosure or use sought to be prevented should be in breach of an obligation to keep the information confidential. It is only where information has been imparted or acquired in circumstances such that its unauthorised use or disclosure would be unconscionable that a remedy to restrain such use or disclosure is available.

Although the law will enforce an obligation of confidence however it arises, the particular source of the obligation may nevertheless be important. This is for two reasons. First, as the House of Lords made clear in *Spycatcher*, the scope of the obligation will in any event depend on the particular circumstances, for example the degree of sensitivity of the information concerned. Secondly, because an obligation of confidence may be qualified by other legal principles. This is most clearly seen in the case of contracts of employment, where express and implied terms as to confidence alike are qualified by the public policy against restraint of trade. For this reason it is useful to consider employment obligations separately from others. This does not mean to say, however, that there is some difference between the nature of an obligation of confidence imposed by contract and the nature of an obligation of confidence imposed by equity: the nature of the obligation is the same, but the scope of the obligation, however imposed, varies according to the particular circumstances.[17]

---

14 *Ibid.* at 319 *per* Lord Griffiths.
15 *Ibid.* at 332 *per* Lord Goff of Chieveley.
16 See *Lac Minerals Ltd v International Corona Resources Ltd* [1990] FSR 441 (Supreme Court of Canada) for an extensive discussion of this question and its potential impact on the remedies that may be awarded.
17 See *Attorney-General v Guardian Newspapers Ltd (No. 3)* [1989] 2 FSR 181 at 220 *per* Scott J, referring to *Lamb v Evans* [1893] 1 Ch. 218. The speeches in the House of Lords are to the same effect.

3.3   THE ELEMENTS OF CONFIDENCE

The clearest statement of the elements necessary to found an action for breach of confidence is contained in a *dictum* of Megarry J in *Coco v Clark*[18] which was quoted with approval by Lord Griffiths in *Spycatcher*:

> First, the information itself . . . must 'have the necessary quality of confidence about it'. Secondly, that information must have been communicated in circumstances importing an obligation of confidence. Thirdly, there must be an unauthorised use of the information to the detriment of the party communicating it.[19]

These three elements will now be considered separately.

3.3.1   Information of a confidential nature

There is no doubt that information which is common knowledge cannot be protected by confidence, however great the precautions taken may be. The classic statement as to the nature of confidential information is that of Lord Greene MR in *Saltman v Campbell*:[20] 'The information, to be confidential, must . . . have the necessary quality of confidence about it, namely it must not be something which is public property and public knowledge.' This, however, is a negative definition which does not assist greatly in identifying positively what information can be confidential. Sir Robert Megarry VC further elaborated on this question in the case of *Thomas Marshall (Exports) Ltd v Guinle*.[21] He acknowledged that: '[i]t is far from easy to state in general terms what is confidential information or a trade secret', but identified four criteria which were of assistance in identifying it:

(1) The information must be information the release of which the owner believes would be injurious to him or of advantage to his rivals or others.
(2) The owner must believe that the information is confidential or secret, that is, that it is not already in the public domain.
(3) The owner's belief under both of the above heads must be reasonable.
(4) The information must be judged in the light of usage and practices of the particular industry or trade concerned.

More specific factors which courts have found of assistance in particular cases are as follows:

(1) The skill or labour which was involved in the creation or assembly of the information.[22]
(2) The measures taken to safeguard confidentiality within the originating organisation.[23]

18   [1969] RPC 41 at 47.
19   *Attorney-General v Guardian Newspapers Ltd (No. 3)* [1989] 2 FSR 181 at 319.
20   (1948) 65 RPC 203 at 215.
21   [1979] FSR 208 at 229 to 230.
22   See *Saltman v Campbell* (1948) 65 RPC 203 at 215, *Marshall v Guinle* [1979] FSR 208.
23   See *G. D. Searle Co.Ltd v Celltech Ltd* [1982] FSR 92.

(3) Whether the information was expressly stated to recipients, for example employees, to be confidential.[24]

(4) The extent to which, and the conditions under which, dissemination of the information outside the originating organisation has occurred.[25]

(5) Whether others are prepared to pay for the information.[26]

It is not entirely clear whether the time as at which the confidentiality of the information is to be assessed is the time at which the information was imparted to or acquired by the confidant or whether it is the time at which the confidant subsequently uses or discloses it or threatens to do so. It appears, however, that the relevant time is the time of acquisition, although subsequent publication of the information may affect the obligation of confidence. The significance of this point is that it appears from the decision of the House of Lords in *Spycatcher* that, if information was confidential when acquired, a duty to keep it confidential may in some circumstances survive publication; whereas if it was public at the time of acquisition, no duty will arise. This point is discussed further below.[27]

It has repeatedly been made clear that the information is not required to be novel (that is in a patent sense), still less inventive.[28] It is perfectly possible for confidential information to be the result of work done on materials which are individually publicly available or even to consist of a compilation of publicly available materials. To put it another way, the accessibility of the information is a relative and not an absolute matter.[29] Thus in *Schering Chemicals Ltd v Falkman Ltd*,[30] the confidential information was public in the sense that it could have been gleaned by a diligent search through scientific literature, yet the defendant, who had not done such a search, was restrained.[31] Although publication of the information by the confider will usually destroy confidentiality,[32] publication of a part of the information concerned does not destroy confidentiality of the whole. For example, it was held in *Ansell Rubber v Allied Rubber*[33] that publication in patent specifications and technical literature of some of the features of an allegedly confidential design did not destroy confidentiality in the design itself. Similarly in *Weir Pumps Ltd v CML Pumps Ltd*,[34] Whitford J held that although individual parts of information contained in manufacturing

---

24 See *Faccenda Chicken Ltd v Fowler* [1987] Ch. 117 at 138.

25 In *Castrol Australia Pty Ltd v Emtech Associates Pty Ltd* (1981) 33 ALR 31 it was held that the confidentiality of a technical report was not destroyed by the publication of advertisements based on the report.

26 See *Potters-Ballotini Ltd v Weston-Baker* [1977] RPC 202 at 206.

27 See paragraph 3.3.2.2.

28 *Saltman Engineering Ltd v Campbell Engineering Ltd* (1948) 65 RPC 203 at 215; *Ansell Rubber Co. Pty Ltd v Allied Rubber Industries Pty Ltd* [1972] RPC 811 (Supreme Court of Victoria); *Terrapin Ltd v Builders Supply Co. (Hayes) Ltd* [1967] RPC 375 at 391.

29 *Franchi v Franchi* [1967] RPC 149 at 152 to 153 *per* Cross J.

30 [1982] QB 1.

31 See also *Ackroyds (London) Ltd v Islington Plastics Ltd* [1962] RPC 97; *Underwater Welders & Repairers Ltd v Street* [1968] RPC 498.

32 *O. Mustad & Son v Dosen (Note)* [1964] 1 WLR 109.

33 [1972] RPC 811 (Supreme Court of Victoria).

34 [1984] FSR 33 at 40.

drawings might be public knowledge, nonetheless the combination of information possessed the necessary quality of confidence.

A distinction which has been developed recently in the cases and which ought to be noticed here is that between trade secrets *stricto sensuo* and confidential information not amounting to trade secrets. This is a distinction that will be discussed in detail below,[35] but for the present it may be roughly defined as follows. A trade secret is a specific, identifiable, distinct item of information which is obviously sensitive, for example a secret formula; while confidential information is lower grade material such as business information. The distinction is primarily of importance in the context of contracts of employment. For the present, it is sufficient to say that it is appears that, subject to any competing legal principle such as that concerning restraint of trade, an obligation of confidence may protect both varieties of information, but the question should not be regarded as finally settled. What is clear, however, is that, first, the quality of information which can be protected depends on the particular circumstances, and secondly, the courts are in general more ready to accept that information should be protected if it is a trade secret or akin to a trade secret.

Another point which will also be returned to below is that of definition.[36] It is normally incumbent on the plaintiff in a confidential information action to specify what it is that he claims to be confidential with some degree of precision. This is of importance for several reasons. The primary reason is that until the alleged confidential information has been properly defined, it is not possible to see whether or not the claim that it is confidential is justified. Nor is it possible to establish whether it has been misused or to what extent. In practice, the process of attempting to specify the confidential information can be quite difficult, and this has the salutary effect of forcing the plaintiff to stop and consider what is truly confidential.

Some examples of information which has been found to be confidential are: an idea for a new type of carpet grip;[37] information contained in manufacturing drawings;[38] chemical formulae;[39] a secret recipe for compounding medicines;[40] secret recipes of mixtures of glass fibres for making filters;[41] aspects of design of aircraft instruments;[42] the design of an electronic circuit;[43] an optimum heat transfer coefficient.[44]

Some examples of information which has been found not to be confidential are: a report on the financial and technical prospects of a company which was expressed to be confidential but had been widely used;[45] the names,

35   See paragraph 3.5.
36   See paragraph 3.6.
37   *Seager v Copydex Ltd* [1967] 1 WLR 923.
38   *Saltman Engineering Ltd v Campbell Engineering Ltd* (1948) 65 RPC 203.
39   *Amber Size and Chemical Co. Ltd v Menzel* [1913] 2 Ch. 239.
40   *Morison v Moat* (1851) 20 LJ Ch. (NS) 513.
41   *Balston Ltd v Headline Filters Ltd* [1990] FSR 385.
42   *Reid & Sigrist Ltd v Moss & Mechanism Ltd* (1932) 49 RPC 461.
43   *System Controls Ltd v Hudson* [1986] IPD 8110.
44   *Industrial Furnaces Ltd v Reaves* [1970] RPC 605.
45   *Dunford & Elliott Ltd v Johnson & Firth Brown Ltd* [1978] FSR 143.

aptitudes and characters of employees of a company who were involved in specialist scientific research;[46] pipe diameters which, although they had been determined as a result of an extensive programme of research, could be ascertained simply by inspection.[47]

Some information may, by its nature, not be protectable as confidential information even if it is in fact secret. Examples of this are information that is mere tittle-tattle;[48] or is nonsensical or useless;[49] or is revealing of iniquity (at least where the disclosure is to a proper authority, and possibly where the disclosure is wider).[50] As a matter of logic, it would appear that there can be no confidence in false information. This point has yet to be expressly decided,[51] but in *Berkeley Administration Inc. v McClelland*[52] it was held that certain financial information was not confidential on the ground that it was not genuine historical or forecast information but rather was pure invention.

It may be observed that showing that information is confidential can be a somewhat artificial process. The true reason why an attempt is made to protect such information is usually because it is of commercial value. Whitford J observed in the case of *Yates Circuit Foil Co. v Electrofoils Ltd* that:

> It may well be that in the end the most important secret in this field as in other fields is that there is really nothing so very secret in what anybody else is doing; but the mere fact that nobody knows what anybody else is doing may have some commercial advantage to it . . . the mere possibility of being able to announce a new treatment may be a not inconsiderable commercial advantage.[53]

Nevertheless, something more than a mere assertion of commercial value is usually required.

With this background, we can turn to consider what information may be confidential in the field of computer software.

---

46 *G. D. Searle & Co. Ltd v Celltech Ltd* [1982] FSR 92.

47 *Alfa Laval Cheese Systems Ltd v Wincanton Engineering Ltd* [1990] FSR 583.

48 *Hubbard v Vosper* [1972] 2 QB 84.

49 *Attorney-General v Guardian Newspapers Ltd (No. 3)* [1989] 2 FSR 181 at 221 (Scott J, referring to *McNicol v Sportsman's Book Stores* [1930] MCC 116), 333 (Lord Goff of Chieveley). See also *Church of Scientology v Kaufman* [1973] RPC 635.

50 See *Gartside v Outram* (1857) 26 LJ Ch. 113 at 115; *Initial Services v Putterill* [1968] 1 QB 396 at 405 to 406; *Fraser v Evans* [1969] 1 QB 349 at 363; *Beloff v Pressdram Ltd* [1973] 1 All ER 214 at 260; *Francome v Mirror Group Newspapers Ltd* [1984] 1 WLR 892; *Lion Laboratories Ltd v Evans* [1985] QB 526 at 550; *Attorney-General v Guardian Newspapers Ltd (No. 3)* [1989] 2 FSR 181.

51 In the *Spycatcher* litigation the defendants did not argue that the information was false, while the Government, although contending that some was false, naturally did not argue the point and in any event conceded that some was true. Sir John Donaldson MR at one point in his judgment suggested that Peter Wright's duty of confidentiality extended to false allegations (*Attorney-General v Guardian Newspapers Ltd (No. 3)* [1989] 2 FSR 181 at 267). Even if this is right, this could only apply in the peculiar circumstances of that case.

52 [1990] FSR 505.

53 [1976] FSR 345 at 357.

3.3.1.1 Source code

On general principles it seems clear that source code which is kept secret may be protectable confidential information. It also seems clear that this can be achieved by an express contractual term.

3.3.1.2 Object code

In the absence of express contractual provision, it is unlikely that object code would in itself be treated as confidential, for it is this that is disseminated to users. This does not, mean, however, that it would not be possible to create a valid express obligation to keep it confidential, particularly where the object code is supplied pursuant to a run-time only licence.

3.3.1.3 Underlying concepts

It has been held that the underlying concepts for a new programme were confidential until published.[54]

3.3.1.4 Algorithms

It would appear likely that the algorithm employed by a particular program is capable of being confidential information. The algorithm could be compared to a secret formula or recipe, both of which have been protected.

3.3.2 Communication of information in confidential circumstances

Mere proof that information is of itself confidential is not sufficient to impose an obligation of confidence on any individual. It is also necessary that the relevant information should have been communicated (or, possibly, acquired) in such circumstances as to import an obligation of confidence. The obligation may be express but frequently will be implied by the courts from the circumstances surrounding its disclosure. In the absence of any contract into which terms as to the permissible use of the information might be implied, the question is whether any equitable obligation of confidence affected the communication. The test to be applied in determining this question was stated by Megarry J in *Coco v Clark* as follows:

> It may be that that hard-worked creature, the reasonable man, may be pressed into service once more; for I do not see why he should not labour in equity as well as at law. It seems to me that if the circumstances are such that any reasonable man standing in the shoes of the recipient of the information would have realised that upon reasonable grounds the information was being given to him in confidence, then this should suffice to impose upon him the equitable obligation of confidence. In particular, where information of commercial or industrial value is given on a business-like basis and with some avowed common object in mind, such as a joint

54 *Cableship Ltd v Williams* (unreported, Hoffmann J, 18 March 1991).

venture or the manufacture of articles by one party for the other, I would regard the recipient as carrying a heavy burden if he seeks to repel a contention that he was bound by an obligation of confidence . . .[55]

In applying this test to the facts of that case, Megarry J observed:

> If the reasonable man is overworked, so is the officious bystander; but just as he provides a convenient touchstone for implied terms in contract, so I think he may perform some useful function in relation to the implied obligation of confidence. If he had said to the parties at the outset, 'Do you not think that you ought to have an express agreement that everything you are discussing is confidential?', I think the parties would have testily suppressed him with a common 'But of course it is' . . . The circumstances of the disclosure in this case seem to me to be redolent of trust and confidence. Business men naturally concentrate on their business, and very sensibly do not constantly take legal advice before opening their mouths or writing a letter, so that business may flow and not stagnate. I think the court, despite the caution which must be exercised before implying any obligation, must be ready to make those implications upon which the sane and fair conduct of business is likely to depend.[56]

Although neither of these passages was cited in the *Spycatcher* case, the approach adopted by the House of Lords to the question of confidential information which comes into the hands of third parties appears to be consistent with them.[57]

Megarry J's formulation of the second element suggests that the information must have been deliberately disclosed by one party (the confider) to another (the confidant). In most cases, this will be the case, and the obligation of confidence will arise either by virtue of an express or implied term of a contract, or because the confider requested the confidant to keep the information confidential or because the nature of their dealings shows that it was implicit that the information would or should be kept confidential. This formulation does not, however, allow for cases where the information is not deliberately disclosed by the confider. One important class of case is where the information is not disclosed by the confider at all, but is created by the confidant himself. This is the case where an employee creates the information himself in the course of his employment. Notwithstanding Megarry J's formulation, it is clear that such information may be confidential to the employer.[58] This leaves two other classes of case, first where the information is improperly or surreptitiously acquired,[59] and secondly where the information is acquired serendipitously.

In the first class of case, although there are *dicta* to the contrary,[60] it now seems clear that a person who improperly or surreptitiously obtains

---

55 [1969] RPC 41 at 48.
56 *Ibid.* at 50 to 51.
57 See in particular the speech of Lord Goff of Chieveley, *Attorney-General v Guardian Newspapers Ltd (No. 3)* [1989] 2 FSR 181 at 332 to 333.
58 See paragraph 3.5.
59 Where this occurs, it may also be possible to establish liability for deceit in appropriate circumstances.
60 See in particular *Malone v Metropolitan Police Commissioner* [1979] Ch. 344 at 376 *per* Sir Robert Megarry VC, although it should be noted that the Vice-Chancellor gave as an alternative ground for his decision on this point the principle that there was no confidence in iniquity.

confidential information will become fixed with an obligation of confidence. Thus in *Lord Ashburton v Pape*,[61] the defendant was restrained from disclosing certain letters or copies thereof which he had obtained by a trick.[62] Swinfen Eady LJ held that:

> The principle upon which the Court of Chancery has acted for many years has been to restrain the publication of confidential information improperly or surreptitiously obtained or of information imparted in confidence which ought not to be divulged.[63]

This *dictum* was applied to similar facts by Warner J in *ITC Film Distributors Ltd v Video Exchange Ltd*[64] and by the Court of Appeal in *Goddard v Nationwide Building Society*.[65]

The second class is exemplified by a series of cases[66] in which documents have accidentally been disclosed to opposing parties during the course of litigation.[67] From these it appears that if the acquirer of the information either receives notice or himself appreciates that the information is confidential so that his conscience is affected, an obligation of confidence will arise. Thus in *English & American Insurance Ltd v Herbert Smith*[68] the papers of counsel for the defendants in an action had been mistakenly returned to the solicitors for the plaintiffs. The plaintiffs' solicitors, having realised what had happened, consulted the Law Society and taken their clients' instructions, proceeded to read the papers and take notes. An injunction was granted to restrain the solicitors from using the information thus obtained and delivery up of the notes was ordered. Sir Nicolas Browne-Wilkinson VC expressly rejected the submission that a third party who had innocently received confidential information could not be restrained from using it.[69] That this is the position is confirmed by the decision in the *Spycatcher* case.[70]

61 [1913] 2 Ch. 469.
62 It is important to note that it is irrelevant that the letters, which were addressed to the plaintiff's solicitor, would have been subject to legal professional privilege in the hands of the plaintiff or his solicitor. Once in the possession of the defendant, the plaintiff's privilege against being compelled to produce them was immaterial (and so they would have been admissible in evidence if the defendant had not been enjoined: *Calcraft v Guest* [1895] 1 QB 759). The confusion between privilege and confidentiality has bedevilled subsequent cases: see Newbold, 'Inadvertent Disclosure in Civil Proceedings' (1991) 107 LQR 99.
63 [1913] 2 Ch. 469 at 475.
64 [1982] Ch. 413.
65 [1987] QB 670. See in particular Nourse LJ at 685.
66 *English & American Insurance Co. Ltd v Herbert Smith* [1988] FSR 232; *Guinness Peat Properties Ltd v Fitzroy Robinson Partnership* [1987] 1 WLR 1027; *Webster v James Chapman & Co.* [1989] 3 All ER 939. See also *Re Briamore Manufacturing Ltd* [1986] 1 WLR 1429 which appears to be wrongly decided.
67 Again, it is a confusing irrelevance that in all cases the documents would have been protected from compulsory production by legal professional privilege if they had not been inadvertently disclosed.
68 [1988] FSR 232.
69 *Ibid.* at 237.
70 *Attorney-General v Guardian Newspapers Ltd (No. 3)* [1989] 2 FSR 181. See in particular Lord Goff of Chievely at 332.

A question which remains to be answered, however, is what the position is of a party who receives information without either being notified or himself realising that it is confidential. As is discussed in paragraph 3.3.2.2, this may depend on whether the recipient has given consideration or not.

In summary, a more general way of formulating the second element is not in terms of the circumstances in which the information was *disclosed*, but in terms of the circumstances in which it was *received*.

3.3.2.1 The period of protection – the 'springboard' principle

It is important to realise that information may not be protectable indefinitely by an obligation of confidence. There may be a period during which information may justifiably be regarded as confidential, but after which such a label is inappropriate even if it has not in fact been published by then. In *Attorney-General v Jonathan Cape Ltd*[71] the British Government sought to restrain publication of the diaries of a former cabinet minister, Richard Crossman, which contained details of past cabinet discussions. Lord Widgery CJ observed that there must be a limit in time after which the confidential character of information, and the duty of the court to restrain its publication, will lapse. In that case the Court was clear that the confidentiality that had subsisted in cabinet discussions which took place over ten years previously had come to an end.[72]

In commercial contracts containing express obligations of confidentiality, it is not uncommon for this principle to be recognised by a term limiting the obligation to a particular period. Although the point has not been tested in court, it is conceivable that a contract which attempted to impose an indefinite obligation in respect of information which only merited, say, a ten-year restraint, would be held to be in restraint of trade. The courts have stressed that the categories of restraint of trade are not closed.[73]

A black-and-white division between information which is confidential and information which has become public or otherwise free from confidence fails, however, to take into account the inequity of the head start that may have been obtained by a defendant during the period in which information was confidential. It has been made clear that where a person has used information obtained in confidence as a 'springboard' for activities detrimental to the confider, the courts are prepared to grant such remedies as will bring him back to a commercial starting line. Thus in *Terrapin v Builders Supply Co (Hayes) Ltd*[74] Roxborough J stated that the springboard remains 'even when all the features have been published or can be ascertained by actual inspection by any member of the public'. The judge specifically dealt with the fact that it would be possible for members of the public, without knowing the confidential information, to dismantle the units embodying it which had

---

71 [1976] QB 752.
72 *Ibid.* at 771.
73 *Esso Petroleum Co. Ltd v Harper's Garage (Stourpourt) Ltd* [1968] AC 269 at 337 *per* Lord Wilberforce.
74 [1967] RPC 375 at 391.

been put on general sale. However, such a 'reverse engineering' operation would not reveal the secrets of the know-how behind the machine, without further tests and construction of a prototype. Therefore the possessor of the confidential information had a long start over any member of the public. Roxborough J held that the possessor of such information 'must be placed under a special disability in the field of competition in order to ensure that he does not get an unfair start'.[75] In *Alfa Laval Cheese Systems Ltd v Wincanton Engineering Ltd*[76] this principle was applied to information which members of the public could only obtain by dismantling the plaintiff's product but not to information as to the diameters of pipes which was apparent to all.

The nature of the 'special disability' is illustrated by *Fisher Karpark Industries Ltd v Nichols*.[77] The defendants had been restrained *ex parte* from using or disclosing confidential information. By the time of the *inter partes* hearing, the injunctions had been running for some five months. The defendants, while not challenging the original grant of the injunctions, suggested that the injunctions granted had already been of sufficient duration to cancel any head start which they might improperly have obtained. Whitford J held that having regard to the precise nature and commercial worth of the information concerned, the injunctions should continue for no more than a total duration of one year. Similarly, in *Roger Bullivant Ltd v Ellis*[78] the Court of Appeal held an interlocutory injunction granted against the plaintiffs' former managing director, who had taken a card index of names and addresses of customers, should be limited to the period of one year which was contained in a restrictive clause of his contract.

3.3.2.2 *The effect of publication other than by the confider*

A question which was intensely debated during the course of the *Spycatcher* litigation was the effect on an obligation of confidence of publication of the confidential information by someone other than the confider. Does this destroy the obligation? Regrettably, the answer is still not entirely clear.

The starting point is that publication of the confidential information by or with the authority of the confider not only prevents any obligation of confidence arising if it occurs before the information is imparted to the confidant but also terminates any obligation of confidence previously imposed if it occurs after the information is imparted, as in the case where a patent specification containing details of the allegedly confidential process was published after proceedings had been commenced.[79]

The next stage is to consider the position if, after information has been imparted in confidence, it is published by a stranger to the confidence. In

75 *Ibid.* at 392.
76 [1990] FSR 583.
77 [1982] FSR 351.
78 [1987] FSR 172.
79 *O. Mustad & Son v Dosen (Note)* [1964] 1 WLR 109.

Speed Seal Products Ltd v Paddington,[80] the Court of Appeal accepted that the case of *Cranleigh Precision Engineering Ltd v Bryant*[81] was authority for the proposition that this 'does not necessarily' terminate the obligation of confidence.[82] This was referred to with approval by Lord Griffiths in the *Spycatcher* case,[83] but criticised by Lord Goff, who pointed out that *Cranleigh* was really a form of springboard case.[84] All of these *dicta* were *obiter*, and so the point remains open for decision. It is submitted, however, that the reasoning of Lord Goff is to be preferred, and if the information is published by a stranger to the confidence, the effect is to destroy the subject-matter of the confidence. It is common practice in confidentiality clauses in commercial contracts to include a provision that the obligation does not apply if the information is published by a third party, and there is good reason for this. It would be commercially wholly unacceptable for one party to be unable to use technical or commercial information which had become widely available through no fault of his own merely because at one time he contracted to another party to keep the same information confidential. This can most clearly be seen by considering the case where the information is a chemical or mathematical formula which is later independently derived by a third party and published by him, a not uncommon occurrence.

The final stage is to consider what is the effect of unauthorised disclosure by or with the authority of the confidant. In the *Spycatcher* case, Scott J at first instance expressly,[85] all three members of the Court of Appeal implicitly,[86] and four members of the House of Lords expressly,[87] held that the worldwide publication of the book would not have prevented the Crown from obtaining an injunction against Peter Wright and his publishers to restrain publication in the United Kingdom. These *dicta* are all *obiter*, not least because neither Wright nor his publishers were parties to the proceedings, and the point does not appear to have been strongly argued, if at all, by the newspapers, for the understandable reason that it was not necessary for them to do so. Nevertheless, the case is strong persuasive authority, and so cannot be ignored. It is therefore worth looking at the reasons given for this.

Two different bases were given for such an injunction. All the members of the Court of Appeal appear to have accepted and Lords Griffiths and Jauncey in the House of Lords clearly did accept that publication did not release Wright from his duty of confidence, that some duty survived. Scott J and Lords Keith and Brightman held that Wright could not benefit by his own wrong. Both Lord Keith and Lord Brightman, on the other hand, expressly

80 [1985] 1 WLR 1327.
81 [1965] 1 WLR 1293.
82 Note 80 above at 1332.
83 *Attorney-General v Guardian Newspapers Ltd (No. 3)* [1989] 2 FSR 181 at 319.
84 *Ibid.* at 336 to 337.
85 *Ibid.* at 235.
86 *Ibid.* at 248 to 249, 266 to 269 (Sir John Donaldson MR), 272 (Dillon LJ), 289, 296, 298 (Bingham LJ).
87 *Ibid.* at 310 (Lord Keith of Kinkel), 317 (Lord Brightman), 321 to 323 (Lord Griffiths), 345 (Lord Jauncey of Tullichettle).

held that no duty of confidence survived publication, without explaining how else the principle that a man could not profit from his own wrong applied. A third basis was canvassed by judges in all three courts, namely that the Crown was the equitable owner of the copyright in *Spycatcher*, but the Crown expressly disclaimed this for reasons that are set out in the judgment of Sir John Donaldson MR in the Court of Appeal.[88]

Given that those members of the House of Lords who held that an injunction would issue against Peter Wright were evenly divided on the question whether his duty survived publication, it is worth quoting the penetrating critique of the proposition that the duty did survive given by Lord Goff (who based his decision that no injunction would issue, however, on the separate[89] point that an injunction would not be in the public interest[89]). As discussed above, Lord Goff began by examining the *Cranleigh* and *Speed Seal* cases, and disapproving the reasoning in the latter. He went on to consider the proposition that a man could not profit by his own wrong:

> The statement that a man shall not be allowed to profit from his own wrong is in very general terms, and does not of itself provide any sure guidance to the solution of a problem in any particular case. That there are groups of cases in which a man is not allowed to profit from his own wrong, is certainly true. An important section of the law of restitution is concerned with cases in which a defendant is required to make restitution in respect of benefits acquired through his own wrongful act – notably cases of waiver of tort; of benefits acquired by certain criminal acts; of benefits acquired in breach of a fiduciary relationship; and, of course, of benefits acquired in breach of confidence. The plaintiff's claim to restitution is usually enforced by an account of profits made by the defendant through his wrong at the plaintiff's expense. This remedy of an account is alternative to the remedy of damages, which in cases of breach of confidence is now available, despite the equitable nature of the wrong, through a beneficent interpretation of the Chancery Amendment Act 1858 (Lord Cairns's Act), and which by reason of the difficulties attending the taking of an account is often regarded as a more satisfactory remedy, at least in cases where the confidential information is of commercial nature, and quantifiable damage may therefore have been suffered.
>
> I have to say, however, that I know of no case (apart from the present) in which the maxim has been invoked in order to hold that a person under an obligation is not released from that obligation by the destruction of the subject matter of the obligation, on the ground that that destruction was the result of his own wrongful act. To take an obvious case, a bailee who by his own wrongful, even deliberately wrongful, act destroys the goods entrusted to him, is obviously relieved of his obligation as bailee, though he is of course liable in damages for his tort. Likewise a nightwatchman who deliberately sets fire to and destroys the building he is employed to watch; and likewise the keeper at a zoo who turns out to be an animal rights campaigner and releases rare birds or animals which escape irretrievably into the countryside. On this approach, it is difficult to see how a confidant who publishes the relevant confidential information to the whole world can be under any further obligation not to disclose the information, simply because it was he who wrongfully destroyed its confidentiality. The information has, after all, already been

---

88   *Ibid.* at 266.
89   *Ibid.* at 341.

so fully disclosed that it is in the public domain: how, therefore, can he be sensibly restrained from disclosing it? Is he not even to be permitted to mention in public what is now common knowledge? For his wrongful act, he may be liable in damages, or may be required to make restitution; but, to adapt the words of Lord Buckmaster,[90] the confidential information, as confidential information, has ceased to exist, and with it should go, as a matter of principle, the obligation of confidence. In truth, when a person entrusts something to another – whether that thing be a physical thing such as chattel, or some intangible thing such as confidential information – he relies upon that other to fulfil his obligation. If he discovers that the other is about to commit a breach, he may be able to impose an added sanction against his doing so by persuading the court to grant an injunction; but if the other simply commits a breach and destroys the thing, then the injured party is left with his remedy in damages or in restitution. The subject matter is gone: the obligation is therefore also gone: all that is left is the remedy or remedies for breach of the obligation.[91]

The view thus expressed by Lord Goff is in agreement with that which had previously been expressed by the Law Commission in its Report on Breach of Confidence.[92]

Finally, however, two things should be noted even if Lord Goff is right. First, publication by the confidant only goes to the question of remedy, and in particular whether an injunction will lie. Secondly, this only applies to cases where the information has actually been published by the defendant; if the defendant has simply used the information, an injunction will still lie.

3.3.2.3 The obligation of confidence and third parties

The central question in the *Spycatcher* case was whether a third party other than the original confidant who receives the confidential information himself comes under an obligation of confidence to the confider, and if so what the scope of that obligation is. Here again, the matter is still not entirely clear.

What is clear from *Spycatcher* is that where a third party comes into possession of confidential information with notice that the information is confidential, then the third party does himself come under an equitable obligation to keep the information confidential.[93] It is not certain what is required to constitute notice, but it appears likely that actual knowledge is not required and that constructive knowledge will suffice. The 'reasonable man' test propounded by Megarry J in *Coco v Clark* may be applicable here.

What also appears to be clear from *Spycatcher*, however, is that the scope of the third party's obligation is not necessarily co-terminous with the original confidant's obligation. The exception to this is where the third party has come by the information by reason of the original confidant's breach of duty

---

90 'The secret, as a secret, had ceased to exist' in *O. Mustad & Son v Dosen (Note)* [1964] 1 WLR 109 at 111.
91 *Ibid.* at 337 to 338.
92 Cmnd 8388 at paragraph 4.30.
93 *Attorney-General v Guardian Newspapers (No. 3)* [1989] 2 FSR 181 at 311 (Lord Keith of Kinkel), 319 to 320 (Lord Griffiths), 332 (Lord Goff of Chieveley) applying *Duchess of Argyll v Duke of Argyll* [1967] Ch. 302.

and was himself a participant in the breach, as in *Schering Chemical Ltd v Falkman Ltd*,[94] where Thames Television, which had received information from Falkman in breach of Falkman's duty to Schering, was restrained as well as Falkman.[95] Where the third party comes by the information without being a participant, then the situation may be different. Thus in *Spycatcher*, the House of Lords held that the *Sunday Times* had come under an obligation of confidence when it had received a copy of the manuscript of the book, and had breached that obligation by publishing the first instalment of a serialisation of it shortly before the book was published in the United States. At this point the *Sunday Times's* obligation was co-terminous with that of Wright. After publication in the United States, however, the *Sunday Times* was free to continue its serialisation and the other newspapers were free to publish, even through Wright himself could not publish in the United Kingdom and even though the newspapers were on notice of the breach of duty. This, as Lord Goff pointed out, is a rather illogical result. A more logical approach would have been to say the third party's duty is co-terminous, but that the newspapers were free to publish because the information was no longer confidential and so no duty subsisted.

One point that remains unclear is the position of the third party who receives confidential information without notice of the confidence but without purchasing it. In other words, does the equitable duty of confidence operate like a property right and bind all recipients of the information except a *bona fide* purchaser for value without notice? During the first round of the interlocutory stage of the case (that is before publication of the book in the US), it was suggested by Nourse LJ that this was the position.[96] During the second round of the interlocutory stage of the case (after the US publication), this suggestion was supported by Sir Nicolas Browne-Wilkinson VC.[97] At trial, it was rejected by Scott J[98] but endorsed on appeal by Sir John Donaldson MR[99] and Bingham LJ.[100] In the House of Lords, none of their Lordships adverted to the point. The authors' view is that since an obligation of confidence is personal and not proprietary, a person who receives confidential information without notice that it is confidential information does not become subject to an obligation of confidence even if he is a volunteer.

3.3.3   Unauthorised use or disclosure of the information

The third element of Megarry J's formulation quoted above is that unauthorised use (or disclosure) of the information is to the detriment of the

94   [1982] QB 1.
95   See the explanation of this case by Lord Oliver of Aylmerton in the second interlocutory round of *Spycatcher*: *Attorney-General v Guardian Newspapers Ltd (No. 2)* [1989] 2 FSR 81 at 160.
96   *Attorney-General v Guardian Newspapers Ltd* [1989] 2 FSR 3 at 26 reiterating the view he had expressed, also *obiter*, in *Goddard v Nationwide Building Society* [1987] QB 670 at 685.
97   *Attorney-General v Guardian Newspapers Ltd (No. 2)* [1989] 2 FSR 81 at 98 to 100.
98   *Attorney-General v Guardian Newspapers Ltd (No. 3)* [1989] 2 FSR 181 at 226 to 228.
99   *Ibid.* at 248.
100   *Ibid.* at 288.

confider, although later in the same judgment he indicated that he was leaving the question of detriment open.[101] In general, any use or disclosure will be unauthorised if it is a use or disclosure otherwise than for the purposes for which the information was imparted.[102] It is worth noting that in some circumstances disclosure would not be authorised whereas use would be.[103] As to detriment, in most cases there will be an obvious detriment to the confider. In some cases, however, it may be less obvious that there is a detriment to the confider.

The question whether it is necessary for the confider to show detriment was considered by some of the members of the House of Lords in *Spycatcher*. Lord Keith pointed out that even, for example, the anonymous donor of a large sum of money to a worthy cause could well have valid reasons for wishing to remain anonymous:

> So I would think it a sufficient detriment to the confider that information given in confidence is to be disclosed to persons whom he would prefer not to know of it, even though the disclosure would not be harmful to him in any positive way.[104]

This, of course, effectively disposes of the requirement for detriment. Lord Griffiths' judgment, on other hand, suggests that detriment is required.[105] Lord Goff, finally, wished to keep the point open, although he indicated that detriment might be widely interpreted.[106]

It is clear from *Spycatcher* and from the Crossman diaries case[107] that preceded it, that where the Government seeks to enforce state confidentiality, then detriment must be shown, in the sense that there must be a public interest which favours non-disclosure. In private law cases, however, the point remains open; but it is doubtful whether the requirement, if it is held to exist, will ever prove much of an obstacle.

3.4 KNOW-HOW LICENCES AND ESCROW AGREEMENTS

In the context of computer software, the information that a software producer is likely to want to keep confidential are the source code and the underlying concepts of the software, particularly algorithms. In order to achieve this aim, it is necessary both to consider external and internal security. There are practical steps that can and should be taken to improve both.

---

101 *Coco v Clark* [1969] RPC 41 at 48.
102 *Saltman v Campbell* (1948) 65 RPC 203 at 213.
103 *R v Licensing Authority ex parte Smith Kline & French Laboratories Ltd* [1989] FSR 440; *Smith Kline & French Laboratories (Australia) Ltd v Secretary for the Department of Community Services and Health* [1990] FSR 617 (Federal Court of Australia).
104 *Attorney-General v Guardian Newspapers Ltd (No. 3)* [1989] 2 FSR 181 at 307.
105 *Ibid.* at 319 to 320, 322.
106 *Ibid.* at 333.
107 *Attorney-General v Jonathan Cape Ltd* [1976] QB 752. See also the Australian cases of *Commonwealth v John Fairfax & Sons Ltd* (1980) 147 CLR 39 (High Court of Australia) and *Smith Kline & French Laboratories (Australia) Ltd v Secretary for the Department of Community Services and Health* [1990] FSR 617 (Federal Court of Australia).

So far as external security is concerned, there are two main issues. The first is supply of source code: don't. The source code should either be retained by the supplier or, if this is not acceptable to the user, deposited with an organisation such as the National Computer Centre under an escrow agreement whereby the source code is released to the user on the occurrence of certain specified events, for example if the supplier goes into liquidation. The second main issue is the nature of the contractual terms on which software is supplied to users. Software should be supplied under licences (sometimes referred to as 'know-how licences' to distinguish them from copyright licences) which strictly define what can and cannot be done with it, and which contain appropriate confidentiality clauses to back up the physical control of the source code.

These questions are discussed further in Chapter 8.

3.5   OBLIGATIONS OF EMPLOYEES

So far as internal security of confidential software is concerned, the main issue is the nature of the obligations of employees. The investment required to produce a particular piece of software may be considerable, and it is not much use to keep the source code secret as between the software house and its customers if the house's employees can easily leave and use their knowledge of the code to produce a cheaper rival package.

The leading case on the obligations of employees is the decision of the Court of Appeal in *Faccenda Chicken v Fowler*.[108] The Court expressed the applicable principles as follows:

> (1) Where the parties are, or have been, linked by a contract of employment, the obligations of the employee are to be determined by the contract between him and his employer . . .
> (2) In the absence of any express term, the obligations of the employee in respect of the use and disclosure of information are the subject of implied terms.
> (3) While the employee remains in the employment of the employer the obligations are included in the implied term which imposes a duty of good faith or fidelity on the employee . . . it may be noted:
> (a) that the extent of the duty of good faith will vary according to the nature of the contract . . .;
> (b) that the duty of good faith will be broken if an employee makes or copies a list of customers of the employer for use after his employment ends or deliberately memorises such a list, even though, except in special circumstances, there is no general restriction on an ex-employee canvassing or doing business with customers of his former employer . . .
> (4) The implied term which imposes an obligation on the employee as to his conduct after the determination of the employment is more restricted in its scope than that which imposes a general duty of good faith. It is clear that the obligation not to use or disclose information may cover secret processes of manufacture such as chemical formulae . . . or designs or special methods of construction . . . and other information which is of a sufficiently high degree of confidentiality as to

108   [1987] Ch. 117.

amount to a trade secret. The obligation does not extend, however, to cover all information which is given to or acquired by the employee while in his employment, and in particular may not cover information which is only 'confidential' in the sense that an unauthorised disclosure of such information to a third party while the employment subsisted would be a clear breach of the duty of good faith . . .

(5) In order to determine whether any particular item of information falls within the implied term so as to prevent its use or disclosure by an employee after his employment has ceased, it is necessary to consider all the circumstances of the case. We are satisfied that the following matters are among those to which attention must be paid:

(a) The nature of the employment. Thus employment in a capacity where 'confidential material' is habitually handled may impose a high obligation of confidentiality because the employee can be expected to realise its sensitive nature to a greater extent than if he were employed in a capacity where such material reaches him only occasionally or incidentally.

(b) The nature of the information itself. In our judgment the information will only be protected if it can properly be classed as a trade secret or as material which, while not properly to be described as a trade secret, is in all the circumstances of such a highly confidential nature as to require the same protection as a trade secret *eo nomine*. The restrictive covenant cases demonstrate that a covenant will not be upheld on the basis of the status of the information which might be disclosed by the former employee if he is not restrained, unless it can be regarded as trade secret or the equivalent of a trade secret . . . It is clearly impossible to provide a list of matters which will qualify as trade secrets or their equivalent. Secret processes of manufacture are obvious examples, but innumerable other pieces of information are *capable* of being trade secrets, though the secrecy of the information may be short-lived. In addition, the fact that the circulation of certain information is restricted to a limited number of individuals may throw light on the status of the information and its degree of confidentiality.

(c) Whether the employer impressed on the employee the confidentiality of the information. Thus though an employer cannot prevent the use or disclosure *merely* by telling the employee that certain information is confidential, the attitude of the employer towards the information provides information which may assist in determining whether or not the information can properly be regarded as a trade secret . . .

(d) Whether the relevant information can easily be isolated from other information which the employee is free to use or disclose . . . For our part we would not regard the separability of the information in question as conclusive, but the fact that the alleged 'confidential' information is part of a package and that the remainder of the package is not confidential is likely to throw light on whether the information in question is really a trade secret.[109]

This decision, which has been applied in a number of subsequent cases, has important implications for those drafting employee contracts. The most important of these is that, since different principles are applicable to the pre- and post-termination of employment situations, these situations should be dealt with separately and by different contractual terms.

109   *Ibid.* at 135 to 138.

3.5.1   Pre-termination terms

So far as pre-termination clauses are concerned, the fact that a term imposing a duty of good faith and fidelity will be implied into any contract of employment means that it is by no means essential to have an express term dealing with the employee's obligations (of confidentiality that is – it is, of course, important to stipulate the employee's other obligations such as what functions he is required to perform, his hours of work and so on). Nevertheless, it may be desirable to include an express term which deals with the question of confidential information, the extent of the employee's access to it and his responsibilities towards it. Such a clause might well be of assistance if it subsequently becomes necessary to prove to a court that the employer's information was indeed confidential.[110] It may also have the practical benefit of making the employee more careful about his handling of his employer's sensitive information, particularly if combined with other measures.

Given the breadth of the implied duty of fidelity, even a widely phrased prohibition on access to or disclosure of sensitive information is likely to be held to be valid so long as it only applies during the currency of the employment. In general, it would be difficult for an employee to challenge an express term of this nature on the ground of restraint of trade unless it were very onerous indeed. One potential pitfall that should be avoided if possible, however, is ambiguity. Clear drafting means that the employee knows what he should and should not do, and that the courts will be more ready to enforce the contract.

3.5.2   Post-termination terms

So far as post-termination clauses are concerned, these fall into two main classes: those which concern trade secrets only, and those which restrict post-employment competition and solicitation. These must be considered separately.

3.5.2.1   Trade secrets clauses

It is important to appreciate that a wide prohibition on use or disclosure of information may be valid insofar as it applies prior to termination, but invalid insofar as it applies after termination.[111] If an express term prohibiting use or disclosure of particular trade secrets after employment is desired, it should be narrowly drawn. In particular, some attempt should be

---

110   See *G. D. Searle & Co. Ltd v Celltech Ltd* [1982] FSR 92. It might also be of material assistance in bringing a prosecution under the Computer Misuse Act 1990 if the employee were, for example, to hack into and damage system levels to which he was not authorised access. See Chapter 10.

111   *Ixora Trading Inc. v Jones* [1990] FSR 251.

made to identify the trade secrets, or the types of trade secrets, that the employee cannot take away with him.

It should be recognised, however, that this may be difficult to achieve. In particular, the employee may well have trade secrets which are not easily separable from the employee's general stock of skill and knowledge. In these circumstances the proper course is to provide a carefully drawn covenant against post-employment competition.[112] The disadvantage of this course is that the employee will become free to use the trade secrets after the expiry of the covenant, while there may be particularly important secrets that the employer wishes to preserve beyond that. In those circumstances the best course is probably to include independent and severable clauses against competition *per se* and against use of the particular trade secrets.[113]

3.5.2.2 Non-competition and non-solicitation clauses

A non-competition clause is a clause which prohibits the employee after the cessation of his employment from entering into competition with his former employer. A non-solicitation clause is a clause with prohibits the employee after the cessation of his employment from soliciting business from his former employer's customers. Both types of clause are in restraint of trade, and so must be carefully drawn, particularly non-competition clauses. Since non-solicitation clauses are less of a restriction, they are less severely judged by the courts.[114]

3.5.2.3 Restraint of trade

Because there is a public policy against restraint of trade, any clause the effect of which is to restrain trade is *prima facie* void and unenforceable. It is therefore for the employer who seeks to enforce such a clause to justify it. Such a clause can only be justified if (1) the employer has an interest which merits protection and (2) the protection given by the clause is no more than is reasonable.[115]

The two principal types of interest which are recognised by the courts as meriting protection are trade secrets and trade connections. Trade connections are where the employee is in a position to build up a personal relationship and influence with customers, such that he would easily be able to take their custom with him when he left. The classic examples of this are hairdressers and solicitors, although the same principle is applicable to other trades and professions.

---

112   *Printer & Finishers Ltd v Holloway* [1965] RPC 239 at 256; *Faccenda Chicken Ltd v Fowler* [1987] Ch. 117 at 137 to 138.
113   An illustration of the practical benefit of this course is *Lawrence David Ltd v Ashton* [1989] 1 FSR 87, where the plaintiffs succeeded in obtaining an interlocutory injunction on the basis of a non-competition clause but failed to obtain one on the basis of a confidentiality clause.
114   See for example *Stenhouse Australia Ltd v Phillips* [1974] AC 391.
115   *Nordenfelt v Maxim Nordenfelt Guns v Ammunition Co. Ltd* [1894] AC 535; *Herbert Morris Ltd v Saxelby* [1916] 1 AC 688.

In considering whether the protection is reasonable, the extent of the restriction will be examined, and in particular the temporal and geographical extent. A clause which is limited in time and area to what is reasonable will be valid and enforceable, one that is not so limited will not. Thus in *Commercial Plastics Ltd v Vincent*,[116] the Court of Appeal held that a covenant which restrained the defendant, a plastics technologist, from being employed by any of their competitors for one year after the termination of his employment was unreasonable and invalid because it was not subject to any geographical limit. A contrast to this in the software field is *SKK (UK) Ltd v Willis*,[117] where a one-year non-competition clause which Nourse J construed as being limited to the software security business in the United Kingdom was held probably to be enforceable.

3.5.2.4 'Garden leave' clauses

A recently-developed alternative to these approaches is the so-called 'garden leave' clause. This is a clause which provides, first, that the contract of employment is only terminable on a certain period's notice; secondly, that during the notice period, the employer is under no obligation to provide any work for the employee; and, thirdly, that during subsistence of the employment the employee may not undertake any other work. Thus if the employee gives notice, the employer can send him home and, provided that the employer performs his side of the contract by continuing to pay the employee and afford him any other contractual benefits, the employee will be in breach of contract if he takes any other employment during the notice period. The rationale for such clauses is that, during the period of 'garden leave', the employee's knowledge of his employer's business will grow stale and out-of-date. This may be particularly valuable in a situation where the employee – such as a senior executive – would ordinarily have access to sensitive business information which does not qualify as a trade secret.

The value of a 'garden leave' clause depends on the ability of the employer to enforce it by obtaining an interlocutory injunction. It used to be thought that no injunction would be granted to enforce a negative covenant in a contract of personal service if the consequence of the injunction would be that the employee was compelled either to carry on working for his former employer or to starve or be idle.[118] In *Provident Group plc v Hayward*,[119] however, the Court of Appeal held that as a matter of principle there was no reason why a 'garden leave' clause should not be enforced. Instead, the Court held that whether the clause is enforceable depends on the particular circumstances of the case. In particular, it depends on the damage that the employer will suffer if the employee is permitted to work for another as

---

116   [1965] 1 QB 623.
117   Unreported, Nourse J, 15 May 1985.
118   *Warner Brothers Pictures Inc. v Nelson* [1937] 1 KB 209.
119   [1989] ICR 160.

against the damage that the employee will suffer through being kept out of work. Thus the effect of this decision is essentially to apply the familiar *American Cyanamid* balance of convenience test.

3.6   ENFORCEMENT

There may be considerable practical difficulties in proving that a breach of confidence has occurred. Having identified the items alleged to be confidential, the plaintiff must then show that these items have been used by the defendant. Difficulties of detection and proof pervade all aspects of software protection and are particularly applicable to actions for breach of confidence. The defendant's use of the information will very often be in private, and evidence of such use may be destroyed when the defendant is challenged.

An important procedural aspect of actions for misuse of confidential information is the need for precise particularisation of the plaintiff's allegations. This was dramatically illustrated in the two *John Zink* decisions. In the first, *John Zink Co. Ltd v Wilkinson*,[120] the statement of claim which had been served set out in very general terms the information alleged to be confidential and the incidences of its alleged use by the defendants. On application by the defendants the Court of Appeal held that 'some condescension to detail' was required of the plaintiffs and ordered that they comply with requests for further particulars to clarify their claims. In the second, *John Zink Co. Ltd v Lloyd's Bank*,[121] the defendants having received the further particulars applied to strike out the case on the grounds of non-compliance with the order of the Court of Appeal and abuse of the process. Templeman J held that there had been compliance since the plaintiffs had done their best to provide the particulars requested, but nevertheless the particulars presented 'the same impenetrable blankness'[122] of generality. The judge was prepared to infer from such generality that the action as a whole was speculative, and found that the defendants could not be certain of the precise nature of the complaint against them. In the circumstances he struck out the Statement of Claim as an abuse of the process.

In *Speed Seal Products Ltd v Paddington*[123] the defendants again applied for particulars, before entering their defence, of the information alleged to be confidential and of which parts of such information it was alleged the defendants had actually used. Such information was listed in a confidential schedule to the statement of claim. On examination of the schedule, however, the judge found that it contained 'jejune observations' which even taken in combination were difficult to conceive of as confidential information.[124]

---

120   [1973] RPC 717.
121   [1975] RPC 385. In the intervening period Mr Wilkinson had died and the bank, which was his executor, was substituted as defendant in his place.
122   *Ibid.* at 389.
123   [1984] FSR 77.
124   *Ibid.* at 79.

Furthermore, the Court rejected the plaintiff's argument that use of confidential information might be inferred from the matters pleaded. The judge observed:

> Once one knows what is confidential, which at present I do not, of that what has been taken? Has the whole of the confidential information been used? Has some part of it been used but in conjunction with other inventions . . .? What is alleged to have been taken?[125]

The plaintiff was ordered to furnish the particulars requested.

The onerous nature of such an order, when applied to a claim for breach of confidence in a computer program, is apparent. To distinguish the precise parts of the software which are confidential as opposed to those parts of the software which are generally known, and further to give particulars of the use that the defendant has made of those parts, is a task of considerable difficulty.

This difficulty is augmented since such particulars are required before discovery in the action, and possibly before the plaintiff has had a chance to inspect the defendant's software. Indeed, the plaintiff may find himself in the Catch-22 position that he cannot give sufficient particulars without inspection, but that he cannot obtain an order for inspection unless he can give particulars of his case, a difficulty that may also be encountered in copyright cases. Thus in *Computer Aided Systems (UK) Ltd v Bolwell*[126] the plaintiffs applied for an interlocutory injunction and for an order for inspection of the defendants' software. Both were refused on the ground that the plaintiffs' case was speculative and lacking in particularity. Similarly, in *Smith Meyers Communications Ltd v Motorola Ltd*[127] an application for inspection of the defendant's hardware before delivery of the statement of claim was refused primarily on the ground that the plaintiff's evidence did not make out an arguable case.

Furthermore, if the plaintiff has failed to give such particulars, quite apart from the effect on his case as a whole, it may prove impossible either to obtain interlocutory relief or to enforce any interlocutory order that may be obtained. In *Lawrence David v Ashton*[128] an interlocutory injunction to restrain misuse of confidential information was refused since the lack of particularity meant that the defendant could not be sure how to obey the injunction. In *P.A. Thomas & Co. v Mould*[129] the plaintiffs were granted an interlocutory injunction to restrain the defendants from divulging or making use of confidential information acquired by them during their employment by the plaintiffs. Subsequent to the grant of the injunction, the defendants circulated details of the plaintiff's scheme to ascertain if it was in fact novel. The plaintiffs applied for committal of two of the defendants for breach of the

125   *Ibid.*
126   IPD April 1990 15.
127   [1991] FSR 262.
128   [1989] FSR 87.
129   [1968] 2 QB 913.

injunction. The motion was dismissed on the grounds that insufficient details of what information was confidential had been provided. O'Connor J held that:

> If the plaintiffs, seeking to protect their know-how, are anxious to enforce any injunction which may be granted to them by seeking the help of the court to punish a breach of it, it seems to me to be quite essential that they should make absolutely clear what it is they are seeking to protect.[130]

The Court was unable to infer the degree of certainty required for a committal from the plaintiffs' affidavits which concealed the precise nature of their confidential information.

If, on the other hand, the plaintiff is able to particularise his confidential information and is able to give particulars of reasons why he says the defendant may be misusing it, he may be reluctant for these to be disclosed to the defendant without any disclosure on the part of the defendant, if in the circumstances it would be possible for the defendant to alter the incriminating part of his program. A possible solution to this difficulty is exchange: the plaintiff gives his particulars of confidential information and of misuse simultaneously with the defendant either allowing inspection of his program or providing particulars of it. In an appropriate case there is no reason why this should not be ordered by the court; but it would be for the plaintiff to persuade the court that the defendant could easily change his program so as to make it necessary.

3.7 PROTECTION OF INFORMATION DISCLOSED IN COURT PROCEEDINGS

It will be apparent that the commencement of an action for breach of confidence involves the disclosure of precisely the information which the plaintiff wishes to keep confidential. This has two aspects: keeping the information confidential from the defendant, and from the public at large. As to the former, many software developers would fear that detailed disclosure of such information will further assist the defendant in his unauthorised activities. As to the latter, this is of importance if the matter gets to court given the provisions of RSC Order 24 Rule 14A and the rule that justice is generally done in open court.[131]

The courts have attempted to strike a balance between plaintiffs' fears of disclosure of confidential information, and defendants' needs to understand the case alleged against them, often by inspection of documents and articles.[132] Such inspection may be ordered subject to safeguards of confidentiality. In *Centri-spray Corp. v Cera International Ltd*[133] Whitford J granted inspection of confidential drawings on an express undertaking that

---

130 *Ibid.* at 922.
131 *Scott v Scott* [1913] AC 417.
132 *Warner-Lambert Co. v Glaxo Laboratories Ltd* [1975] RPC 354.
133 [1979] FSR 175.

no use would be made of the information disclosed thereby save for the purposes of litigation. He further ordered that the drawings should not be taken away, nor should copies be made of them.

The direct application of such safeguards to computer software was shown in the case of *Format Communications Mfg Ltd v ITT (United Kingdom) Ltd.*[134] The plaintiffs, who were alleging breach of confidence and infringement of copyright following the termination of a joint venture, were unwilling to allow discovery and inspection of their most recent source code listing, which they had developed subject to termination of the joint venture. Having held that the source code listing was a relevant document in the action, the Court of Appeal ordered discovery subject to a variety of safeguards to protect confidentiality. A similar course was followed in *Atari Inc. v Phillips Electronics and Associated Industries Ltd.*[135]

It is to be noted that in all three of the cases discussed above the Court did not feel it necessary for an independent expert to be appointed to perform the inspection. Since the subject matter was such that a substantial amount of time would be spent in familiarising an independent expert sufficiently to perform such an inspection, an expert employed by the party seeking inspection or (in the *Atari* case) an independent contractor who was the author of the defendants' program was permitted access to the confidential documents. If there is especially sensitive material, however, it may be possible to insist that there be inspection only by an independent expert.

Of course, it is not just plaintiffs who will be reluctant to disclose their confidential information. A defendant who is accused of breach of confidence will be equally reluctant, even if innocent, to reveal his software to a competitor. If inspection by or on behalf of the plaintiff is ordered, the defendant will also be entitled to appropriate safeguards. In these circumstances the court may be more ready to insist on inspection by an independent expert since the defendant, unlike the plaintiff, is not a voluntary party to the litigation.[136]

An extreme example of disclosure by a defendant is *Leisure Data v Bell.*[137] In that case there was a dispute between the parties over the ownership of copyright in certain software. The Court of Appeal upheld a mandatory interlocutory injunction requiring the defendant to disclose source codes to the plaintiff's expert, and even to permit the plaintiff's expert to maintain and modify them, upon the giving of rigorous undertakings by the plaintiff (including a provision as to the copyright in the modifications).

It may be observed that in considering what measure of disclosure should be made and on what terms, the court will have regard to the particular circumstances of each case, in particular the degree of confidentiality of the information, and the likelihood of misuse of such information following inspection.[138] It is therefore difficult to provide any general guidance.

---

134   [1983] FSR 473.
135   [1988] FSR 416.
136   See *Computer Aided Systems (UK) Ltd v Bolwell* IPD April 1990 15.
137   [1988] FSR 367.
138   See *Warner-Lambert Co. v Glaxo Laboratories Ltd* [1975] RPC 354 at 358 to 360 *per* Buckley LJ.

3.8   REMEDIES

The remedies for breach of confidence are an injunction, delivery up, damages or an account of profits. Interlocutory remedies are available on normal principle. These remedies are discussed in Chapter 9.

3.9   PRACTICAL MEASURES TO SAFEGUARD CONFIDENTIALITY

It will be apparent from the foregoing discussion that, although confidentiality is potentially a very powerful weapon, it is beset with potential pitfalls. The following is a list of practical suggestions for attempting to avoid these pitfalls:

(1) Where possible, software should be supplied only in the form of object code under a run-time licence. Source code should be retained and kept secret. Alternatively the source code should be placed in escrow.

(2) All software licences should contain express confidentiality clauses, in particular in respect of the object code. These clauses should be carefully drafted.

(3) All employees should have contracts of employment with express trade secret protection clauses and express non-competition covenants where appropriate. Such terms should again be carefully drafted.

(4) Some attempt should be made to identify and specify trade secrets and confidential information in advance. This should not be left until the need to sue someone arises.

(5) Employees should be made aware of what information is sensitive and how to treat it. Where appropriate hierarchies of access should established. Again where appropriate, security measures such as identity cards and so forth should be put in place.

(6) If contract programmers and the like are engaged, their contracts should contain confidentiality provisions.

(7) Care should be taken about publishing information, for example at exhibitions or in manuals or in magazine articles.

(8) Records should be kept of the time, money and effort invested in particular pieces of software, of the qualifications of the creators of the software, of particular problems encountered and solved. All of these may assist in persuading a court that you have valuable confidential information.

(9) Reviews of confidentiality should be conducted on a regular basis, for example annually.

4   Subsistence of Copyright

4.0   INTRODUCTION

The Copyright, Designs and Patents Act 1988 ('the 1988 Act') contains a number of provisions which specifically relate to computer programs. The legislature has given a far more detailed consideration to the subsistence and infringement of copyright in computer software than was provided in previous United Kingdom copyright enactments. Indeed, it is fair to say that the Copyright (Computer Software) Amendment Act 1985 ('the 1985 Amendment Act') was only intended as a temporary measure, until this major review of intellectual property law had been completed. The 1988 Act has repealed in their entirety a number of statutes, including the Copyright Act 1956 and the 1985 Computer Amendment Act.[1] In those circumstances it might be assumed that it has now become unnecessary to consider the position of computer software under those previous enactments. However, as discussed below,[2] as a result of certain transitional provisions in the 1988 Act, at least the 1985 Computer Amendment Act remains relevant in relation to programs written before the coming into force of the new Act.[3]

4.1   TRANSITIONAL PROVISIONS

Transitional provisions are contained in Schedule 1 of the 1988 Act. Paragraph 5(1) of Schedule 1 provides that: 'copyright subsists in an existing work after commencement only if copyright subsisted in it immediately before commencement'. An 'existing work' is defined as a work made before commencement; and, in the case of a work the making of which extended over a period, such work is taken to have been made when it was completed.[4]

1   See section 303(2) and Schedule 8.
2   See paragraphs 4.3.2 and 4.3.3 below.
3   The previous enactments are also relevant to the questions of authorship and first ownerships of such programs; and in relation to infringements committed before coming into force of the 1988 Act. See paragraphs 5.3 and 5.4 below.
4   Schedule 1 paragraph 1(3).

'Commencement' (unless otherwise qualified) is defined as the date on which the new copyright provisions come into force.[5] The copyright provisions of the 1988 Act came into force on 1 August 1989.[6]

It is further provided that every work in which copyright subsisted under the 1956 Act immediately before commencement shall be deemed to satisfy the requirements of Part 1 of the 1988 Act as to qualification for copyright protection.[7]

Accordingly, the subsistence of copyright in a computer program made before 1 August 1989 will be determined in accordance with the law in force prior to the 1988 Act.

4.1.1 The law prior to the 1988 Act

The 1985 Amendment Act expressly states that the Copyright Act 1956 shall apply in relation to a computer program as it applies in relation to a literary work, whether or not copyright would subsist in that program apart from the Amendment Act. Further, it is stated that this amendment applies to computer programs made before the commencement of the Act, as well as to programs made after that date.[8]

In *Milltronics Ltd v Hycontrol Ltd*[9] the Court of Appeal held that these words made it clear that the 1985 Act was retrospective in its operation. Its provisions in relation to subsistence applied to programs made before its commencement as well as those made thereafter.[10]

Accordingly, the question of subsistence of copyright in computer programs under the 1956 Act prior to amendment is of interest only insofar as decisions under that statute may shed light on the meaning of the more recent enactments. This is an important consideration, however, as section 172(3) of the 1988 Act provides that:

> Decisions under the previous law may be referred to for the purpose of establishing whether a provision of this part departs from the previous law, or otherwise for establishing the true construction of this Part.

In the circumstances this chapter contains a consideration of the case law under the 1956 Act, as well as the more recent statutes.

4.1.2 Modifications and improvements

Modifications and improvements to computer programs, if sufficiently substantial, may result in the creation of fresh copyright works.[11] If the

---

5 Schedule 1 paragraph 1(2).
6 See the Copyright, Designs and Patents Act 1988 (Commencement No. 1) Order 1989 (SI 1989 No. 816).
7 Schedule 1 paragraph 35.
8 Copyright (Computer Software) Amendment Act 1985 section 1.
9 [1990] FSR 273.
10 *Ibid. per* Nicholls LJ at 282.
11 In relation to the meaning of 'originality' in the Copyright Acts, see paragraph 4.2.1.

first version of a computer program is made prior to August 1989, and modified versions are made after that date, subsistence of copyright in the first version will be considered under the law before the 1988 Act, whereas subsistence of copyright in subsequent versions will be decided under the new statute.

4.2 SUBSISTENCE OF COPYRIGHT – GENERAL CONSIDERATIONS

Before giving detailed consideration to the different questions which may arise under the various statutes referred to above, it is useful to consider certain facts which must be established in order to prove subsistence of copyright under all of those enactments.

4.2.1 Originality

Originality continues to be a requirement for subsistence of copyright under the 1988 Act, just as it was under the previous law.[12] It is submitted that there is no difference in the meaning of 'originality' between the 1988 Act and the 1956 Act.[13]

The classic statement of the concept of originality in copyright law is contained in the judgment of Peterson J in *University of London Press Limited v The University Tutorial Press Limited*:

> The word 'original' does not in this connection mean that the work must be the expression of original or inventive thought. Copyright Acts are not concerned with the originality of ideas, but with the expression of thought, and, in the case of 'literary works' with the expression of the thought in print or writing. The originality which is required relates to the expression of thought. But the Act does not require that the expression must be an original or novel form, but that the work must not be copied from another work – that it should originate from the author.[14]

4.2.1.1   *The* Lego *case*

A detailed consideration of the requirement of originality is set out in the judgment of Lord Oliver of Aylmerton in the recent case of *Interlego AG v Tyco International Inc.*[15] He observed that the statement of Peterson J is incomplete because there may clearly be an original work which makes use of material obtained by the author from pre-existing sources.

---

12   Copyright, Designs and Patents Act 1988 section 1(1)(a); Copyright Act 1956 sections 2 and 3.
13   There is no change of expression in this respect between the 1956 Act and the 1988 Act.
14   [1916] 2 Ch. 601 at 608 to 609.
15   [1989] AC 217 at 256 to 266.

Lord Oliver cited with approval certain passages from the opinion of the Privy Council delivered by Lord Atkinson in *Macmillan & Co. Ltd v Cooper*:

> It is the product of the labour, skill and capital of one man which must not be appropriated by another, not the elements, the raw material, if one may use the expression, upon which the labour and skill and capital of the first has been expended. To secure copyright for this product it is necessary that labour, skill and capital should be expended sufficiently to impart the product some quality or character which the raw material did not possess and which differentiates the product from the raw material.[16]

Further, Lord Oliver cited a passage from the judgment of Lord Kinloch in *Black v Murray*:

> I think it clear that it will not create copyright in a new edition of a work, of which the copyright has expired, merely to make a few emendations of the text, or to add a few unimportant notes. To create a copyright by alterations of the text, these must be extensive and substantial, practically making a new book. With regard to notes, in like manner, they must impart an addition to the work which is not superficial or colourable, but imparts to the book a true and real value, over and above that belonging to the text.[17]

In the *Lego* case it was suggested that engineering drawings, which were very largely copied from previous drawings, but represented an updating of the pre-existing designs by the incorporation of small but technically significant modifications, were original copyright works. The Privy Council rejected this argument. It was held that skill, labour or judgment merely in the process of copying cannot confer originality. There must in addition be some element of material alteration or embellishment which suffices to make the totality of the work an original work. Lord Oliver observed that even a relatively small alteration or addition quantitatively, may, if material, suffice to convert that which is substantially copied from an earlier work into an original work. Whether it does so or not is a question of degree having regard to the quality rather than the quantity of the addition.

The modifications in issue in the *Lego* case primarily consisted of new manufacturing instructions which were technically significant and were the result of considerable labour and expertise. However Lord Oliver held that the essence of an artistic work is that which is visually significant. As there were no visually significant alterations between the previous drawings and the modified drawings, the Privy Council held that the modified drawings did not constitute original artistic works.

---

16 [1924] 40 TLR 186 at 188.
17 (1870) 9 Macph. 341 at 355 (also relied upon by Lord Atkinson in the *Macmillan* case).

4.2.1.2   The application of the Lego *case to computer programs*

A degree of caution needs to be exercised in any attempt to apply the *Lego* judgment in the context of literary works, including computer programs. In particular, certain observations of Lord Oliver support the proposition that there may be a distinction in the requirement of originality between literary works and artistic works. Lord Oliver observed that originality in the context of literary copyright has been said in several well-known cases to depend upon the degree of skill, labour and judgment involved in preparing a compilation.[18] However, he stated that to apply that test as a universal test of originality in all copyright cases (and in particular in the case of artistic copyright in the Lego drawings) was not only unwarranted by the context in which the observations were made, but palpably erroneous.[19]

Nonetheless it is submitted that, as a result of the *Lego* decision, it will be more difficult to establish originality in subsequent versions of literary works which include minor modifications on earlier works, simply by reference to the amount of skill and labour expended in making the modifications.[20]

This may be of considerable significance in relation to computer software, where it would otherwise be possible to prolong the period of the copyright monopoly by slight modifications to a program. The reasoning behind the following statement of Lord Oliver would appear to be of general application to all copyright works:

> Moreover it must be borne in mind that the Copyright Act 1956 confers protection on an original work for a generous period. The prolongation of the period of statutory protection by periodic reproduction of the original work is an operation which requires to be scrutinised with some caution to ensure that that for which protection is claimed really is an original artistic work.[21]

Summary

It is submitted that the *Lego* case lends support to the following propositions in relation to computer programs:

(1) In order to qualify for copyright protection a computer program does not have to be novel. It does not have to be proven that the way in which the program is expressed is new, nor a departure from the prior art.

---

18   [1989] AC 217 at 262, citing *G.A. Cramp & Son Ltd v Frank Smythson Ltd* [1944] AC 329 and *Ladbroke (Football) Ltd v William Hill (Football) Ltd* [1964] 1 WLR 273 at 277, 285 and 287.

19   *Ibid*. See also the suggestion at 261 that the opportunities for the creation of an original work by way of compilation of existing materials are more limited in the case of artistic copyright than in the case of literary copyright.

20   Prior to the *Lego* case, it was frequently argued that substantial copies of earlier works were original, since skill, judgment and labour were expended in making the subsequent work.

21   [1989] AC 217 at 263.

However, it is necessary to show that the expression originated with the author of the program and is the author's own work.

(2) A computer program may still be original even if it includes material taken from pre-existing sources provided that the author has added improvements to that pre-existing material whether consisting of alterations to plan, arrangement or text.

(3) Equally the creation of modified versions of a computer program may give rise to a fresh copyright work.

(4) However in order for copyright to subsist in the situations referred to in paragraphs (2) and (3) above the alterations must be substantial and must have a material effect on the program.

(5) The substantiality of a modification or improvement is judged by its quality rather than its quantity. Even a relatively small alteration or addition quantitatively may, if sufficiently material, suffice to convert that which is substantially copied from an earlier work into an original. By contrast, an alteration which required considerable skill and labour in its execution may not create a new work if it does not affect a material change in the form of expression of the computer program.

4.2.1.3 Originality of 'pirated' works

The *Lego* case was concerned with works which were legitimately copied from earlier works. This does not answer the question of whether copyright may subsist in a work which comprises an unauthorised copy of some or all of a previous work. This issue was specifically considered in *Warwick Film Productions Ltd v Eisinger*.[22] This case concerned certain books and films based upon the trials of Oscar Wilde. It was argued by the defendants that the author of the work relied upon by the plaintiffs had copied a previous work entitled 'Three Times Tried' without permission from anyone who had been proven to be the owner of the copyright therein. It was argued that the subsequent work must be regarded as piratical, and that no copyright exists in a pirated book or, at any rate, in the pirated part of that book.[23]

Plowman J rejected this argument. In considering the problem of a literary work which included part original and part pirated material, he followed the approach of the House of Lords in *Ladbroke (Football) Ltd v William Hill (Football) Ltd*.[24]

In the *Ladbroke* case the argument was rejected that because the fragments of a compilation, taken separately, would not qualify for copyright protection, the whole could not be the subject of copyright. It was held that the correct approach was first to determine whether the plaintiff's

---

22 [1969] Ch. 508 at 530.
23 In support of this submission the following cases were relied on: *Cary v Faden* (1799) 5 VS 24; *Cary v Longman* (1801) 1 East 358; *Walter v Steinkopff* [1892] 3 Ch. 489; *Walter v Lane* [1900] AC 539, *per* Lord Brampton; as well as certain United States authorities.
24 [1964] 1 WLR 285.

work as a whole was original and protected by copyright, and then to en-quire whether the part taken by the defendant was a substantial part. Lord Pearson summarised the law on this subject in the following passage:

> The reproduction of a part by itself that has no originality will not normally be a substantial part of the copyright and therefore will not be protected. For that which would not attract copyright except by reason of its collocation will, when robbed of that collocation not be a substantial part of the copyright and therefore the court will not hold its reproduction to be an infringement. It is this, I think, which is meant by one or two judicial observations that 'there is no copyright' in some unoriginal part of a whole that is copied. They afford no justification, in my view, for holding that one starts the enquiry as to whether copyright exists by dissecting the compilation to component parts instead of starting it by regarding the compilation as a whole and seeing whether the whole has copyright. It is when one is debating whether the part reproduced is substantial that one considers the pirate portion on its own.[25]

In applying that test in the Oscar Wilde case, Plowman J held that the work relied on by the plaintiffs did attract copyright, in spite of the fact that it contained much unoriginal material. However, he held that the defendant's film did not reproduce a substantial part of the plaintiff's book since although considerable use had been made of unoriginal material in that book, this had attracted copyright only by collocation with edited passages and taken alone could not constitute a substantial part of the book; the defendant's use of the original material was very limited and did not infringe the plaintiff's copyright.

The application of this doctrine to computer software

If a computer program relied upon by a plaintiff in a copyright action is itself an unauthorised copy of an earlier computer program, this may provide a defence in the action. However, it is submitted that, unless the work relied upon is a slavish copy of the earlier work with only minor modifications, it is likely that copyright will subsist in the plaintiff's computer program. However, the allegations of non-originality may be used to rebut the claim that the defendant has reproduced a substantial part of the plaintiff's computer program.

4.2.2   Qualification for copyright protection

Copyright will only subsist in a work if it qualifies for protection under the 1988 Act. A work will qualify for protection either by reference to its author, or by reference to the place where the work was first published.

Under schedule 1 paragraph 35 of the 1988 Act a work made before commencement qualifies for protection if it qualified for protection under the 1956 Act. Accordingly it is necessary to consider the qualification provisions under both statutes.

---

25   *Ibid.* at 293.

4.2.2.1   *Qualification under the 1988 Act*

Pursuant to section 154 of the 1988 Act a work qualifies for protection if the author was a qualified person at the material time. Qualified persons include:

(a) British Citizens, together with various categories of British overseas citizens and British protected persons
(b) Individuals domiciled or resident in the United Kingdom or in another country to which the relevant provisions of the statute *extend*
(c) Books incorporated under the law of a part of the United Kingdom or of another country to which the relevant provisions *extend* (emphasis added)

Works are also protected if at the material time the author was a citizen or subject of, or an individual domiciled or resident in, or a body incorporated under the law of any country to which the Act is *applied* by Orders in Council made pursuant to section 159.

Pursuant to section 155 of the 1988 Act, a work also qualifies for protection if it is first published in the United Kingdom or in another country to which the Act extends or is applied. 'Publication' means the issue of copies to the public, and includes, in the case of a literary, dramatic, musical or artistic work, making it available to the public by means of an electronic retrieval system.[26]

In summary, in most cases a work will qualify for protection either because the author is a qualified person, or because he is a citizen of or resident or domiciled in a country to which the Act has been applied. It is only where neither of these criteria can be fulfilled that it is necessary to rely on the place of first publication of the work.

4.2.2.2   *Qualification under the 1956 Act*

The qualification provisions under the 1956 Act were very similar to the new legislation considered above. The principal difference of relevance to computer programs is that under the 1956 Act, it was possible for an unpublished work to lose its protection on publication, if it was first published in a country to which the Act did not extend and had not been applied.[27]

This is no longer the case under the 1988 Act, since section 153(3) provides that if the qualification requirements are once satisfied in respect of a work, copyright does not cease to subsist by reason of any subsequent event.

It was held by the Court of Appeal in *Milltronics Limited v Hycontrol Ltd*[28] that the provisions for qualification under the 1956 Act also applied to the 1985 Computer Amendment Act.

---

26   1988 Act section 175(1).
27   Copyright Act 1956 section 2(2)(a).
28   [1990] FSR 273.

4.3   SUBSISTENCE OF COPYRIGHT IN COMPUTER PROGRAMS UNDER THE VARIOUS COPYRIGHT STATUTES

4.3.1   The 1988 Act

The 1988 Act specifically provides that 'literary work' means any work, other than a dramatic or musical work, which is written, spoken or sung, and of course includes a computer program.[29]

No definition of 'computer program' is provided. It may be thought that the absence of a definition is desirable, since a definition would limit the scope of the section and might well be rendered obsolete by advances in technology.

Nonetheless the absence of a definition is likely to lead to considerable argument as to whether a particular manifestation of computer software is a 'computer program' within the meaning of section 3(1)(b) of the 1988 Act. In the absence of judicial consideration of this section conclusions on the meaning of this phrase are speculative. However it is submitted that some guidance as to the meaning of 'computer program' may be derived from references to this phrase in other parts of the Act.

In particular, section 21(4) of the 1988 Act, which deals with infringement by making adaptations, provides that:

> In relation to a computer program a 'translation' includes a version of the program in which it is converted into or out of a computer language or code or into a different computer language or code otherwise than incidentally in the course of running a program.

This section is concerned with infringement as opposed to subsistence of copyright. Nonetheless, it does appear to contemplate different versions of a computer program in different languages or codes. This suggests that computer software will fall within the ambit of section 3(1)(b), whether first written in source, assembler or object code.

This conclusion is reinforced by the statutory definitions of 'writing' contained in section 178 of the 1988 Act. This provides that 'writing' includes any form of notation or code, whether by hand or otherwise and regardless of the method by which, or medium in or on which, it is recorded.

A possible area of debate is whether microcode stored in a ROM can properly be regarded as computer programs. It is submitted that the code stored within such media can generally be described as a computer program. The fact that it may also form part of the machine would appear to be of no relevance under the 1988 Act. Further support for this view is derived from the Australian *Apple Computer* case discussed below.

---

29   Section 3(1).

It is submitted, that the courts are likely to take a broad view of the meaning of computer program in the new Act. In the absence of any statutory definition the meaning of the phrase is likely to be determined by evidence from persons skilled in the art – would a particular embodiment be described as a computer program?

Under previous legislation, the requirement that a literary work should be expressed in material form created difficulties in relation to computer software. By contrast section 3(2) of the 1988 Act provides that:

> Copyright does not subsist in a literary, dramatic or musical work unless and until it is recorded, in writing or otherwise; and references in this part to the time at which such a work is made are to the time at which it is so recorded.

It would appear from this section that copyright will subsist in a computer program once it has been recorded, irrespective of the medium in which it is recorded. The phrase 'in writing or otherwise' is not limited to any specific medium.

The word 'recorded' is not defined in the 1988 Act. It seems clear that whenever a computer program is recorded in permanent form the requirement of section 3(2) will be satisfied. However, where a program is simply written into RAM, and only exists in transient form, there may be some doubt as to whether it can be said to have been 'recorded'. While the 1988 Act specifically resolves the question of works stored in RAM in relation to infringement of copyright, it does not do so in relation to subsistence.

However, since any copyright action is likely to concern computer programs of which there is at least one hard copy, the point is probably of academic interest only.

4.3.2 The 1985 Computer Amendment Act

Section 1(1) of the 1985 Amendment Act states that:

> The Copyright Act 1956 shall apply in relation to a computer program (including one made before the commencement of this Act) as it applies in relation to a literary work and shall so apply whether or not copyright would subsist in that program apart from this Act.

Section 2 of the Act provides that references in the Copyright Act 1956 to the reduction of any work to a material form shall include references to storage of that work in a computer.

The combined effect of these sections is that a number of questions raised under the old law in relation to subsistence of copyright in computer programs would appear to be settled. Under the 1985 Act, a computer program is treated as a literary work, and is reduced to material form within the meaning of section 49(4) of the 1956 Act by storage of the program. While it is suggested that this was already the law under the 1956 Act, nonetheless a clear statutory recognition of this fact is to be welcomed.

As in the 1988 Act, no definition of 'computer program' is provided. However, it is submitted that some guidance as to the meaning of 'computer program' is to be found in the remaining sections of the Computer Amendment Act.

Section 1(2) of the 1985 Act is similar in terms to section 21(4) of the 1988 Act. It states that:

> A version of the program in which it is converted into or out of a computer language or code, or into a different computer language or code, is an adaptation of the program.

This subsection deals purely with the meaning of 'adaptation', rather than 'computer program'. Nonetheless, it does appear to contemplate different versions of a computer program, in different languages or codes.

Section 3 of the 1985 Act applies certain criminal remedies in the 1956 Act 'whether an infringing copy of a computer program consists of a disc, tape or chip or any other device which embodies signals serving for the importation of the program or part of it.'

Again, it may be argued that while section 3 only deals with infringing copies, the section contemplates that a computer program may be embodied in a disk, tape or chip. This suggests that computer software falls within the ambit of section 1, irrespective of the memory medium, such as ROM floppy or hard disk, in which it is first stored.

On the other hand, section 2 of the Act specifies that a work is reduced to material form when it is stored '*in a computer*' (emphasis added). This phrase suggests that whereas a work stored in the internal memory of the computer is afforded protection under the Act, works stored in external memory media, such as punched cards or floppy disks, have not been reduced to a material form within the meaning of section 2.

As with the 1988 Act, it is submitted that courts are likely to consider the meaning of 'computer program' in the Computer Amendment Act from the standpoint of the man skilled in the art. It should be noted that the Computer Amendment Act is expressly intended to apply copyright to computer programs, whether or not such copyright subsisted under the old Law.

4.3.3   The 1956 Act

This section has been retained because arguments raised under the old Act may prove of relevance to the true construction of the new statute; and in particular to the position of object code under the present law.

The issue of the subsistence of copyright in the various levels of languages of a computer program, and of precisely what acts constitute infringement of such copyright, has never been the subject of a full decision in the United Kingdom. In two interlocutory decisions made prior to the 1985 Amendment Act it was held that a computer program is a 'literary work' within the meaning of section 2(1) of the Copyright Act 1956.

However in the recent case of *Milltronics Ltd v Hycontrol Ltd*[30] the Court of Appeal declined to decide this issue as it was not necessary for the resolution of the case before them.

In the case of *Sega Enterprises Ltd v Richards*[31] the plaintiffs, who claimed to own the copyright in the computer game called *Frogger*, sought interlocutory relief to restrain, *inter alia*, the reproduction of their program in machine readable form by the manufacture of logic boards. The defendants admitted that their program was based on that of the plaintiffs, but argued that copyright in computer programs *per se* was not known to English law. Goulding J rejected the defendants' contention and stated:

> On the evidence before me in this case I am clearly of the opinion that copyright under the provisions relating to literary works in the Copyright Act 1956 subsists in the assembly code program of the game Frogger. The machine code program derived from it by the operation of part of the system of the computer called the assembler is to be regarded, I think, as either a reproduction or an adaption of the assembly code program and accordingly for the purposes of deciding this motion I find that copyright does subsist in the program.[32]

The *Sega* case was followed by Megarry VC in the interlocutory decision of *Thrustcode v W.W. Computing.*[33]

Further, in the South African case of *Northern Office Microcomputers (Pty) Ltd v Rosenteins*[34] Marais J had no doubt that under the South African Copyright Act 98 of 1978, a computer program was a literary work and has been 'written down, recorded or otherwise reduced to material form' within the meaning of section 2(2)(b) of that Act. On a further finding that substantial skill and effort had been spent in the development of the program sufficient to give it an original character, he held that the program, both in source code and on floppy disk, was entitled to copyright protection.[35]

In Australia, the matter was considered in detail in *Apple Computer Inc. v Computer Edge Pty Ltd.*[36] At first instance, Beaumont J held that neither source nor object code had sufficient literary character to qualify as a literary work.[37] His decision was reversed on appeal by a majority of the Federal Court, who held that source code was a literary work, and that object code was an adaptation of source code within the meaning of the Australian Copyright Act 1968.[38] They did not decide the question of whether object code was itself a literary work. Shortly after the Federal Court decision, the Australian Copyright Act was amended specifically to include protection for source and object code.[39]

30 Note 9 above.
31 [1983] FSR 73.
32 *Ibid.* at 75.
33 [1983] FSR 502.
34 [1982] FSR 124.
35 *Ibid.* at 133 to 134.
36 At first instance [1984] FSR 246; (1984) 50 ALR 581. On appeal [1984] FSR 481.
37 [1984] FSR 246 at 256 to 257.
38 But see the dissenting judgment of Sheppard J [1984] FSR 481 at 532 to 544.
39 Copyright Amendment Act 1984 (No. 43 of 1984). See Lahore, [1984] 7 EIPR 196.

In view of these decisions it is of importance to consider the nature of the works for which protection has been sought.

4.3.3.1   Literary works

Section 2(1) of the Copyright Act 1956 includes original literary works among the categories of those works in which copyright may subsist. No comprehensive definition of 'literary work' is provided in the Act. Section 48(1) gives a non-exclusive definition, providing that the expression includes 'any written table or compilation'.[40]

There is, however, a substantial body of authority on the meaning of the word 'literary'. In the absence of statutory amendment expressly to include computer software[41] the question of whether source or object code can appropriately be described as 'literary' depends on resolution of the following issues:

(1) whether a functional work, intended for utilitarian purposes, can be described as literary;
(2) whether a literary work must have some aesthetic merit;
(3) whether a literary work must at least be comprehensible to human beings;
(4) whether a computer program is more aptly described as a 'machine part' rather than literary work;
(5) whether a literary work must be in writing;
(6) whether computer software is expressed in 'material form'.

4.3.3.2   Functional works

The distinction has frequently been drawn in case law between purely functional works, which are intended to be used, and works of literary merit, which are intended to educate or amuse.[42] In the Australian *Apple Computer* case, Beaumont J held that copyright did not subsist either in source or object code. He relied on *dicta* from English authorities which drew a distinction between functional and literary works.[43]

It is important to appreciate that subsistence of copyright does not depend on the purpose for which a work is intended. The fact that a

---

40   Similarly the Australian Copyright Act 1968 section 10(1) states that 'literary work' includes a 'written table or compilation'.
41   That is, prior to the 1985 and 1988 Acts.
42   See *Hollinrake v Truswell* [1894] 3 Ch. 420; *Exxon Corporation & Others v Exxon Insurance Consultants Limited* [1982] RPC 69 at 88; cf. *D.P. Anderson & Co. Ltd v The Leiber Code Company* [1917] 2 KB 469; *Mirror Newspapers Ltd v Queensland Newspapers Ltd* (1982) 59 FLR 71; *British Leyland Motor Corp. v Armstrong Patents Co. Ltd* [1984] FSR 591 at 609 to 610.
43   [1984] FSR 246 at 256; citing in particular *Hollinrake v Truswell*, Note 39 above, and *Exxon Corporation & Others v Exxon Insurance Consultants International Limited* [1982] RPC 69.

literary work is used for a functional purpose, such as a maintenance manual for a motor car,[44] does not prevent it from being 'literary' in the copyright sense. This point was made by the Australian Federal Court in the *Apple Computer* decision. Lockhart J noted that the purpose of computer programs was to control the sequence of operations carried out by the computer. He held that utilitarian purpose did not deprive the work of protection by copyright law.

> Copyright is essentially concerned with the expression of ideas in composition or language, rather than the function or purpose of those ideas.[45]

It would be an extremely difficult task to distinguish between different kinds of software on an assessment of the function or purpose for which they were intended. If this were the correct test of subsistence of copyright, then an operations program could be denied protection of copyright, whereas an applications program might be protected as a literary work. Such a distinction would have no basis in copyright law, since the degree of skill and labour required in the expression of the program is entirely independent of whether it is intended as an operations or applications program. The distinction between operations and applications programs has accordingly been rejected as 'arbitrary' and 'not very useful' for copyright purposes.[46]

4.3.3.3   The aesthetic value of literary works

Support may be found among old authorities for the view that a literary work must amuse or educate its readers.[47] Beaumont J in the *Apple Computer* case relied on such authorities:[48]

> In my view a literary work for this purpose is something which was intended to afford 'either information or instruction or pleasure in the form of literary enjoyment.'

The finding that literary merit is required for a literary work in copyright law is a surprising one. There is no doubt that works which have no pretensions whatsoever to literary style have long been protected under copyright law in the United Kingdom and the Commonwealth.[49] In *University of London Press Ltd v University Tutorial Press Ltd*[50] copyright protection was held to extend to examination papers for the University of London as 'original literary works' under the Copyright Act 1911. Peterson J stated that:[51] 'In my view the words "literary work"

---

44   For subsistence of copyright in instruction leaflets see *Elanco Products Ltd v Mandops (Agrochemical Specialists) Ltd* [1979] FSR 46.
45   [1984] FSR 481 at 522.
46   *Ibid*. at 491 *per* Fox J.
47   See Note 39 above.
48   [1984] FSR 246 at 256.
49   D.P. *Anderson*, Note 39 above; *Ager v P & O Steam Navigation Co.* (1984) 26 Ch.D. 637; *Masson, Seeley & Co. Limited v Embosotype Manufacturing Co.* (1924) 41 RPC 160; *Pitman v Hine* [1884] TLR 39.
50   [1916] 2 Ch. 601.
51   *Ibid*. at 608.

cover work which is expressed in print or writing, irrespective of the question of whether the quality or style is high.'

He went on to observe that originality did not mean that the work must be an expression of original or inventive thought but merely that the work must not be copied from another work – it should originate from the author.[52]

The House of Lords expressly approved this *dictum* in *Ladbroke (Football) Ltd v William Hill (Football) Ltd*[53] where it was held that football pools, the devising of which involved substantial skill and labour were protected by copyright as original literary works. Lord Reid observed that with regard to a compilation, originality is 'a matter of degree depending on the amount of skill, judgment or labour that has been involved in making the compilation'.[54]

It is clear from the above cases that the courts make no assessment of the literary value of the work provided that labour, time and skill have been expended in its production, and that such efforts can be demonstrated to have originated with the plaintiffs. Accordingly throughout England and the Commonwealth a wide variety of works have been held to be 'literary', including telegraph codes,[55] the rules of a game,[56] a system of shorthand[57] and instructions for leaflets for a herbicide.[58]

On the other hand, support for the view that literary merit is required for a literary work may be found in the case of *Hollinrake v Truswell*.[59] The plaintiff claimed copyright in a cardboard pattern sleeve containing scale figures and descriptive words. The purpose of the sleeve was for use in dressmaking as a chart to dispense with any calculations beyond simple measurements of the arm. The case contained certain *dicta* as to the limitations of the Copyright Act then in force in respect of literary works. Davey LJ stated that:

> A literary work is intended to afford either information and instructions or pleasure in the form of literary enjoyment. The sleeve chart before us gives no information or instruction. It does not add to the stock of human knowledge and it is not designed to give any instruction by way of description or otherwise: and it certainly is not calculated to afford literary enjoyment or pleasure . . . It is intended not for the purpose of giving information or pleasure but for practical use in the art of dress making.[60]

This *dictum* was cited with approval by the Court of Appeal in *Exxon Corporation & Others v Exxon Insurance Consultants International Ltd*.[61] In that case the specific question before the Court of Appeal related to whether the invented corporate name 'Exxon' was an original literary

---

52   *Ibid.* at 609.
53   [1964] 1 WLR 273.
54   *Ibid.* at 277 to 278.
55   *D.P. Anderson*, Note 39 above.
56   *Caley (A.J.) & Son Ltd v Garnett & Sons Ltd* [1936–45] MCC 99.
57   *Pitman v Hine* (1884) 1 TLR 39.
58   *Elanco v Mandops* [1979] FSR 46.
59   Note 39 above.
60   *Ibid.* at 428.
61   Note 40 above.

work within the meaning of section 2(1) of the Copyright Act 1956. The Court doubted whether the word could be said to be a work at all, but were clearly of the opinion that it could not be said to be a literary work. Stevenson LJ quoted from *Hollinrake v Truswell*, and stated that the view that a literary work was intended to afford either information or pleasure appealed to him 'as stating the ordinary meaning of the words "literary work" '.[62]

In spite of the *dicta* referred to above, the better view appears to be that a literary work does not require literary merit.

Hollinrake v Truswell was decided under the Copyright Act 1842[63] and the Court was specifically considering whether the chart in question could be described as a book, and in particular a 'map, chart or plan' within section 2 of that Act. The preamble to the 1842 Act states that protection was given 'to afford a greater encouragement to the production of literary works *of lasting benefit to the World*' (emphasis added). Literary merit is clearly implied. Davey LJ derived specific assistance from the preamble in ascertaining the class of works which were intended to be protected as books.[64]

Again, in the *Exxon* case, the Court of Appeal was not considering the question of copyright in computer software, but was addressing itself to the issue of copyright in a single invented word or name. English courts have tended to shun monopoly protection in invented names or words, apart from such protection as is afforded by the Trade Marks Act 1938.[65]

The Australian Federal Court in the *Apple Computer* case did not regard the decisions of *Holinrake v Truswell* and *Exxon* as helpful on the question of literary copyright in computer programs. The Court was unanimously of the view that the statement that a literary work should be for information, instruction or literary pleasure could not be an exhaustive definition.[66] It is submitted that it would clearly be unhelpful to apply *obiter dicta* from authorities under copyright legislation which has now been repealed, and to regard those *dicta* as a bar to the subsistence of copyright in computer software under the 1956 Act.

4.3.3.4 Intelligibility of literary works

Acceptance of the view that a literary work does not need literary merit does not, however, necessitate the conclusion that computer software is a literary work. The question still remains as to whether a literary work

62 *Ibid.* at 88.
63 5 & 6 Vict. c.45; repealed by the Copyright Act 1911 1 & 2 Geo. 5, c.46.
64 It was stated: 'Although I agree that the clear enactment of a statute cannot be controlled by the preamble, yet I think that the preamble may be usefully referred to for the purpose of ascertaining the class of works it was intended to protect.' See [1894] 3 Ch. 420 at 428.
65 See *Day v Brownrigg* (1878) 10 Ch.D 294; *Burberrys v J. Cording & Co. Ltd* (1909) 26 RPC 693; *Wombles Ltd v Wombles Skips Ltd* [1977] RPC 99; *Taverner Rutledge Ltd & Another v Trexapalm Ltd* [1977] RPC 275.
66 See, for example, Lockhart J [1984] FSR 481 at 522; also Whitford J in *Express Newspapers Plc v Liverpool Daily Post & Echo Plc & Others* [1985] FSR 306.

must be comprehensible and intelligible to human beings. The point is particularly relevant to object code. While source code is in eye readable form, object code is machine readable. Shepherd J in a dissenting judgment in the Australian Federal Court in the *Apple Computer* case,[67] held that while programs in source code were literary works, programs in object code were not. He held that while a literary work does not require literary merit, it must be 'capable of being seen or heard'. He stated:[68]

> In my opinion the programs in object code are not literary works. Fixed as they are in the ROMs they are unable to be seen in that code. True it is someone could write them out so as to show them symbolically in binary notation or hexadecimal notation. The computer itself can show them symbolically in hexadecimal notation. But all of that is irrelevant. The important point is that it is only the machine itself, that is, the microprocessor, which can 'understand' or 'see' and thus deal with, the object code.

There is no express statutory requirement that a literary work must be 'intelligible'. Shepherd J, however, formed his view from the natural meaning of the word 'literary' and the context in which the word was used in the Australian Copyright Act.[69]

However, collections of letters or symbols which are in themselves meaningless may nonetheless be the subject of copyright as literary works. Furthermore, while object code is undoubtedly machine readable it can nonetheless be read and understood by persons sufficiently skilled in the art of computer programming.

In *D.P. Anderson & Co. Ltd v The Lieber Code Company*[70] the plaintiffs published a code of invented words for sending telegraph messages. Each word was of itself meaningless but was chosen with a degree of skill and care to avoid errors in transmission. The defendants argued that the code was not an original literary work within the meaning of the Copyright Act 1911 inasmuch as it was a mere compilation of meaningless words. They argued that nothing could be 'literary' which did not involve an appreciation of the meaning of words.

Bailhache J rejected this argument. He summarised the defendant's contentions as follows:

> The words in the code are not words in the ordinary sense at all, but merely collections of letters which are in themselves meaningless and are made up in a merely mechanical way. I cannot accede to that argument. The words, I call them so for want of a better name, are for use for telegraphic purposes and to each of them a meaning can be attached by the person sending the message and also by the addressee provided, of course, he is informed of the meaning attached to it by the sender.[71]

---

67   [1984] FSR 481 at 532 to 543.
68   *Ibid.* at 538 to 539.
69   No definition of 'literary work' is contained in the Australian Copyright Act 1968. Section 10(1) merely states that the phrase includes 'a written table or compilation'.
70   Note 39 above.
71   *Ibid.* at 471.

It is submitted that there is no substantial difference, in the copyright sense, between telegraphic code and object code. Both are machine readable and are 'made up in a merely mechanical way'. Both are made up from, and are equivalent to, humanly intelligible language from which they are compiled.

It is of importance that in the *Apple Computer* case itself, it was possible to obtain a print out of the object code in visible hexadecimal form. It was further found that that object code could be understood by a person sufficiently skilled in the art. Lockhart J summarised the position as follows:

> The object code into which the source code has been translated can be reproduced in written form and examined by a human being to see whether or not it is a faithful version of the source code . . . Object code is not a mysterious language which only computers can read. It is a language devised and developed by persons skilled in computer science which they can read, and indeed translate, into various computer languages, mainly assembly languages.[72]

In those circumstances there would appear to be an overwhelming case for saying that the *Apple Computer* object code satisfied in full any requirement of 'intelligibility'. However, many object codes are found only in machine readable form and are difficult to decompile into source code. Again, it is submitted that this is no reason for disqualifying such object codes from copyright protection. The contention that a literary work must be visually or actually intelligible is supported neither by authority nor by the words of the statute.

4.3.3.5 *Machine parts as opposed to literary works*

It is clear that while copyright law may protect the expression of an idea, whether that expression is intended for functional or aesthetic purposes, it may not protect a machine part. A manufacturing drawing of a functional part, for example an exhaust pipe,[73] has frequently been held to be an artistic work under the Copyright Act 1956, despite its functional purpose. However, copyright does not subsist in the exhaust pipe itself. It is a part of a machine and such protection as may be available must be sought in the law of patents. This distinction may again be found in the case of *Hollinrake v Truswell*. Lord Herschell LC stated that:

> What the plaintiff has sought to protect under the Act for the protection of literary production is not a literary production but an apparatus for the use of which certain words and figures must necessarily be inscribed upon it. Such a thing may possibly, if novel and useful, be good subject matter for a patent but I cannot bring myself to hold that it is a map, chart or plan within the meaning of the Copyright Act.[74]

It might be suggested that computer software whether in a high or low level language is in fact a machine part. The instructions are written to do work within a machine. This argument may be put more forcefully in relation to object code, which is exclusively machine readable. Again, this

---

72   Note 64 above at 523 to 524.
73   *British Leyland Motor Corp. v Armstrong Patents Co. Ltd* [1986] AC 577.
74   Note 39 above at 424.

view was adopted by Beaumont J at first instance in the *Apple Computer* case. He held that a source program was 'a mechanical device'. The case was still stronger in relation to an object program which was 'a more advanced stage of the process of controlling the sequence of operations carried out by a computer'.[75]

It is submitted that the view of a computer program, whether in high or low level language, as a machine part is technically and legally incorrect.

The question to be answered for the purpose of copyright law is whether an idea has been expressed in material form.[76] In source code a series of commands are expressed in eye readable form. The description of 'mechanical contrivance' is as little suited to a source listing as it is to any other form of written code.

The object program is the identical expression of the idea contained in the source program, but in a form which communicates only with machines – machine readable language. The outer manifestation of the expression has been changed, but each source code instruction is reproduced in object code. Object code remains the expression of an idea.

In respect of source code the description of mechanical contrivance was rejected by the Australian Federal Court in the *Apple Computer* decision. Fox J held that:

> I do not myself doubt that the programs in source code were literary works . . . it is incorrect to describe them simply as components of a machine . . . there is a distinct and recognised difference between a computer program and the electromagnetic functioning of a machine.[77]

The Federal Court made no finding as to whether the object code was itself a mechanical contrivance.[78] It is submitted that there is no logical basis for differentiating between source and object code in this respect. As discussed above, object code consists of the same instructions expressed in the source listing, held in a different medium.

4.3.3.6 *The requirement of writing in literary works*

Section 48(1) of the Copyright Act 1956 specifically includes any written table or compilation within the meaning of a 'literary work'. 'Writing' includes any form of notation by hand or printing, typewriting or any similar process.[79] It seems clear that a printout of high level computer

---

75 [1984] FSR 246 at 257.
76 *Ladbroke (Football)*, Note 50 above at 277.
77 [1984] FSR 481 at 495 to 496.
78 Lockhart J stated at page 524: 'My fourth question is whether the programs in object code . . . answer the description of original literary works in which copyright subsists . . . Although I recognise some force in the view that the programs in object code are originally literary works in which copyright subsists I have considerable reservations about the correctness of the view, but need not decide the question.'
79 Section 48(1) Copyright Act 1956.

language could constitute writing within the meaning of the above definition. It would further appear that object code printout in hexadecimal or binary form would be equally capable of constituting writing.[80] Other forms of secondary storage media, such as punched cards, would also be capable of being regarded as writing under the statutory definition as being a form of notation produced by a similar process to printing or typewriting.[81]

The real question arises where the programmer has not made any printed record of his work whether in high or low languages, but has merely retained the work stored in a ROM. The difficulty would become acute where, unlike the *Apple Computer* case, it is difficult to obtain a printout of source or object code from the ROM.

Where the work is held solely in electronic storage it is arguable that the 'notation' is not produced by any similar process to printing or typewriting. However, it should be observed that the definition of literary work within section 48(1) is not intended to be comprehensive but merely gives examples of what may constitute a literary work. For instance, books and magazines are not included within the definition. Similarly, the definition of writing is inclusive as opposed to exclusive.

Furthermore, section 49(4) of the Copyright Act 1956 states that a literary work is made at such time as 'it was first reduced to writing or *some other material form*' (emphasis added). This section provides support for the view that a literary work may be reduced to some material form other than writing and that writing is merely an example of a medium in which such work may be expressed.

4.3.3.7 The question of material form

Under section 49(4) of the Copyright Act 1956 a literary work must have 'material form'. However, it has been suggested above that the combined effect of sections 48(1) and 49(4) of the Act is that writing is not required for a literary work, but as soon as the expression of an idea takes on any material form, it is protected by the laws of copyright. It is, however, necessary to consider whether software in all its manifestations may be said to have material form. It would appear that certain media in which the computer program may be expressed clearly have material form, such as floppy disks, printouts, tapes, etc. Where a program is stored in a ROM, that storage would also seem to have material form. The matter was considered by the Federal Court in *Apple Computer* in relation to ROMs and EPROMs.[82] Lockhart J observed that the Apple object codes

---

80 See *Gates v Swift* [1982] RPC 339. Graham J appears to have accepted at page 340 that 'the Act does not require writing at all; any material form of fixation (such as magnetic recording) suffices.'
81 See *Copinger and Skone James on Copyright*, Sweet & Maxwell, 1991 (13th edn), paragraph 3-49.
82 The point was considered in relation to infringement by reproduction 'in material form'. See [1984] FSR 481 at 525 to 526. The definitions of terms such as ROM and EPROM are given in Chapter 1.

were stored in ROMs and EPROMs by means of fused or unfused wires or of a permanent presence or absence of relatively large numbers of electrons. He stated that the silicon chips represent the material form in which the codes are embodied and that the code might be ascertained from the chips by having the programs reproduced in a written form.[83] He went on to state that:[84] . . . 'whichever means of storage is adopted, each is in a material form'.

Even where information is merely entered into a RAM and is retained therein for the short period during which the machine is turned on, such storage effects an alteration in the arrangement of electrons held within the memory and as such does possess a material form. The only difference between the RAM and ROM storage is that the former can more easily be erased. The fact that a work is erasable or fragile does not deprive it of copyright protection. For example, copyright would appear to subsist in a literary work, irrespective of whether it is written on rice paper or on parchment.

This question is sometimes expressed as a matter of permanence. It may be suggested that a copyright work has to be 'fixed' and 'permanent'. However, a degree of permanence is not a requirement of 'material form' in the Copyright Act 1956. Since that Act requires material as opposed to *permanent* or *tangible* form, it is submitted that the point does not arise.[85]

4.3.3.8   Conclusion

It appears from the foregoing that copyright subsists in computer software as a 'literary work' under the unamended Copyright Act 1956. This conclusion is based on the following premises:

(1) A consideration of whether a work is intended for a functional purpose is irrelevant to the question of whether it is 'literary'.

(2) A literary work, within the meaning of the Copyright Acts, does not need to possess aesthetic merit.

(3) There is no requirement in copyright law that a literary work should be intelligible to human beings. In so far as such a requirement may exist, computer code is 'intelligible'.

(4) It is inappropriate to describe a computer program as a machine component.

(5) Computer software is expressed in 'writing'. In any event, a literary work does not have to be expressed in writing. Other material forms of expression are protected as literary works.

(6) The essential requirements for a literary work are that:

(a) the work is expressed in some material form;
(b) the creation of that material form required skill and labour on the part of its author.

---

83   [1984] FSR 481 at 525 to 526.
84   *Ibid.* at 526.
85   This view is expressed in Laddie, Prescott and Vitoria, *The Modern Law of Copyright*, Butterworth, 1980, paragraph 2.143, note 4.

The composition of a program in whatever code it is expressed satisfies both those requirements.

4.4 SEPARATE COPYRIGHT IN OBJECT CODE

In certain circumstances, it would appear that copyright may subsist in object code either as a literary work, or as a translation of a literary work, both under the 1988 Act and the 1985 Computer Amendment Act. The subsistence of copyright in object code, however, is dependent on whether its creation involved a degree of skill and labour.

4.4.1 Subsistence of copyright in object code as a literary work

In some cases, a program may not be written in source code. It is possible for a program to be initially devised in hexadecimal code. In those cases, it is submitted that the hexadecimal code may be protected as a literary work, since its expression will have involved a significant degree of human endeavour.[86]

Similarly, were a program to be first devised as a series of binary numerals, those numerals could constitute a literary work.[87]

However, object code is frequently produced within a microprocessor, by compilation from a source listing. In those cases human skill is not required to create the program in object form. It is doubtful whether such object code is 'original' within the meaning of the Copyright Act.[88]

4.4.2 Subsistence of copyright in object code as a translation

The question was considered in the *Apple Computer* decision as to whether object code is an adaptation, or more specifically a translation, of source code within the meaning of the Australian Copyright Act.[89] This question is particularly relevant to infringement, and is discussed in more detail under that heading (see Chapter 5). For the present, suffice it to say that since each instruction of source code is translated, or transliterated, into object code, there is a very strong case for saying that object code is a translation of the source code. As stated by Fox J:[90] 'The object codes contained in the Apple ROMs are a straight-forward electronic translation into a material form of the source codes, and it would be entirely within ordinary understanding to say that they are translations of the source code.'

---

86 This view was accepted on an *ex parte* application in *Gates v Swift*, Note 77 above.
87 Works of a numerical character, for example mathematical tables, have been considered to be literary works, *Southern v Bailes* (1894) 38 SJ 681.
88 *Ladbroke (Football)* Note 50 above, cf. Express Newspapers, Note 63 above.
89 Australian Copyright Act 1968 section 10(1).
90 [1984] FSR 481 at 496.

Aside from being literary works in themselves, it may be possible to argue that copyright subsists in object code as an adaptation or translation of the source code. This argument seems to have considerable force in the light of the amendments made by section 21(4) of the 1988 Act, and section 1(2) of the 1985 Computer Amendment Act, where the act of converting from code to code is stated to be an adaptation.

It seems clear that where a work is translated by a change of medium, the work in a different medium may itself enjoy the protection of copyright as a literary work. For example, in *Walter v Lane*[91] the Court of Appeal held that a shorthand writer who reported a speech verbatim was the author of that report, which was a literary work. Similarly in *Byrne v Statist Co.*[92] Baillhache J granted protection to a translation of a literary work as a copyright work in itself. He observed that a translator of a literary work had for many years been held to be the author of that translation.[93]

However, it is nonetheless difficult to regard object code as entitled to a separate copyright as a translation of source code. Translations have in the past been protected where a significant degree of skill and labour is involved in their formation.

In *Wood v Boosey*[94] it was held that the arrangement of an existing opera score for the pianoforte was entitled to copyright as an adaptation of that work. This entitlement arose from the fact that the adaptation involved labour and intelligence, which made it into a new work.

Object code is frequently translated from source code by means of the assembler in the computer itself. The translation does not require any skill or labour on the part of the programmer or computer operator. Lockhart J observed in *Apple Computer* that:

> The fact that a program in object code is a result of the computer's interpretation of that program in source code, and in that sense is a mechanical result without the intervention of a human being, does not in my view prevent the object code answering the description of a translation of the source code.[95]

As will be discussed, this statement appears to be perfectly accurate from the point of view of infringement.[96] For the purposes of infringement a translation does not have to be of itself an independent copyright work. However, when object code is produced within the computer without human skill and labour, it is difficult to say that that translation is itself an independent copyright work.

In cases where object code does not enjoy an independent copyright from source code, the object code is not deprived of protection by copyright.

91   [1899] 2 Ch. 749.
92   [1914] 1 KB 622.
93   *Ibid.* at 627.
94   (1867) LR 2 QB 340.
95   [1984] FSR 481 at 523.
96   See Chapter 5 at paragraph 5.4.1.8.

It is strongly arguable that an unauthorised copy of such object code is either a reproduction in material form, or a translation, of source code, and amounts to an infringement of copyright in the source listing.[97]

4.4.3 Summary

The following is a summary of the position of object code under the 1988 Act and the 1985 Amendment Act:

(1) If a computer program is first written in object or hexadecimal code, then it is submitted that copyright will subsist in such code under both statutes.

(2) If a computer program is first written in source code, then a separate copyright will only subsist in the object version if a degree of human skill and labour was expended in the conversion from source to object code.

(3) However, even if a separate copyright does not subsist in object code derived from source code, it is submitted that copying of the object code would constitute a reproduction of a translation of the source code, and as such, an infringement of copyright.

4.5 STATUTORY PROVISIONS ON OWNERSHIP

The 1988 Act sets out a new statutory scheme in relation to ownership of copyright. In certain respects, changes have been made to the previous law which are directed at specific problems in relation to computer software. However, under the transitional provisions to the 1988 Act, the identities of the author and first owner of copyright in an existing work are to be determined in accordance with the law in force at the time when the work was made.[98] Accordingly questions of authorship and ownership of copyright in works made after 1 August 1989 will be determined pursuant to the provisions of the 1988 Act; by contrast, if a computer program was made before that date, then those questions will be determined pursuant to the 1956 Act, which contains the law then in force.

4.5.1 Authorship and ownership under the 1988 Act

Section 7 of the 1988 Act deals with authorship of copyright works. 'Author' is defined as the person who creates the work. Section 9(3) provides that:

> In the case of a literary, dramatic, musical or artistic work which is computer-generated the author shall be taken to be the person by whom the arrangements necessary for the creation of the work are undertaken.

97 See Chapter 5 generally.
98 Schedule 1 paragraphs 10 and 11.

The expression 'computer generated' is defined in section 178 as meaning that the work is generated by computer in circumstances such that there is no human author of the work.

Section 10 defines a 'work of joint authorship' as a work produced by the collaboration of two or more authors in which the contribution of each author is not distinct from that of the other author or authors. References to the 'author' of a work, save where otherwise provided, are to be construed as references to all the authors of a joint work.

Section 11 of the 1988 Act provides that the author of a work is the first owner of any copyright in it, subject to certain specified exceptions.[99] Significantly, section 11(2) provides that where a literary, dramatic, musical or artistic work is made by an employee in the course of his employment, his employer is the first owner of any copyright in the work subject to any agreement to the contrary. 'Employment' refers to employment under a contract of service or apprenticeship.[100]

It is apparent that different provisions as to ownership apply, depending on whether a work is classified as a computer program, or as a computer generated work. It is important to note that the definition of computer generated work is limited to cases where there is no human author of the work. Accordingly, computer aided designs, such as engineering drawings produced on computer, may not be regarded as computer generated works as a result of the human skill and labour involved in their creation.

If a work is classified as a computer program, then the author is the person who created the work.[101] By contrast, the author of a computer generated work is the person by whom the arrangements necessary for the creation of the work were undertaken. The treatment of computer generated works is equivalent to the treatment of cinematograph films under the 1956 Act. It is a welcome provision, which in many cases may avoid technicalities in securing title. It is perhaps unfortunate that this provision was not applied to computer programs in general.

If the author is identified as the person who arranged for the creation of the work, it is not necessary to identify every person who participated in the creation of the work. In the case of a complex computer program, which may have been marketed in several versions, numerous different persons may have participated in its creation. All such persons may be authors or joint authors of the work. This fact can cause serious problems in the prosecution of any action for infringement of copyright.

It is essential to secure title to copyright. In order to do so, it is necessary to identify the authors of the program. This can prove difficult, or even impossible, in the absence of documented records. However, since cases

99   See also section 11(3), which exempts Crown Copyright, Parliamentary Copyright, and copyright of certain international organisations from the operation of section 11.
100   *Per* section 178.
101   Or persons, in the case of joint authors.

are decided on a balance of probabilities, it may be sufficient to adduce evidence that all such persons were qualified persons acting in the course of their employment under contracts of service with the plaintiff company. Unfortunately, it is not always possible to adduce such evidence of fact.

Assuming that the authors can be identified then it may still be necessary to prove that the plaintiff, as opposed to the identified individuals, is the owner of the title to copyright. In some cases, this may not present a problem. Contracts with the individual authors may specifically provide that title to copyright vests in the plaintiff. In the absence of such contractual provisions, it is necessary to establish whether each such individual was an employee of the company or an independent contractor.

In the case of an employee, if reliance is placed on section 11(2) of the 1988 Act, it is necessary to prove that the work was made in the course of his employment under a contract of service. This may be the fundamental issue in the action. For example, in *Missing Link Software v Magee*[102] the first defendant was previously the software development manager of the plaintiff company. It was contended that he had written a substantial part of the defendant's system while employed by the plaintiff; and that the plaintiff was owner of the legal title to copyright in that part of the defendant's system. It was held that the plaintiff had an arguable case that the composition by the defendant of a program for a rival business, while employed to write such programs for the plaintiff, would make the new work a work created in the course of employment; and an injunction was granted against the distribution of the defendant's program until trial.

It may be possible for a company who has commissioned an independent contractor to write its software or some part thereof to commence an action on the basis that the company is the equitable owner of title to the copyright. Indeed, it is possible to obtain an interlocutory injunction on the basis of an equitable title.[103] In order to obtain final judgment however it is necessary to perfect title by obtaining an assignment from the legal owner.[104] Any such assignment must be in writing and signed by or on behalf of the assignor.[105]

In some cases, however, it may not be possible to establish equitable ownership simply as a result of commissioning the work. Essentially, the claim is that the author of the work holds the title for the benefit of the commissioning company on a constructive trust. In order to make good such a claim, it is necessary to adduce evidence of all of the surrounding circumstances of the relationship. Evidence that the work was done as a part of a larger work created by the commissioner, or under the direction or instructions of the commissioner, is of assistance in this respect.

---

102 [1989] FSR 361.
103 See *Merchant Adventurers Ltd v M. Grew & Co.* [1972] Ch. 242; *Leisure Data v Bell* [1988] FSR 367.
104 *Performing Right Society Ltd v The London Theatre of Varieties Ltd* [1924] AC 1.
105 Copyright, Designs and Patents Act 1988 section 90(3).

The author of the work may be unwilling to enter into an assignment of title. Indeed the author, being an ex-employee or independent contractor, may be the defendant in the action. In such cases it is possible to seek an order that title be assigned, as a part of the relief claimed in the action. The basis for such a claim is that the author holds title on trust for the plaintiff, and is required to assign it at the request of the equitable owner.

4.5.2   Statutory presumptions

The 1988 Act contains certain presumptions in relation to subsistence and title, which may be of assistance to producers of computer software.[106] Specifically, section 105(3) provides that in proceedings brought with respect to a computer program where copies of the program are issued to the public in electronic form bearing a statement that a named person was the owner of copyright in the program at the date of issue of the copies, the statement is admissible as evidence of the facts stated and shall be presumed to be correct until the contrary is proved.

This provision raises at least three questions which have yet to be answered by the courts:

(1) Is it necessary for the statement itself to be in electronic form, or is it sufficient if the statement appears on the packaging of a copy which is itself in electronic form?
(2) What words must be used in the 'statement' in order to satify the presumption?
(3) What degree of proof must be offered by the defendant in order to rebut the presumption?

While no definitive answer can be given in the absence of case law, it is submitted that the following is a likely interpretation of the scope of the presumption:

(a) It is not necessary for the statement itself to be in electronic form. The reference to electronic form relates to the copies issued to the public, and there would appear to be no purpose in requiring the statement to be in any particular form, as long as it is visible to the public.
(b) It is possible to argue that the 'statement' must reflect precisely the words of the section. However, on a purposive construction it is difficult to see why a court should so conclude. Provided that the statement conveys the meaning set out in the section, the precise language seems immaterial.
(c) It is possible to suggest that the statutory presumption may not be relied on if any evidence to the contrary is offered by the defendant. However,

---

106   See generally sections 104 and 105 of the 1988 Act.

the words 'until the contrary is proved' are to be read in their statutory context and may be contrasted with the presumption in section 104(5) which only applies 'in the absence of evidence to the contrary'. It is submitted that the presumption in section 105(3) is stronger than the presumptions as to title and subsistence under the 1956 Act, and operates to shift the onus to the defendant to disprove the relevant facts.

5   Infringement of Copyright

5.0   INTRODUCTION

The Copyright, Designs and Patents Act 1988 has clarified many of the doubtful issues which existed under previous statutes in relation to infringement of copyright in computer programs. However, as is the case with provisions dealing with subsistence of copyright, the earlier law still remains relevant in relation to infringing acts committed before the coming into force of the new Act.[1]

Specifically Schedule 1 paragraph 14 of the 1988 Act provides that:

> The provisions of Chapters II and III of Part 1 as to the acts constituting an infringement of copyright apply only in relation to acts done after commencement; the provisions of the 1956 Act continue to apply in relation to acts done before commencement.

Since the 1985 Amendment Act is legislation which amended the 1956 Act, it constitutes a part of 'the provisions of the 1956 Act'. However, by section 4(4) of the 1985 Amendment Act it is provided that its provisions do not affect any question as to whether anything done before its commencement was an infringement of copyright. Accordingly, depending on the date when an alleged infringement has been committed, the issue of liability may be decided under the 1988 Act, the 1985 Amendment Act, or the 1956 Act prior to amendment. The position may be summarised as follows:

(1) In relation to acts committed after 1 August 1989, the infringement provisions of the 1988 Act will apply.

(2) In general the issue of infringement in relation to acts committed prior to 1989 will be determined under the provisions of the 1985 Amendment Act.

(3) However, the issue of infringement, in relation to acts committed prior to 16 September 1985, will be determined under the provisions of the unamended Copyright Act 1956.

---

1   For a detailed discussion of the effect of the transitional provisions, see Chapter 4 paragraph 4.1.

(4) By reason of the Limitation Acts[2] the situation contemplated in (3) above will become increasingly rare. It can only arise in actions commenced prior to 16 September 1991. However, this may still be of significance in relation to quantum of damages in actions commenced before that date.

In the circumstances, both old and new law continue to be relevant to issues of infringement of copyright in computer software.

This chapter is divided into the following parts:

(1) General principles of infringement of copyright.
(2) Infringement of copyright in computer software under the 1988 Act.
(3) Infringement of copyright in computer software under the Copyright (Computer Software) Amendment Act 1985.
(4) Infringement of copyright under the unamended Copyright Act 1956.

5.1 GENERAL PRINCIPLES

5.1.1 Scope of copyright protection

The law of copyright cannot be used to prevent independent development, even if that development produces an identical article to the copyright work. The scope of copyright protection prevents copying of a work without the licence of the copyright owner. Accordingly, and save where specifically discussed below, it is not an infringement of copyright to use, as opposed to reproduce, a copyright work.[3]

5.1.1.1 *Ideas and their expression*

The courts have frequently expressed this principle by stating that the law of copyright protects the expression of an idea, as opposed to the idea itself.[4] Accordingly, to copy the idea or principle behind a work, as opposed to the way in which it is expressed, is not an infringement of copyright. A copyright owner does not have a monopoly in the idea behind his work. This is because, unlike patent protection, novelty and inventiveness are not prerequisites of copyright protection. This principle was expressed by Bradley J in the American case of *Baker v Selden*[5] recently

---

2 The writ must be issued within six years of the date when the cause of the action accrued.
3 See for example *Brigid Foley Limited v Ellott & Others* [1982] RPC 433; *Thrustcode v W.W. Computing* [1983] FSR 502.
4 *Ladbroke (Football) Ltd v William Hill (Football) Ltd* [1964] 1 WLR 273; *L.B. (Plastics) Ltd v Swish Products Ltd* [1979] RPC 551.
5 (1879) 101 US 99.

cited with approval by Oliver LJ in the Court of Appeal in *British Leyland Motor Corp. v Armstrong Patents Co. Ltd*:

> The copyright of the book, if not pirated from other works, would be valid without regard to the novelty, or want of novelty, of its subject matter. The novelty of the art or thing described or explained has nothing to do with the validity of the copyright. To give the author of the book an exclusive property in the art described therein, when no examination of its novelty has ever been officially made, would be a surprise and a fraud upon the public. That is the province of letters patent.[6]

5.1.1.2 Expression dictated by function

Since copyright does not give to its owner a monopoly in an idea, the degree of copyright protection varies from work to work. Copyright may be severely limited in a work which, due to its function, can only be expressed in one way.[7] To protect that expression is to protect the idea behind it. Wills J observed in *Kenrick & Co. v Lawrence & Co.*, in relation to a very simple drawing:[8] 'With such a drawing . . . the copyright must be confined to that which is special to the individual drawing over and above the idea . . . a square can only be drawn as a square, a cross can only be drawn as a cross . . .'

It may be argued that these general statements limit the scope of copyright protection for computer software. The argument may be put in the following alternative ways:

(1) That reproduction of computer software is reproduction of an idea, rather than the expression of an idea.

(2) That since a computer program is an entirely functional work, nothing will be a reproduction which is not an exact copy of the original.

5.1.1.3 Reproduction of expression

The distinction between ideas and their expression was considered in the case of *L.B. (Plastics) Ltd v Swish Products Ltd*.[9] The plaintiffs (appellants) claimed infringement of copyright in drawings of plastic drawers. The defendants (respondents) had successfully argued in the Court of Appeal that all that they had adopted was the appellants' 'concept' or 'idea' which was not an infringement of copyright. Lord Hailsham accepted as 'trite law' that there was no copyright in mere ideas. However, he stated:[10]

> It all depends on what you mean by 'ideas'. What the respondents in fact copied was no mere general idea. It was, to quote the respondents' own language 'to follow the pattern principle in part or in whole with minor changes to the design'.

6　[1984] FSR 591 at 608.
7　This view was adopted by the United States Supreme Court in *Apple Computer Inc. v Franklin Computer Corporation*, No.82-1582, 30 August 1983; and in *Whelan Inc. v Jaslow Dental Laboratories* [1987] FSR 1 by the Third Circuit Court of Appeals.
8　(1890) 25 QBD 99 at 104.
9　Note 4 above.
10　*Ibid.* at 629.

It may be observed that it is particularly difficult to define where 'idea' ends and 'expression' begins.[11] It has been suggested that this distinction is an unhelpful generalisation which leads to confusion.[12] The principle is perhaps best illustrated by reference to decided cases.

On the one hand, if a rival takes the concept underlying a particular work, and expresses it in a different way in his own work, then it may well be that he has used no more than the idea in the source work, which is not protected by copyright. In *Cuisenaire v South West Imports*[13] the plaintiff was the owner of copyright in a book teaching arithmetic which described a method of teaching by coloured rods. The defendant, in order to apply the plaintiff's method, constructed the described rods and was sued for infringement of copyright. The plaintiff failed, since the expression of his idea had not been copied, only the idea itself had been used. The Court relied on the dictum of Pape J in the Australian case of *Cuisenaire v Reid*:[14] 'If the law were otherwise everyone who made a rabbit pie in accordance with the recipe of "Mrs Beeton's Cookery Book" would infringe the literary copyright in that book.'

More recently, in the case of *Brigid Foley Ltd v Ellott & Others*[15] the plaintiff alleged on motion that its copyright in knitting guides had been infringed by the defendants' knitted garments. The knitting guide contained a series of instructions for production of the garments. It was argued that the garments, when produced according to these instructions, reproduced the instructions in a material form.

Megarry VC rejected this contention. The instructions were not reproduced, they were executed:[16] 'It seems to me quite plain that there is no reproduction of the words and numerals in the knitting guides in the knitted garments produced by following the instructions.'

So the distinction would appear to lie between cases where the instructions of a functional work are reproduced, and where such instructions are executed. In the former case the expression of the copyright work is reproduced. In the latter, while the idea behind the work may have been copied, its mode of expression is shed.

In applying this distinction to computer software it is essential to remember that in each stage of the computer program the expression of the programmer remains. A series of commands are expressed in eye readable form in source code. That expression remains in object code, which is in fact the identical expression of the idea contained in the source code, but in machine readable language.

It is therefore incorrect to regard object code merely as the execution of the source program instructions. It is in fact a translation of the expression of the idea in the source program into another medium.

11 See generally Laddie, Prescott and Vitoria, *The Modern Law of Copyright*, Butterworth, 1980, paragraphs 2.50 to 2.62.
12 *Ibid.* at paragraph 2.50.
13 [1969] SCR 208.
14 [1963] VR 719 at 735.
15 Note 3 above.
16 *Ibid.* at 434.

It may therefore be suggested that the object program is not the 'rabbit pie' of Pape J's example, nor is it the 'knitted garment' which was held not to reproduce the instructions for its manufacture. It is rather a tape recording of the recipe or the instructions themselves – the same expression in machine readable form. The source listing instructions are not 'shed' in object form, but are reproduced in another medium.

5.1.1.4   The degree of copying of a functional work

If the scope of copyright in functional work is limited to slavish copies, then it would be possible to avoid infringement of copyright where minor changes have been made in a program, which have little effect on its end result.

The degree of copying is a matter of fact which will, of course, vary from case to case. However, it appears to be clear that in the United Kingdom, in deciding whether a 'reproduction' within the meaning of copyright statutes has been made, there is no ground for distinguishing between works which are purely functional and works with some aesthetic appeal. In *British Leyland v Armstrong Patents*, the defendants in the Court of Appeal relied on the fact that the idea behind a copyright work is not protected. The defendants submitted that:

> Whilst in the case of works with a genuinely artistic or aesthetic appeal one can conceive of a variety of ways, including three-dimensional models, in which the substance of the work may be reproduced, in the case of an engineering drawing of a piece of purely functional equipment . . . nothing will be a reproduction which is not a literal and exact copy of the original.[17]

The Court of Appeal specifically rejected this approach. Oliver LJ stated:

> The question in every case is, no doubt, whether a given three dimensional object 'reproduced' the substance of the two dimensional drawing or drawings, but I can see nothing in the Act which justifies a distinction being drawn, so far as the ambit of 'reproduction' is concerned, between drawings which are purely functional, and drawings which have some aesthetic appeal. I can find no context at all for giving the word some different and more extended or more restricted meaning according to the intention, of the author, or the emotional response of the beholders.[18]

The House of Lords affirmed this aspect of the Judgment of the Court of Appeal, albeit with undisguised reluctance. Lord Scarman observed as follows:

> The Copyright Act 1956 is, I gladly hear, presently under review. This case illustrates that more than redrafting with a view to clarification is needed; nothing less than an overhaul of some of the principles of the modern extended law is necessary.[19]

17   [1984] FSR 591 at 609.
18   *Ibid.* at 609 to 610.
19   [1986] AC 577 at 613. The decision of the Court of Appeal that the manufacture of spare parts for BL motor cars constituted an infringement of copyright was reversed by the House of Lords on other grounds.

This 'overhaul' has, of course, now been completed. Its result is the 1988 Act. It is submitted that this has clarified and strengthened copyright protection for computer software.

5.1.1.5 *Non-textual copying*

The difficulty in deciding where 'idea' ends and 'expression' begins is particularly acute when one considers the issue of non-textual copying of computer software. If no individual lines of code have been reproduced, but the underlying structure or arrangement of the program has been copied without authorisation, does this amount to an infringement of copyright? This problem has been considered in numerous decisions in the United States, where the courts have held that copyright in computer software is infringed if the 'look and feel' of a program has been copied.[20]

It is submitted that, while the English courts are unlikely to adopt the 'look and feel' approach, non-textual copying of a literary work is a well-recognised concept in United Kingdom copyright law. In a number of decisions, the arrangement and incidents of plot have been regarded as a compilation, which required skill and labour on the part of the author to devise and assemble, and which is entitled to protection. The question has arisen in particular in relation to the non-textual copying of works of reference, for example historical or scientific works. In the early case of *Jarrold v Houlston*[21] Page Wood VC described the illegitimate use of a work of reference in the following terms:

> . . . if, knowing that a person whose work is protected by copyright has, with considerable labour, complied from various sources a work in itself not original, but which he has digested and arranged, you, being minded to compile a work of a like description, instead of taking the pains of searching into all the common sources, and obtaining your subject matter from them, avail yourself of the labour of your predecessor, adopt his arrangements, adopt moreover the very questions he has asked, or adopt them with but a slight degree of colourable imitation, and thus save yourself pains and labour by availing yourself of the pains and labour which he has employed, that I take to be illegitimate use.[22]

The case of *Poznanski v London Film Productions Ltd*[23] concerned the alleged copying of incidents, chronology and characterisation of a play in a film which dealt with the same subject-matter. Crossman J rejected the allegation of infringement, essentially because similarities resulted from

---

20 It is important to distinguish between copying of the structure, sequence and order of code; and the copying of screen outputs. The latter is commonly referred to as part of the 'look and feel' of the program and is not the same copyright work as the underlying code. See the discussion of the relevant decisions below and see Chapter 6 paragraph 6.7.
21 [1857] 3 K & J 708.
22 *Ibid*. at page 714. The expression 'not original' in this context means that the work was assembled from sources available to the public.
23 [1937] MCC 107.

coincidence as opposed to copying. He referred to the distinction between ideas and their expression in the following terms:

> I find that if and insofar as there are similarities between the play and the film, the similarities are mainly in ideas, which are not the subject matter of copyright, and that the treatment and development of these ideas in the film are quite different from the treatment and development in the play.[24]

Nonetheless, Crossman J clearly accepted that similarities in incidents and situations could afford *prima facie* evidence of copying.[25]

The case of *Harman Pictures N.V. v Osborne*[26] concerned the alleged copying of the incidents and situations of the plot of a book entitled *The Reason Why* in the script of the film *The Charge of the Light Brigade*, written by John Osborne. Goff J found that there was a *prima facie* case of infringement of copyright, and granted an interlocutory injunction against release or distribution of the film. This was again a case of non-textual copying. While there was some evidence of quotations common to both works, the judge gave great weight to the unexplained similarities of plot:

> . . . on comparing the book and the script, I was, and remain, impressed by the marked similarity of the choice of incidents, and the relative importance of those which are common and those in the script only and by the juxtaposition of ideas.[27]

Non-textual copying was considered by the Court of Appeal in the case of *Elanco Products Ltd v Mandops (Agrochemical Specialists) Ltd.*[28] The plaintiffs claimed copyright in a leaflet which set out detailed instructions on the use of a particular herbicide. They argued that the leaflet constituted a compilation of relevant information extracted from literature available to the public. The defendants argued that they were entitled to take any information available to the public, provided that they did not take the same form or language as the plaintiff's literature. It was held that the defendants were not entitled to save themselves the effort and cost of assembling their own information, and making their own selection of material, and an interlocutory injunction was granted.[29]

In *Ravenscroft v Herbert & Another*[30] the Court considered a case where there was a degree of textual copying; but in addition the same characters, incidents and interpretations of the significance of events existed in both the plaintiff's and the defendant's works. It was held that the combination of elements taken constituted a substantial part of the plaintiff's work.

---

24   *Ibid.* at 111.
25   As observed by Goff J when considering the *Poznanski* case in *Harman Pictures N.V. v Osborne* [1967] 1 WLR 723 at 737.
26   See Note 25 above.
27   *Ibid.* at 735.
28   [1979] FSR 46.
29   See in particular Buckley LJ at 57.
30   [1980] RPC 193.

5.1.1.6 *M.S. Associates Ltd v Power & Others*[31]

In this case the issue of infringement of copyright in computer software was considered where only a minimal amount of code contained any similarities. This action concerned computer programs which translated BASIC into 'C' language. Such programs consisted of a translator section and a library section. The plaintiff alleged that the defendants' 'B-tran' library section infringed its copyright in its 'C-Gen' library section. An application for interlocutory relief was heard by Falconer J and the motion was decided under the provisions of the 1985 Amendment Act.

The plaintiff had inspected some 9,000 lines of the defendants' program. However they only relied upon textual similarities between the two programs in 43 lines. The plaintiff further alleged that there were 'many objective similarities in structure and in detail between the two programs', and also pointed to certain errors in the plaintiff's program which were alleged to have been reproduced in the defendants' program.

The defendants argued that the plaintiff had failed to show that there was a serious question to be tried. It was argued that the parts of the plaintiff's program alleged to have been copied did not constitute a substantial part of the plaintiff's program. The plaintiff had not described the overall structure of the library in their C-Gen program, the structure of which was alleged to be reproduced. Therefore, it could not be said that those passages constituted a substantial part of the structure of the plaintiff's work.

Falconer J rejected the defendants' argument, and held that there was a serious question to be tried. The plaintiff had relied upon similarities in structure between the functions known as GET in each program. In the plaintiff's program this function comprised 91 lines of code, and in the defendants', 25 lines. Falconer J stated that:

> It does not seem to me that, on any footing, and to take only a part of their program, the 'GET' function could be regarded *prima facie* as otherwise than a substantial part and I have no difficulty in forming that view from a consideration of the 'GET' function itself.[32]

Nonetheless, the learned judge declined to grant the relief sought by the plaintiff on the basis that the balance of convenience was against the grant of an injunction.

The *M.S. Associates* decision, in its approach to the question of 'substantial part', may be contrasted with the case of *Thrustcode v W.W. Computing*.[33]

The plaintiff alleged infringement of copyright and breach of confidence in two of its computer programs by a similar program produced by the defendant, and sought interlocutory relief. At the hearing of the motion,

31 [1988] FSR 242.
32 *Ibid.* at 250.
33 [1983] FSR 502.

the plaintiff produced in evidence neither its complete source code nor its complete object code but relied on some 75 lines of source code. Megarry VC held that there was no arguable case of infringement and dismissed the motion.

The Vice-Chancellor envisaged that it would normally be necessary to have a printout of both the plaintiff's and the defendant's programs, or of substantial parts of both, to make a direct comparison between the two. As, in the case before him, insufficient portions of the plaintiff's programs had been exhibited, and the argument of infringement was based on inference from the functions of the programs rather than on direct evidence of similarities, the Vice-Chancellor's primary finding was that there was no arguable case of infringement.[34]

It is possible to reconcile these cases on the basis that in *M.S. Associates*, the Court was satisfied that there was a serious question to be tried that the small passages relied on constituted a substantial part of the whole. However, it would appear that in order to prove its case at trial, a plaintiff would need to make a far more wide-ranging comparison of the programs in dispute.

The importance of the *M.S. Associates* decision lies in the recognition that copyright may be infringed if a substantial part of the 'structure' of the plaintiff's program has been copied. This form of non-textual infringement may be regarded as an application of those authorities concerned with the copying of the plot of a literary work.[35]

The test of marked similarities between the choice and relative importance of incidents[36] is just as applicable to a comparison of computer programs as to other literary works. In *Computer Aided Systems (U.K.) Limited v Bolwell*[37] Hoffmann J accepted for the purposes of the application for an interlocutory injunction that the structure of a computer program is a form of literary expression in which copyright can subsist. He relied upon the United States decision in *Whelan Inc. v Jaslow Dental Laboratories Inc.*[38] as persuasive authority in support of this proposition. However, on the facts of that case Hoffmann J held that the evidence of structural similarities amounted to no more than speculation. He held that there was no arguable case of infringement, and dismissed the motion.

5.1.1.7   *The* Total Information *case*

The case *Total Information Processing Systems Limited v Daman Limited*[39] is of considerable interest, since it is the first decision in the United Kingdom in which consideration has been given to the question of copying of an interface program. The case did not concern similarities in

---

34   *Ibid.* at 508.
35   Discussed in detail in paragraph 5.1.1.4 above.
36   *Per* Goff J in *Harman Pictures N.V. v Osborne* [1967] 1 WLR 723 at 735.
37   IPD April 1990 15.
38   [1987] FSR 1.
39   [1992] FSR 171.

the user interface, but rather in a program written in order to link one software package with another.

The dispute concerned rights in computer software for use in particular in the buildings and construction industry. The software included a costing program which was specifically designed to operate with other programs. Its purpose was to perform calculations relating to the costing of contracts using data fed into it from other programs, and in particular from the payroll program. The data was passed through a part of the costing program known as the interface file. This consisted of the field and record specifications of the costing program written as part of the source code. It operated to ensure that data from the payroll program was directed correctly to the record files in the costing program. The defendants owned the rights in the interface file, and sought an interlocutory injunction against the plaintiffs (TIPS) to restrain them from copying that file. TIPS admitted that they had copied those parts of the source code as were necessary to link their own software to the costing program.

Judge Paul Baker QC held that the defendants had not shown an arguable case of infringement of copyright. He held that the part of the interface file which had been copied could be likened to a table of contents and could not be described as a substantial part of the program as a whole.

The part of the interface file which had been copied was a very small part of the commands in the program as a whole, and was akin to the idea of the program, rather than its expression.

It is of interest, however, that the learned judge rejected the submission that TIPS were entitled to copy the interface file in the public interest.

5.1.1.8 *United States decisions*

A full consideration of the United States authorities on copyright infringement in computer programs is beyond the scope of this book. However, certain of the leading cases are briefly considered below, in order to highlight where the approach of the United Kingdom courts is likely to be similar, and where it is likely to diverge.

In *Whelan v Jaslow*[40] the Court of Appeals for the Third Circuit specifically addressed the question of whether copyright in a computer program would be infringed in the absence of copying of the literal code, if the structure and organisation of the program had been copied.

The Court pointed to the fact that the copyright in other literary works can be infringed even where there is no substantial similarity between the works' literal elements. By analogy the copyright in a computer program could be infringed in the absence of literal copying if the structure was part of the expression of the idea behind a program rather than the idea itself.[41]

40   [1987] FSR 1.
41   *Ibid.* at 16 to 17.

It was held that the line between idea and expression could be drawn by reference to the end sought to be achieved by the work in question, so that the purpose or function of a utilitarian work would be the work's idea, and everything that was not necessary to that purpose or function would be part of the expression of the idea. Where there were various means of achieving the desired purposes, the particular means chosen were not necessary to the purpose, and hence were expression, not idea.

The Court was able to conclude that the structure of the plaintiffs' program was not necessary to its purpose (that is, was not the only way in which the purpose could be carried out) in that there were competing programs which performed the same function but had different structures.

It is important to note that the Court arrived at its finding of infringement by a comparison of the structures of the codes of the programs in issue. Similarities in screen outputs could not be direct evidence of copyright infringement in code, but only indirect or inferential evidence. It was pointed out that there is necessarily a causal relationship between screen outputs and the underlying programs, and therefore evidence of similarities was admissible. However, it was clear that the Court was cautious as to the weight to be attached to such evidence, since different structures of code could produce the same 'results'.[42]

By contrast, certain other US decisions have applied a 'look and feel' test to the question of infringement. 'Look' refers to the screen outputs or sequence of screen outputs displayed on the VDU. 'Feel' concentrates on the operation of the program by the user, for example the sequence of required keystrokes. In *Broderbund Software Inc. v Unison World Inc.*[43] it was held that the defendant had infringed copyright in the appearance, structure and sequence of the audio-visual displays of the plaintiff's program. This conclusion was reached in the absence of a comparison of the program codes. Similarly in *Lotus Development Corporation v Paperback Software International*[44] the Court held that copyright had been infringed because the plaintiff's 'user interface' had been copied. The user interface included screen displays and their associated menus, long prompts and macro commands. Again the Court found infringement on the basis of a comparison of the screens and menus of the programs, and in the absence of code comparison.

All of the above decisions have been the subject of criticism in numerous articles and other writings. However, it is important to stress that there is an important distinction between the *Whelan* decision and the *Broderbund* and *Lotus* cases. *Whelan* was concerned with a code comparison. It is submitted that the same approach to copying of structure is likely to be adopted by the courts in the United Kingdom, and the analogy with the

42   *Ibid.* at 28 to 29.
43   648 F. Supp. 1127 (N.D.Calif. 1986).
44   740 F. Supp. 37 (D. Mass. 1990).

plots of other literary works is a persuasive one. From a policy standpoint, it is difficult to find a convincing reason why a programmer should be entitled to misappropriate the skill, labour and ingenuity of another by copying the structure of a program, so long as he avoids literal copying, where there are other ways of achieving the same result.

The *Broderbund* and *Lotus* cases were concerned with a comparison of similarities apparent to the user, for example screens and menus. It is submitted that this approach may be acceptable, *provided that* it is understood that this is a consideration of copyright works which are *separate* from the underlying code.

The screen displays of a program may well constitute literary or artistic works, or even cinematograph films,[45] which works are susceptible of infringement. However, the dangers of the look and feel test can be summarised as follows:

(1) It cannot necessarily be concluded that the copyright in code has been infringed by a comparison of extrinsic similarities in programs. Such similarities are at best inferential evidence of copying, which needs to be confirmed by a comparison of the program codes.

(2) Care needs to be taken to avoid undue restrictions on fair competition. Software suppliers should be permitted to offer programs which have similar functions without fear of copyright infringement.

(3) It is desirable that the law should not restrict the development of programs which are compatible with other successful software packages. It is most unlikely that courts in the United Kingdom would restrict such development, in the absence of copying of expression. However, a concentration on protection of the user interface, and a broad approach to the question of look and feel, could be used in certain cases to produce precisely that result. It is submitted that the courts should be astute to avoid any such conclusions.

5.1.1.9 *Substantial part*

It is a requirement of both the 1956 and 1988 copyright statutes that a substantial part of the plaintiff's work must have been reproduced, copied or adapted, in order to establish infringement.[46] It will be apparent from the above discussion of non-textual infringement that the issue of 'substantial part' can be determinative of the success or failure of an action.

The standard citation on the meaning of 'substantial part' is the statement of Lord Pearce in *Ladbroke (Football) Ltd v William Hill (Football) Ltd*[47] (a case concerned with infringement of copyright in football pools): . . . 'whether a part is substantial must be decided by its quality rather than its quantity'. However, this test merely poses the question, it does not answer it.

---

45 See Chapter 6 paragraph 6.7.
46 Copyright Act 1956 section 49(1); Copyright, Designs and Patents Act 1988 section 16(3).
47 [1964] 1 WLR 273 at 292.

In two recent cases, despite a finding that the defendant had copied certain features of the plaintiff's design, it was concluded that these features did not constitute a substantial part and that accordingly there had been no infringement of copyright.

In *Johnstone Safety Ltd v Peter Cook (Int) Plc & Another*[48] (a case concerned with alleged infringement of copyright in drawings of road traffic cones) Whitford J found that the defendant's designer had deliberately adopted two design features of the plaintiff's design; and that his denial of copying in these respects was not to be believed.

The judge held that those features constituted a substantial part of the plaintiff's design. This decision was reversed by the Court of Appeal. The Appellate Court did not disturb the finding of the trial judge as to the credibility of the relevant witness; and considered the issue of infringement on the basis that two design features had been copied. However, it was held that a substantial part of the plaintiff's drawing had not been reproduced.

Whitford J had considered it significant that one feature which had been reproduced (a step and lip in the skirt of the cone) was an important design feature of the plaintiff's successful design. In the Court of Appeal, Ralph Gibson LJ held that the judge had applied the wrong test:

> . . . whether a substantial part of the plaintiff's drawing was reproduced by the defendants must be considered essentially with reference to the visual images of the drawing and the defendants' cone respectively, as a matter of fact and degree. The presence in the defendants' cone of the step and lip in the skirt, is not more potent for demonstrating that a substantial part of the plaintiff's drawing has been reproduced because that step with lip in the skirt was in functional terms an important design feature of the plaintiff's successful design.[49]

The decision was considered and explained by Hoffmann J in *Billhofer Maschinenfabrik GmbH v T.H. Dixon & Co. Ltd.*[50] Again the Court was faced with the issue of whether copied features constituted a substantial part of the plaintiff's drawings. The judge explained that the question of whether features visually depicted on a drawing were sufficiently important to be a substantial part must depend upon their significance to the kind of person to whom the drawing was addressed. In considering the *British Leyland* decision, he observed:

> To whom, one asks, would the flow line have been the salient feature and the dimensions crucial? Not to a visitor observing the exhaust pipe mounted on a plinth at the Tate Gallery but to the engineer wanting to make an exhaust which would fit under a Marina.[51]

Hoffmann J explained that in previous cases such as *Johnstone Safety*, the importance of the functional feature lay in its idea, and not in the

48   [1990] FSR 161.
49   *Ibid*. at 177.
50   [1990] FSR 105.
51   *Ibid*. at 122.

particular form in which it was expressed. The idea was important but it was not visually significant to the drawing.

Johnstone Safety and *Billhofer* were both concerned with the issue of substantial part of artistic works, and considerable care must be exercised in considering their applicability to literary works. Nonetheless the following summary may be of assistance when preparing expert evidence in copyright actions in relation to computer software:

(1) Whether a particular section of a program constitutes a substantial part is to be determined by the quality of that section, and not its quantity.

(2) This question depends upon the importance of the particular section to the person to whom the code is addressed, that is the computer programmer.

(3) In order to constitute a substantial part, the importance of the section must lie in the way in which it is expressed, as opposed to the technical idea which it embodies.

5.2 INFRINGEMENT OF COPYRIGHT IN COMPUTER SOFTWARE UNDER THE COPYRIGHT, DESIGNS AND PATENTS ACT 1988

It is proposed to confine consideration of infringement under the 1988 Act to those sections which raise special questions in relation to computer software.

5.2.1 Copying

Section 16(1)(a) gives the owner of copyright the exclusive right to copy the work in the United Kingdom. The copying of a work is defined in section 17(2) as 'reproducing' the work in any material form. Pursuant to section 16(3)(a) it is an infringement to reproduce the whole or any substantial part of the work.

A consideration of section 17 shows substantial differences from the 1956 Act. Section 17(2) provides that copying includes storing the work in any medium by electronic means. Section 17(6) provides that copying includes the making of copies which are transient or are incidental to some other use of the work.

It is clear from these sections that the 1988 Act gives to the copyright owner the right to prevent unauthorised use of his computer program. Whenever a program is loaded from disk to RAM, the contents of the disk are stored in the computer by electronic means. The fact that this copy is transient, in that it will only remain while the machine is turned on, is immaterial. A copy has still been made. While it is submitted that a 'use right' may well have existed under the 1956 Act, both before and after amendment[52], the position is undoubtedly much clearer under the 1988 Act.

5.2.2   Issuing of copies to the public

Section 18 creates a new right for copyright owners to control the issue of copies of their work. This right is of particular importance to software developers, for the reasons discussed below, and did not exist under previous legislation.[53]

Pursuant to section 18(1), the issue of copies to the public is an act restricted by copyright. The restricted act is further defined in section 18(2) as the putting into circulation of copies not previously put into circulation, in the United Kingdom or elsewhere. It is provided that the restricted act does not apply to:

(a) any subsequent distribution, sale, hiring or loan of those copies or
(b) any subsequent importation of those copies
except that in relation to sound recordings, films and computer programs the restricted act of issuing copies to the public includes any rental of copies to the public.

'Rental' is widely defined as an arrangement under which a copy of a work is made available for payment and on terms that it will or may be returned.[54]

The effect of this somewhat convoluted section may be summarised as follows:

(1) It is an infringement of copyright to issue any copy of a copyright work to the public in the United Kingdom without consent, if that copy has not previously been put into circulation in the United Kingdom or elsewhere.

(2) In general, this right does not apply to any subsequent distribution or importation of copies already in circulation.

(3) However, in relation to computer programs it is an infringement to rent to the public any copy of the program without consent, whether or not such copy has previously been circulated.

This section has the effect of giving to the software developer the right to prevent unauthorised sublicensing of his program, a right which was previously dependent on contractual provisions in the main licence.

5.2.3   Sales or gifts of licensed software

Section 18 does not, however, extend to cases where the licensee makes an outright sale of the copy which he had been given, nor to cases where he

---

52   See paragraphs 5.3 to 5.4 below.
53   *Infabrics Ltd v Jaytex Ltd* [1982] AC 1.
54   Copyright, Designs and Patents Act 1988 section 178.

gives away such copy without any consideration. If he transfers by either of those methods a licensed copy, the article itself is not made in infringement of copyright, nor is such transfer caught by the rental right.

It is arguable, however, that any such unauthorised act by a licensee would amount to an authorisation to the recipient to copy the program within the meaning of section 17 of the 1988 Act. Any person who supplies another with a copy of a program is likely to authorise its use (in the absence of special circumstances) since that is the purpose of the supply.[55] Any such use will result in storage of the contents of the disk in computer memory by electronic means, even if only in transient form. The authorisation of such an act without consent would constitute an infringement of copyright.

Further support for this argument is provided by the limited statutory licence contained in section 56 of the 1988 Act. This applies in circumstances where a copy of a work in electronic form has been purchased on terms which, expressly or impliedly or by virtue of any rule of law, allow the purchaser to copy the work or to adapt it or make copies of an adaptation in connection with his use of it.

It is provided that anything which the purchaser was allowed to do may also be done without infringement by a transferee.[56]

There are a number of important limitations on the scope of this licence.

(1) It only applies where copies have been purchased, and not where copies have been licensed. The use of the word 'purchased' in this section is to be contrasted with the definition of rental in section 178. A purchaser is not likely to be bound by terms that he will or may return the software. Since it is the industry practice to license software, section 56 would appear to be of limited application.

(2) The effect of section 56 can be excluded by express terms to the contrary in the licence agreement.

The existence of the limited licence suggests that transfers which do not fall within the scope do constitute infringements of copyright. The statutory licence must be intended to render lawful acts which would otherwise be unlawful.

5.2.4 Translation

Section 21 of the 1988 Act states that the making of an adaptation of a work is an act restricted by the copyright therein. The copyright owner is also given the exclusive right to copy, issue copies to the public, and make adaptation of an adaptation of his work.[57]

---

55 *Monckton v Pathé Frères Pathephone Ltd* [1914] 1 KB 395. Cf. *CBS Songs Ltd v Amstrad Consumer Electronics plc* [1988] AC 1013.
56 But any copy, adaptation or copy of an adaptation made by the purchaser which is not also transferred is treated as an infringing copy for all purposes.
57 Section 16(1)(e) of the 1988 Act.

'Adaptation', in relation to a literary work, includes making a translation of the work.[58] 'Translation' in relation to a computer program is specifically dealt with in section 21(4) in the following terms:

> In relation to a computer program a 'translation' includes a version of the program in which it is converted into or out of a computer language or code or into a different computer language or work, otherwise than incidentally in the course of running the program.

This limitation is to be contrasted with section 17(6), from which it appears that copying includes the making of copies which are incidental to some other use of the work.[59]

The exclusion of incidental running from the limitation of 'translation' may constitute a limitation on the right to restrict the unauthorised use of a computer program in the following circumstances:

If a program is run by a process of conversion from one language to another, and the language in which the program is written is not copied into the computer memory, then the unauthorised use of such program would not amount to an infringement of copyright. This limitation seems somewhat arbitrary since the unauthorised use of a program where the language or a substantial part thereof is copied into memory prior to conversion does constitute an infringement of copyright.

It is noteworthy that the 1985 Amendment Act gives wider rights to the copyright owner in this respect than the 1988 Act.[60]

Illustrations of the translation right
The translation right has a wide application to computer software. This may be illustrated by a number of examples:

> (1) A software house originally writes a program in BASIC, and subsequently converts the program into a different language to enable it to be used on other machines. The subsequent version constitutes a translation within the meaning of section 21, and it is an infringement of copyright to copy such a translation.
>
> (2) A computer programmer, without consent, converts a program written in BASIC into a different language. The resulting program will not constitute a reproduction of the original, since the language will appear quite different. It will, however, amount to an infringement of copyright, since it constitutes an unauthorised translation of the work.
>
> (3) Object code is loaded into computer memory without consent, in order to use the program. This constitutes copying of the object code within the meaning of section 17. If the program was originally written in source code, and subsequently converted to object code,

---

58   *Ibid.* section 21(3)(a)(i).
59   Section 21(5) provides that no inference shall be drawn from section 21 as what does or not does not amount to copying a work.
60   See paragraph 5.3.2.

unauthorised use also constitutes the copying of a translation of the literary work.

5.3   INFRINGEMENT OF COPYRIGHT IN COMPUTER SOFTWARE UNDER THE COPYRIGHT (COMPUTER SOFTWARE) AMENDMENT ACT 1985

In cases where the question of infringement is governed by the provisions of the 1985 Amendment Act,[61] many of the problems raised under the unamended Copyright Act 1956 have been clarified.

5.3.1   Translation of source code to object code

Section 1(2) of the Amendment Act states that for the purposes of the application of the Copyright Act 1956 in relation to a computer program: '. . . a version of the program which is converted into or out of a computer language or code, or into a different language or code, is an adaptation of the program'.

It would therefore appear that the reproduction of source code in object code is an adaptation, and specifically a translation of the source code within the meaning of section 2(6) of the Copyright Act 1956. If done without consent, such an act amounts to an infringement of copyright in the source code.

5.3.2   Translation incidental to running

Section 1(2) states that the conversion of a computer program, whether into a different code or into the same code, amounts to an adaptation of the program. The translation right is wider under the 1985 Amendment Act than under the 1988 Act since translation incidental to running the program is not excluded.

5.3.3   Reproduction in a material form

Section 2 of the 1985 Amendment Act states that references in the Copyright Act 1956 to the reproduction of work in a material form shall include references to the storage of that work in a computer.

It would therefore appear that under the 1985 Amendment Act the principle of visual similarity based on the decision of *Boosey v Whight*[62] has no application. This argument is supported by the fact that section 3 of the 1985 Amendment Act specifically refers to infringing copies of a computer program consisting of 'a disc, tape or chip or any other device

---

61   In other words, in relation to acts committed between 16th September 1985 and 1 August 1989.
62   See paragraphs 5.4.1.2 to 5.4.1.5 below.

which embodies signals serving for the impartation of the program or part of it'. This suggests that the question of whether a program is a 'copy' is to be decided irrespective of the particular storage medium in which it is held. It would therefore seem that where source code is converted into object code such conversion amounts to reproduction in a material form within the meaning of section 2(5)(a) of the Copyright Act 1956, since the object code will be stored, at least for a temporary period, in the computer.

5.3.4   Infringement by use of a copyright program

It is submitted that the effect of section 2 of the 1985 Amendment Act is to render unauthorised use of a copyright program an infringement of copyright. The contents of the disk are stored within a computer whenever such disk is loaded. Since every program must be loaded before use, it would appear that use of the disk constitutes a reproduction in material form of the object code contained on the disk within the meaning of section 2(5)(a) of the Copyright Act 1956, as amended by section 2 of the 1985 Amendment Act.

Further, since conversion of source code to object code is an adaptation of the source code within section 1(2) of the 1985 Act, it would appear that unauthorised loading of a program amounts to reproduction of an adaptation of the source code. Such act would constitute an infringement of copyright under section 2(5)(a) of the Copyright Act 1956.

5.4   INFRINGEMENT OF COPYRIGHT IN COMPUTER SOFTWARE UNDER THE UNAMENDED COPYRIGHT ACT 1956

5.4.1   The acts of infringement

Specific acts restricted by copyright in a literary work are listed in sections 2 and 5 of the Copyright Act 1956. It is proposed to confine consideration of infringement to those acts which occasion specific problems in relation to computer programs.

5.4.1.1   *Reproducing the work in any material form*

Under Section 2(5)(a) of the Copyright Act 1956, reproducing a literary work in any material form is one of the acts restricted by copyright.

It is clear from the case law that the word 'reproduction' involves the act of copying. In the *Ladbroke (Football)*[63] case Lord Reid expressly held that reproduction meant copying, and excluded cases of substantial

---

63   [1964] 1 WLR 273.

similarity which had been achieved independently. In *Francis Day & Hunter Ltd v Bron*[64] the Court of Appeal defined two stages in the inquiry as to copying, the first objective, the second subjective. The objective question is purely one of fact – a judgment of the degree of similarity between the works dependent on the perception of the judge and on expert evidence tendered to him.[65] The subjective stage is also a question of fact, whether the defendant has actually copied the plaintiff's work or whether it is an independent work of his own. For example, proof that the defendant had not had access to the copyright work in question would show that even complete identity was a coincidence.

It is to be observed that while copying is clearly a prerequisite of reproduction, the phrase 'reproduction in any material form' would appear to contemplate copying by change of medium.[66] Provided the two-stage factual inquiry as to copying is answered in the affirmative, change of form does not prevent the infringement from being a reproduction.

5.4.1.2 The definition of 'copy'

In the United States prior to legislative amendment which specifically removed the problem,[67] the scope of copyright infringement in computer software was substantially reduced by a restricted definition of 'copy'. That definition was based *inter alia* on English authority. In the case of *Data Cash Systems Inc. v JS & A Group Inc.*[68] it was held that a copy of an object program did not infringe copyright in a source program, since it was not visibly perceptible as a copy. The Court's conclusion was based on the definition of copy at common law and under the Copyright Act 1909. Citing the English decision of *Boosey v Whight*,[69] the US case of *White-Smith v Apollo Publishing Co.*,[70] and the 1909 Act itself,[71] Flaum J held that a copy must have 'appeal to the eye'. Since the object program was not in a form which could be seen and read with the naked eye it was not a copy under the Act and its reproduction was not an infringement of copyright. The question therefore arises as to whether the same principle would be applied by the English courts under the unamended Copyright Act 1956.

5.4.1.3 Limitation of visual intelligibility

This argument does not concern the subsistence of copyright. It would clearly be wrong to assert that every copyright work must have appeal to

---

64 [1963] Ch. 587.
65 *Per* Upjohn LJ at 618.
66 See below at paragraph 5.4.1.9.1.
67 In December 1980 section 117 of the United States Copyright Act 1976 was amended to include specific reference to software.
68 203 USPQ 735 (1980).
69 [1900] 1 Ch. 122.
70 209 US 1 (1908).
71 US Copyright Act 1909 section 1(a).

the eye. The point concerns the question of infringement of copyright, specifically the definition of copy under the Copyright Act. Furthermore, the judgment cannot be interpreted to say that a copy of a copyrighted work must be visually perceptible. A copy of a sound recording need not be reduced to writing to constitute an infringement. The principle is rather a copy of a visually perceptible work must have appeal to the eye — must be visibly similar.

5.4.1.4   *The test of copying under the Copyright Acts 1709–1842*

An early definition of copy was provided by Bayley J in the case of *West v Francis*[72] decided under the Statute of Anne 1709: 'A copy is that which comes so near to the original as to give every person seeing it the idea created by the original.'

The tests suggests that the similarity between the two works is by the eye, and that the degree of resemblance should be gauged by visible indicia.

This definition was specifically adopted in the case of *Boosey v Whight*,[73] where the Court of Appeal decided that perforated rolls were not 'copies' of sheet music within the terms of the Copyright Act 1842. Lindley MR held that the reproduction of a work in machine readable form is not a copy of that work, since a copy must be in a form which others can see and read.[74]

It is possible to argue that this principle prevents a machine readable reproduction of a source program from infringing copyright. This would severely limit the scope of copyright protection. The value of the computer program lies in its machine readable form — when it is working in the computer. If the object program is obtained and copied, the source program becomes, to all intents and purposes, unnecessary.

5.4.1.5   *The status of* Boosey v Whight

It would appear that the *Boosey v Whight* judgment has no binding effect on courts in England and the Commonwealth when they come to consider the issue of infringement of copyright in computer software.

First, consideration of the judgments of the case in subsequent authorities suggest that its *ratio* was confined to musical works.[75]

Secondly, the specific effect of the decision has been overruled by statute. Perforated rolls and phonograph records, left unprotected by *Boosey v Whight*, were expressly protected under the Copyright Act 1911 in the United Kingdom.[76] The binding effect of principles drawn from cases

72   (1822) 5 B & Ald. 737.
73   Note 69 above.
74   *Ibid.* at 124.
75   See below Notes 79 and 80.
76   Copyright Act 1911 section 1(2)(d).

whose specific decisions have been overruled by statute has been doubted both by the Court of Appeal and the House of Lords in the United Kingdom.[77]

There are certain *dicta* in *Boosey v Whight* which might be applied by analogy to computer software: Lindley MR held that:[78] 'To play an instrument from a sheet of music which appeals to the eye is one thing: to play an instrument with a perforated sheet which itself forms part of the mechanism which produces the music is quite another.'

Subsequent judicial statements on *Boosey v Whight* regard its principle as being restricted to sound recordings.

In *Newmark v National Phonograph Co.*[79] Sutton J held that '*Boosey v Whight* decided that sounds produced mechanically did not come within the Copyright Act at all.'

Again in *Thompson v Warner Bros*[80] Lawrence LJ stated that the decision was 'generally accepted as laying down the principle that the sole right to multiply copies of a musical work did not include the sole right to reproduce the work by mechanical means.'

In *Boosey v Whight* Romer LJ concurred in the conclusion that perforated rolls were not copies of sheet music. He held that the legislature could not have contemplated that the author's copyright in published music would entitle him to stop the use in private of mechanical instruments. This was because 'mechanical instruments for producing music were well known at the date of the Act'. He referred to musical boxes as an example.[81] It would therefore appear that mechanical contrivances which were entirely unknown at the date of the Act would not be included within the *ratio* of *Boosey v Whight*.

5.4.1.6 *Reversal by statute of the consequences of a decision*

Where the consequences of a decision have been overruled by statute, that decision is no longer 'good law'.

This principle was clearly expounded by the House of Lords in *Thomson v Moyse*.[82] The *ratios* of two earlier cases favoured the plaintiff, who was claiming that he had been unfairly assessed for tax purposes.[83] The result of these cases had been reversed by statute.[84] All of the Law Lords thought that the cases were therefore irrelevant, and decided for the defendant.

---

77 *Thomson v Moyse* [1961] AC 967.
78 Note 69 above at 124.
79 [1907] 23 TLR 439 at 445.
80 [1929] 2 Ch. 308 at 328.
81 Note 69 above at 126.
82 Note 77 above.
83 *Hull v Marians (No. 2)* (1935) 19 TC 582; *IRC v Gordon* [1952] AC 552.
84 Finance Act 1953 section 24.

Lord Radcliffe stated with reference to the earlier authorities:[85]

> Whether this is the right way to treat the facts . . . is not now of any importance, since the legislature has intervened after the *Gordon* case to reverse the consequence of that decision. It would be a mistake in the circumstances to build any principles on the basis of those two decisions.

Lord Denning further stated:[86] 'They can no longer be regarded as of binding authority, nor can the reasons on which they were based.'

5.4.1.7   The test of copying under the Copyright Acts 1911–1956

It may be observed that the subject-matter before the Court in *West v Francis* was an artistic work. An artistic work appeals to the eye, and therefore it seems logical to judge the similarity of an alleged copy by appeal to the eye. The question remains, however, as to whether this definition should be applied across the board, to test the similarity between the works which communicate to senses other than the ocular. If, as has been suggested,[87] works in any material form may be protected by the law of copyright, it seems entirely illogical to effect a visual comparison.

It may be observed that more recent cases under the Copyright Act 1956 have not applied the test of visible similarity in relation to infringement. In the field of commercial design it has been held that as a resemblance may be due to common subject-matter or stock designs, it is necessary to consider a variety of factors to judge if there has been an infringement.[88]

Even in the field of artistic works, which appeal to the eye, visible similarity is no longer the sole criterion of infringement. In the case of *Krisarts S.A. v Briarfine*[89] Whitford J adopted a wide test of infringement, as suggested by *Copinger and Skone James*:[90] 'The degree of resemblance between the two works is not in itself a test of infringement but is only one factor in determining whether an unlawful use of a plaintiff's work has been made.'

In the light of these more recent decisions, it would appear that a reproduction of a visually perceptible work in machine readable form would be regarded as a copy of that work, despite lack of visible similarity. Resemblance is merely one indicator in a test of whether the defendant has substantially reproduced the plaintiff's work in material form. Accordingly it is concluded that the test of copying is wider than a mere assessment of visible similarities. It is a factual inquiry to determine whether a defendant has reproduced, in whatever medium, a substantial part of a copyright work.

85 [1961] AC 967 at 999.
86 *Ibid.* at 1006.
87 See above Chapter 4 paragraph 4.3.3.7.
88 *Kenrick*, Note 8 above; *Merchant Adventures Ltd v M. Grew & Co. Ltd* [1973] RPC 1.
89 [1977] FSR 557 at 562.
90 *Copinger and Skone James on Copyright*, Sweet & Maxwell, 1980 (12th edn) at paragraph 458.

The effect of this test may be seen in the Australian *Apple Computer* decision, where the Federal Court held that a copy of object code was a reproduction in material form of an adaptation of the source code from which it was assembled.[91]

5.4.1.8 Translation

Under section 2(5)(f) of the Copyright Act 1956, the acts restricted by the copyright in a literary work include making any adaptation of that work. Under section 2(6) 'adaptation' is defined to include a 'translation' of the work.

The development of a computer program is a process of translation from high level to low level language. It is translated from one language to another – from human readable computer language to machine readable code.

The object program is the identical expression of the idea contained in the source program but in a form which communicates only with the machine – machine readable language. The other manifestation of the expression has changed, but the way in which the program ideas are expressed remains the same.

It would therefore appear that conversion of source code to object code may be a translation of the source code under the 1956 Act.

5.4.1.8.1 Translation of source code to object code

The translation argument, in relation to computer software, was specifically considered in the United States pursuant to section 1(b) of the US Copyright Act 1909.[92] This provision, which was in substantially similar form to translation rights in the United Kingdom and Commonwealth, gave to the copyright owner the exclusive right 'to translate the copyright work into other language, or to make any other version thereof, if it be a literary work'.

The argument was put in *Synercom Technology v University Computing Co.*[93] that the production of a computer program using the plaintiff's copyrighted input formats was a translation within section 1(b).

It was held that the preparation of a program from input formats was not a translation. Input formats were merely material to aid the user of the software, closer to a general description of a problem to be solved rather than specific instructions:[94]

> The formulation of a problem in sufficient detail with sufficient precision to enable it to be converted into an unambiguous set of computer instructions requires

---

91 [1984] FSR 481.
92 USC Title 17, now repealed by the United States Copyright Act 1976.
93 199 USPQ 537 (1978).
94 *Ibid.* at 543.

substantial imagination and creativity, and the resulting program can in no way be said to be merely a copy or version of the problem statement.

But what if the fully developed program were copied from one language to another? In that event the Court held that there would be an infringement of section 1(b).[95] It is as clear an infringement to translate a computer program from for example, FORTRAN to ALGOL, as it is to translate a novel or play from English to French.

The question then remains as to whether it is 'as clear an infringement' to translate from source to object code – from human readable to machine readable languages. In *Synercom* developed computer programs were held not to infringe the copyright in input formats as the formats were merely the idea from which the programs had been developed. The better defined the expression of this idea becomes the more likely is the making of another version of it to be an infringement of translation rights. The object program is the final state of computer software where the expression of the idea is at its most developed.

It would appear to be an infringement of the translation right to make an unauthorised version of a program in object form since as in a translation from English to French, only the external manifestation of the expression changes.

This view was adopted by the Australian Federal Court in the *Apple Computer* case. Fox J stated:

> I am satisfied that the object codes in the Apple II ROMs are adaptations . . . of the original literary works constituted by the programs in source codes. This is, I think, because they can fairly be described as translation. Trans-literation may more precisely explain what happens but this is plainly comprehended within 'translation'. This term doubtless normally suggests translation from one language to another, but its ordinary meaning is wider and it is necessary to apply it with due regard for modern technology. The object codes contained in the Apple ROMs are a straightforward translation of the source codes and it would be entirely within ordinary understanding to say that they are translations of the source code.[96]

It is therefore concluded that it is an infringement of copyright to assemble object code from source code without the consent of the owner of copyright in the source code.

5.4.1.8.2   *Translation of object code from object code*

Reproduction of a program in object code from object code amounts to a reproduction of a translation of source code. Sections 2(5)(g) of the Copyright Act 1956 makes it clear that reproduction of an adaptation[97] of a literary work is included among the acts restricted by copyright.[98]

---

95 *Ibid.* at 543 note 5.
96 Note 91 above at 496.
97 'Adaptation' includes a translation of the work: Copyright Act 1956 section 2(6)(a)(iii).
98 Also under the Australian Copyright Act 1968 sections 31(i)(a)(vi) and 10(1): considered in the *Apple Computer* decision.

Accordingly, the reproduction of object code from object code without the consent of the copyright owner is an infringement of copyright subsisting in the source code.

5.4.1.9 *Infringement by use of a copyright program*

Prior to the 1985 Amendment Act, a variety of committees in the United Kingdom considered the question of the adequacy of copyright law for the protection of computer software and recommended that additional rights should be added to the Copyright Act. A majority of the Whitford Committee recommended that a supplementary use right should be provided to prevent unauthorised use of a computer program.[99] The Green Paper on Copyright preferred a loading restriction.[100]

From a commercial point of view, the cases where unauthorised use, as opposed to reproduction, would inflict substantial harm on a software developer are minimal. Obviously, unauthorised sales or leasing of the program would be impossible without reproduction. Use in private of the program would only escape infringement if the misappropriated copy was not recorded and retained for future use.

In any event, even under the 1956 Act it is arguable that every time a program is loaded into a computer memory, a reproduction in material form,[101] and a translation of the program,[102] is made. If the act of loading takes place without the consent of the copyright owner, such act would be an infringement of his exclusive rights. A specific instance of 'use' of object code may illustrate this point. Where a program is loaded from disk to memory the contents of the disk, that is, object code, are 'reproduced in a material form' within the meaning of the Copyright Act 1956 Section 2(5)(a). As has been suggested, mere change of medium from magnetic to electronic does not prevent infringement.[103] Accordingly, such use would amount to an unauthorised reproduction of the object code, which may arguably be, of itself, a literary work.[104]

Furthermore, the object code is a translation of the source code, and retranslation into electronic form is an infringement of the copyright in the source code under section 2(5)(g) of the Copyright Act.[105]

99   Whitford Committee Report (1977) (Cmnd 6732) at page 133.
100   Government Green Paper on Copyright Reform (1981) (Cmnd 8302).
101   See paragraphs 5.4.1.4 to 5.4.1.7.
102   Or alternatively reproduction of a translation.
103   See paragraph 5.4.1.1.
104   See Chapter 4 paragraph 4.4.1.
105   See paragraph 5.4.1.8.2.

6 Rights in Semiconductor Topographies and Copyright in Visual Displays

6.0 INTRODUCTION

This chapter is concerned with the copyright-style protection that is available for computer software other than the literary copyright in the actual programs. There are two principal subjects for discussion. The first is the protection that is available for hardware, and in particular semiconductor topographies, which are now protected by a modified form of design right. This form of protection is becoming increasingly important given the accelerating trend towards the 'hardwiring' of computer software, that is to say, the manufacture of semiconductor chips with specially-designed logical circuits for carrying out particular sequences of instructions (sometimes referred to as application-specific integrated circuits or ASICs). More and more software for larger computers is being supplied in this way or in the form of 'microcode', which means code for sequences of hardwired instructions. The second subject is the protection that is available for the output of computer programs – the products of their operations – and in particular the screen displays generated for visual display units (VDUs). This is still an underexplored area in the United Kingdom.

It should be remembered that where computer software is being copied without a licence, particularly in cases of 'piracy' or counterfeiting, there may well be other intellectual property rights that can be relied upon in addition to rights in or related to the software itself. Thus there may be copyright in the musical soundtrack played by the software while operating[1] or in the artwork of the packaging, registered or unregistered trade marks and so on which can be relied upon. The principles which are applicable in such cases are in no way peculiar to computers or computer software, however, and so the coverage in this chapter is concentrated on the two areas which are special to computers.

The subject of ownership of copyright which was discussed in this chapter in the first edition is now dealt with in Chapter 4.

---

1   See *Atari Inc. v Philips Electronics and Associated Industries Ltd* [1988] FSR 416 – a case about *Pac-Man*.

6.1 SEMICONDUCTOR CHIPS

The design and manufacture of semiconductor chips or integrated circuits is essentially an exercise in the art of reduction. A semiconductor chip is a miniature electronic circuit containing a number of individual logic components, for example, gate transistors. Large numbers of such components can be condensed into an area of no more than a few microns. Chips can be used in computers as general processing units, as storage for programs or data or to contain specific sets of instructions.

Semiconductor chips are made from semiconductor materials such as silicon, germanium or gallium arsenide. Of these silicon is the most popular. Manufacture of a silicon chip begins with the slicing of a wafer of silicon from a crystal. This wafer of silicon is then doped in predetermined places with trace elements which modify the conductivity of the silicon to create particular components. Other components are created, and the components linked together in circuits, by the deposition of layers of conductive metal or insulators on the surface of the silicon.

The design of the chip involves two distinct stages: first, the translation of the functional requirements of the chip into an electronic circuit; and second, the translation of the electronic circuit into a series of layers to be deposited onto the surface of the silicon wafer. The process can be visualised by imagining a series of transparencies each of which has certain marks drawn on it in a coloured pen. When all the transparencies are superimposed one on top of the other, the various coloured marks will form a complex three-dimensional pattern. This pattern is the semiconductor topography.

To deposit each layer onto the wafer, the silicon is coated with a photo-resistant material. A negative image of the design of the layer is then placed on top of the photo-resistant material. This negative is known as the 'mask' since it screens portions of the photo-resistant material, and it may be produced either by photographing a positive drawing or directly. Light or some other radiation is directed onto the exposed areas of the resistant surface, which are not screened by the mask. Those areas harden and become resistant to acid. The wafer is then dipped in an acid bath. The areas which have not been rendered acid-resistant are etched away, leaving a positive image of the desired layer etched onto the wafer. This may be treated as desired. The acid-resistant material may then be removed. This process is repeated until the complete topography has been built up. Instead of using a physical mask, a directed light beam may be used instead.

Chip design is now carried out using computer-aided design techniques which have advanced to the stage of automatically translating functional designs into detailed layouts or masks. Nevertheless, the investment required for chip design is still very substantial, and chips are vulnerable to copying for a fraction of the cost of the design process.

6.2 FORMS OF LEGAL PROTECTION OF SEMICONDUCTOR CHIP DESIGNS

Consideration of the legal protection available for semiconductor chip designs is complicated by the fact that there are three different forms of protection which are potentially applicable:

(1) Copyright in artistic works under the Copyright Act 1956 as modified by the Copyright, Designs and Patents Act 1988.
(2) A bespoke topography right created by the Semiconductor Products (Protection of Topographies) Regulations 1987.
(3) A specially modified version of the unregistered design right under Part III of the 1988 Act.

The effect of the transitional provisions of the 1988 Act and of the statutory instruments is that which of these three applies depends on the date when the particular semiconductor topography was created.

6.3   EFFECT OF THE TRANSITIONAL PROVISIONS

The effect of the transitional provisions can be seen by considering topography designs created on different dates:

(1) *Designs created before 7 November 1987*

Topography designs created before 7 November 1987 (when the 1987 Regulations came into force) are protected, if at all, by copyright in artistic works.

Under the 1988 Act, the new design right does not subsist in any design which was made before the commencement of Part III on I August 1989.[2] In respect of designs made before that date, there is a complex system of transitional provisions by virtue of which copyright protection continues to be available until 31 July 1999.[3] This applies to topography designs made before 7 November 1987. Unlike copyrights in other types of design created prior to 1 August 1989,[4] however, licences of right for topography designs are not available for the last five years of this ten-year term.[5] From 1 August 1999, copyright protection is excluded in relation to designs,[6] and so topography designs made before 7 November 1987 will then be free of any form of protection.

---

2   Copyright, Designs and Patents Act 1988 section 213(7) and Copyright, Designs and Patents Act 1988 (Commencement No. 1) Order 1989, SI 1989 No. 816.
3   *Ibid.*, Schedule 1, paragraph 19(1), which provides that section 51 of the 1988 Act (exclusion of copyright protection in relation to designs) does not apply for ten years from commencement of Part I of the Act.
4   *Ibid.*, section 237 and Schedule 1, paragraph 19(2), (3).
5   Design Right (Semiconductor Topographies) Regulations 1989, regulation 10(3).
6   Copyright, Designs and Patents Act 1988 section 51.

(2) Designs created between 7 November 1987 and 29 June 1989 inclusive

Topography designs created between 7 November 1987 and 29 June 1989 are subject to the Semiconductor Products (Protection of Topographies) Regulations 1987.

The 1987 Regulations came into force on 7 November 1987 and were revoked on 29 June 1989.[7] Presumably this revocation was without prejudice to accrued rights,[8] so that proceedings for infringements of rights under the 1987 Regulations which occurred between 7 November 1987 and 29 June 1989 may be brought up to 29 June 1995.[9]

So far as topography designs created between 7 November 1987 and 31 July 1989 are concerned, the ten-year delay on the exclusion of copyright protection from application to designs[10] does not apply.[11] Thus copyright protection is already excluded so far as these designs are concerned.

(3) Designs created between 30 June 1989 and 31 July 1989 inclusive

The combination of the various provisions has the anomalous effect that topography designs created between 30 June 1989 and 31 July 1989 inclusive are not protected by any of these forms of protection: copyright is not available because of the exclusion of copyright protection, rights under the 1987 Regulations are not available because the Regulations had been revoked and design right is not available because it had not come into force. It seems clear that this result was unintended, but it appears to be inescapable.

(4) Designs created from 1 August 1989 onwards

So far as topography designs created from 1 August 1989 onwards are concerned, the only form of protection available is design right under Part III of the 1988 Act as modified by the 1989 Regulations.

6.4   COPYRIGHT IN ARTISTIC WORKS

It is well established that copyright may subsist in an artistic work such as a drawing regardless of artistic quality.[12] Copyright may therefore subsist in a blueprint or other manufacturing drawing for a functional article, and will do if the requirements of originality[13] and qualification[14] are

---

7   Design Right (Semiconductor Topographies) Regulations 1989, regulation 10(1).
8   See Interpretation Act 1978 section 16(1)(c).
9   Limitation Act 1980 section 2.
10   Copyright, Designs and Patents Act 1988 section 51 and Schedule 1, paragraph 19(1).
11   Design Right (Semiconductor Topographies) Regulations 1989, Regulation 10(2).
12   Copyright Act 1956 section 3(1)(a); Copyright, Designs and Patents Act 1988 section 4(1)(a).
13   In the case of artistic works, this means that the work must be the product of skill and labour, but skill and labour in copying an antecedent work is not enough – there must be some difference in the visual image: *Interlego AG v Tyco Industries Inc.* [1989] AC 217. See Chapter 4 paragraph 4.2.1.1.
14   These are the same as for literary works, as to which see Chapter 4 paragraph 4.2.2.

satisfied. Under the Copyright Act 1956, it was held in a series of cases[15] that if articles were made which were reproductions in three dimensions of the drawing, and those articles were copied by a competitor, the competitor indirectly copied the drawing and so infringed the copyright in it unless it would not appear to a person who was not an expert in articles of that description that the allegedly infringing article was a reproduction of the drawing (the section 9(8) defence). Thus copyright afforded protection to the design even of the most functional articles. Given the low threshold of originality for subsistence of copyright, given the length of time for which copyright subsisted and given the remedies that were available for infringement (especially that of conversion damages), it came to be felt that this protection was excessive.

Copyright in artistic works is now governed by Part I of the Copyright, Designs and Patents Act 1988, which came into force on 1 August 1989.[16] In the long term, this will radically change the law of industrial designs, effectively abolishing the application of copyright in artistic works and substituting a new right, called the design right.[17] For a transitional period of ten years from 1 August 1989, however, the law applicable to designs created before that date remains much as it was under the 1956 Act,[18] although both the section 9(8) defence and the remedy of conversion damages have been abolished[19] and licences are available as of right during the last five years of the period.[20] In particular copyright only subsists in such existing works if it subsisted under the 1956 Act.[21] It is worth noting, however, that there is a noticeable trend towards a more restrictive application of the law by the courts in industrial design cases.[22]

So far as semiconductor topography designs are concerned, the transitional provisions under the 1988 Act are modified so that any copyright in artistic works will only be applicable if the work was created before 7 November 1987. Any such copyright will cease to be applicable after 31 July 1999. Unlike other categories of work, however, licences of right are not available during the last five years of this period.

There are four categories of artistic works which may attract copyright so as to afford protection for topography rights. These are:

(1) Circuit diagrams.
(2) Layouts and masks.

---

15   See for example *Dorling v Honor Marine Ltd* [1965] Ch. 1; *L.B. (Plastics) Ltd v Swish Products Ltd* [1979] RPC 611; *British Leyland Motor Corp. v Armstrong Patents Co. Ltd* [1986] AC 577.

16   Copyright, Designs and Patents Act 1988 (Commencement No. 1) Order 1989, SI 1989 No. 816.

17   Copyright will continue to subsist in artistic works, but manufacturing an article will no longer be an infringement. Instead, it will be an infringement of any design right that subsists.

18   This is the combined effect of section 51 and Schedule 1, paragraph 19(1) of the 1988 Act.

19   Except in existing proceedings: Copyright, Designs and Patents Act 1988, Schedule 1, paragraph 31(2).

20   *Ibid.*, section 237 and Schedule 1, paragraph 19(2), (3).

21   *Ibid.*, Schedule 1, paragraph 5(1). See Chapter 4 paragraph 4.1.

22   See in particular *Interlego AG v Tyco Industries Inc.* [1989] AC 217, and *Johnstone Safety Ltd v Peter Cook plc* [1990] FSR 161.

(3) Each etched layer on the surface of the chip.
(4) The complete topography.

Each of these merits separate consideration.

6.4.1 Circuit diagrams

An 'artistic work' is defined in the 1956 Act to include a 'drawing',[23] which is in turn defined to include 'any diagram, map, chart or plan'.[24] A circuit diagram is therefore clearly an artistic work. If it is original and meets the qualification requirements, copyright will subsist.

Whether such a copyright would be infringed by the copying of a silicon chip embodying a topography made in accordance with the circuit diagram seems very doubtful, however. It is not sufficient for infringement that the alleged infringement be derived from the copyright work relied upon, in the sense that there is a causal connection (although this is necessary): there must also be a reproduction of a substantial part of the copyright work. In *Johnstone Safety Ltd v Peter Cook plc*,[25] the Court of Appeal emphasised that what mattered was not whether there was a taking of functionally important features, but whether there was a substantial visual similarity between the alleged infringement and the copyright work relied upon. This is because copyright is primarily concerned with expression in the medium in question rather than with an underlying idea. In that case the Court held that, notwithstanding that the defendants had copied functional features of the plaintiffs' product and lied in denying that they had done so, the alleged infringement did not reproduce a substantial part of the drawing relied upon.

Even though it is proper where technical works are concerned to assess visual similarity through the eyes of a technical man rather than a layman,[26] given the process by which circuit diagrams are translated into the layers of a semiconductor topography, there is little visual resemblance between the two. Rather the position is somewhat analogous to a recipe for a cake and a cake baked from the recipe: the one is derived from the other, but there is no reproduction of the recipe. Similarly, in *Brigid Foley Ltd v Ellott*[27] Sir Robery Megarry VC held that knitted garments were not reproductions of the instructions from which they were made:

> By a process of counting up the number of stitches . . . in the knitted garment, one might be able to work back and produce the knitting instructions, but that is a very different matter from saying that the garment is a reproduction of those instructions.[28]

23 Copyright Act 1956 section 3(1)(a).
24 *Ibid.*, section 48(1).
25 [1990] FSR 161.
26 *Billhofer Maschinenfabrik GmbH v T.H. Dixon & Co. Ltd* [1990] FSR 105.
27 [1982] RPC 433.
28 *Ibid.*, at 434. See Chapter 5 paragraph 5.1.1.3.

Accordingly it is unlikely that a court would find that a chip infringed the copyright in a circuit diagram.

Prior to the coming into force of the 1988 Act, an alternative route to this conclusion would have been the application of the section 9(8) defence. Thus in *Guildford Kapwood Ltd v Embsay Fabrics Ltd*[29] Walton J held that the defendants who had copied the plaintiffs' fabric had not infringed the copyright in a lapping diagram which showed the movement of a warp knitting machine during production of the fabric since section 9(8) provided a complete defence. Now that the section 9(8) defence is no longer available, it is likely that the court would arrive at the same result on the basis that no substantial part had been reproduced.

If the copyist engaged in a process of reverse engineering as a part of which he made his own circuit diagram, and this circuit diagram resembled the originator's circuit diagram, then it might well be possible to argue that the making of the second circuit diagram constituted an infringement.

6.4.2   Layouts and masks

As discussed above, a mask may be produced by photographing a layout which has been drawn or it may be produced directly. Layouts are undoubtedly artistic works. As for masks, 'artistic work' also includes a photograph,[30] which is defined to mean:

> . . . any product of photography or of any process akin to photography, other than part of a cinematograph film.[31]

This definition is wide enough to include masks.

Given that layouts and masks are now frequently produced by computer, it is worth pointing out that this does not mean that they cannot attract copyright,[32] although they must satisfy the requirement of originality in the ordinary way.[33] Where an artistic work is computer-generated, however, the 'author' will presumably be the person by whom the arrangements necessary for the creation of the work are undertaken.[34]

Where the mask is produced by photographing a layout rather than directly, it is possible that it will not be regarded as sufficiently original for

---

29   [1983] FSR 567.
30   Copyright Act 1956 section 3(1)(a).
31   *Ibid.*, section 48(1).
32   See *British Leyland Motor Corp. v Armstrong Patents Co. Ltd* [1986] AC 577, where copyright was held to subsist in drawings produced by computer-aided design; and *Express Newspapers plc v Liverpool Post & Echo plc* [1985] FSR 306 where copyright was held to subsist in data generated by a computer program.
33   *Bauman v Fussell* [1978] RPC 485.
34   Cf. Copyright, Designs and Patents Act 1988 section 9(3).

copyright to subsist, for the mask will be a precise visual reproduction of the layout, albeit in negative.[35] This should not matter, however, for copyright will subsist in the layout if this is original. Thus one or other ought to be protected.

Unlike a circuit diagram, a layout or mask will normally be broadly similar in appearance to the layer of the chip in the manufacture of which it is employed. If a chip has been copied, therefore, it may be argued that each layer of the second chip is an infringing copy of the layout or mask from which the first chip was made. This involves notionally sectioning the second chip into its component layers, however, rather than comparing the layout or mask with the entire topography of the second chip, in which case little resemblance may be apparent. That this exercise is permissible is suggested by the decision of the Court of Appeal in *Solar Thompson Engineering Co. Ltd v Barton*,[36] where it was held that a rubber ring was an infringement on the basis of a comparison of the ring when sectioned with the drawing relied upon (which was of a section). Alternatively, it may be permissible to consider all the layouts/masks for the first chip together, and to compare them *en masse* with the topography of the second chip. This would appear to be possible from decisions of the Court of Appeal and the House of Lords in the *British Leyland* case,[37] where the defendants' exhaust pipe was held to reproduce the plaintiffs' set of drawings rather than any one particular drawing.

6.4.3   Etched layers

'Artistic work' also includes any 'engraving', which is defined to include 'any etching, lithograph, woodcut, print or similar work'.[38] According to the *Chambers Dictionary of Science and Technology*,[39] 'etching' is: 'The process of dissolving, with an acid, portions of a surface, such as copper or zinc sheet, where it is not protected by a resist.' As discussed above, each layer of a silicon chip is produced by a process of etching. Accordingly it would appear to be arguable that each layer is an etching and thus an artistic work for the purposes of the 1956 Act. The contrary arguments would be that the layers do not have a permanent existence in that they have other layers superimposed upon them, and that the layers are not created for anything resembling artistic purposes. Neither of these arguments is very strong.

It is difficult, however, to see that such etchings would satisfy the requirement of originality so that copyright subsisted. Although skill and labour may be employed in the making of the etching, the net result is that the etching is visually a copy of the mask from which it was made, albeit

35   See *Interlego AG v Tyco Industries Inc.* [1989] AC 217.
36   [1977] RPC 537.
37   [1986] AC 577.
38   Copyright Act 1956 section 48(1).
39   W.R. Chambers Ltd, 1974.

in negative. If the mask was made from a layout, the etching will be an exact copy of the layout.

6.4.4 Topographies

It is difficult to see that a complete semiconductor topography design, as opposed to its component layers, is a work in which copyright is capable of subsisting under the 1956 Act. There are two reasons for this. The first is that the topography is three-dimensional. The definition of 'graphic work' suggests that it only includes two-dimensional works. Even if this were not a problem, one would usually have difficulty pointing to a single work which embodied the entire design and from which the chips derived. Topography designs usually consist of layers which only come together in the intended three-dimensional relationship on the surface of the chip; although data comprising the three-dimensional co-ordinates will exist beforehand, there will not be any one artistic work which embodies the whole design; or if there is one such work, it will exist for record purposes and will not form part of the chain of causation. Traditional artistic copyright is not well-suited to protecting a set of three-dimensional relationships in these circumstances.

If, however, it happened to be the case that a particular topography design was made by drawing it out on paper (say, in different coloured inks for each layer) and from that drawing masks were made from which chips were produced which were copied by a copyist, then there would appear to be no reason why copyright should not subsist in the drawing which the copied chips would infringe.

6.5   SEMICONDUCTOR TOPOGRAPHY RIGHT

By the mid-1970s it was widely felt that there was a need for special protection for semiconductor topographies. Although in the United Kingdom it was at least arguable that chip designs would be protected as artistic works under the Copyright Act 1956, in the United States it was thought that copyright did not provide protection. The chips themselves could not be the subject of copyright as three-dimensional works since they were merely utilitarian objects. As to the mask, which might be protectable as a drawing, any copyright in this would not be infringed by the reproduction of the circuits depicted. Attempts to provide suitable protection by means of amendments to what became the US Copyright Act 1976 were unsuccessful, and ultimately the Semiconductor Chip Protection Act 1984 was passed. This provided for a unique form of protection for 'mask works', defined as:

> . . . a series of related images, however fixed or embodied, having or represent-
> ing the predetermined three-dimensional pattern of metallic, insulating or

semiconductor material present or removed from the layers of a semiconductor chip product.[40]

The 1984 Act provided that mask works originating from countries outside the United States were only protected in the United States if the country of origin provided equivalent protection under its domestic legislation. As a consequence, similar bespoke regimes were introduced in a number of other countries in order to qualify for reciprocal protection under the 1984 Act.[41] In particular the Council of the European Communities issued a Directive to this end.[42] This was implemented in the United Kingdom by the introduction of the Semiconductor Products (Protection of Topographies) Regulations 1987[43] made under section 2(2) of the European Communities Act 1972 which came into force on 7 November 1987.

The 1987 Regulations created a new *sui generis* intellectual property right akin to copyright, the semiconductor topography right. This was defined as the exclusive right to reproduce the whole or a substantial part of an original topography, or to deal in a reproduction of it or in a semiconductor product incorporating such a reproduction.[44] 'Topography' was defined as the design of the pattern fixed or intended to be fixed on a layer of a semiconductor product, or on a layer of other material (for example, a mask) to be used in the manufacture of such a product, including the arrangement of the layers of a semiconductor product.[45] For the topography right to subsist, the topography was required to be the result of the creator's intellectual efforts, and not commonplace in the art.[46]

As a result of the advent of the new design right under Part III of the Copyright, Designs and Patents Act 1988 and of the transitional provisions of the Regulations applying this to semiconductor topography right,[47] the topography right only applies to designs created between 7 November 1987 and 29 June 1989. It is therefore of limited importance, and will not be considered further.

6.6 SEMICONDUCTOR TOPOGRAPHY DESIGN RIGHT

The unique form of protection provided by the 1987 Regulations has now been repealed and replaced by the Design Right (Semiconductor

40 Semiconductor Chip Protection Act 1984 section 901(a)(2)(A).
41 Ironically the result of this process was the rapid adoption of a WIPO Treaty on the Protection of Intellectual Property in Respect of Integrated Circuits at Washington in May 1989 in the face of a vote by the United States *against* the final text.
42 Directive 87/54/EEC (OJ L24/36 27 January 1987).
43 SI 1987 No. 1497.
44 Semiconductor Products (Protection of Topographies) Regulations 1987, regulation 4(1).
45 *Ibid.*, regulation 2(1)
46 *Ibid.*, regulation 3(3).
47 See paragraph 6.3.

Topographies) Regulations 1989,[48] which apply to all designs created after 31 July 1989. These assimilate the semiconductor topography right with the design right under Part III of the Copyright, Designs and Patents Act 1988, with certain modifications.[49] Although this has the desirable effect that semiconductor topography rights are now within the domestic statutory framework of intellectual property rights rather than being free-standing, it appears that there have been few changes in the substantive law, with the result that there are certain anomalies in the protection of semiconductor topographies compared with other designs.[50]

6.6.1   Definition of semiconductor topography

'Semiconductor topography' is defined in the 1989 Regulations as:

> . . . a design within the meaning of section 213(2)[51] of the Act[52] which is a design of either of the following:

> (a) the pattern fixed, or intended to be fixed, in or upon –
>   (i) a layer of a semiconductor product, or
>   (ii) a layer of material in the course of and for the purpose of the manufacture of a semiconductor product, or
> (b) the arrangement of the patterns fixed, or intended to be fixed in or upon the layers of a semiconductor product in relation to one another.[53]

'Semiconductor product' is defined as an article the purposes, or one of the purposes, of which is the performance of an electronic function and which consists of two or more layers, at least one of which is composed of semi-conducting material and in one or more of which is fixed a pattern appertaining to that or another function.[54]

This definition of semiconductor topography differs from those which appear in both the US 1984 Act and in the EC Directive in that there is no reference to a series of related images which represent the three-dimensional pattern of the product's layers. It does not appear that the difference is of much practical effect, however. Thus, although it has been suggested that a list of the functional requirements of an application-specific integrated circuit (ASIC) would qualify,[55] this does not seem correct, for such a list would not convey either a pattern or an arrangement of patterns.

---

48   SI 1989 No. 1100.
49   For which reason, perhaps, the 1989 Regulations, like the 1987 Regulations, have been made under section 2(2) of the European Communities Act 1972 rather than under the 1988 Act.
50   An effect which has not, however, been formalised by making the Regulations under Part III of the 1988 Act.
51   See below at paragraph 6.6.2.
52   That is the Copyright, Designs and Patents Act 1988.
53   Design Right (Semiconductor Topographies) Regulations 1989, regulation 2(1).
54   *Ibid.*
55   Hart and Reed in Reed (ed.), *Computer Law*, Blackstone Press, 1990 at 132.

6.6.2 Application of design right to semiconductor topographies

Design right is a new species of intellectual property akin to copyright which is created by Part III of the Copyright, Designs and Patents Act 1988. Section 213 of the Act provides that:

(1) Design right is a property right which subsists in accordance with this Part in an original design.

(2) In this Part 'design' means the design of any aspect of the shape or configuration (whether internal or external) of the whole or part of an article.

(3) Design right does not subsist in –

(a) a method or principle of construction,

(b) features of shape or configuration of an article which –

(i) enable the article to be connected to, or placed in, around or against, another article so that either article may perform its function, or

(ii) are dependent upon the appearance of another article of which the article is intended by the designer to form an integral part, or

(c) surface decoration.

As can be seen from the definition set out above, the 1989 Regulations are framed upon the assumption that a semiconductor topography is a design in which design right is capable of subsisting by virtue of section 213. Instead of an express stipulation that Part III of the 1988 Act shall apply semiconductor topographies, it is simply provided that 'in its application to a design which is a semiconductor topography, Part III of the 1988 Act shall have effect subject to regulations 4 to 9' of the 1989 Regulations.[56] Furthermore, it is provided that except where the context otherwise requires, the 1989 Regulations shall be construed as one with Part III of the 1988 Act.

There is no exclusion of section 213(3) in the Regulations. Although subsubsection (c) is probably inapplicable on the ground that 'surface decoration' must be something visible to the naked eye, subsections (a) and (b)(i) may be of some importance. Subsection (a) would prevent a chip designer from monopolising, for example, a particular way of constructing layers to create a particular electronic component. Subsubsection (b)(i) would appear to have the effect that chip designers cannot use the design of the input/output connections of a chip to prevent interoperability, although this has yet to be tested.

In a number of other respects, Part III is substantially modified in its application to semiconductor topographies. In particular, the Regulations contain special versions of the following sections: sections 215 (ownership), 216 (duration), 217 and 220 (qualification), 226 (infringement). Furthermore certain sections are provided not to apply: sections 219 (qualification) and 236 (licences of right).

6.6.3 Subsistence of design right

In order for design right to subsist, three conditions must be satisfied: (1) the design must be original; (2) the design must have been fixed; and (3) the design must qualify for protection.

---

56 Design Right (Semiconductor Topographies) Regulations 1989, regulation 3.

6.6.3.1　Originality

A design is not 'original' for the purposes of Part III if it is commonplace in the design field in question at the time of its creation.[57] This provision is new to the 1988 Act, and represents departure from the law under the Copyright Act 1956, where the requirement for originality in respect of an artistic work was interpreted as no more than a requirement that the work should not have been copied from a pre-existing work.[58] It is not easy to predict how the courts will interpret the exclusion of 'commonplace' designs. It seems clear that this imports a requirement for some degree of innovation on the part of the designer, but it is not clear how demanding a test of innovation will be imposed. It does seem clear, however, that a computer-generated design is as capable of being original as any other.

6.6.3.2　Fixation

Design right does not subsist unless and until the design has been recorded in a design document or an article has been made to the design. This again represents a departure from the law under the 1956 Act which, as interpreted by the courts, accorded functional designs protection against copying but subject to the technical requirement that the design be contained in a drawing or other artistic work. Thus an equally meritorious design which was not made in the form of a drawing but merely by making an article was not protected. This distinction is abolished in the case of design right.

'Design document' is widely defined as meaning any record of a design, whether in the form of a drawing, a written description, a photograph, data stored in a computer or otherwise.[59]

So far as semiconductor topographies are concerned, this should have the result that the difficulties over treating the complete topography as an artistic work[60] are avoided with design right.

6.6.3.3　Qualification

Under Part III of the 1988 Act, a design may qualify for design right protection in either of two basic ways. First, the designer or the person by whom the design was commissioned or the person by whom the designer was employed may qualify. Secondly, the person by whom and the country in which articles to the design were first marketed may qualify. The 1989 Regulations contain modifications to these provisions as they are set out in Part III of the 1988 Act. In particular, it is not possible for designs to qualify by reference to the person who commissioned the design or employed the designer if the designer is the first owner of the design

---

57　Copyright, Designs and Patents Act 1988 section 213(4).
58　See *Interlego AG v Tyco Industries Inc.* [1989] AC 217.
59　Copyright, Designs and Patents Act 1988, section 263(1).
60　See paragraph 6.4.4.

right.[61] The result is a rather complicated set of rules, which are tabulated below:

A. *Qualification by reference to designer or commissioner or employer*

(1) *Design not created pursuant to commission or employment*
The design qualifies if the designer is a qualifying individual or, in the case of a computer-generated design, a qualifying person.[62]
(2) *Design created pursuant to commission or employment but designer first owner of design right*
The design qualifies if the designer is a qualifying individual or, in the case of a computer-generated design, a qualifying person.[63]
(3) *Design created pursuant to commission or employment and commissioner or employer first owner of design right*
The design qualifies if the commissioner or employer is a qualifying person.[64]

B. *Qualification by reference to first marketing*

The design qualifies if the first marketing of articles made to the design is by a qualifying person who is exclusively authorised to put such articles on the market in every EEC Member State and takes place in a Member State.[65]

C. *'Qualifying individual'*

A 'qualifying individual' is defined as a citizen or subject of, or an individual habitually resident in, a qualifying country.[66] In the case of the United Kingdom, the requirement that the individual be a citizen or subject means that he must be a British citizen.[67]

D. *'Qualifying person'*

A 'qualifying person' is defined as any of the following:[68]

(a) a qualifying individual;
(b) a body corporate which has a place of business at which substantial business activity is carried on in any qualifying country or in Gibraltar;
(c) a British Dependent Territory citizen;
(d) a citizen, subject or habitual resident of any of the following: Japan, Switzerland, United States of America, Austria, Finland, French overseas territories, Iceland, Norway, Sweden, the Isle of Man, the Channel Islands or any British colony;

---

61 Design Right (Semiconductor Topographies) Regulations 1989, regulation 4(3).
62 Copyright, Designs and Patents Act 1988 section 218(1), (2).
63 *Ibid.*, section 218(2) as modified by Design Right (Semiconductor Topographies) Regulations 1989, regulation 4(3).
64 *Ibid.*, section 219(1).
65 *Ibid.*, section 220(1) as substituted by regulation 4(4).
66 *Ibid.*, section 217(1) as substituted by regulation 4(2).
67 *Ibid.*, section 217(4) as substituted by regulation 4(2).
68 *Ibid.*

(e) a firm or body corporate formed under the law of any of the following: the United Kingdom, Gibraltar or any EEC Member State; or (f) a firm or body corporate formed under the law of any of Japan, Switzerland or the United States of America with a place of business within any such country at which substantial business activity is carried on.

E. 'Qualifying country'

A 'qualifying country' is any EEC Member State.[69]

6.6.3.4 Formalities

Like copyright, and unlike say patents, there are no formalities which need to be observed for design right to subsist. In particular, there is no requirement for any form of registration.

6.6.4 Duration of design right

Design right in semiconductor topographies subsists for ten years from the end of the calendar year in which the topography or articles made to it were first made available for sale or hire anywhere in the world by or with the licence of the owner of the design right.[70] If neither the topography nor articles made to the topography are made available within 15 years of the making of the design, design right subsists for 15 years from the making of the design.[71] Thus if the design was made on 1 January 1990, and articles made to it are marketed on 31 December 2005, design right will subsist until 31 December 2015.

In determining whether the topography or articles made to it have been made available, a single sale or hire of the topography or an article made to it subject to an obligation of confidence in respect of the topography is not to be taken into account.[72]

6.6.5 Ownership of design right

Except where the design is created pursuant to a commission or in the course of employment, the first owner of any design right in a topography design is the designer.[73] Where the design is created pursuant to a commission, the person who commissions the design is the first owner of the design right subject to any agreement in writing to the contrary.[74] Where the design is created by an employee during the course of employment (but

---

69   *Ibid.*, section 217(3) as substituted by regulation 4(2).
70   *Ibid.*, section 216(a) as substituted by regulation 6(1).
71   *Ibid.*, section 216(b) as substituted by regulation 6(1).
72   Design Right (Semiconductor Topographies) Regulations 1989, regulation 7(a).
73   Copyright, Designs and Patents Act 1988 section 215(1) as substituted by Design Right (Semiconductor Topographies) Regulations 1989, regulation 5.
74   *Ibid.*, section 215(2) as substituted by regulation 5.

not pursuant to a commission), the employer is the first owner of the design right subject to any agreement in writing to the contrary.[75] The foregoing provisions do not apply, however, if the design qualifies for design right by virtue of articles made to the design having been first marketed in an EEC Member State by a qualifying person who is exclusively authorised to put such articles on the market in every Member State:[76] in that case, the person by whom the articles are first marketed is the first owner of the design right.[77]

6.6.6 Dealings in design right

Design right may be assigned and licensed in much the same way as copyright.[78] As with copyright, an exclusive licensee has his own right of action for infringement.[79]

6.6.7 Infringement of design right

As with copyright, there are two basic forms of infringement of design right: primary infringement and secondary infringement.

Primary infringement of design right in a topography design consists of reproducing the design in either of two ways: by making articles to the design or by making a design document recording the design for the purpose of enabling such articles to be made to the design.[80] This is subject to two exceptions: (a) reproduction privately for non-commercial aims; and (b) reproduction for the purpose of analysis or evaluation.[81]

Secondary infringement of design right in a topography design consists of importing into the United Kingdom for commercial purposes, possessing for commercial purposes or selling, hiring, offering or exposing for sale or hire in the course of a business any article which is, and which the dealer knows or has reason to believe is, an infringing article,[82] except where the article in question has been sold or hired either within the UK by or with the licence of the design right owner or within another EEC Member State by or with the consent of the person entitled to sell or hire in that State.[83]

75 *Ibid.*, section 215(3) as substituted by regulation 5.
76 *Ibid.*, section 220(1) as substituted by regulation 4(4).
77 *Ibid.*, section 215(4) as substituted by regulation 5.
78 See Copyright, Designs and Patents Act 1988 sections 222 to 225.
79 *Ibid.*, sections 234 to 235.
80 Copyright, Designs and Patents Act 1988 section 226(1) as substituted by Design Right (Semiconductor Topographies) Regulations 1989, regulation 8(1).
81 *Ibid.*, section 226(1A) as substituted by regulation 8(1).
82 *Ibid.*, section 227(1).
83 Design Right (Semiconductor Topographies) Regulations 1989, regulation 8(2).

Any act which would be an infringement if done in relation to the whole of a topography design is also an infringement if done in relation to a substantial part of the design.[84]

6.6.7.1   'Reproduce'

'Reproduction' is defined in relation to making articles to a design as meaning copying the design so as to produce articles exactly or substantially to the design.[85] There is no corresponding definition of reproduction in relation to making a design document; but it seems clear that it must be construed *mutatis mutandis*. Reproduction may be direct or indirect, and it is immaterial whether any intervening acts themselves amount to an infringement.[86]

6.6.7.2   Non-commercial aims

It is not an infringement of design right to reproduce a topography design privately for non-commercial aims.[87] This would presumably cover, for example, reproduction for the purposes of academic research.

It should be noted that the effect of this exception is different to that contained in the unmodified version of section 226 of the 1988 Act, which applies to designs for other articles. The unmodified version excepts reproduction other than for 'commercial purposes', which is defined as being with a view to selling or hiring the article in question.[88] Thus it would not be infringement of ordinary design right for a company to make articles in house. This will be an infringement of design right in topography designs, however.

6.6.7.3   Analysis or evaluation

It is not an infringement of design to reproduce a topography design for the purpose of analysing or evaluating the design or analysing, evaluating or teaching the concepts, processes, systems or techniques embodied in it.[89] Nor, for good measure, is it an infringement to create another original topography as a result of the analysis or evaluation of the topography or of the concepts, processes, systems or techniques embodied in the first topography or to reproduce that other topography.[90]

This is a limited 'reverse engineering' exception akin to that for experiments under the Patents Act 1977, but on the face of it of much

---

84   *Ibid.*, regulation 8(5).
85   Copyright, Designs and Patents Act 1988 section 226(2).
86   *Ibid.*, section 226(4).
87   Copyright, Designs and Patents Act 1988 section 226(1A)(a) as substituted by Design Right (Semiconductor Topographies) Regulations 1989, regulation 8(1).
88   *Ibid.*, section 263(3).
89   *Ibid.*, section 226(1A)(b) as substituted by regulation 8(1).
90   Design Right (Semiconductor Topographies) Regulations 1989, regulation 8(4).

wider ambit than the 1977 Act provision as it has been interpreted by the courts. In particular, it permits reproduction for commercial purposes, provided that these are limited to analysis and evaluation and subsequent creation of an original design. This recognises and sanctions what most designers would regard as good design practice, namely examining, and learning from, what the designer's competitors are doing (provided that the designer does not go further and copy). It is therefore somewhat curious that this exception appears in the modified version of Part III that applies to semiconductor topography designs, but not in the unmodified version that applies to other designs.

6.6.7.4 'Infringing articles'

An infringing article is an article the making of which was an infringement of design right or (in the case of articles which have been or or are proposed to be imported into the United Kingdom) would have been infringement if it had been made in the UK.[91] In the case of topography designs, a design document can be an infringing article for this purpose.[92]

6.6.8 Territoriality

Design right extends to the whole of the United Kingdom.[93] Like copyright, it is a territorial right, so that acts committed outside the United Kingdom do not infringe UK design right.[94]

6.6.9 Remedies

The remedies available for infringement of design right are injunctions, orders for delivery up and forfeiture,[95] damages (including statutory additional damages)[96] and accounts of profits. There are two 'innocence' defences: ignorance that design right subsisted is a defence to damages,[97] while ignorance that an article was an infringing article is a defence to any remedy other than a reasonable royalty.[98] Interlocutory relief is available on the usual principles. These remedies are discussed in Chapter 9.

6.6.10 Threats

In common with patents and registered designs, but in contrast to copyright,[99] unjustified threats of proceedings for infringement of design

---

91 Copyright, Designs and Patents Act 1988 section 228(1).
92 Design Right (Semiconductor Topographies) Regulations 1989, regulation 8(3).
93 Copyright, Designs and Patents Act 1988 section 255(1).
94 *Def Lep Music v Stuart-Brown* [1986] RPC 273.
95 Copyright, Designs and Patents Act 1988 sections 230, 231.
96 *Ibid.*, section 229(3).
97 *Ibid.*, section 233(1).
98 *Ibid.*, section 233(2), (3).
99 *Granby Marketing Services Ltd v Interlego AG* [1984] RPC 209.

right made against persons other than manufacturers or importers of the articles in question are actionable.[100]

6.7 COPYRIGHT IN VISUAL DISPLAYS

There has been considerable controversy in recent years over the protection of the 'look and feel' of computer programs, particularly in the light of certain decisions of courts in the United States. It is important to distinguish the copying of the 'look and feel' of a program from other forms of copying, for different issues are involved. In particular, it is important to distinguish copying of 'look and feel' from copying of 'structure, sequence and organisation',[101] another controversial area. Although there have been cases in which allegations of copying of structure, sequence and organisation have come before the courts in the United Kingdom,[102] there has yet to be a true case of copying of 'look and feel' in the UK.

It is quite possible for two programs to exist the source and object codes of which are each radically dissimilar to the other, yet the operation of which as perceived by the user sitting at the visual display unit of a computer is very similar. Conversely, the fact that two programs operate in manners that appear to the user to be similar does not establish that the source or object code of one program has been copied from another. Thus in *Thrustcode v W.W. Computing*[103] Sir Robert Megarry VC declined to draw an inference that one program had been copied from another from the the the fact that the two programs performed similar functions.

Even if one concentrates on the structure, sequence and organisation (SSO) of a program rather than upon its literal code (its 'plot' rather than its 'text'), it is quite possible for different SSOs to be employed to produce similar end results.

It therefore seems reasonably clear that literary copyright in a computer program does not protect the visual displays generated by that program in use (although if the underlying software is copied there will be a remedy for that). It is possible, however, that the visual displays may themselves constitute protectable copyright works. Although there has yet to be any English authority on the point, this appears to be the effect of certain United States decisions.

6.7.1 United States decisions

It is clear that under US law screen displays can be copyrighted as audio-visual works separately from the underlying program.[104] In *Digital*

100 Copyright, Designs and Patents Act 1988 section 253.
101 As to which see Chapter 5 paragraph 5.1.1.6.
102 For example *M.S. Associates Ltd v Power* [1988] FSR 242 and *Computer Aided Systems (UK) Ltd v Bolwell* IPD April 1990 15.
103 [1983] FSR 502.
104 *Midway Manufacturing Co. v Artic International Inc.* 704 F.2d 109 (7th Cir. 1983).

Communications Associates v Softklone Distributing Corp.,[105] it was held that although copyright in a display might be copied by copying the underlying program, copyright in the underlying program was not infringed by merely copying the display. In the earlier case of *Broderbund Software Inc. v Unison World Inc.*,[106] however, the plaintiff had registered the screen displays as an audio-visual work, and 'the eerie resemblance between the screens of the two programs' led the Court to find that there had been infringement.

The most recent US authority is *Lotus Development Corp. v Paperback Software International*.[107] The plaintiff alleged that the defendant had infringed its copyright in the Lotus 1-2-3 spreadsheet program by copying various elements of the user interface, including the menu structure, the macro language and the choice of particular keys to perform particular functions. The Court held that although some parts of the user interface, such as the choice of particular keys to perform particular functions, were not protectable by copyright since they were properly to be categorised as 'ideas' rather than as 'expression', the menu structure and the macro language were protectable. Although this decision does not deal with screen displays *solus*, it tends to confirm that copying displays can constitute infringement, at least where the display can be regarded as 'expression' rather than 'idea'. The acid test here seems to be whether competitive programs use different displays: if they do, then the displays will be 'expression'.

6.7.2   United Kingdom law

6.7.2.1   *Individual screen displays*

It does not appear that an individual screen display on a VDU is *per se* a work in which copyright is capable of subsisting under Part I of the Copyright, Designs and Patents Act 1988 apart from the program that generates the display. Section 1(1) of the Act limits the categories of works in which copyright subsists to literary works, dramatic works, musical works, artistic works, sound recordings, films, broadcasts, cable programs, and typographical arrangements. Although an individual screen display may well have literary content this will almost certainly be contained within the program. It is therefore unlikely that the screen display will attract separate protection.

The component of the screen display for which separate protection will generally be desired is the 'artistic' content – the visual image. It is unlikely, however, that the screen display itself will qualify as an artistic work. It is not a photograph, sculpture or collage. Nor would it seem to be a graphic work within the meaning of section 4(2) of the Act, for

105   659 F.Supp 449 (N.D.Ga. 1987).
106   648 F.Supp 1127 (N.D.Ca. 1986).
107   740 F.Supp 37 (D.Mass. 1990).

although the definition of 'graphic work' is inclusive rather than definitive, all the examples given have in common the fact that they are executed on paper or some other physical two-dimensional medium.

As for the other categories of work, none of these seems appropriate for an individual screen display.

So far as individual screen displays are concerned, therefore, one is thrown back upon more orthodox antecedent works, if any exist. If the screen display was first designed by drawing it with pen and paper, and then a program was written to produce that result on a VDU, then it is arguable that a person who copied what appeared on the VDU by writing another program to produce the same result would infringe any copyright that subsisted in the drawing. The drawing would be an artistic work in which copyright was capable of subsisting in the normal way. If it was original and made by a qualifying person or first published in a qualifying country, then copyright would subsist. Assuming derivation and identical or substantial reproduction, and given that the 1988 Act expressly provides that reproduction in a material form includes storing the work in any medium by electronic means,[108] that copying includes the making of copies that are transient[109] and that indirect copying is an infringement whether or not any intervening acts infringe,[110] it would seem very arguable that the copyright in the drawing would be infringed.

It is unlikely, however, that many screen displays are designed in this way, and so obtaining protection for individual displays apart from any protection afforded by the copyright in the program would appear to be difficult. In the case of computer game programs, on the other hand, it may be the case that, even if complete screens are not drawn, then individual characters appearing in the game may be drawn.[111] Copyright in such character drawings might well be infringed in the manner just discussed.

6.7.2.2   Sequences of screen displays

It may, however, be possible to protect sequences of screen displays as films.[112] The point may be illustrated by reference to the visual display of a computer game. A computer game normally consists of an 'attract' mode and 'play' mode. In the attract mode, visual images appear in a pre-ordained sequence, which explain the operation of the game to the player. In the play mode, the sequence of images on the VDU is determined, within limits dictated by the program, by the intervention of the player.

108   Copyright, Designs and Patents Act 1988 section 17(2).
109   *Ibid.*, section 17(6).
110   *Ibid.*, section 16(3).
111   It appears that a case of this nature was pleaded in the *Pac-Man* case, *Atari Inc. v Philips Electronics and Associated Industries Ltd* [1988] FSR 416 at 417 and in *Sega Enterprises Ltd v Richards* [1983] FSR 73. No decision was reached on the point in either case, however.
112   Again it appears that this was alleged in the *Atari* and *Sega* cases: *ibid.*

It is at least arguable that the attract mode is a film within the meaning of the 1988 Act. 'Film' is defined as: . . . 'a recording on any medium from which a moving image may by any means be reproduced'.[113] The difficult part of the definition for this purpose is 'recording', which is not itself defined in Part I. At first blush a computer program which produces a particular sequence of displays is not obviously a 'recording' in the way that, say, a videotape is. It seems clear, however, that in context 'recording' is intended to mean no more than something that has been recorded, that is to say something that has been stored or preserved. In this wide, general sense a computer program which in operation produces a particular sequence of screen displays would appear to be a 'recording'. The 'medium' will be the medium in which the program (or the visual data it outputs) is stored. As for the sequence of screen displays, there is no reason which this should not qualify as a 'moving image'. A VDU is, after all, the same as a television set.

By contrast, it is much more difficult to argue that the play mode of the game is a film. 'Recording' implies that the film should be the same each time it is shown, whereas the play mode is different on each occasion, although stock visual images will be employed.

If a computer game is pirated, and if it is right that at least the attract mode constitutes a film in which copyright may subsist, there is no reason why the copying of the program to produce the same sequence of images should not amount to an infringement.

What if a person writes a program the source and object code of which is entirely different to the original game program, but which produces the same sequence of images (and there are no antecedent works such as drawings upon which the originator can rely)? It is then more difficult to say that there is an infringement, for although the *images* have been taken, the *recording* has not been copied. The traditional conception of copyright law is that one man's copyright in, say, a photograph of Westminster Abbey does not prevent another man from going through the same exercise – using the same type of camera, the same type of film, standing in the same place – to produce the same result, it only prevents actual copying. The rationale for this is that copyright is not a true monopoly, it is merely a prohibition on taking a short cut by appropriating another's skill and labour. If it were physically possible to replicate a film by going through the same processes as the original film-maker, it may be argued, the same position would apply: it would not be an infringement. The contrary argument would be that there was nevertheless an appropriation of the original film-maker's *creativity* if not of his skill and labour, and that the second film could not have assumed the form that it did if the first had never existed. Given that the traditional bias of English law is to protect the copyright owner's economic interests rather than his artistic

113   *Ibid.*, section 5(1).

interests,[114] however, this argument is not likely to meet with great favour. On the other hand, although the copyist would have the same development costs as the originator, and thus would not be taking a short cut, it is still possible that he could pose an economic threat to the originator. Nevertheless, in conclusion, the authors consider it unlikely that a programmer who did as postulated would be found to infringe.

114 Only with the enactment of the 1988 Act have authors be accorded moral rights by English law, and these are still rather limited. Indeed, moral rights are excluded from application to computer programs: Copyright, Designs and Patents Act 1988 sections 79(2)(a) and 81(2).

7 Patents

7.0 INTRODUCTION

The grant of a patent gives the holder of the patent, the patentee, a monopoly over the patented invention. Patents thus have the advantage, for patentees, that enforcement is not dependent on proof of copying by the infringer as is the case with copyright. They also have the advantages, for the rest of the community, that they are registered, so that it is possible to find out whether a patent exists and if so who owns it, and that the scope of the rights conferred by a patent is more-or-less definite. It might therefore be expected that patent protection would be widely sought for computer software. In fact, patent protection has been relatively unpopular until recently. There are two basic reasons for this, one statutory and one practical. The statutory reason is that the Patents Act 1977 contains a specific exclusion from patentability of computer programs as such. The practical reason is that patents are expensive compared with copyright: expensive and time-consuming to apply for and obtain, costly to maintain and expensive to enforce.

Recently, however, there has been a trend towards attempts to patent computer programs. The fundamental reason for this is that it is increasingly the case that new technology utilises microprocessors and thus some form of software. In other words, many inventions now are implemented by means which include software, even if the software is not the heart of the invention. This trend has been greeted by a greater readiness on the part of patent offices and courts to accept the patentability of such inventions. Furthermore, an important step has been taken to provide a less expensive forum for enforcing patents in the United Kingdom with the creation of a patents county court.

At the time that the first edition of this book was written, there was very little authority on the patentability of computer programs under the Patents Act 1977. Accordingly, decisions under the Patents Act 1949 were reviewed for possible guidance. Since then, there have been several decisions of the European Patent Office under the corresponding provisions of the European Patent Convention, and two decisions of the Court of Appeal under the 1977 Act itself, *Merrill Lynch's Application*[1]

1 [1989] RPC 561.

and *Gale's Application.*[2] In the *Merrill Lynch* case, the Court of Appeal held that decisions under the previous Act were not relevant to issues under the 1977 Act.[3] The discussion of cases under the 1949 Act has therefore not been reproduced. Interested readers are referred to the first edition.

Since the trend of these decisions is towards a greater readiness to permit the patenting of computer programs in appropriate cases, a brief survey of the questions of novelty, inventive step, application, duration, ownership and infringement has been included for the first time.

7.1   PATENTABILITY

7.1.1   Excluded subject-matter under the Patents Act 1977

Section 1 of the Patents Act provides that:

> (1) A patent may be granted only for an invention in respect of which the following conditions are satisfied, that is to say −
> (a) the invention is new;
> (b) it involves an inventive step;
> (c) it is capable of industrial application;
> (d) the grant of a patent for it is not excluded by subsections (2) and (3) below.
> (2) It is hereby declared that the following (among other things) are not inventions for the purpose of this Act, that is to say, anything which consists of
> (a) a discovery, scientific theory or mathematical method;
> (b) a literary, dramatic, musical or artistic work or any other aesthetic creation whatsoever;
> (c) a scheme, rule or method for performing a mental act, playing a game or doing business, or a program for a computer;
> (d) the presentation of information
> but the foregoing provision shall prevent anything from being treated as an invention for the purposes of this Act only to the extent that a patent or application for a patent relates to that thing as such.

Thus anything within the list of excluded subject-matter is not an invention for the purposes of the Act, and so cannot be patented even if it satisfies the other criteria for patentability of novelty, inventiveness (non-obviousness) and industrial application.

An important point to note is that there is some overlap between the various categories of excluded matter, and in a particular case it may well be necessary to consider more than one category. In particular, it will frequently be the case that an invention which is objected to on the ground that it is a computer program is also objected to on the ground that it is a mathematical method.

A similar point which does not appear to have been taken yet is that, given that it is now widely accepted that computer programs qualify for

2   [1991] RPC 305.
3   Note 1 above at 569.

copyright protection as literary works,[4] objection could be taken under paragraph (b) of subsection (2). Presumably the reason why it has not been is that such an objection is redundant in the light of the express exclusion in paragraph (c).

7.1.2 The European Patent Convention

Section 1(2) of the 1977 Act is derived from the European Patent Convention. Article 52 of the Convention provides as follows:

(1) European patents shall be granted for any inventions which are susceptible of industrial application, which are new and which involve an inventive step.

(2) The following in particular shall not be regarded as inventions within the meaning of paragraph 1:
(a) discoveries, scientific theories and mathematical methods;
(b) aesthetic creations;
(c) schemes, rules and methods for performing mental acts, playing games or doing business, and programs for computers;
(d) presentations of information.
(3) The provisions of paragraph 2 shall exclude patentability of the subject-matter or activities referred to in that provision only to the extent to which a European patent application or European patent relates to such subject-matter or activities as such.

As can be seen, the list of exclusions in section 1(2) and the proviso thereto is almost identical to the list of exclusions in Article 52(2) and the proviso in Article 52(3).

Although decisions of the European Patent Office under the EPC are not binding on English courts, section 130(7) of the 1977 Act declares that a number of sections of the Act, including section 1, are so framed to have:

. . . as nearly as practicable, the same effects in the United Kingdom as the corresponding provisions of the European Patent Convention . . . have in the Territories to which those Conventions apply.

Furthermore, section 91(1)(c) of the 1977 Act provides that judicial notice shall be taken of decisions or expressions of opinion by the relevant convention court on questions arising under the relevant convention. 'Relevant convention court' is defined in terms which include the Boards of Appeal of the European Patent Office (EPO).[5] Thus the guidelines and decisions of the EPO are of considerable persuasive authority.

7.1.3 European Patent Office Guidelines

To begin with, the EPO took a narrow view on the patentability of computer programs. The original Guidelines for Examination issued by

---

4 See Chapter 4.
5 Patents Act 1977 section 130.

the EPO stated:

> A computer program may take various forms, e.g. an algorithm, a flow-chart or a series of coded instructions which can be recorded on a tape or other machine-readable record-medium, and can be regarded as a particular case of either a mathematical method . . . or a presentation of information . . . If the contribution to the known art resides solely in a computer program then the subject-matter is not patentable in whatever form it may be presented in the claims. For example, a claim to a computer characterised by having the particular program stored in its memory or to a process for operating a computer under control of the program would be regarded as objectionable as a claim to the program *per se* or the program when recorded on magnetic tape.[6]

The statement that if the contribution to the prior art resided solely in a computer program then the subject-matter was not patentable in whatever form it was presented was very restrictive, for it had the result that if an otherwise novel and inventive process happened to be implemented by computer program rather than by mechanical or electronic means, the process would not be patentable.

In 1985, however, the Guidelines were revised to read as follows:

> *General*
> In considering whether the subject-matter of an application is an invention within . . . Art. 52(1), there are two general points the Examiner must bear in mind. Firstly, any exclusion from patentability . . . applies only to the extent to which the application relates to the excluded subject-matter as such. Secondly, the Examiner should disregard the form or kind of claim and concentrate on its content in order to identify the real contribution which the subject-matter claimed, considered as a whole, adds to the known art. If this contribution is not of technical character, there is no invention within Art. 52(1). Thus, for example, if the claim is for a known manufactured article having a painted design or certain written information on its surface, the contribution to the art is as a general rule merely an aesthetic creation or presentation of information. Similarly, if a computer program is claimed in the form of a physical record e.g. on a conventional tape or disk, the contribution to the art is still no more than a computer program. In these cases the claim relates to excluded subject-matter as such and is therefore not allowable. If, on the other hand, a computer program in combination with a computer causes the computer to operate in a different way from a technical point of view, the combination might be patentable . . .
>
> *Programs for computers*
> The basic patentability considerations here are exactly the same as for the other exclusions listed in Art. 52, para. 2. However, a data-processing operation can be implemented either by means of a computer program or by means of special circuits, and the choice may have nothing to do with the inventive concept but be determined purely by factors of economy or practicality. With this point in mind, examination in this area should be guided by the following approach:
> A computer program claimed by itself or as a record on a carrier, is not patentable irrespective of its content. The situation is not normally changed when the computer program is loaded into a known computer. If however the subject-matter as claimed makes a technical contribution to the known art, patentability should not be denied merely on the ground that a computer program is involved

6   OJ 1/1978.

in its implementation. This means, for example, that program-controlled machines and program-controlled manufacturing and control processes should normally be regarded as patentable subject-matter. It follows also that, where the claimed subject-matter is concerned only with the program-controlled internal working of a known computer, the subject-matter could be patentable if it provides a technical effect. As an example, consider the case of a known data-processing system with a small fast working memory and a larger but slower further memory. Suppose that the two memories are organised under program control, in such a way that a process which needs more address space than the capacity of the fast working memory can be executed at substantially the same speed as if the process data were loaded entirely in that fast memory. The effect of the program in virtually extending the working memory is of a technical character and might therefore support patentability.

Where patentability depends upon a technical effect the claims must be so drafted as to include all the technical features of the invention which are essential for the technical effect.

Where patentability is admitted then, generally speaking, product, process and use claims should be allowable.[7]

These passages, which represent a less restrictive approach, have been retained in the latest issue of the Guidelines.[8]

In an article about the 1985 Guidelines and computer programs,[9] the Director of Legal Affairs at the EPO claimed that Article 52 was never intended to do more than restate the generally accepted proposition that ideas and methods could not be patented otherwise than in a particular application. He also emphasised that it was immaterial that the only novel element in an invention was the computer program if the invention as a whole was not excluded from being patentable. Thus if it exhibited a technical result an invention passed the test of being an invention, whether or not it included a computer program. The invention, as a whole, was then to be considered from the point of view of novelty and obviousness, so that it did not matter at that stage that these characteristics derived exclusively from the program.

An example might be a chemical process for the manufacture of a particular chemical from particular starting materials. Suppose that a plant has been set up to operate this process, and the plant is controlled by computer, so that by reprogramming the computer the temperature, timing and so on can be changed. Suppose further that a program is written to control the process which by manipulation of these variables in a particular way achieves a much higher yield of the product than anyone had previously obtained. If this is non-obvious, the invention will be patentable, for the fact that the desired technical result is achieved by use of a computer program is neither here nor there.

7 OJ 3/1985 84.
8 Guidelines for Examination in the European Patent Office, Part C, Chapter IV. See European Patents Handbook (CIPA), 2nd edn, Volume 2, Chapter 56 at 295.
9 Gall, 'European Patent Office Guidelines 1985 on the Protection of inventions relating to computer programs', (1985) 2 *Computer Law and Practice* 2.

7.1.4   European Patent Office decisions

The approach set out in the revised Guidelines was adopted by the Technical Board of Appeal of the EPO in *VICOM/Computer-related invention*,[10] where the application related to a method and apparatus for improving the quality of, and increasing the speed of, digital image processing. The process involved the physical manipulation of electrical signals representing the image in accordance with an algorithm. The Board overturned the view of the Examination Division that the process was an unpatentable mathematical method and/or computer program. The Board considered the questions both whether the application should be rejected as a mathematical method as such and whether it should be rejected as a computer program as such.

As to the first question, it held that the invention was more than just a mathematical method but was a technical process:

> There can be little doubt that any processing operation on an electrical signal can be described in mathematical terms. The characteristics of a filter, for example, can be expressed in terms of a mathematical formula. A basic difference between a mathematical method and a technical process can be seen, however, in the fact that a mathematical method or a mathematical algorithm is carried out on numbers (whatever these numbers may represent) and provides a result also in numerical form, the mathematical method or algorithm being only an abstract concept prescribing how to operate on the numbers. No direct technical result is produced by the method as such. In contrast thereto, if a mathematical method is used in a technical process, that process is carried out on a physical entity (which may be a material object but equally an image stored as an electrical signal) by some technical means implementing the method and provides as its result a certain change in that entity. The technical means might include a computer comprising suitable hardware or an appropriately programmed general purpose computer.
>
> The Board, therefore, is of the opinion that even if the idea underlying an invention may be considered to reside in a mathematical method a claim directed to a technical process in which the method is used does not seek protection for the mathematical method *as such*.[11]

As to the second question, the Board applied the same reasoning. So far as the method claims were concerned, the Board held that:

> The Board is of the opinion that a claim directed to a technical process which process is carried out under the control of of a program (be this implemented in hardware or software), cannot be regarded as relating to a computer program *as such* within the meaning of Article 52(3) EPC, as it is the application of the program for determining the sequence of steps in the process for which in effect protection is sought. Consequently such a claim is allowable under Article 52(2)(c) and (3) EPC.[12]

So far as the apparatus claims were concerned, the Board held that:

> Generally claims which can be considered as being directed to a computer set up to operate in accordance with a specified program (whether by means of hardware

10   Decision T208/84, [1987] EPOR 74.
11   *Ibid.* at 79, Reasons paragraphs 5 and 6.
12   *Ibid.* at 80, Reasons paragraph 12.

(d) where the term excludes or restricts any liability if some condition is not complied with, whether it was reasonable at the time of contract to expect that compliance with that condition would be practicable;

(e) whether the goods were manufactured, processed or adapted to the special order of the customer.[30]

In *Mackenzie Patten & Co. v British Olivetti Ltd*,[31] it was held that the requirement of reasonableness was not satisfied where a solicitor who was ignorant about computers dealt with a computer salesman. It appears from this that the respective expertise of the parties is also a relevant consideration. In addition, another consideration which has been held to be relevant is which party may most easily insure against the loss.[32]

Where the customer either deals as a consumer or deals on the supplier's written standard terms, then any clause purporting to exclude or limit liability for breach of contract (that is not just breach of the statutory implied terms) is subject to the test of reasonableness.[33]

Liability for death or personal injury due to the supplier's negligence cannot be excluded or limited at all, while other loss due to negligence can only be excluded or limited to the extent that is reasonable.[34]

It is sometimes suggested that, where software is supplied under a software licence (that is the supply agreement is not separate), sections 2 to 4 of the Unfair Contract Terms Act do not apply, due to the operation of Schedule 1, paragraph 1(c):

Sections 2 to 4 of this Act do not extend to –

(c) any contract insofar as it relates to the creation or transfer of a right or interest in any patent, trade mark, copyright, registered design, technical or commercial information or other intellectual property, or relates to the termination of any such right or interest.

It is not clear, however, that a mere licence (as opposed to an assignment or charge) qualifies as 'right or interest'. Even if it does, the provision only excludes sections 2 to 4 'insofar' as the contract relates to creation or transfer of a right or interest. Insofar as the contract relates to other matters, such as the supply of the software and its quality or fitness for purpose, then it appears that the provision does not apply.

8.1.7 Drafting a software supply agreement

8.1.7.1 *Defining the specification*

As has already been commented, it is of the greatest importance where bespoke software is to be supplied that the supply agreement should

30 *Ibid.*, Schedule 2.
31 Unreported, Michael Davies J, 11 January 1984. See Staines, 'Computer Sales: Caveat Distributor', (1985) 48 MLR 344.
32 *George Mitchell (Chesterhall) Ltd v Finney Lock Seeds Ltd* [1983] 2 AC 803.
33 Unfair Contract Terms Act 1977 section 3.
34 *Ibid.*, section 2.

specify what the supplier is to supply and what facilities, information and assistance the customer is to provide. If a specification of requirements has already been drawn up, then the supplier can contract to supply software complying with the specification. If a proper specification has not been drawn up before the contract is entered into, then the first stage of the project must be to define the specification.

Example clauses
(1) The Supplier shall within 28 days of execution of this Agreement draw up a full Specification of Requirements for the Software in accordance with the outline specification contained in the First Schedule hereto.
(2) The Customer shall provide such facilities, information and assistance to the Supplier for the purpose of drawing up the Specification of Requirements as the Supplier shall reasonably require.
(3) Upon completion of the Specification of Requirements the Supplier shall deliver the same to the Customer for approval. The Customer shall within 14 days after delivery thereof communicate to the Supplier such amendments (if any) as it shall require. If no amendments are communicated within the said period the Customer shall be deemed to have accepted the Specification unamended.
(4) The Supplier shall within 14 days of receipt of the Customer's amendments deliver a revised Specification incorporating such amendments to the Customer.

8.1.7.2   Requests for specification changes

It is a common experience of software suppliers that as a project proceeds the customer requests changes to the specification. There may be a number of reasons for this. The customer may realise that the original specification did not accurately reflect his business, the customer's business may change, the customer may discover that points he thought the supplier had understood had not been understood, the feedback from the supplier may make the customer realise that he would benefit more from computerisation if certain things were changed. Whatever the reason, however, requests for changes can cause severe problems if a proper procedure for handling them is not laid down by the contract. Among the points that should be provided for are the following:

(1) A change request should only be made in writing, in an agreed form, authorised by an appropriately senior representative of the customer.
(2) Each change request should specify in detail the nature of the change and the reason for it.
(3) Provisions should be made for dealing with the cost and time implications of each change. In general, requests for changes lead to increased expense and to delay in delivery of the completed software. These should both be provided for, for example, by a stipulation that a change request will only be accepted when a price for the change and an extension to any delivery deadline have been agreed.

Example clauses
(1) If after acceptance of the Specification by the Customer and prior to acceptance of the Software by the Customer the Customer shall desire any changes to be made to the Specification the Customer shall deliver to the Supplier a duly completed and authorised Change Request Form specifying the same and the reason therefor in the form set out in the Second Schedule hereto.
(2) Within 14 days of receipt of any Change Request Form the Supplier shall supply the Customer with an estimate of the extra cost (if any) which will be occasioned by the changes requested and of the postponement (if any) of the delivery date of the Software that will be necessitated by the changes requested.
(3) The Supplier shall not be obliged to implement any Change Request unless its estimates of cost and delay are accepted by the Customer, in which case the Change Request will take effect upon acceptance as a variation of this Agreement.

8.1.7.3 Acceptance tests

It is increasingly common for customers to insist upon some form of acceptance testing. This means that once the software has been developed by the supplier, it is installed on the customer's hardware and tested, preferably with real data, for a certain period before it is accepted by the customer. The significance of this is that once software has been accepted by the customer, the customer cannot reject it for breach of condition and his remedy for any defects is limited to damages for breach of warranty.[35]

Example clauses
(1) Upon completion of the Software the Supplier shall install the same upon the Hardware and shall run the acceptance tests specified in the Third Schedule hereto.
(2) Upon passing the acceptance tests the Software shall be deemed to be accepted by the Customer and shall be delivered to the Customer together with appropriate documentation.

8.1.7.4 Ownership of copyright

It should be made clear that the copyright in the software to be supplied will vest in the supplier (otherwise it may subsequently be argued that the customer has acquired equitable title to the copyright by virtue of having commissioned the software).[36]

35 Sale of Goods Act 1979 section 11(4).
36 As in *Saphena Computing Ltd v Allied Collection Agencies Ltd* (unreported, Mr Recorder Havery QC, 22 July 1988), where the argument failed.

Example clause
The copyright and all other intellectual property rights (as defined in section 72 of the Supreme Court Act 1981) in all Software developed or supplied pursuant to this Agreement shall vest in and be the absolute property of the Supplier.

8.1.7.5 Warranties

It may be desirable for an express warranty as to the performance of the software to be given, particularly if exclusion or limitation clauses are included in the agreement.

Example clause
The Supplier warrants:

(a) that the Software to be supplied pursuant to this Agreement shall substantially comply with all requirements expressly contained in the Specification together with any Change Requests which have been implemented as provided by clause [change clause];
(b) that it will correct by patch or new release (at its option) any defects in the Software notified by the Customer to the Supplier within 3 months of acceptance of the Software by the Customer, 'defects' being defined for the purpose of this warranty as deviations from the requirements expressly contained in the Specification, provided that such defects have not been caused by any modification or addition to the Software not made by the Supplier or caused by the incorrect use or corruption of the Software or by use of the Software on hardware other than the Hardware specified in the First Schedule hereto.

8.1.7.6   Exclusion and limitation clauses

The Supplier may wish to attempt to exclude or limit its liability.

Example clauses
(1) Save as expressly warranted in clause [warranty clause], the Supplier does not warrant the quality, fitness for purpose or performance of the Software and any and all such warranties, whether implied, statutory or otherwise are hereby excluded.
(2) The Supplier shall not in any circumstances be liable for loss or corruption of data or other software nor for any lost business or profits or anticipated savings or other consequential loss caused by any defect in the Software or any breach of its obligations under this Agreement.
(3) If either or both of the foregoing provisions shall for any reason be held to be invalid or unenforceable in whole or in part, it is hereby agreed that the Supplier's liability to the Customer for any loss or damage caused by any defect in the Software or any breach of the Supplier's obligations under this Agreement shall be limited to and shall not exceed the sum of

£100,000. The Supplier's liability for any loss caused by the negligence of the Supplier, its employees or agents shall in any event be limited to the said sum.

(4) The foregoing provisions shall not apply to the Supplier's liability for death or personal injury to the extent that the same is due to the negligence of the Supplier, its employees or agents.

(5) It is hereby agreed that it shall be the responsibility of the Customer to obtain appropriate insurance for any defects in the Software and for any loss and damage that may be caused by any breach of the Supplier's obligations under this Agreement and in particular to obtain insurance against loss or corruption of data or other software.

8.1.7.7   *Use of the software supplied*

Use of the software when supplied should be made subject to the terms of a licence agreement, as discussed below. If desired, the supply and licence agreements can be combined into one.

8.2   SOFTWARE LICENCE AGREEMENTS

8.2.1   What is a software licence?

A licence is a permission or consent to do something, usually something that would be unlawful without such permission. In the case of software which is the subject of copyright, it is almost impossible to use it without infringing the copyright unless a licence has been obtained.[37] It is worth stressing, however, that in no sense is the subsistence of copyright a condition precedent to a valid licence. It is open to any software supplier to supply software only if the user enters into a licence agreement. Thus although software copyright may provide the basis for a licence, it is not essential.

Where copyright does subsist, a licence is to be distinguished from an assignment. An assignment is a conveyance of property rights in the things assigned. A licence is a bare permission to use.

The main objects of a software licence are as follows:

(1) To give the user permission to use the software, thus enabling him not to infringe.

(2) To limit the nature and extent of the use.

(3) To regulate the terms on which use is made, for example, financial terms.

(4) To impose other terms for the benefit of the parties, for example, governing confidentiality or liability for defects.

A licence may be express or it may be implied. A licence will be implied in the same way as any other contractual term, namely where it is

---

37 See Chapter 5.

necessary to give the agreement business efficacy. It will be appreciated that it is better to have express terms than to wait to find out what terms a court will imply.

8.2.2   Shrink-wrap licences

It is increasingly the case that software which is intended for widespread distribution is sold on a retail basis in exactly the same way as other consumer products. A cassette or disk containing a copy of the software is displayed on a shelf in a shop, the customer picks it up, goes to the till and pays for it. In these circumstances it is not possible for a licence agreement to be individually negotiated with each purchaser. It may also be commercially undesirable to require a purchaser even to sign a standard form contract incorporating conditions which impose limitations on copying and use.

Starting in the United States, attempts have been made to circumvent this problem by imposing conditions by means of devices known as 'shrink-wrap licences'. Essentially, a licence containing standard conditions is printed on the top of the package and can be seen through clear plastic film. It is stated on the package that the purchaser is deemed to accept those conditions if he opens the package and breaks the film. In England, however, there are considerable legal difficulties with this approach.

8.2.2.1   Completion of a contract – offer and acceptance

In English law, a contract is completed at the time when one party accepts an offer made by the other party with the intention of creating a legal relationship.[38]

The time of completion of a contract of sale in a retail outlet was considered by the Court of Appeal in *Pharmaceutical Society of Great Britain v Boots Cash Chemists (Southern) Ltd*.[39] The defendants ran a number of self-service retail chemists shops. A customer, on entering the shop, was provided with a wire basket and, having selected from the shelves the articles which he wished to buy, he placed them in the basket and took them to the cashier's desk, where the cashier stated the total price and received payment. It was held that the display of goods on shelves did not amount to an offer to sell, but was merely an invitation to the customer to offer to buy. Accordingly the contract was not complete until the customer's offer to buy was accepted by the cashier. The offer to buy would usually be constituted by the tendering of money and the acceptance by the acceptance of that money.

38   *Chitty on Contracts*, Sweet & Maxwell, 1989 (26th edn), Volume 1, paragraph 42.
39   [1953] 1 QB 401.

Similarly it has been held that display of articles in a shop window[40] and commercial advertisements for articles[41] amount to invitations to treat rather than offers for sale.

It follows that when goods are purchased in a retail outlet, conditions may be incorporated into the contract of sale at any time up until the acceptance of money by the cashier. Once the contract is complete, however, no further conditions may be incorporated. In *Thornton v Shoe Lane Parking Ltd*[42] a series of conditions was printed on the back of a car park ticket which was automatically received on payment of money by the customer. The Court of Appeal held that the customer was not bound by the terms printed on the ticket. Lord Denning MR said:

> The offer is made when the proprietor of the machine holds it out as ready to receive the money. The acceptance takes place when the customer put his money into the slot. The terms of the offer are contained in the notice placed on or by the machines stating what is offered for the money. The customer is bound by those terms so long as they are sufficiently brought to his notice before-hand, but not otherwise. He is not bound by the terms printed on the ticket if they differ from the notice, because the ticket comes too late. The contract has already been made; the ticket is no more than a voucher or a receipt for the money that has been paid . . . on terms which have been offered and accepted before the ticket is issued.[43]

In the case of a shrink-wrap licence, the statement that the customer is deemed to accept the licence conditions by breaking the film is ineffective to incorporate those conditions into the contract of sale, for this will not happen until after the contract is complete.

This is not the end of the matter, however. Firstly, it may be possible to incorporate the terms before completion of the contract of sale. This depends on giving the purchaser reasonable notice of the terms sought to be imposed before he pays for the software.

Secondly, it may be possible to create an independent contract. The contract of sale is a contract between the retailer and the purchaser. It may be possible by means of a shrink-wrap licence to create an independent contract between licensor and licensee.

Both of these possibilities are discussed below.

8.2.2.2 *Reasonable notice*

In order to incorporate terms into the contract of sale, they must be displayed by the seller with sufficient prominence and reasonable efforts must have been made to to bring them to the attention of the purchaser.[44] It is not necessary to prove that the conditions have bean read by the purchaser or that he is subjectively aware of their meaning and effect, on the other hand.[45]

40 *Fisher v Bell* [1961] 1 QB 394.
41 *Partridge v Crittenden* [1968] 1 WLR 1204.
42 [1971] 2 QB 163.
43 *Ibid.*, at 169.
44 *Olley v Marlborough Court Ltd* [1949] 1 KB 532; *Thornton v Shoe Lane Parking Ltd* (above).
45 *Chitty on Contracts*, Sweet & Maxwell, 1989 (26th edn), Volume 1, paragraph 781.

In some circumstances it may be sufficient to display a prominent notice at the point of sale, particularly if the purchaser's attention is drawn to it.[46] On the other hand, printing conditions on the back of a document without sufficient reference to them on its face is likely to be insufficient.[47] What is necessary will depend to some extent on the nature of the terms sought to be imposed:

> Some clauses which I have seen would need to be printed in red ink on the face of the document with a red hand pointing to it before the notice could be held to be sufficient.[48]

The following arrangements may be considered in order to achieve incorporation of conditions into contracts of sale of software in retail shops:

(1) Conditions sought to be imposed should not be so numerous or so complex as to render it unreasonable to expect a purchaser to consider them prior to completion of the contract. For example they might be limited to the following three conditions:

> (a) That the purchaser shall not copy and shall not procure, authorise or permit others to copy any part of the software package without the prior consent in writing of the software supplier.
> (b) That the purchaser shall not disassemble, alter or modify any part of the software package.
> (c) That the purchaser shall use the software only on specified and compatible machines.

(2) Each of these conditions should be prominently displayed on the front of the package. Notices should also be placed in prominent positions in the shop, and in particular at the cash till drawing the purchaser's attention to the conditions on the package.
(3) The conditions and notices should not attempt to refer to any other terms or documents which are not clearly on display at the time of making the purchase.

8.2.2.3   An independent contract

Incorporation of the terms of a licence into the retail contract of sale has the disadvantage that, even if it is successful, the contract remains one between retailer and purchaser. It is therefore not enforceable at the instance of the software supplier. It is therefore preferable to attempt to create an independent contract directly between the software supplier and the user. It is this which the shrink-wrap licence is primarily directed to. The idea is that by breaking the film, the user creates a new contract between himself and the supplier.

---

46   *Birch v Thomas* [1972] 1 WLR 294.
47   *White v Blackmore* [1972] 2 QB 651 to 664.
48   *J. Spurling Ltd v Bradshaw* [1956] 1 WLR 461 at 466 *per* Denning LJ.

There are two difficulties with this, even assuming that the terms of the new contract are sufficiently brought to the user's attention before he breaks the film (as to which see above). The first is that it is a general rule that a contract cannot be imposed upon another by construing silence as an acceptance of an offer.[49] While it is arguable that acceptance by breaking the film and loading the program is sufficient, it is not clear that this argument would succeed. Of course, the terms of the licence may require the user to fill in and return a registration card, which could be construed as a positive acceptance, but the problem is what happens where the user neglects to do this.

The second difficulty is that of consideration. In English law, a contract is only enforceable if it is supported by consideration. Where the user has purchased the software from a retailer, the most obvious forms of consideration are exchanged to support the contract of sale: the purchaser gives consideration by paying money, and the retailer gives consideration by permitting the purchaser to acquire at least possession of and usually title to the physical cassette or disk containing the software. It is rather less obvious what consideration may move in either direction to support a shrink-wrap licence contract.

In order to achieve this, it is suggested that the licence should begin with the prominent statement that the purchaser may not load or use the software without the consent of the software supplier, and that the supplier does not consent unless the purchaser accepts the terms and conditions of the licence. Thus, if the purchaser breaks the film and loads the program, it can be argued that a contract is created in which the supplier gives consideration by consenting to the loading and use of the program, and the purchaser gives consideration by promising to obey the terms of the licence. The supplier may also give additional consideration, for example by promising to replace faulty diskettes.

Considered from the perspective of copyright law, this is entirely reasonable: there is no reason why a contract of sale of goods between retailer and purchaser should necessarily carry with it a licence of copyright licence, and equally there is no reason why the copyright licence should not be the subject of a separate agreement. Indeed, from a copyright perspective a separate contract is entirely logical.

Considered from the perspective of sale of goods law, however, this is more problematical. The purchaser may reasonably ask what he has acquired in return for the money he has paid the retailer if it does not entitle him to use the software. As a matter of logic, the answer must be that he has acquired nothing more than title to the physical cassette or disk, and the possibility of entering into a licence to use the software. Given that the purchaser will have paid rather more than he would for a blank cassette or disk, however, he may well expect to have acquired rather more. In other words, the purchaser might contend that it was implicit in the contract of sale that he acquired the right to use the

49 *Felthouse v Bindley* (1862) 11 CB (NS) 869.

software, and if not there was a total failure of consideration. By analogy, it might be said, the purchaser of a book acquires the right to read it, and the purchaser of a record acquires the right to play it. The difference, however, is that neither of these acts is an infringement of copyright. By contrast, it is impossible to use a computer program without infringing the copyright in it if the user is not licensed. Thus it may be said that the true analogy is not with the purchase of a record for playing in the privacy of the purchaser's home, but the purchasing of a record for playing at a discothèque: the purchase of the record does not carry with it any licence under the performing right, which must be obtained separately from Phonographic Performance Ltd. On the other hand, the discothèque operator can still play the record at home, whereas the software is useless without a licence.

Another analogy is with patent law. It is well established in patent law that a patented article may be sold subject to a limited licence restricting its use which will run with the goods provided that the purchaser has notice of the restrictions.[50] For use outside the scope of the licence, a separate licence has to be obtained. A similar approach would appear to be available in the case of copyright software.

There has yet to be any reported English case in which the enforceability of a shrink-wrap licence has been tested, and so it remains to be seen what the attitude of the courts will be.

8.2.3   Drafting a software licence

8.2.3.1 The grant

The agreement should state at the outset the premises on which the agreement is made and the basic function of the agreement, which in the present case is the grant of a licence. From the point of view of the software house, the licence granted should be expressly and strictly limited.

Example clauses
THIS AGREEMENT is made the . . . day of . . . . between SOFTWARE HOUSE LIMITED of [address] (hereinafter called 'the Licensor') of the one part and PROGRAM USER LIMITED of [address] (hereinafter called 'the Licensee') of the other part

W H E R E A S:
A. The Licensor has developed a computer program together with instruction manuals and other materials as specified in the Schedule hereto (hereinafter called 'the Software')
B. The Licensee wishes to use the software for the purposes specified in the Schedule hereto

---

50 See *Terrell on Patents*, Sweet & Maxwell, 1982 (13th edn), paragraph 9.66.

C. The Licensor is willing to grant the customer and the Licensee is willing to accept a licence to use the Software for the said purposes subject to the terms and conditions of this Agreement

NOW IN CONSIDERATION of the aforesaid premises and of the terms and conditions hereinafter contained IT IS HEREBY AGREED as follows:

(1) *Grant of licence*
The Licensor hereby grants to the Licensee a non-exclusive licence to use the Software only:

(i) for the purposes specified in the Schedule;
(ii) in the premises and on the machines specified in the schedule.

8.2.3.2 *Ownership*

It is desirable to include an express term in the licence making it clear that title to the software and all rights therein is vested in the supplier.

Example clause
The Licensor is the owner of the copyright and all other intellectual property rights (as defined in section 72 of the Supreme Court Act 1981) which subsist in the Software and any copies thereof.

8.2.3.3 *Restrictions on use*

As well as a limitation on the scope of the licence, it is a good idea to include a positive obligation not to use the software other than as licensed.

Example clause
The Licensee shall not use the Software or any copy thereof in any premises or on any machine other than those expressly referred to in the Schedule hereto.

8.2.3.4 *Restrictions on copying*

It is also a good idea to include general restrictions on copying. On the other hand, the customer will want to be able to make back-up copies and it may be unreasonable to attempt to prevent this.[51]

Example clause
The Licensee covenants that it shall not copy, and shall not procure, authorise or assist others to copy, whether in eye readable or machine readable form, any part of the software without the prior written consent of the Licensor PROVIDED THAT the Licensee shall be entitled to make one back-up copy of the Software in machine readable form to be used only in the event that the primary copy thereof fails to function.

---

51 It will soon be impossible to do so, for under Article 5(2) of the EC Directive on Protection of Computer Software this is forbidden. See Chapter 2 paragraph 2.9.1.2.

8.2.3.5   Confidentiality

As discussed in Chapter 3, it is desirable to impose express confidentiality restrictions.

Example clauses

(1) The Licensee covenants that it shall keep the Software, whether in machine readable or eye readable form, and all information relating thereto confidential and shall not communicate or procure, authorise or assist any person to communicate any part thereof to any person without the prior written consent of the Licensor.

(2) Nothing in the foregoing covenant shall prevent the Licensee from disclosing the Software or any part thereof to those of its directors officers or employees to whom such disclosure is reasonably necessary in order for them to use the Software in the course of their employment.

8.2.3.6   Modifications and improvements

In *Saphena Computing Ltd v Allied Collection Agencies Ltd*,[52] Mr Recorder Havery QC held, applying the reasoning of *British Leyland Motor Corp. v Armstrong Patents Co. Ltd*,[53] that it was an implied term of an agreement for the supply of bespoke computer software that the customer was licensed under the copyright in the software to 'repair' the software. That is to say, the customer was impliedly licensed to make copies of the software – of the object code and of the source code if the latter had been supplied – for the purpose of fixing bugs. The learned recorder even appears to have held that this implied licence extended to improving the software. He also held, however, that there was no obligation upon the software supplier to facilitate such repairs or improvements, and in particular no obligation on the supplier to supply or license reproduction of the source code if all that has been supplied is the object code.

This aspect of the learned recorder's decision was not ultimately challenged on appeal, and it remains to be seen exactly what the extent of any such implied licence might be. In the circumstances, the best course is for any software licence expressly to delimit the rights granted to the licensee in respect of repairs and improvements. The importance of this becomes particularly acute if, as was the case in *Saphena*, there is a dispute between the parties over the supply agreement.

Although it is not uncommon for software licences to contain express restrictions on disassembling object code, it must now be doubted whether these are valid.

Example clauses

(1) During the subsistence of this Licence the Licensee shall be entitled (whether acting by its directors officers servants agents or independent

52   Unreported, 22 July 1988.
53   [1986] AC 577.

contractors) to make such modifications to the Software as may be necessary for the purpose of correcting errors in the same and to make such copies of the Software as are necessary for that purpose. The Licensor shall be under no obligation to facilitate the making of such modifications, whether by supplying or providing access to the source code of the Software or otherwise.

(2) During the subsistence of this Licence the Licensee shall be entitled (whether acting by its directors officers servants agents or independent contractors) to make improvements to the Software on condition that all such improvements are forthwith disclosed to the Licensor. The Licensee hereby grants to the Licensor an irrevocable perpetual licence to reproduce such improvements with power to sub-license other licensees of the Software. The Licensor shall be under no obligation to facilitate the making of such improvements, whether by supplying or providing access to the source code of the Software or otherwise.

8.2.3.7 *Detection of infringement*

It is of assistance to the supplier contractually to bind the customer to inform it of any infringement of rights in the software so that action may be taken without delay.

Example clause
The Licensee covenants that it shall forthwith upon learning of any unauthorised reproduction, use, disclosure or modification of the Software (whether existing or planned) inform the Licensor of the same.

8.2.3.8 *Assignment and sub-licensing*

It is desirable to make clear the extent to which, if at all, assignment and/or sub-licensing is permitted.

Example clause
This Agreement is personal to the Licensee and may not without the written consent of the Licensor be assigned or sub-licensed.

8.2.3.9 *Term and termination*

It is also desirable to specify the term of licence and the precise circumstances in which it may be terminated. On termination of the agreement, the supplier must be able to continue to take action against the customer for any infringement of rights in the software. Risk of infringement should be minimised by provisions for return of all copies of the software.

Example clauses
(1) After the expiry of a period of six months from the delivery date specified in the Schedule hereto, either party may terminate this Agreement

by giving three months notice in writing to the other party of such termination.

(2) The Licensor shall have the right to terminate this Agreement forthwith by notice in writing to the Licensee in any of the following circumstances: (a) if any sum payable hereunder is in arrears for more than three months after the date upon which payment of such sum is due; (b) if the Licensee shall commit any breach of any of the covenants specified in this Agreement.

(3) Termination of the Agreement (for whatever reason) shall be without prejudice to any rights of either party accrued prior to termination or to any rights in respect of events occurring after termination. Upon such termination the Licensee shall forthwith cease to use the Software, and any improved software made pursuant to clause [improvements clause]. Such termination shall be without prejudice to the covenants by the Licensee under this Agreement which shall continue in force.

(4) Upon termination of this Agreement the Licensee shall forthwith deliver up to the Licensor all articles and documents containing any part of the Software or of any improved software made pursuant to clause [improvements clause] whether in eye readable or machine readable form, and shall cause every part of the Software or the improved software to be deleted and erased from all processing units, magnetic media and other means of storage in its possession power or control. Upon completion of such delivery up deletion and erasure the Licensee shall certify in writing to the Licensor that it has complied in full with the requirements of this clause.

8.2.3.10   *Law and jurisdiction*

Finally it is desirable, particularly where companies of more than one nationality are concerned, to specify the law of the contract and which courts are to have jurisdiction over any dispute or whether such a dispute is to be arbitrated and if so who is to appoint the arbitrator(s).

Example clause
This Agreement shall be subject to the Law of England and Wales and both parties hereby agree to submit to the exclusive jurisdiction of the High Court of Justice in the event of any dispute.

8.3   SOFTWARE MAINTENANCE AGREEMENTS

8.3.1   What is a software maintenance agreement?

It is sometimes surprising to people to find that software can and does go wrong. Although most people readily accept that hardware, like any other form of machine, may be subject to malfunction or breakdown, for example if parts fail or wear out, some assume that software will not be subject to such problems. This is understandable, but mistaken. The reason is simple: human error. Software is still largely created by human beings, and human beings make mistakes. In the context of computer software, these are called 'bugs'. Although a competent software supplier will attempt to de-bug software before supplying it to a customer, it is frequently the case that it is only when the software is exposed to the stresses and strains of real users and real data that faults emerge. It is therefore unrealistic, at least with bespoke or customised software, to expect it to be error-free. Even with a standard package, it is impossible to be 100 per cent confident that it is wholly bug-free.

This problem becomes multiplied when different programs or packages are used together, particularly when they have been developed by different suppliers. Predicting how the combination will behave in all circumstances is very difficult and so bugs are almost inevitable.

Another problem is that when the user begins to use the system, he may find that it does not quite work in the way that he expects (for example, because of the differences between computerised and manual systems) or that it does not do things that he wants it do or that it does things that he does not want it to or that its operation is deficient in some ways (for example, it is too slow). Assuming that the supplier has complied with his obligations under the supply contract, this may occur because of an insufficiently detailed specification of requirements, or it may happen because once the user becomes familiar with the system he begins to appreciate what more he would like it to be able to do. Strictly speaking, such problems are not bugs. They can be equally frustrating to the user, however.

Finally, there is the ever-increasing problem of viruses. These may cause damage to software or (more usually) to data or both. Users may well require assistance first to eradicate the virus and secondly to restore the system (so far as this is possible). Damage may also be caused by hackers or by power surges and the like.

Even if the software contains no defects, a new user may well find that he needs advice and assistance in using it over and above the training he has received as part of the supply agreement.

For all these reasons, it is a good idea to have a software maintenance contract. Although the supplier may be obliged to correct bugs under the supply agreement, it is convenient to have a maintenance contract to fall back on so that the software can be fixed first and responsibility assigned afterwards. This is particularly important where the supply agreement contains an express warranty that bugs will only be fixed for a defined period such as three months. As for the second and third categories of problems mentioned above, these are unlikely to be the supplier's fault.

A maintenance agreement should provide the user with support assistance in such eventualities. If the agreement is with the supplier, provision may also be made for the supply of new and updated versions of the software.

8.3.2   Drafting a software maintenance agreement

8.3.2.1   *Levels of support*

It is a good idea to specify the levels of assistance which will be provided, for example telephone advice, on-line support through a modem and on-site attendance. Different levels of support are usually charged for at different rates.

Example clauses
(1) *Telephone support.* The Contractor shall provide support by telephone as follows. The Customer's Representatives may telephone the Contractor during normal working works (Monday to Friday, 9am to 5pm, excluding public holidays) for assistance in identifying investigating and resolving any problem. It is the responsibility of the Customer to communicate sufficient information and other material to the Contractor to enable the Contractor to understand the nature of the problem and where appropriate to duplicate it. Where telephone support is provided, the Contractor shall attempt to identify investigate and resolve the problem as soon as reasonably practical. Where appropriate, the Contractor shall give an estimate of the time which may be required to solve the problem. The Contractor shall keep the Customer reasonably informed of the progress of the Contractor's attempts to resolve the problem.
(2) *On-line support.* Where on-line support is specified in the Schedule, the Contractor shall provide on-line support in the following circumstances. Where the problem is urgent and the Contractor in its sole discretion judges that it would be appropriate to attempt to investigate or resolve the problem on-line, the Contractor shall supply on loan a modem[54] for on-line investigation of the problem and such loan shall be charged for at the Contractor's standard rate for the time being. An urgent problem is one of the following: failure or degradation of the System, defective Software distribution media or performance substantially inconsistent with documentation.
(3) *On-site support.* Where on-site support is specified in the Schedule, the Contractor shall provide on-site support in the following circumstances. Where the problem is urgent and cannot be resolved by telephone support or (if appropriate) on-line support, the Contractor shall attend at the Customer's Site to assist in identifying investigating and resolving the problem. It is the responsibility of the Customer to communicate sufficient information and other material to the Contractor to enable the Contractor to understand the nature of the problem and where appropriate to duplicate it. Where telephone support is provided, the Contractor shall attempt to identify investigate and resolve the problem as soon as reasonably practical. Where appropriate, the Contractor shall give an estimate of the time which may be required to solve the problem. The Contractor shall keep the Customer reasonably informed of the progress of the Contractor's attempts to resolve the problem.

54   This may be unnecessary if the Customer already has a modem link to the Contractor.

8.3.2.2 Extent of support

It is a good idea to define the extent of the support to be provided.

Example clauses
(1) The support provided by the Contractor under this Agreement shall be limited to support of the Software expressly listed in the Schedule operating on the Hardware expressly listed in the Schedule at the Site(s) specified in the Schedule and shall not extend to any other software or hardware or site(s).
(2) The support provided by the Contractor under this Agreement shall not extend to Software which has been modified or added to by the Customer nor shall it extend to support of versions of Software older than the latest version released by the Contractor or the Supplier and the version immediately preceding the latest version.
(3) The support provided by the Contractor under this Agreement shall not extend to the retrieval or rectification of lost or corrupted data unless such loss or corruption is due to the negligence of the Contractor its employees or agents.
(4) The support provided by the Contractor under this Agreement shall not extend to the identification investigation or resolution of problems not associated with the Software nor to problems caused by use of the Software otherwise than in accordance with the design or specification of the same as laid down in any manual or other documentation supplied with the Software.
(5) Where the Software the subject of the problem is software developed by the Contractor, the Contractor may in its sole discretion correct errors by patch or by new version. Where the Software the subject of the problem is software developed by the Supplier, the Contractor shall to the extent that it is permitted to by law or by any agreement with the Supplier correct errors by patch. Where correction of errors by patch by the Contractor is for any reason not permitted the Contractor's responsibility shall be limited to reporting the error to the Supplier and requesting the Supplier to correct the same.
(6) This Agreement shall not be interpreted as a guarantee or warranty that the Contractor will be able to resolve any or all problems either at all or within any period of time. The Contractor's obligations under this Agreement are limited to exercising reasonable endeavours and reasonable skill and care in attempting to resolve problems.

8.3.2.3 Customer obligations

It is also a good idea to define the customer's obligations.

Example clauses
(1) The Customer undertakes to follow the Contractor's problem reporting procedure, a statement of which is available upon request.

(2) The Customer undertakes to provide the Contractor or the supplier as appropriate with such dumps or code or data as may reasonably be requested for the purpose of identifying investigating or resolving any particular problem.

8.3.2.4   *Exclusion and limitation clauses*

The contractor may wish to include exclusion or limitation clauses in the agreement. The issues are essentially the same as in software supply agreements, discussed above.

8.4   ESCROW AGREEMENTS

8.4.1   What is an escrow agreement?

In the context of computer software, an escrow agreement is an agreement where the supplier deposits the source code for software with a third party and agrees that the third party shall release it to the customer upon the occurrence of certain specified events, for example the insolvency of the supplier. The escrow agreement is a three-way agreement between the supplier, customer and escrow agent which defines their respective obligations. Usually the escrow agreement is ancillary to a software licence. The National Computer Centre provides an escrow deposit service. Alternatively, a lawyer, accountant, bank or trade association may be asked to act as escrow agent.

An elementary point is that escrow deposit services are not provided free. Accordingly one term of the escrow agreement should be a term stipulating who bears the cost of it. Since the escrow agreement is for the benefit of the customer it is usually the responsibility of the customer; alternatively the cost may be shared between the customer and the software supplier.

If, as is usually the case, the software is going to be updated in any way, there is little point in having the original source code in escrow unless the source code of the updates is also deposited. Therefore the escrow agreement should provide for this to be done on a regular basis as well.

8.4.2   Drafting an escrow agreement

8.4.2.1   *Deposit of the source code*

Early escrow agreements simply obliged the licensor to deposit the source code with the escrow agent. More recently, some licensees have become reluctant to rely upon such a 'blind faith' arrangement and have begun to insist upon verification provisions. If verification is to be carried out by the escrow agent, this will of course mean that the escrow agent must have the requisite technical skills. It will also mean that the cost of the escrow will increase.

Example clauses
(1) Within 14 days of the execution of this Agreement, the Licensor shall present to the Escrow Agent one copy of the Code in the form specified in the First Schedule hereto for verification at the Licensee's premises. The Licensor shall give the Escrow Agent such assistance in verifying the Code as the Escrow Agent shall reasonably require. When the Escrow Agent is satisfied as to the completeness and accuracy of the Code the Escrow Agent and the Licensor shall execute a Certificate of Verification in the form set out in the Second Schedule hereto. If the Escrow Agent is not satisfied as to the completeness and accuracy of the Code the Licensor shall be liable for all fees and expenses incurred by the parties in carrying out the procedure.
(2) Upon execution of the Certificate of Verification the Escrow Agent shall accept the Code for deposit.
(3) At intervals of six months after the date of deposit of the Code the Licensor shall present for verification and deposit in like manner all updates to the Code (including all modifications and new versions thereof) made during the preceding six months.

8.4.2.2   Escrow Agent's obligations

It is as well to spell out the escrow agent's obligations under the agreement.

Example clauses
(1) The Escrow Agent shall store the Code and any updates thereto deposited under the terms of this Agreement in a safe and secure place at its premises.
(2) The Escrow Agent shall not release deposited Code or updates thereto except as provided by this Agreement.
(3) The Escrow Agent shall not use or copy deposited Code or updates thereto or any part thereof for any purpose whatsoever.
(4) The Escrow Agent shall keep deposited Code and updates thereto strictly confidential and shall not disclose the same or allow access thereto except upon release as provided by the Agreement.

8.4.2.3   Release of the source code

The most important clause in an escrow agreement is the clause which specifies the circumstances in which the source code is to be released to the licensee.

Example clauses
(1) The Escrow Agent shall release the Code to the Licensee and shall only release the Code to the Licensee upon the occurrence of any of the following events and upon receipt from the Licensee of the appropriate written notice specified in this Agreement together with such supporting documentation as the Escrow Agent may reasonably require:
(i)   If the Licensor shall be in default of any term of the Licence or of this Agreement and have failed to remedy such default (if capable of remedy) within 14 days.

(ii)   If the Licensor, being a body corporate, shall present a petition or have a petition presented by a creditor for its winding up, or convene a meeting to pass a resolution for voluntary winding up, or shall enter into any liquidation (other than for the purposes of a bona fide reconstruction or amalgamation), or shall have a receiver of all or any of its undertakings or assets appointed, or shall be deemed by virtue of section 123 of the Insolvency Act 1986 to be unable to pay its debts.

(iii) If the Licensor, being a firm or sole trader shall be dissolved or commit any act of bankruptcy or have any receiving order made against it or him or make or negotiate for any composition or arrangement with or assignments for the benefit of its or his creditors.

(2)   If the Licensee desires the Escrow Agent to release the Code upon the occurrence of one of the events listed in (1) above the Licensee shall give the Escrow Agent written notice thereof specifying the nature of the event and giving reasonable particulars thereof and shall send a copy of such notice to the Licensor. Together with such notice or thereafter the Licensee shall provide the Escrow Agent with such supporting documentation as the Escrow Agent shall reasonably require.

(3)   After the expiry of 14 days from receipt by the Escrow Agent of any such notice as is mentioned in (2), the Escrow Agent shall release the Code and any Updates to the Licensee subject always to payment of the Licensee's portion of any outstanding fees and charges owing to the Escrow Agent as at the release date.

(4)   In the event of any dispute between the Licensee and the Licensor as to the validity of any such notice as mentioned in (2), the Escrow Agent shall take such action (including, but without limitation, arbitrating the dispute or referring the dispute to such arbitration as it shall consider appropriate) as it shall in its sole discretion consider fit but shall not be obliged to take any action.

8.4.2.4   *Termination of the agreement*

It is also necessary to provide for termination of the agreement in circumstances other than those which trigger release of the source code.

Example clause

This Agreement shall terminate and the Escrow Agent shall be discharged of its obligations hereunder (save those which are expressed to continue after termination) in any of the following circumstances:

(i)   the Code is released to the Licensee as provided by [the relevant clause];

(ii) termination of the Licence otherwise than upon default of the Licensor;

(iii) if the Escrow Agent or the Licensor and Licensee jointly give 90 days' written notice of termination of this Agreement;

(iv) if the Code is lost, destroyed or corrupted.

8.5 PERSONNEL CONTRACTS

As discussed in Chapter 3,[55] it is not much use for a software house to go to great lengths to protect its valuable software against misuse by its customers and others if its own employees (or sub-contractors) are free to use their inside knowledge of the software to produce a competing product.

8.5.1 Employment contracts

8.5.1.1 Pre-termination clauses

During the subsistence of the employment contract, a wide express duty of fidelity may be imposed.

Example clauses
(1) The Employee shall not pursue or undertake any activity which interferes with or is likely to interfere with the performance by him of his duties hereunder and shall not, without the prior written consent of the Company, engage in any other business or employment whatsoever. Such consent shall not be unreasonably withheld by the Company, provided that such other business or employment does not in any way compete or conflict with any activity in which the Company its subsidiaries or affiliates may from time to time be or have been engaged.
(2) The Employee shall not at any time during his employment, except with the prior written consent of the Company or where it is reasonably necessary for him to do so to carry out his duties in the course of his employment with the Company, disclose to any person (whether employed by the Company or not) any secret or confidential information concerning the company's business or products which he has devised, discovered, learnt or otherwise acquired during the course of his employment with the Company.
(3) The Employee shall use his best endeavours to prevent any unauthorised disclosure of any secret or confidential information by any person and shall forthwith upon learning of any such unauthorised disclosure (whether existing or planned) inform the Company of the same.

8.5.1.2 Post-termination clauses

After termination of an employee's employment, care should be taken not to draft the ex-employee's obligations too widely or else they will be void and unenforceable for restraint of trade.

8.5.1.2.1 Non-competition covenant

Example clause
For the period of 12 months after the termination of his employment (for whatsoever reason) the Employee shall not without the prior written consent of the Company enter the employment of or otherwise participate or

---

55 See paragraph 3.5.

assist in the business of any company firm or individual which is in competition with the Company within the geographical area specified in the Schedule hereto.

8.5.1.2.2 Non-solicitation covenant

Example clause
For the period of 24 months after the termination of his employment (for whatever reason) the Employee shall not without the prior written consent of the Company solicit canvass or deal with any company firm or individual who was a customer of the Company during the period of the Employee's employment and with whom the Employee dealt.

8.5.1.2.3 Trade secrets clause

Example clause
The Employee shall not at any time after the termination of his employment without the prior written consent of the Company disclose to any other person or use for his own benefit any trade secrets of the Company. For the purposes of this clause 'trade secrets' shall mean: any customer list of the Company, any algorithm used in the Company's products which is not in the public domain, [other examples] and other confidential information which the Employee is specifically directed during the course of his employment by the Company to regard as a trade secret.

8.5.2 Independent contractors

It is quite common for software houses and others to engage systems analysts and programmers on a contract-hire basis rather than to employ them. In these circumstances the analysts are independent contractors rather than employees. A software house which engages independent contractors in this way needs no less protection so far as confidential information is concerned than it does in respect of its employees. Therefore contracts for such persons should contain similar provisions as for those employees, with appropriate changes. In addition, however, it will be necessary to ensure that the software house gets the full benefit of the contractors' work and in particular that it acquires the copyright. Difficulties can be avoided if proper provision for this is made in advance. The best course is for the contract to contain an assignment of future copyright. In this way the necessity to take a later assignment of legal title can be avoided.

Example clause
It is agreed and understood that the copyright and all rights in the nature of copyright in all works which may be created by the Contractor during the course of this Contract shall vest in and be owned by the Company and the Contractor hereby irrevocably assigns to the Company his entire right

title and interest in all such copyrights and other rights throughout the world for the entire term thereof together with the right to take proceedings for any infringements thereof and to recover relief in respect of the same.

8.6 EEC COMPETITION LAW[56]

The competition rules of the Treaty of Rome raise important considerations for the distribution and licensing of computer software. Competition law within the EEC is perceived not only as a means of controlling competitive conduct but also as a means of integrating the common market. It is this added dimension of policy that has resulted in the sometimes harsh application of the competition rules to the distribution or licensing of products. The imposition of export bans, allocation of markets or attempts to maintain different pricing policies for different national markets will *prima facie* infringe the competition rules of the Treaty and a reliance upon national intellectual property rights will not necessarily provide a defence.

There is a distinction in the application of the EEC competition rules to distribution agreements on the one hand and to licensing agreements on the other. Insofar as software may be sold under a distribution or under a licensing agreement, it is necessary to consider the relevant rules with regard to both. First, however, the general principles applied by the Commission under Articles 85 and 86 of the Treaty of Rome will be considered.

8.6.1 The scope of the competition articles

The competition rules of the EEC are set out in Articles 85 to 94 of the Treaty of Rome. The most important of these are Articles 85 and 86. Article 85 prohibits as incompatible within the common market agreements and practices which have as their object or effect the prevention, restriction or distortion of competition with the common market. Article 86 prohibits as incompatible with the common market any abuse of a dominant position within the common market or in a substantial part of it insofar as it may affect trade between Member States.

Both Articles are of broad application. The importance which it is perceived that they have for the successful integration of the common market is clear from the reference made to them in Article 3 of the Treaty, which sets out the activities of the Community for the purposes of establishing the common market.[57] This explains the strict attitude of the European Commission to anti-competitive activity which involves the

---

56 See generally Bellamy and Child, *Common Market Law of Competition*, Sweet & Maxwell, 1987 (3rd edn and Supp.) to which the authors are indebted.
57 Article 3(f) includes among these 'the institution of a system ensuring that competition in the common market is not distorted'.

erection or maintenance of barriers to interstate trade such as market-sharing agreements or restrictions on parallel trade, whether direct or indirect.

In relation to distribution and licensing agreements, Article 85 is of primary importance. Where companies are involved which have such a share of the market as to be in a dominant position, Article 86 will also be relevant.

8.6.2   Article 85

8.6.2.1   Article 85(1)

Article 85(1) applies where three elements are present:

(1) There must be either an agreement between undertakings, a decision by an association of undertakings or a concerted practice. Unilateral conduct *per se* is not within the scope of Article 85(1),[58] although it may infringe Article 86. An 'undertaking' is any entity which engages in commercial activities,[59] regardless of legal form, and includes individuals. The distinction between 'agreement', 'decision' and 'concerted practice' is of little or no importance.[60] It is not necessary for the agreement to be in writing[61] or to take any particular form or indeed to be legally binding.[62] It is sufficient that one of the parties voluntarily undertakes to limit its freedom of action with regard to the other.[63] Standard form contracts, including standard conditions of sale,[64] are as much within the scope of Article 85(1) as any other. The mere exercise of a legal right, such as bringing an action for infringement of copyright, does not *per se* fall within Article 85(1); but the position may be different if the action is brought pursuant to some agreement or concerted practice and has objectionable effects.[65]

(2) The agreement, decision or practice must have, as its object or effect, the prevention, restriction or distortion of competition within the common market. Although in many cases the Commission and the European Court do not clearly distinguish between object and effect, the correct course is first to consider the object of the agreement.[66]

---

58   *Ford v Commission (No. 1)* Cases 228 & 229/82 [1984] ECR 1129 at 1160.
59   *Polypropylene* OJ 1986 L230/1.
60   *Van Landweyck v Commission* Cases 209/78 etc. [1980] ECR 3125 at 3310.
61   See, for example, *Tepea v Commission* Case 28/77 [1978] ECR 1391 at 1412 to 1417.
62   See, for example, *ACF Chemiefarma NV v Commission* Case 41/69 [1970] ECR 661 at 693.
63   *Franco-Japanese Ballbearings* [1975] 1 CMLR D8.
64   See, for example, *Distillers Company v Commission* Case 30/78 [1980] ECR 2229.
65   See, for example, *Coditel v Cine-Vog Films (No. 2)* Case 262/81 [1982] ECR 3381.
66   *Technique Minière v Maschinenbau* Case 56/65 [1966] ECR 235 at 249.

This is a matter of objective assessment and does not depend on the parties' subjective intentions. Thus it is no defence to argue that an agreement is intended to promote trade. Certain types of agreements have been held by their nature to have the object of restricting competition. These include 'horizontal agreements' which fix prices, partition markets or confine dealings to particular channels and 'vertical agreements' such as exclusive distribution agreements, franchise agreements and the like which impose export bans or other restrictions on buyers' freedom to deal in goods. If there is a plain intention to restrict competition, it is unnecessary to show that there has in fact been such an effect.[67] In cases where this is not obvious, the effects of the agreement must be examined. This involves consideration of what competition there would be in the absence of the agreement. Whether the parties are potential competitors is important, as is whether third parties are affected. In order to infringe Article 85(1), the effect on competition must be an appreciable one.[68] A rough test of this applied by the Commission is that an agreement does not have an appreciable effect if the undertakings concerned do not have a market share of more than 5 per cent in the relevant product and geographical market and their combined turnover does not exceed 200 million ECUs.[69]

(3) There must be an effect on trade between Member States. This requirement is common to Articles 85 and 86. The purpose of it is to define the jurisdiction of Community law. If there is no effect on trade between Member States, then the matter is one for the application of the relevant national law. The threshold for establishing an effect is a low one. The basic test is whether the agreement alters the normal pattern or flow of trade.[70] It is sufficient that the products concerned are traded across at least one frontier between Member States.[71] Even where the conduct complained of takes place entirely within one Member State, there may be an effect if export disincentives are involved. Furthermore, an agreement between an undertaking in a Member State and an undertaking in a non-Member State may be deemed to affect trade between Member States, for example if the non-Member State party is prohibited from exporting to a common market country[72] or if the Member State is prohibited from exporting to a non-common market country from which re-importation into the common market would be likely.[73]

---

67   See, for example, *Miller v Commission* Case 19/77 [1978] ECR 131.
68   *Völk v Vervaecke* Case 5/69 [1969] ECR 295.
69   Notice on Agreements of Minor Importance OJ 1986 C231/2.
70   See, for example, *Frubo v Commission* Case 71/74 [1975] ECR 563.
71   See, for example, *Cooperative Vereniging Suiker Unie v Commission* Cases 40/73 etc. [1975] ECR 1663.
72   See, for example, *EMI v CBS* Case 51/75 [1976] ECR 811 at 848.
73   See, for example, *Re the Agreements of Davide Campari-Milano SpA* Case 78/253 [1978] 2 CMLR 397.

8.6.2.2　*Article 85(2)*

If an agreement, decision or practice infringes Article 85(1), then, unless it is exempted under Article 85(3), Article 85(2) provides that it is automatically void and unenforceable.

The effect of the nullity of terms prohibited by Article 85 on the rest of the agreement is a question of national law.[74] Under English law, this raises the possibility of severance of the offending provisions. Thus in *Chemidus Wavin v TERI*[75] the Court of Appeal enforced a minimum royalties provision in a patent licence between a British licensor and a French licensee even though other terms of the licence arguably infringed Article 85(1).

8.6.2.3　*Article 85(3)*

An agreement, decision or practice which would otherwise fall foul of Article 85 may be exempted from its application under Article 85(3) if four criteria are satisfied (two positive, two negative):

(1) It contributes to improving the production or distribution of goods or promotes technological or economic progress. Agreements of the types in respect of which block exemptions have been granted provide examples of this.

(2) It allows consumers a fair share of the resulting benefit. 'Consumers' in this context includes trade purchasers.[76] In practice, what this means is that there must be a reasonable probability that the benefits of the agreement will be passed on to consumers, rather than that the agreement will simply benefit the parties.

(3) It does not impose restrictions on the undertakings concerned which are not indispensable to the attainment of the objectives set out under (1) and (2). The general principle is that the parties should adopt the least restrictive provisions consistent with achieving the aims of the agreement.[77] The 'black-listed' restrictions in the block exemptions provide examples of restrictions which the Commission regards as 'not indispensable'.

(4) It does not afford the undertakings concerned the possibility of eliminating competition in respect of a substantial part of the market in the products in question.

Exemptions may be granted either individually or on a block basis. Individual exemptions are obtained by notification of the agreement in

---

74　*Soc. de Vente de Ciments et Betons v Kerpen & Kerpen* Case 319/82 [1983] ECR 4173 at 4184 to 4185.
75　[1978] 3 CMLR 514.
76　*GEC/Weir* [1978] 1 CMLR D42.
77　See, for example, *GEC/Weir*, Note 76 above.

question to the Commission. Block exemptions consist of carefully drafted regulations issued by the Commission setting out a code of conduct and granting exemption to all those who bring themselves within its terms. If an agreement is covered by a block exemption, it need not be notified to the Commission.

8.6.2.4 *Individual exemptions and negative clearance*

In order to obtain individual exemption, the Commission must be notified of the agreement, decision or practice in question. Only the Commission has power to grant or refuse an exemption.[78] It may do so for a specified period only, and it may attach conditions.[79] The burden of establishing that the agreement satisfies the requirements for exemption lies upon the notifying party or parties.[80] Even where the normal criteria for exemption are satisfied, exemption may be refused if one of the parties is engaged in anti-competitive practices, even if these are extrinsic to the agreement for which exemption is sought.[81]

An alternative to notification is to apply for negative clearance. Negative clearance is a declaration by the Commission that in the light of the information available to it the agreement falls outside Article 85 altogether.[82] This is therefore different from an exemption, but the procedure is similar. In practice, an application for negative clearance is usually accompanied by an application for exemption in case negative clearance is not granted.

Before granting exemption or negative clearance, the Commission must publish a summary of the agreement in the Official Journal and invite comments from third parties.[83] Instead of granting formal exemption, the Commission may write an 'informal comfort letter' stating that it sees no need to take action. Alternatively, a 'formal comfort letter' may be written, stating that the agreement falls outside Article 85(1) or satisfies Article 85(3), but that the Commission does not feel it is necessary to proceed to a formal decision to that effect.

The decision whether or not to notify an agreement is not an easy one. While there is no obligation to notify, failure to do so means that the benefits of notification will not be obtained. On the other hand, the Commission is very slow in reaching decisions – two to three years is typical, it may require considerable quantities of information to be supplied, and the publicity may be unwelcome.

If an agreement is notified, it is important to make full and accurate disclosure in the notification. If this is not done, a fine may be imposed.[84]

---

78 Regulation 17, Article 9(1). See *L'Oréal v Niuwe AMCK* Case 31/80 [1980] ECR 3775.
79 Regulation 17, Article 8.
80 *Consten and Grundig v Commission* Cases 56 & 58/64 [1966] ECR 299.
81 *Ford v Commission (No. 2)* Cases 25 & 26/84 [1985] 3 CMLR 528.
82 Regulation 17, Article 2.
83 Regulation 17, Article 19(3).
84 Regulation 17, Article 15(1)(a).

More importantly, the Commission may decide that the agreement was not duly notified (and so not eligible for exemption) or that subsequent activities were outside the limits of the notification (and so not immune from fines).[85]

8.6.2.5   Block exemptions

Since in practice the Commission grants few individual exemptions and obtaining such exemptions is a slow and uncertain business, the block exemptions are of much greater importance. The following block exemptions exist:

(1) Bilateral exclusive distribution agreements (Regulation 1983/83). This grants block exemption, subject to certain conditions, to agreements to which only two undertakings are party whereby one party agrees to supply only to the other certain goods for resale within the whole or a defined area of the common market.

(2) Bilateral exclusive purchase agreements (Regulation 1984/83). This grants block exemption, subject to certain conditions, to agreements lasting no more than five years to which only two undertakings are party whereby one party agrees to purchase certain goods for resale only from the other or from a connected undertaking or from another undertaking which the supplier has entrusted with the sale of his goods. The essential distinction between an exclusive distribution agreement and an exclusive purchase agreement is that in the latter there is no contract territory allotted to one distributor.

(3) Patent licences (Regulation 2349/84). This grants block exemption, subject to certain conditions, to patent and combined patent and ancillary know-how licences to which only two undertakings are party under which the licence is exclusive and the licensee accepts certain limitations on his freedom to sell licensed products elsewhere in the common market.

(4) Franchise agreements (Regulation 4087/88). This grants block exemption, subject to certain conditions, to franchise agreements for the retailing of goods or services to which only two undertakings are party and which oblige the franchisor not to grant other franchises in the franchisee's territory or which oblige the franchisee to exploit the franchise only from certain premises, not to solicit custom outside his territory and not to deal in competitive goods or services.

(5) Know-how licences (Regulation 556/89). This grants block exemption, subject to certain conditions, to pure know-how licences and to mixed patent and know-how licences not falling within Regulation 2349/84 lasting up to 10 years.

---

85   See, for example, *AEG v Commission* Case 107/82 [1983] ECR 3151, where a selective distribution system which, as notified, was unobjectionable was in fact operated in manner different from that put forward in the notification. The Commission, upheld by the Court, held that the way in which the system was actually operated infringed Article 85(1) and no protection was given by the notification. A fine of 1 million ECU was imposed.

(6) Specialisation agreements (Regulation 417/85). This grants block exemption, subject to certain conditions, to agreements whereby undertakings accept reciprocal obligations not to manufacture certain products or to have them manufactured, but to leave it to other parties to do so or to manufacture certain products or have them manufactured only jointly. (7) Research and development agreements (Regulation 418/85). This grants block exemption, subject to certain conditions, to agreements between undertakings for joint research and development of products and processes and/or joint exploitation of the fruits of such research and development.

Some of these block exemptions are discussed further below. In addition, there is a block exemption for selective distribution agreements in the motor trade and more product- or service-specific exemptions are proposed.

8.6.2.6 *Consequences of breach*

Apart from the avoidance of the agreement or part of it, breach of Article 85 may lead to the imposition of fines by the Commission and possibly to civil remedies at the suit of third parties.

The Commission is empowered under Article 15(2) of Regulation 17 to impose fines of up to 10 per cent of the preceding year's turnover of undertakings that are in breach of Article 85. Although a fine of this level has not yet been imposed, some substantial fines have been levied.[86] The level of fine is fixed in each case according to the gravity of the conduct – practices involving export bans, for example, attract high fines owing to their significance for community integration. Aggravating conduct (for example, repeated violations) may lead to an increased fine. Mitigating conduct (for example, co-operation with the Commission, willingness to reform) may lead to a moderation in the level of fine.

Immunity from fines can be achieved by notification.[87] The immunity will then last for the duration of the Commission's investigation of the matter.

The question of civil remedies is discussed in relation to Article 86. It appears that the position under Article 85 is the same.

8.6.3 Article 86

8.6.3.1 *Application of Article 86*

Article 86 applies where three elements are present:

(1) There must be a dominant position held by one or more undertakings in the common market or a substantial part of it. A dominant

---

86 For example in *ECS v Akzo (No. 2)* OJ 1985 L374/1 the Commission imposed a fine of 10 million ECU (£6 million).
87 Regulation 17, Article 15(5).

position is a position of economic strength enjoyed by an undertaking which enables it to hinder the maintenance of effective competition in the relevant market by allowing it to behave to an appreciable extent independently of its competitors and customers.[88] Showing that an undertaking enjoys a dominant position can be broken down into four steps: (i) defining the relevant market; (ii) showing that the undertaking has a persistently high share of that market; (iii) showing that there is no real likelihood of rivals eroding the position of the undertaking; and (iv) showing that the dominant position exists in at least a substantial part of the common market. What is the relevant market depends on the extent to which there is 'demand substitutability' – whether consumers regard other products as reasonable substitutes for the one in question[89] – and 'supply substitutability' – whether other suppliers are able to supply the product in question.[90] In one case, the relevant market was limited to spare parts for machines made by one undertaking required by other undertakings for servicing machines in competition with the manufacturer.[91] A high share of the market indicating dominance is typically taken to be 40 per cent or more. As to what is a substantial part of the common market, this may be less than the whole of a Member State.[92]

(2) There must be an abuse of the dominant position. Abusive conduct can take a number of forms, some examples of which are listed in Article 86: (a) directly or indirectly imposing unfair purchase or selling prices or other unfair trading conditions; (b) limiting production, markets or technical development to the prejudice of consumers; (c) applying dissimilar conditions to equivalent transactions with other trading parties, thereby placing them at a competitive disadvantage; (d) making contracts subject to supplementary obligations which have no connection with the subject of the contracts. In general, abusive conduct is conduct which either is anti-competitive or is unfair to persons who depend on the dominant undertaking for the supply or acquisition of the relevant goods or services. In the *IBM* case,[93] the abuses alleged by the Commission were: (i) failing to supply other manufacturers in sufficient time with the technical information needed to permit competitive products to be used with System/370 ('interface information'); (ii) not offering System/370 CPUs (central processing units) without a capacity of main memory included in the price ('memory bundling'); (iii) not offering System/370 CPUs without the basic software included in the price ('software bundling'); and (iv) discriminating between users of IBM software by

88   *Michelin v Commission* Case 323/81 [1983] ECR 3461.
89   *Ibid.*
90   See, for example, *Europemballage and Continental Can v Commission* Case 6/72 [1973] ECR 215.
91   Case 22/78 *Hugin v Commission* [1979] ECR 1869.
92   Case 40/73 *Suiker Unie* [1975] ECR 1663.
93   See the Fourteenth Report on Competition Policy (1985) at pages 77 to 79.

refusing to supply IPOs (installation productivity options) to users of non-IBM CPUs.

(3) There must be an effect on trade between Member States. This is the same requirement as under Article 85(1).

8.6.3.2 Consequences of breach

Where a breach of Article 86 is found, the Commission has power to impose a fine up to the same limit as under Article 85. The Commission also has power to order the undertaking or undertakings concerned to cease the objectionable practice.[94] Where there is (a) a strong *prima facie* case of breach; (b) an urgent need for relief; and (c) the likelihood of irreparable harm to an injured party if no relief is granted, the Commission has power to adopt interim measures pending a final decision.[95]

In addition, it has been held by the House of Lords in *Garden Cottage Foods v Milk Marketing Board*[96] that it is arguable that Article 86 imposes a duty akin to a statutory duty breach of which gives rise to a civil cause of action on the part of anyone who suffers damage as a result. In *Bourgoin SA v Ministry of Agriculture Fisheries and Food*[97] the Court of Appeal held, albeit *obiter*, that this was indeed the case. Thus although the matter has yet finally to be determined, it appears that a civil action for an injunction and damages may be brought. Certainly the matter is sufficiently arguable for an interlocutory injunction potentially to be available as a remedy.

8.6.4 Exclusive distribution agreements

In an exclusive distribution agreement, a producer of software or other products agrees with a distributor that, within a given geographical area, the producer will supply his goods only to that distributor. Such agreements are very common. The element of exclusivity is usually required by the distributor who seeks protection from intra-brand competition within his territory in return for his investment in marketing the goods. The producer is prepared to grant exclusivity in order to ensure that the distributor devotes maximum attention to the promotion of the goods, and may exact an obligation from the distributor not to deal in competitive products as a *quid pro quo*.

In a distribution network, where one producer supplies a number of distributors each of whom has been granted his own geographical area of exclusivity, it is usual to impose on each distributor an obligation not to sell the goods in the territory of other distributors in the network. The

---

94 Regulation 17, Art. 3(1). This also applies to breaches of Article 85.
95 *Camera Care Ltd v Commission* Case 792/79R [1980] ECR 119.
96 [1984] AC 130.
97 [1985] 3 WLR 1027. See also *An Bord Baine v Milk Marketing Board* [1988] 1 CMLR 605.

natural result of this is not merely the exclusion of intra-brand competition but also the establishment of a series of barriers to interstate trade.

Notwithstanding the obvious threats that such arrangements pose to trade within the common market, the Commission has recognised that exclusive distribution agreements do have justifying benefits:

> Exclusive distribution agreements facilitate the promotion of sales of a product and lead to intensive marketing and to continuity of supplies while at the same time rationalising distribution; they stimulate competition between the products of different manufacturers. The appointment of an exclusive distributor who will take over sales promotion, customer services and carrying of stocks is often the most effective way, and sometimes the only way, for the manufacturer to enter a market and compete with other manufacturers already present . . .[98]

Accordingly, exclusive distribution agreements have been granted block exemptions, first by Regulation 67/67 and now by Regulation 1983/83.

8.6.4.1 The block exemption

Article 1 of Regulation 1983/83 provides:

> Pursuant to Article 85(3) of the Treaty and subject to the provisions of this Regulation, it is hereby declared that Article 85(1) of the Treaty shall not apply to agreements to which only two undertakings are party and whereby one party agrees with the other to supply certain goods for resale within the whole or a defined area of the common market only to that other.

Thus this exemption does not apply to services, nor does it apply if the goods are processed in some way that adds significant value to them. Thus it does not apply to OEM (Original Equipment Manufacturer) purchase agreements.[99]

8.6.4.2 The white list

Article 2 contains a 'white list' of restrictions which may be included in an exclusive distribution agreement without losing the benefit of the block exemption conferred by Article 1. These are:

(1) An obligation on the producer not to supply the contract goods directly to users within the contract territory.[100]

(2) An obligation on the distributor not to manufacture or sell competing goods.[101]

(3) An obligation on the distributor to obtain all contract goods for resale from the producer.[102]

(4) An obligation on the distributor not actively to sell the contract goods outside the contract territory.[103]

---

98 Preamble to Regulation 83/83, paragraph 6.
99 *ICL/Fujitsu*, Sixteenth Report on Competition Policy (1987), point 72.
100 Regulation 83/83, Article 2(1).
101 *Ibid.*, Article 2(2)(a).
102 *Ibid.*, Article 2(2)(b).
103 *Ibid.*, Article 2(2)(c).

(5) Minimum purchase obligations on the distributor or obligations to purchase whole product ranges.[104]

(6) An obligation on the distributor to sell the goods under specified trade marks or in accordance with the producer's packaging or presentational requirements.[105]

(7) An obligation on the distributor to take specific measures to promote sales, for example by the employment of technically qualified staff.[106]

Exclusive distribution agreements containing restrictions not sanctioned by Article 2 do not qualify for block exemption. In particular, restrictions on 'passive' trading are not permitted – the distributor must remain free to respond to unsolicited orders from outside the contract territory. Furthermore, the producer must remain free to deliver contract goods outside the contract territory to end users based in the territory, even if the end user intends to import the goods into the territory for resale there.

8.6.4.3   The black list

Article 3 contains a 'black list' of situations where the block exemption is not available. These are:

(1) Reciprocal exclusive distribution agreements between producers of identical or equivalent goods.[107]

(2) Non-reciprocal exclusive distribution agreements between producers of identical or equivalent goods where either party has an annual turnover of over 100 million ECUs.[108]

(3) Where consumers cannot obtain the contract goods from a source other than the exclusive distributor.[109] The point of this is that exemption is only available where parallel imports are possible.

(4) Where either or both parties inhibit parallel trade in the contract goods, particularly by the exercise of intellectual property rights.[110] The mere grant of trade mark rights in a distribution agreement does not deprive it of the block exemption, however. There must an exercise of, or an intention to exercise, the rights to impede parallel imports.[111]

---

104   *Ibid.*, Article 2(3)(a).
105   *Ibid.*, Article 2(3)(b).
106   *Ibid.*, Article 2(3)(c).
107   *Ibid.*, Article 3(a).
108   *Ibid.*, Article 3(b).
109   *Ibid.*, Article 3(c).
110   *Ibid.*, Article 3(d).
111   *Hydrotherm v Compact* Case 170/83 [1984] ECR 2999.

8.6.5   Selective distribution agreements

In certain industries, it is common for suppliers to sell goods only through a network of authorised dealers. This is known as 'selective distribution'. Selective distribution is particularly attractive where, as is generally the case with computer software, the supplier wishes to ensure that the products are sold only through outlets that possess a minimum level of technical expertise. Unlike exclusive distribution agreements, there is no general block exemption for selective distribution agreements, although there is a block exemption which is specific to the motor vehicle sector.[112] There is, however, a reasonably well-developed body of case law.

8.6.5.1   Applicability of Article 85(1)

The first question is whether Article 85 applies at all. It is now reasonably well established that, save in exceptional circumstances, a selective distribution system does not fall within Article 85(1) if the following criteria are satisfied:

(1) The resellers must be selected solely on the basis of objective qualitative criteria relating to their technical ability to handle the goods and the suitability of their premises.[113]
(2) The qualitative criteria applied must be reasonably necessary to ensure an adequate distribution of the goods in question.[114]
(3) All properly qualified resellers must be admitted to the system.[115]
(4) The supplier must not take measures likely to obstruct parallel imports or exports.[116]

Article 85(1) may apply, however, if selective distribution is not justified by the nature of the goods, or if qualified resellers are excluded or their numbers limited by quantitative criteria or measures to limit parallel imports are taken.

In the *IBM PC* case,[117] IBM notified the terms of its selective distribution agreement which included requirements, *inter alia*, of sales staff experienced in the business use of microcomputers and trained, or ready to be trained, in use of the PC, appropriate space for demonstration and display of the computers and keeping at least one computer available for demonstration purposes. The Commission approved the agreement as not being caught by Article 85(1) and stated:

> Computers are not simple products. Moreover, apart from the simplest computer bought for use as it were as a toy at home, they are not even single products, but rather a range of different products used together, as are the amplifier, the

---

112   Regulation 123/85.
113   See, for example, *Metro v Commission (No. 1)* Case 26/76 [1977] ECR 1875.
114   See, for example, *L'Oréal v Niuwe AMCK* Case 31/80 [1980] ECR 3775.
115   See, for example, *Hasselblad (GB) Ltd v Commission* Case 86/82 [1984] ECR 883.
116   See, for example, *Ford v Commission (No. 2)* Cases 25 & 26/84 [1985] 3 CMLR 528.
117   [1984] 2 CMLR 342.

turntable and loudspeakers in a hi-fi system. The capabilities and price of the IBM personal computer make the business or professional user the most likely customer. In order first to choose and then operate a computer for business or professional purposes, the buyer must have, or be able to obtain, information or advice on a number of different topics . . .[118]

Notwithstanding the developments in the personal computer market in the intervening period, the same attitude is likely to apply today.

8.6.5.2 *Exemption*

Even if Article 85(1) does apply, it may be possible for a selective distribution agreement to gain exemption under Article 85(3). In *Metro v Commission (No. 1)*[119] the Court held that certain promotional obligations which were imposed on the dealers went further than merely qualitative requirements so that Article 85(1) applied, but nevertheless could be exempted under Article 85(3). These included obligations to enter into six-month supply contracts, to maintain stocks and to achieve adequate turnover in the contract goods.

Where quantitative limits on the numbers of dealers in a particular area are imposed, the Commission has stated[120] that exemptions under Article 85(3) will only be granted in exceptional cases. Nevertheless, exemptions have been granted in four such cases.[121]

8.6.6 Patent licences

8.6.6.1 *The block exemption*

Like Regulation 1983/83 in respect of exclusive distribution agreements, Regulation 2349/83 provides block exemption for patent licences to which only two undertakings are party and which contain one or more of a list of obligations. These include an obligation on the licensor not to license other undertakings to exploit the licensed territory within the common market insofar as a licensed patent remains in force, an obligation on the licensee not to manufacture or use the licensed product or use the patented process in territories within the common market which are licensed to other licensees insofar as the licensed product is protected in those territories by parallel patents and similar provisions.[122] The Regulation also applies to agreements where ancillary know-how is licensed,[123] but not if the know-how is the dominant element.[124]

---

118 *Ibid.*, at 347.
119 Case 26/76 [1977] ECR 1875.
120 Fifth Report on Competition Policy (1976), points 12 and 13.
121 *Omego* [1970] CMLR D49; *BMW* [1975] 1 CMLR D44; *Ivoclar* OJ 1985 L369/1; *Austin Rover Group/Unipart* OJ 1988 L45/34.
122 Regulation 2349/84, Article 1(1).
123 *Ibid.*
124 *Boussois/Interpane* OJ 1987 L50/30. Agreements where know-how is the dominant element are now covered by Regulation 556/89.

8.6.6.2   *The white list*

Article 2 of Regulation 2349/84 contains a 'white list' of obligations which may be included in the licence without losing the benefit of the block exemption, in the same way as Regulation 1983/83. The structure of Article 2 is that, in effect, it is declared that the white-listed terms are not within Article 85(1) but provided that, if by reason of particular circumstances they are, then they are exempted under Article 85(3).[125]

8.6.6.3   *The black list*

Again, Article 3 contains an extensive 'black list' of provisions that must not be included if the block exemption is to apply.

8.6.6.4   *The opposition procedure*

An innovation in Regulation 2349/84 is the provision of an opposition procedure by which agreements which do not fall within Articles 1 and 2 of the Regulation, and are not caught by Article 3, may be notified to the Commission and, if the Commission does not oppose within six months, are automatically given individual exemption.[126]

8.6.7   Know-how licences

8.6.7.1   *The block exemption*

Regulation 556/89 provides block exemption to pure know-how licences and to mixed know-how and patent licences which are not exempted by Regulation 2349/84 to which only two undertakings are party and which contain one or more of the obligations listed in Article 1(1). These include an obligation on the licensor not to license other undertakings to exploit the licensed technology in the licensed territory, an obligation on the licensee not to manufacture or use the licensed product or use the licensed process in territories within the common market which are licensed to other licensees and similar provisions. The exemption is only available where the know-how is identified in an appropriate form and for so long as it remains secret and substantial,[127] and it lasts for 5 years or 10 years depending on the nature of the obligations.[128] The exemption extends to agreements which contain ancillary provisions relating to trade marks or other intellectual property rights.[129]

---

125   Regulation 2349/84, Article 2(2).
126   Regulation 2349/84, Article 4.
127   Regulation 556/89, Article 1(3).
128   *Ibid.*, Article 1(2).
129   *Ibid.*, Article 1(1).

8.6.7.2 *The white list*

Article 2 sets out a 'white list' of permitted obligations in the same way as Article 2 of Regulation 2349/84. Again, the structure of the Article is that it is stipulated that the obligations do not fall within Article 85(1), but if due to particular circumstances they do, they are exempted under Article 85(3).

8.6.7.3 *The black list*

Article 3 sets out a 'black list' of prohibited obligations, the inclusion of which nullifies the block exemption, in the same way as Article 3 of Regulation 2349/84.

8.6.7.4 *The opposition procedure*

As with Regulation 2349/84, Article 4 provides for an opposition procedure for agreements that are not covered by Articles 1 and 2, but excluding those within Article 3. The opposition period is again six months.

8.6.8 Copyright licences

Although block exemptions have now been promulgated for patent licences, know-how licences and franchise agreements, there is no block exemption which applies to copyright licences. Furthermore, there is as yet relatively little case law on the subject.[130] Such case law as there is, however, shows that copyright licences are capable of infringing Articles 85 and 86. In *Coditel v Ciné Vog Films (No. 2)*[131] the Court of Justice held that an exclusive licence to exhibit a film in cinemas within a Member State did not of itself infringe Article 85(1), but did not rule out the possibility that Article 85(1) might apply if there was some unreasonable exercise of copyright. In *Film Purchases by German Television Stations*[132] the Commission held that Article 85(1) did apply to agreements for the purchase of exclusive rights to broadcast MGM films throughout most of German-speaking Europe since the large number of films affected by, and the duration of, the agreements constituted artificial barriers to competition from other undertakings. Exemption was granted under Article 85(3), however, after the agreements were amended to enable third parties to gain greater access to the films. In *Ministère Public v Tournier, Lucazeau v SACEM*[133] the Court held that the charging of excessive royalties under copyright licences by a collecting society was capable of being an abuse of a dominant position under Article 86. In the

---

130 Most copyright cases which have come before the European courts have been concerned with the application of Articles 30 to 36.
131 Case 262/81 [1982] ECR 3381.
132 OJ 1989 L284/36. Under appeal.
133 Cases 395/87, 241 and 244/88 [1991] CMLRAR 248.

TV Listings cases,[134] the Court of First Instance held that the refusal of the broadcasters to grant copyright licences so as to prevent the marketing of a pan-Irish television guide was an abuse of a dominant position.

On general principles, one may expect that copyright licences which contain export bans, no-challenge clauses, non-competition clauses and the like will potentially infringe Article 85(1). This is confirmed by the statement of the Commission that it regards copyright licences as analogous to patent licences.[135] It remains to be seen precisely what attitude will be taken by the Commission and the Court to copyright licences for computer software, however. For example, it is uncertain whether Article 85(1) could apply to such common restrictions in software licences as limitations to specified hardware and locations. It is arguable that these restrictions are legitimate exercises of the copyright owner's rights which are necessary to protect his interests, and so are not caught.

Given that most of the software industry depends on licences under copyright rather than on patent or know-how licences, the uncertainty of the present position is unsatisfactory. The best solution would be for the software industry to lobby for an appropriate block exemption. This is unlikely to be feasible until the Directive on the Protection of Computer Software is in effect, however.

134   *Radio Telefís Éireann v Commission* Case T69/89 [1991] CMLRAR 586; *British Broadcasting Corporation v Commission* Case T70/89 [1991] CMLRAR 669; *Independent Television Publications Ltd v Commission* Case T76/89 [1991] CMLRAR 743.
135   Twelfth Report on Competition Policy (1983), paragraph 878.

9 Remedies

9.0 INTRODUCTION

In this chapter, consideration is given to the general principles governing the following remedies, and to their specific application to computer software:

(1) The interlocutory injunction;
(2) Anton Piller relief;
(3) The Mareva injunction;
(4) Inquiry as to damages for infringement;
(5) An account of profits for infringement;
(6) Statutory remedies under the 1988 Act;
(7) Conversion damages;
(8) Remedies in criminal law.

Interlocutory remedies are considered in detail, because of their paramount importance in this field.

9.1 THE INTERLOCUTORY INJUNCTION

The interlocutory injunction is a vital remedy in the protection of intellectual property. Very frequently a considerable number of years will pass between issue of a writ and trial of the action. If, during that period, software may be copied without restraint, then by the time the case is heard, it may not be possible to repay the damage that had been done to the developer of the program. This is particularly so in the case of programs intended for a mass market. Such programs frequently appeal to the public by reason of their novelty, and often have a limited useful commercial life.

On learning that a program is being copied, the owner of the software may wish to obtain immediate interim relief from the courts. However, at this early stage in the litigation it will not be possible for the court clearly to determine the merits of the case. Accordingly, a set of guidelines were laid down by the House of Lords in *American Cyanamid Co. v Ethicon Ltd*[1] to be considered when deciding whether or not to grant interim relief

---

1   [1975] AC 396.

until trial. The essential principle behind these guidelines is that the court should attempt to do justice between the parties by a consideration of their potential losses pending trial.

Six factors are taken into consideration:[2]

(1) Whether the plaintiff can show that he has a serious case to be tried.

(2) Whether, if successful at trial, damages would be an adequate remedy for the plaintiff.

(3) Whether, if an injunction is granted, the plaintiff's cross-undertaking in damages would adequately compensate the defendant for his loss.

(4) If damages would not adequately compensate either party, who would be more inconvenienced by the grant or refusal of an order pending trial (the balance of convenience).

(5) If the balance of convenience is evenly divided, whether the *status quo* is preserved by grant or refusal of an injunction.

(6) Where all other factors are evenly balanced the court may take into account the relevant strength of each party's case as revealed by affidavit evidence.

9.1.1   A serious question to be tried

In the *American Cyanamid* decision Lord Diplock indicated that a plaintiff does not have to go very far to show that there is a serious question to be tried. He rejected the view that the plaintiff must show a *prima facie* case or a probability that he will succeed. He stated:[3] 'The court no doubt must be satisfied that the claim is not frivolous or vexatious; in other words, that there is a serious question to be tried.'

If all the plaintiff has to do is show that his case is not frivolous or vexatious, then an interlocutory injunction could be granted where there is little real prospect of success at trial. The term 'frivolous or vexatious' has been considered in a number of cases,[4] and it has been held that a claim is frivolous or vexatious if it is obviously ridiculous, groundless or manifestly fictitious. It is clear that an action may stand little chance of success without being frivolous or vexatious.

In *Mothercare Ltd v Robson Books Ltd*[5] Megarry VC held that the burden on the plaintiff at the interlocutory stage was substantially higher than merely to show that his claim was not ridiculous. He indicated that it was undesirable to use the term 'frivolous' or 'vexatious', as the plaintiff

---

2   *Ibid. per* Lord Diplock at 407 to 409.
3   *Ibid.* at 407.
4   On applications to strike out a claim under RSC Order 18 rule 19(l)(b). See for example *Norman v Matthews* (1916) 85 LJKB 857 at 859 and *Day & William Hill (Park Lane) Limited* [1949] 1 KB 632.
5   [1979] FSR 466.

must show that he has real and substantial prospect of success at trial. An honest but hopelessly optimistic claim was not sufficient.[6]

In *Re Lord Cable*,[7] Slade J made it clear that a plaintiff must produce clear evidence at the interlocutory stage to back up the contention that there was a serious question to be tried. He stated that:

> In my judgment it is still necessary for any plaintiff who is seeking interlocutory relief to adduce sufficiently precise factual evidence to satisfy the court that he has a real prospect of succeeding in his claim for a permanent injunction at the trial. If the facts adduced by him in support of his motion do not by themselves suffice to satisfy the court as to this, he cannot in my judgment expect it to assist him by inventing hypotheses of fact upon which he might have a real prospect of success.[8]

In Australia[9] and in South Africa[10] courts have declined to follow the *American Cyanamid* approach in so far as it relieves the plaintiff from showing that he has a substantial prospect of success at trial.

It should be noted, however, that *American Cyanamid* does not require a defendant to show that his defence has a serious prospect of success at trial in order to defeat an interlocutory injunction. It is sufficient for the defendant to satisfy the court that he has a genuine intention to defend the action; and consideration will then proceed to the adequacy of damage for each party.[11] If a plaintiff considers that there is no arguable defence to the action, then the appropriate course is to apply for summary judgment under RSC Order 14, rather than an interlocutory injunction.

9.1.2 The preparation of interlocutory evidence in software litigation

It is clear from the above authorities that it is not sufficient for a plaintiff to seek interlocutory relief without giving a careful explanation in evidence of the merits of the case. However, there are particular difficulties in the preparation of affidavit evidence for interlocutory relief in computer software cases.

The difficulties of proof of infringement at the interlocutory stage of proceedings, which takes place before discovery in the action, is well illustrated by the case of *Thrustcode v W.W. Computing*.[12] The plaintiff alleged infringement of copyright and breach of confidence in two of its computer programs by a similar program produced by the defendant, and sought interlocutory relief. At the hearing of the motion, the plaintiff produced in evidence neither its complete source code nor its complete object code but relied on some 75 lines of source code. Megarry VC held that there was no arguable case of infringement and dismissed the motion.

---

6 *Ibid.* at 473 to 474.
7 [1977] 1 WLR 7. This was approved by the Court of Appeal in *Moran v Lloyd's* [1981] 1 Ll.R 423.
8 *Ibid.* at 19 to 20.
9 *Firth Industries Ltd v Polyglas Engineering Pty Ltd* [1977] RPC 213.
10 *Beecham Group Ltd v B.M. Group Pty Ltd* [1977] RPC 220.
11 *Quantel Ltd v Shima Seiki Europe Ltd* [1990] RPC 436.
12 [1983] FSR 502.

He found it impossible to say that either source or object code had been copied, in the absence of sufficient evidence of the source or object codes alleged to have been reproduced or of any evidence in relation to the allegedly infringing source and object codes.[13]

It is clear from the *Thrustcode* decision that it is not possible to establish infringement of copyright in a program merely by reliance on the fact that the alleged infringement performs the same function. Where the claim is to copyright in the program itself, the results produced by operation of the program should not be confused with the program instructions in which copyright is claimed.

The Vice-Chancellor went on to point out that it is necessary to compare the copyright work with the alleged infringement to see if copying has actually occurred. If both works are invisible then normally they must be reproduced in visible form, or in a form that is in some way perceptible, before it can be determined whether one infringes the other.[14]

He envisaged that it would normally be necessary to have a printout of both the plaintiff's and the defendant's programs, or of substantial parts of both, to make a direct comparison between the two. As, in the case before him, insufficient portions of the plaintiff's program had been exhibited, and the argument of infringement was based on inference from the functions of the programs rather than on direct evidence of similarities, the Vice-Chancellor's primary finding was that there was no arguable case of infringement.

The Vice-Chancellor observed that any plaintiff may experience grave practical difficulties in obtaining any interlocutory relief whatsoever in copyright claims for software infringement. With reference to the necessity to compare printouts of both the plaintiff's and the defendant's programs, it was observed that there should be no real difficulty for a plaintiff to exhibit a printout of the program alleged to have been infringed. He went on to suggest, however that:

> The Plaintiff may encounter grave difficulties in relation to the defendant's program at the interlocutory stage, before there has been any discovery, for he may well be quite unable to demonstrate in any direct way that what is in the defendant's software is in breach of the plaintiff's copyright. In this case, the plaintiff unsuccessfully sought access to the defendant's programs, and the position of other plaintiffs may well be similar.[15]

This suggests that a plaintiff must include in his evidence in support of an interlocutory injunction a visibly perceptible representation of the contents of the defendant's software. However, the only way he can obtain such a representation may be from the defendant himself, who at that stage may be under no obligation to disclose such a document.

13   *Ibid. per* Megarry VC at 507 to 508.
14   *Ibid.* at 505 to 506.
15   *Ibid.* at 508.

The Vice-Chancellor's concerns in this respect have been justified by subsequent cases. In *Computer Aided Designs (UK) Ltd v Bolwell*[16] the plaintiff unsuccessfully applied for inspection of the defendant's source listings at the *inter partes* hearing for an interlocutory injunction. Both applications were refused as the plaintiff had failed to demonstrate a real prospect of success at trial.

By contrast, in *M.S. Associates Ltd v Power & Another*[17] the defendant had voluntarily given the plaintiff access to parts of his program prior to commencement of the litigation. In the circumstances, the plaintiff was able to present a detailed comparison as a result of initial inspection, and an order for a further inspection was agreed prior to the *inter partes* hearing.

Assuming that a defendant is not willing to grant access to his source code, the problem with an application for inspection prior to discovery is that it is necessary for the plaintiff to demonstrate an arguable case of infringement in order to obtain such an order;[18] and yet the very purpose of the application may be to assist in showing an arguable case in an application for an interlocutory injunction.

One method of overcoming this problem is suggested by the judgment of Hoffmann J in the *Bolwell* case discussed above. Counsel for the plaintiff had argued that the refusal of the defendant to give inspection suggested that it had something to hide. The judge considered that there would have been force in this point if the plaintiff had suggested inspection by an independent expert before commencing proceedings. However, in the *Bolwell* case, the plaintiff had not taken this course, but had launched proceedings together with an application for inspection by the plaintiff itself (later modified to inspection by an agent). In the circumstances the defendant could not be blamed for leaving the plaintiff to justify its claims for interlocutory relief and inspection on the evidence which it had available.

This indicates that a request for inspection by an independent expert prior to commencement of proceedings is an important first step; refusal of inspection by such an expert may lead to adverse inferences against the defendant.

Other methods of presentation of evidence to overcome this problem are considered below.

9.1.3 Presentation of affidavit evidence

The *Thrustcode* decision is indicative of the way in which affidavit evidence may be presented in order to show an arguable case of infringement. A plaintiff will generally have access to no more than the defendant's program in object form (whether on disk or otherwise). The evidence which it will be necessary to adduce will depend entirely on the way in

---

16   IPD April 1990 15.
17   [1988] FSR 242.
18   *Unilever Ltd v Pearce* [1985] FSR 475; *Smith Myers Communications Ltd v Motorola Ltd* [1991] FSR 262.

which it is alleged that the defendant has copied the plaintiff's program. If the defendant has merely made a slavish copy of the object program then it would be a simple matter to exhibit printouts of both object codes in hexadecimal or binary form. Points of similarity would be immediately apparent on visual examination.

The case becomes more complex where the allegation is that the defendant has had access to, and has copied, the plaintiff's source code. The object code might appear entirely different, depending on which compiler was used, even if the source code had been closely copied. For this reason it is not normally possible to work back from object to source code. An alternative approach to the proof of copying is for the plaintiff to work forward from his own source code, using different compilers to produce a variety of object code printouts. Experiments with a variety of available compilers may produce an object code of substantial similarity to the defendant's if source code has in fact been copied.

The problem is more complex where the case does not depend on textual copying, but rather on copying of structure, sequence and order. How is it possible to present an arguable case of infringement, in the absence of inspection of source code?

The best method available, at least to present evidence in support of an application for inspection, may be to rely upon similarities in structure, sequence and order of the program as perceived by the user. It is an obvious fallacy to draw firm conclusions as to the structure of the code from screen output; on the other hand there is a causal relationship between the screen output and the underlying code. The more detailed the similarities between screen outputs, the more likely it may appear that the respective codes will exhibit structural similarities.[19]

Evidence of this nature may be presented in the form of an expert report and will be considerably strengthened by a comparison of the programs in issue with third-party programs, showing that the similarities relied upon are not present in those programs. Furthermore, the court may attach considerable weight to the reproduction of errors or capricious features in the programs in issue.[20]

Such evidence should be accompanied by proof of the defendant's access to the plaintiff's source code, and of the opportunity to copy.

This approach would be likely to be insufficient to prove a case of copying at trial. However, inferential evidence of this nature may require the defendant to accede to inspection of his source listing, particularly if he intends to support a denial of copying with a positive case of independent development.

---

19   In *Whelan Inc. v Jaslow Dental Laboratory Inc.* [1987] FSR 1, the Court was prepared to treat similarities of screen outputs as inferential evidence of copying. See Chapter 5 paragraph 5.1.1.6 for a more detailed discussion.
20   *Per* Hoffmann J in *Billhofer Maschinenfabrik GmbH v T.H. Dixon & Co. Ltd* [1990] FSR 105.

9.1.4 Damages as an adequate remedy

9.1.4.1 *Irreparable harm to the plaintiff*

Where both plaintiff and defendant are substantial companies, where the plaintiff's goods are firmly established and identified in the market, and where there is no suggestion that the inferior quality of the defendant's goods is likely to be confused with and damage the plaintiff's reputation, it may well be that the plaintiff will be compensated by payment of damages which the defendant will be able to pay. In *T.J. Smith & Nephew Ltd v 3M U.K. Plc*[21] Lawton LJ observed as a general principle that where a plaintiff has been in the habit of granting licences and accepting royalty payments, that may well entitle the court to infer that damages would be an adequate remedy at the end of the day, and that royalty payments are a useful method of assessing the quantum of such damages.[22]

On the other hand there are numerous cases when damages would simply not provide an adequate remedy for the plaintiff. This is particularly the case where the plaintiff's legal rights are limited to a short period of time. In *Corruplast Ltd v George Harrison (Agencies) Ltd*[23] the plaintiff was the owner of a patent which had 14 months to run before the grant of licences of right. Due to substantial investment in the product the plaintiff had just reached the point where the market was beginning to turn in its favour. The Court of Appeal held that at this delicate point in its business, damages could not compensate the plaintiff for the disruption that the launch of the defendant's product would cause it.

The same point may be taken when the useful commercial life of a product is limited in duration. In *Graff Electronic Machines Ltd v Dawoodey & Others* Walton J stated:

> The crucial matter is, in all advanced electronic equipment, lead time. A person can produce the most effective market leader, but he will only have the market to exploit to the full for a comparatively short period during which time his rivals will be thinking up ways of doing exactly the same thing . . . so that any new product only has a comparatively short time in which it is the market leader . . . and that is the very point which the plaintiff has just reached. The defendants are now threatening to put their product on the market.[24]

In those circumstances, damages would clearly not be an adequate remedy for destruction of the plaintiff's market lead.

9.1.4.2 *Irreparable harm to the defendant*

On the other hand, damages will seldom be an adequate remedy for a defendant who is prevented from selling a product for a number of years.

---

21 [1983] RPC 92.
22 *Ibid.* at 102.
23 [1978] RPC 761.
24 6 April 1984 (unreported).

If the defendant has just entered the market, it will be particularly difficult to assess how many articles he would have sold but for the grant of the injunction. This is a relevant factor in the consideration of a grant of an interlocutory injunction. In *Brupat Ltd & Another v Sanford Marine Products Ltd* Templeman LJ observed:

> The second question is whether the defendant can be protected by damages. The answer to that, in my judgment, is no. No one can establish the number of sales which the defendants would have made if they had not been restrained from selling the Seaclaw. There is no past history on which to base any estimates. The defendants are beginning their venture selling the Seaclaw anchor and so there is no past experience.[25]

9.1.5   The balance of convenience

Assuming that both sides are likely to suffer damage which cannot be compensated in money, the court will be compelled to consider the balance of convenience. Factors relevant to the balance of convenience vary from case to case. In each case, the court attempts to balance irreparable harm to the plaintiff against irreparable harm to the defendant. One matter of importance in computer software cases is likely to be the financial status of the defendant. Very frequently, a large company will be claiming that an individual or software house of limited resources has made unauthorised copies of their software.

It has long been accepted by the courts that the inability of a defendant to meet an award of damages is a factor to be taken into account in finding where the balance of convenience lies. If a plaintiff is able to assert that because of a defendant's impecuniosity, the defendant will be unable to pay such damages as may be awarded at trial, then he can allege with some justification that even loss which is quantifiable in money terms becomes uncompensatable. On this thesis, every sale by the defendant pending trial does irreparable harm to the plaintiff.

9.1.6   Payment into joint accounts

In order to mitigate the potential severity of this argument against impoverished defendants, the courts have become increasingly willing to accept offers by defendants to pay a percentage of the selling price of each article sold by them into a joint bank account, pending trial. The payment in of such sum provides the plaintiff with some security for his damages and therefore the offer itself becomes another factor to be weighed in the balance of convenience. It has proved particularly effective where a defendant has been able to show that were an interlocutory injunction to be granted the company would be forced into liquidation, and therefore he would be denied the opportunity to argue his case at trial.

---

25   [1983] RPC 61 at 64.

In the case of *Vernons v UPC*[26] the Vice-Chancellor accepted an undertaking by impoverished defendants to pay 5 per cent of the selling price of each of the disputed articles sold by them into a bank account, and on that basis refused to grant an injunction. He stated:

> It would be intolerable if the *Cyanamid* case was allowed to become a charter of success for all rich companies who seek interlocutory injunctions against poor companies, in cases in which damages would be an adequate remedy enabling them to obtain an injunction merely on showing that there is a serious question to be tried.

It is of interest that in the *Vernons* case the 5 per cent figure was considered acceptable. The action, could, if successful have entitled the plaintiff to damages which concerned infringement of copyright and breach of confidence, for conversion under section 18 of the Copyright Act 1956. Conversion damages could have amounted to the entirety of the defendant's turnover in the disputed articles.[27] Of course, it would be pointless for a court to insist on a payment in of too substantial a percentage of turnover pending trial, since such a requirement would be just as certain to drive the defendant into liquidation as the grant of an injunction. It would appear then that in assessing the quantum of a payment in, the court takes into consideration the comparative effects on both parties.

The question of payment in was considered by the Court of Appeal in *Brupat Ltd & Another v Sanford Marine Products Ltd*.[28] The plaintiffs sought an interlocutory injunction to restrain infringement of patent against the defendants, who were a £2 company and not able to provide any security out of their existing assets. On the other hand, the defendants' entire business consisted of manufacture and sale of the product in dispute, and there was no doubt that an interlocutory injunction would force them into liquidation. At first instance, Falconer J granted an injunction. The Court of Appeal allowed the defendants' appeal on their undertaking to set aside in a bank account in the joint names of the respective solicitors 7 per cent of all the moneys which they obtained as a result of the sale of alleged infringements.

Again, the percentage figure that was acceptable to the Court is of interest in this case. The plaintiffs argued that the defendants should pay in a figure of 40 per cent of their gross profits, the profit figure which the plaintiffs themselves made on their goods. The Court of Appeal rejected this figure as too high. Templeman LJ stated that:

> In any event it would be unfair to require 40 per cent security for all Sea Claw anchors which the defendants manage to sell because *non constat* that the

---

26 [1980] FSR 179.
27 See for example *Lewis Trusts v Bamber Stores Ltd* [1983] FSR 453.
28 [1983] RPC 61.

plaintiffs would in fact have lost sales. The defendants would be making their own commercial campaigns and as far as appears from the evidence they would be competing and taking orders away from manufacturers other than the plaintiffs. They may even be persuading people to buy more anchors. The 40 per cent figure is not particularly helpful in the present case where what is offered is a percentage of all anchors which the defendants make whether or not they have been made at the cost of sales by the plaintiffs.[29]

However, where a court regards the defendant's fears of liquidation as exaggerated, or where the defendant's conduct in commencing his business has been in such disregard of the plaintiff's right that liquidation may really be said to be his own fault, then the court may be minded to grant an injunction despite an offer to pay in. In *Belfast Ropework Company Limited v Pixdane Limited* [30] the plaintiff was a substantial manufacturing company which owned a patent in the United Kingdom for agricultural twine. The defendant, a company with scant resources, began to import cheap twine from Portugal into the United Kingdom, and the plaintiff moved for an interlocutory injunction. The defendant had been warned of the existence of the patent about one month before it began the acts complained of.

A guarantee of £15,000 was offered to the plaintiff by way of security, and the defendant gave evidence that it would go into liquidation if injuncted pending trial. At first instance, Whitford J refused to grant the injunction, but was overruled on appeal.

The Court of Appeal was clearly influenced by the fact that the judge had found that the plaintiff had 'an immensely arguable case'.[31] Furthermore, the Court took the view that the defendant had courted litigation by starting on that course of trading in the first place:

> It is said that if the injunction is granted, the defendant company will be unable to finance the defence of the action and that the action will go unfought. If that is the position, it is perhaps a misfortune which attends starting a venture of this kind in the circumstances in which this venture was started, knowing that it would almost inevitably involve the defendant company in litigation.[32]

Most importantly, the Court did not accept that the grant of an injunction would be likely to result in the defendant's liquidation. The defendant was no more than a dealer in the alleged infringements, and had no large capital sums tied up in plant or machinery. In the circumstances there seemed no particular reason why it should not simply diversify its business into other goods pending trial.

It should be emphasised that both in *Vernons* and in *Brupat* the Court was satisfied that the offer to pay in would protect the plaintiff against substantially all unquantifiable loss pending trial. In neither case would the plaintiff's goodwill or market be damaged by the defendant's activities.

---

29   *Ibid.* at 66.
30   [1976] FSR 337.
31   *Ibid. per* Buckley LJ at 340.
32   *Ibid.* at 342.

The problem arose in a more acute form in the case of *Roba GmbH &
Others v Cubematic Ltd.*[33] The plaintiffs alleged infringement of patent
by the manufacture of kebab-making machines and obtained *ex parte* relief
against the defendants, who were a £2 company with no assets. At first
instance Falconer J accepted that quite apart from the defendants'
impecuniosity the plaintiffs were likely to suffer unquantifiable damage
pending trial. In particular the plaintiffs were the only manufacturers of
the relevant machines until the defendants commenced their business. The
plaintiffs had only recently begun to establish their market, and alleged
that they were in a particularly delicate position. They also alleged that
they were likely to lose the confidence of their distributors if they were
unable to restrain the defendants pending trial. Furthermore the defendants were undercutting the plaintiffs' selling price on all machines sold by
over £250.

On the other hand, the defendants were a one-product manufacturing
company, who would have gone into immediate liquidation had the injunction been continued.

On a detailed consideration of the *Brupat* case the judge accepted an
offer by the defendant to pay in 10 per cent of their selling price (£45) to
a joint account pending trial. The principles of his judgment were affirmed
by the Court of Appeal who, however, admitted further evidence as to the
plaintiffs' loss of profit and increased the quantity of the payment into
court.[34]

9.1.7 Conclusions

Conclusions on this aspect may be summarised as follows:

(1) The fact that a defendant is impecunious and will be unable to
meet any award of damages made against him at trial is a relevant
factor on the balance of convenience.

(2) The courts have proved increasingly receptive to undertakings
from such defendants to pay money into court pending trial, and have
refused to grant injunctions in the light of such an offer.

(3) An offer of payment in is merely one factor to be weighed in the
balance of convenience. Such offer does not have to protect a plaintiff
entirely against all irreparable harm, but merely to render his potential
harm less than that of the defendant. Any other conclusion would
mean that a test more onerous than *American Cyanamid* would be
applied to impoverished defendants, which the courts have clearly
rejected.

(4) However, where the court regards the defendant's fears of liquidation as exaggerated, or where the defendant's conduct in commencing his business has been in such disregard of the plaintiff's rights

33 2 April 1984 (unreported): see Carr, [1984] 9 EIPR at 250.
34 19 June 1984 (unreported).

that liquidation may really be said to be his own fault, then an injunction may be granted despite the defendant's undertaking.

9.1.8   Preserving the *status quo*

Where irreparable damage to both sides appears to be equally balanced the court will attempt to preserve the *status quo*. The *status quo* is particularly relevant where one party has been long established in the market, and the other is just about to commence on his activities. In those circumstances the *status quo* militates against commencement of new activities. In the *Corruplast* case Goff LJ observed:

> It would not be right that the defendant should be allowed to build up a business which they have only just started, and create a bridge head to enable them . . . to start off from the position of an established business, instead of starting off as a new competitor just coming into the market.[35]

In *Garden Cottage Foods Ltd v Milk Marketing Board*[36] it was stated by Lord Diplock that the *status quo* is assessed at the time immediately preceding the issue of the writ. If there has been an unreasonable delay between the issue of the writ and the motion for an interlocutory injunction, then the *status quo* is assessed at the period immediately preceding the motion.

9.1.9   Delay

An interlocutory injunction is an emergency remedy where the plaintiff claims that he cannot wait for relief until trial. In those circumstances if he has delayed in bringing complaint to the attention of the defendants, that delay militates against grant of an injunction. On the other hand, delay of itself may not disqualify the plaintiff from interlocutory relief. The defendant must show that he has been prejudiced by the delay. In *Radley Gowns Ltd v Costas Spyrou*[37] the plaintiff had delayed for six weeks before sending a letter of complaint about the defendant's activities and then had waited for another two months before the writ was issued. Oliver J disapproved of what he described as 'a somewhat leisurely stroll to the door of the court'. Nonetheless, he granted the injunction in the absence of evidence that the defendant had materially changed position for the worse during the period of delay.[38]

9.1.10   *Ex parte* injunctions

The normal procedure, when seeking interlocutory relief, is for the plaintiff to issue a writ and give the defendant two clear days' notice of his

---

35   Note 23 above at 766.
36   [1984] AC 130.
37   [1975] FSR 455.
38   *Ibid.* at 468 to 469.

application for such relief. However, in a case of extreme urgency, the court has power to grant an *ex parte* injunction for a short period, even before issue of the writ.[39] When seeking such *ex parte* relief the plaintiff will have to satisfy the court that his case is of such great urgency that were he to follow the normal procedure, irreparable damage would be done before his case could be heard. A typical instance might be where the plaintiff learns that unauthorised copies of his computer programs are about to be exhibited at a major exhibition in the next few days. If he were to give normal notice of his application, the exhibition would take place before the case could be heard. In those circumstances, he may seek specified relief to prevent the display of unauthorised reproductions of his software over a limited period, for example, seven days.

Where the plaintiff is seeking *ex parte* relief any delay on his part is likely to be fatal to the application.[40]

9.2 THE ANTON PILLER ORDER

The court has jurisdiction under its rules to make an order for the detention or preservation of the subject-matter as a cause of action and of documents relating thereto.[41] The rules also provide that such application for detention or preservation must be made after giving notice to the defendants.[42]

However, where there is firm evidence of real dishonesty, the courts have been prepared to recognise that if a defendant were warned of the plaintiff's case, he would simply destroy the evidence. Accordingly, in such cases, it is the practice of the courts to hear an *ex parte* application by the plaintiffs in camera. Orders have been granted requiring the defendant to allow the plaintiff and his legal advisers to enter his premises and remove articles and documents which are evidence of infringements.

The grant of this form of *ex parte* order for entry and removal was approved by the Court of Appeal in *Anton Piller K.G. v Manufacturing Processes Ltd & Others*.[43] The plaintiffs were foreign manufacturers who owned the copyright in the design of a high frequency converter used in computers. They learned that the defendants, their English agents, were planning to supply rival manufacturers with confidential information and drawings of their machines.

The available evidence made it clear that there was a strong *prime facie* case that an infringement of the plaintiffs' rights was about to take place.

At first sight, an order of the court made in civil proceedings requiring a defendant to open his doors and to allow the plaintiff and his legal

39 RSC Order 29 rule 1(2) and (3).
40 *Bates v Lord Hailsham of St Marylebone* [1972] 3 All ER 1019.
41 RSC Order 29 rule 2(1).
42 RSC Order 29 rule 2(5).
43 [1976] Ch. 55.

advisers to search and remove large quantities of documents from his premises seems to be a gross invasion of liberty. The relief seems particularly extreme when one considers that the defendant will not have been warned of the application and will not, when the order is made, have had a chance to present his own case. Lord Denning in the *Anton Piller* case was anxious to distinguish the Anton Piller order from a criminal search warrant which would enable the police forcibly to enter premises and remove evidence:

> The order sought in this case is not a search warrant. It does not authorise the plaintiffs' solicitors or anyone else to enter the defendants' premises against their will. It does not authorise the breaking down of any doors nor the slipping in by the back door or getting in by an open door or window. It only authorises entry and inspection with the permission of the defendants.[44]

However, as Lord Denning went on to point out, the order does bring pressure to bear on the defendants to give that permission since if they refuse they may be guilty of a contempt of court, and fined or committed to prison.

The limitations on the grant of such an order are clear. Lord Denning stated that:

> It should only be made where it is essential that the plaintiff should have inspection so that justice can be done between the parties; and when if the defendant were forewarned there is a grave danger that vital evidence will be destroyed, that papers will be burnt and lost or hidden, or taken beyond the jurisdiction so that the ends of justice be defeated: and when the inspection would do no real harm to the defendant or his case.[45]

Certain safeguards were laid down as to the method of execution of an Anton Piller order. The plaintiff should be attended by his solicitor, an officer of the court. The defendant must be served with all the evidence as well as the order and have a reasonable opportunity to consider the order and consult his own solicitor. The defendant is given specific liberty to apply to discharge the order if he has grounds for thinking it has been improperly obtained.[46]

9.2.1   *Ex parte* orders for disclosure

The scope of Anton Piller orders was extended by the Court of Appeal in *EMI Ltd & Another v Sarwar & Haidar*.[47] EMI discovered that infringing copies of cassette recordings were being sold at a low price in a number of shops. In addition to an order requiring entry and removal of documents, they sought an order that the defendants disclose forthwith the names and addresses of the suppliers of the infringing material. The Court

44   *Ibid.* at 60.
45   *Ibid.*
46   *Ibid. per* Lord Denning MR at 61.
47   [1977] FSR 146.

of Appeal regarded this as a legitimate extension of the Anton Piller relief. Lord Denning stated:

> If the retailer is innocent, he has nothing to fear . . . If the retailer is guilty, there is all the more reason for the order: so that he should give the name of the maker and not give him advance warning of the steps being taken to discover him and his works.[48]

This extension is a vital adjunct to Anton Piller relief. Very often in dealing with a large and concerted organisation, the plaintiff finds it particularly difficult to track down the primary source of supply of infringing goods. The ability to find out this identity may enable him to tackle the organisation at its roots.

9.2.2 Anton Piller orders and computer programs

An Anton Piller order may be the only effective form of relief to prevent the illicit marketing of computer software which has achieved widespread popularity. In *Gates v Swift*[49] the plaintiffs were the authors and publishers of a series of computer games written in assembly language. The plaintiffs obtained an Anton Piller order requiring the defendants to admit the plaintiffs' representative to remove all recordings, in magnetic or other computer readable form, embodying any substantial part of their computer programs. The defendants were also required to disclose the whereabouts of all such reproductions, and to display or print out on a computer any such reproductions in computer readable form. They were further required to disclose the names of their suppliers and of the persons to whom they had supplied unauthorised copies.[50]

Obviously, evidence obtained on an Anton Piller order may be invaluable support for an allegation of copyright infringement in computer software. It is of particular difficulty, at an interlocutory stage, to show that the defendant has actually copied the code of the plaintiff's program. The defendant may allege with some force that he has achieved the same result by different programming. However, where it is possible to obtain a printout of his program, or even the source listing of such program, difficulties of proof may well disappear.

On the other hand, a plaintiff should not apply for an Anton Piller order unless it is clear that such order is necessary. In *Systematica Ltd v London Computer Centre Ltd*[51] the plaintiffs obtained an Anton Piller order to search for and remove infringing copies of their computer program. The plaintiffs had evidence of one sale of an unauthorised copy program. It subsequently emerged as a result of the execution of the Anton

---

48 *Ibid.* at 147.
49 [1982] RPC 339.
50 *Ibid.* at 341.
51 [1983] FSR 313.

Piller order that other programs sold by the defendants were not made in infringement of copyright of the plaintiffs' material.

The case is illustrative of the circumstances in which it is appropriate to apply for Anton Piller relief. In *Systematica* the plaintiffs had good grounds for believing that their programs were being copied. On the other hand, it did not appear that the defendants' operation was being conducted in a clandestine and secretive manner or that evidence was likely to be destroyed. Following execution of the Anton Piller order the matter was brought back to court. Whitford J refused to award the plaintiffs their costs. He observed:

> A situation is developing where I think rather too free use is being made by plaintiffs of the *Anton Piller* provision. I do not say that there are not many cases where, without *Anton Piller* relief, the plaintiffs would be in a hopeless position. However, where alleged infringement is taking place and the alleged infringer is operating perfectly openly in his business, as this was . . . where there is nothing to show that the business is being conducted in so underhand and so surreptitious a way that there may be a very good ground for supposing that unless *Anton Piller* action is taken at the end of the day there would be nothing left to fight on, applications of this kind will be made the the peril of the plaintiff so far as the question of costs is concerned.[52]

9.2.3   Non-disclosure of material facts

It should also be noted that, since the plaintiff makes his application without the defendant having a chance to present his case, there is a very high burden on the plaintiff to present all material facts to the court. 'Material' facts include those which are adverse to the plaintiff's case or to the granting of the application. If the plaintiff fails to disclose all material facts, the defendant can apply to the Court for the Anton Piller order to be discharged on this ground. There was a series of cases involving such applications in the late 1980s, from which it appears that the following principles are applicable:

> (1) If the non-disclosure is not concerned with the merits of the plaintiff's case (for example, it is concerned with the plaintiff's ability to give a worthwhile cross-undertaking in damages) and so need not be investigated at trial, the Anton Piller order may be discharged prior to trial.[53]
>
> (2) If the non-disclosure concerns the merits of the case and requires lengthy investigation of evidence, the proper course is for the application to be made at trial.[54]

---

52   *Ibid.* at 316 to 317.
53   *Wardle Fabrics Ltd v G. Myristis Ltd* [1984] FSR 263; *Lock International plc v Berwick* [1989] 1 WLR 1268.
54   *Booker McConnell plc v Plascow* [1985] RPC 425; *Dormeuil Frères SA v Nicolion International (Textiles) Ltd* [1988] 1 WLR 1362.

(3) Even where a material non-disclosure is established on an *inter partes* application prior to trial, the Court retains a discretion not to discharge the Anton Piller order and to continue injunctive relief.[55]

9.2.4 *Columbia Pictures v Robinson*

The judgment in *Columbia Pictures Inc. v Robinson & Others*[56] contains a detailed and biting criticism of the manner in which Anton Piller and Mareva relief was obtained and executed. Since this judgment, it has become far less common for the courts to grant Anton Piller orders, and, when granted, they are accompanied by still further safeguards and undertakings.

The facts of the case were as follows. The defendant ran a business hiring and selling video tapes as well as genuine tapes. His stock contained a large quantity of pirate tapes. The defendant permitted the chief investigation officer of the plaintiff's trade organisation to inspect and take away tapes to check if they were pirated. They had further meetings in which the defendant supplied the officer with information about video pirates. The plaintiff then applied for Anton Piller relief and a Mareva injunction. Its solicitor's affidavit did not refer to the defendant's meetings with the investigation officer, and gave no indication that there was a legitimate side to the defendant's business.

A number of items seized in the raid were lost while in the custody of the plaintiff's solicitors. As a result of the Anton Piller order and Mareva injunction, the defendant ceased trading.

On the defendant's motion for the order to be set aside and for damages, Scott J criticised the plaintiff's solicitors for failing in their duty to make full and frank disclosure of all relevant matters; and concluded that in a number of respects the plaintiff and its solicitors had acted oppressively and in abuse of their powers. He ordered the plaintiff to pay £10,000 damages to the defendant.

The case highlights the dangerous incursion into civil liberties which these type of orders had come to represent during the 1980s. Scott J characterised Anton Piller orders as 'draconian and essentially unfair' and observed:

> . . . a decision whether or not an Anton Piller order should be granted requires a balance to be struck between the plaintiff's needs that the remedies allowed by the civil law for the breach of his rights should be attainable and the requirement of justice that a defendant should not be deprived of his property without being heard. What I have heard in the present case has disposed me to think that the practice of the court has allowed the balance to swing too far in favour of plaintiffs and that Anton Piller orders have been too readily granted and with insufficient safeguards for respondents.[57]

55 *Brinks Mat Ltd v Elcombe* [1988] 1 WLR 1350.
56 [1987] Ch. 38.
57 *Ibid.* at 76.

The *Robinson* case illustrates not only the dangers in applying for relief of this nature, but also the heavy responsibility which is borne by legal advisers in the presentation and execution of such orders. It may well be that the perceived danger of destruction of documents may be met by an immediate order for delivery up, which does not permit a search of the defendant's dwelling house, with the consequent humiliation and family distress which that frequently involves.[58]

9.3   THE MAREVA INJUNCTION

Where there is evidence that software is being copied on a large scale, and that such copying is extremely well organised, a potential defendant may be likely to take measures beyond destruction of evidence. If he is warned that the plaintiff has discovered his activities, he may attempt to transfer assets out of the jurisdiction or otherwise dispose of moneys to prevent execution of judgment against him. The Mareva injunction is a remedy to freeze assets, which has been developed specifically to prevent such deliberate disposals.

This form of injunction was first granted in a shipping dispute. In *Mareva Companie Naveria S.A. v International Bulk Carriers S.A. 'The Mareva'*[59] the Court of Appeal affirmed the grant of an injunction restraining the defendants from removing or disposing out of the jurisdiction moneys standing in their bank account in London.

The width of Mareva injunctions has been substantially broadened since the *Mareva* decision. It is now specifically provided by statute that Mareva injunctions are not restricted to cases where a foreign defendant is likely to transfer his assets abroad.[60] Such an injunction may be granted against any defendant where there is a real fear that he is likely to dispose of or dissipate his assets in order to defeat the plaintiff's claim.

Like Anton Piller relief, an application for a Mareva injunction is normally heard *ex parte* and in camera. The plaintiff must make a full and frank disclosure of all material facts, and must show that he has a good case against the defendant which is likely to succeed at trial. He must further show that the defendant has some assets in the country, and that there is a real risk that he will dispose of those assets before the judgment is executed.[61]

The court also has the power to order a defendant to disclose what his assets are and where they may be found. This additional discovery has been regarded as necessary for the effective operation of the injunction.

---

58   *Per* Hoffmann J in *Lock Plc v Beswick* [1989] 1 WLR 1268 at 1281.
59   [1980] 1 All ER 213.
60   Supreme Court Act 1981 section 37(3).
61   *Per* Mustill J in *Third Chandris Corporation v Unimarine S.A.* [1979] QB 645.

The court retains a discretion notwithstanding proof of material to non-disclosure, nevertheless to continue the order or to make a new order with varied terms.[62]

The operation of the Mareva injunction in cases of infringement of copyright is shown by the case of *CBS U.K. Ltd v Lambert & Another.*[63] The case concerned piracy of records and cassettes. It was discovered that although one of the defendants was pretending to be unemployed he was spending large sums of money on assets, such as motor cars, which could be easily disposed of. CBS was granted a combined form of Anton Piller and Mareva relief, to enter and search the defendant's premises, and to restrain disposal of assets. The Court was prepared to freeze all manner of disposable assets including motor vehicles, jewellery, works of art and other valuables. Further, the Court ordered that the motor cars should be delivered up to the plaintiff's solicitors pending trial and that the defendant should disclose the value, nature and whereabouts of all his assets, including bank accounts.

A combination of Anton Piller and Mareva relief may have a disastrous effect on a defendant's business. His premises will be searched and amounts of articles and documents will be removed. His bank accounts and other assets will be frozen, and his weekly spending may be limited to some small provision for day to day and legal expenses.

A plaintiff, when obtaining any form of interlocutory relief, is required to give a cross-undertaking in damages, promising to pay the defendant any damage that he has suffered if the court subsequently decides that the order should not have been granted. This cross-undertaking may have particular importance in cases where Anton Piller and Mareva relief have been obtained where damages suffered is very great.[64]

In summary, remedies of the most extreme form have been developed by the courts to combat infringement of copyright. The remedies available in civil actions appear at present to be more effective to combat software piracy than those offered by the criminal law.[65] However, it should be borne in mind that those orders are dangerous weapons. They should not be applied for unless the plaintiff is very certain of the full facts and of the strength of his case.

---

62   See for example *Brinks Mat Ltd v Elcombe* [1988] 1 WLR 1350.
63   [1983] Ch. 37.
64   In *Jeffrey Rogers Knitwear Productions Ltd v Vinola (Knitwear) Ltd* [1985] FSR 184, Whitford J gave leave for the defendants to proceed on an inquiry as to damages on the cross-undertaking without waiting for the trial of the action. See also the *Robinson* case discussed above.
65   But extended powers of search and seizure under criminal law have been applied to computer programs: Copyright (Computer Software) Amendment Act 1985 section 3 and Copyright, Designs and Patents Act 1988 sections 108 and 109.

9.4   COMPENSATION FOR LOSS OF PROFITS

It is standard practice in copyright and patent actions to claim an inquiry as to damages or an account of profits in the alternative in relation to acts of infringement. Election between these remedies may then be postponed until the trial has been heard. It is therefore necessary to consider the principles on which damages and accounts of profits are assessed, and the application of those principles to computer programs.

9.4.1   An inquiry as to damages

Damages for infringement of copyright, infringement of patent and breach of confidence are assessed on a tortious measure.[66] The general principles of assessment of infringement damages were made clear by Lord Wilberforce in the case of *General Tire & Rubber Co. v Firestone Tyre & Rubber Co. Ltd*:[67] 'The measure of damages is to be, so far as possible, that sum of money which will put the injured party in the same position as he would have been in if he had not sustained the wrong.'

On any inquiry as to damages the plaintiffs have the burden of proving their loss. Damages are assessed liberally against the defendants, since they are wrongdoers, but the object is to compensate the plaintiffs and not to punish the defendants.

No specific rule of law can be laid down as to assessment of damages, since each case depends on its own facts. However, it is possible to define three broad categories of cases in software litigation where the courts may assess the measure of damages on differing principles.[68]

9.4.1.1   *Where the developer of a computer program has not granted licences*

Where a plaintiff has not granted licences to third parties then the measure of damages for infringement will normally be the profit which would have been realised by the plaintiff if the defendant's sales had been made by him.

This may be the case even where only part of the profits are directly attributable to the infringement. In *United Horse Shoe & Nail Ltd v Stewart & Co.*,[69] the defendants had manufactured nails by use of machines which were held to infringe the plaintiff's patent. It was observed:[70] 'I think it nothing to the purpose to show, if it is shown, that the defenders might have made the nails equally good, and equally cheap, without infringing the pursuers' patent at all.'

---

66   On assessment of damages for breach of confidence see Jones, 'Restitution of Benefits Obtained in Breach of Another's Confidence', [1970] LQR 463.
67   [1976] RPC 197.
68   *Ibid. per* Lord Wilberforce at 212.
69   (1888) 5 RPC 260.
70   *Ibid.* at 264.

Where a software developer exploits his software exclusively by manufacture and sale and does not grant licences to third parties then he may claim that each sale gained by the defendant is a sale lost to him. In those circumstances the measure of damages will normally be the profit which would have been realised by the software developer if all of the defendant's sales had been made by him.[71]

9.4.1.2 *Where licences have been granted*

Where a software house, in the course of its business, has licensed others to manufacture a computer program, then the percentage obtained by it by way of royalty is a convenient figure for the court to adopt when assessing damages for infringement. In the case of *Meters Ltd v Metropolitan Gas Meters Ltd*[72] Fletcher-Moulton LJ propounded the following principle which has subsequently been approved by the House of Lords in the *General Tire* case. He observed that where the owner of a patent had granted licences at a certain figure, every one of the infringing articles might have been rendered non-infringing by applying for and getting that permission. In those circumstances:[73]

> The court takes the number of infringing articles and multiplies that by the sum that would have had to be paid in order to make the manufacture of that article lawful and that is the measure of the damage that has been done by the infringement.

9.4.1.3 *Cases in which no established practice exists*

There is a third category of cases in which it may not be possible to show that there is a normal rate of profit on sales of a particular program, or that any granted licence represents a normal and established commercial royalty figure. In these circumstances a court is likely to assess a reasonable notional royalty that is fair in all the circumstances.[74] Falconer J gave detailed consideration to the question of a reasonable notional royalty in *Catnic Components Ltd & Others v Hill & Smith Ltd*.[75] The following factors influenced him in the determination of a royalty rate:

(1) The plaintiffs had pioneered and developed a market for their product, and dominated that market.
(2) The plaintiffs had ample production capacity and had no need to grant licences to anyone.

---

71 Unless the defendants are able to prove to the contrary; *per* Falconer J, *Catnic Components Ltd & Others v Hill & Smith Ltd* [1983] FSR 512.
72 [1911] 28 RPC 157.
73 *Ibid. per* Fletcher-Moulton LJ at 164.
74 *General Tire* Note 67 above, *per* Lord Wilberforce at 214.
75 Note 71 above at 530.

(3) The plaintiff's evidence was that they would not have granted a licence unless they could have guaranteed that the licensee would not impinge on their market.

While every case is dependent on its own facts, the above considerations are indicative of evidence that it would be useful to introduce on an inquiry as to damages for infringement of proprietary rights in computer software.

9.4.2   An account of profits

In contrast to an inquiry as to damages the object of ordering an account of profits is not to compensate the plaintiff for loss that he has suffered by reason of the tort. It is rather to deprive the defendant of the profits which he has improperly made by his acts of infringement and to transfer such profits to the plaintiff.[76]

Such general principles may be stated very simply. However, because of uncertainties in the results of the application of this doctrine, plaintiffs more usually elect for damages.

Two leading cases in which the principles of accountability for profits have been discussed in relation to patent infringement are *Crosley v The Derby Gas Light Co.*[77] and *Siddell v Vickers.*[78] In both of these cases the defendants were not held accountable for the entire profits made on their sales of infringing articles but only for that proportion of their profits attributable to the infringements. In other words, the Court compared the cost of producing the infringing products with the cost that would have been incurred by the defendants if they had manufactured non-infringing articles. The difference between the two was held to be the measure of account of profits.

By contrast an alternative approach was adopted in the case of *Peter Pan Manufacturing Corporation v Corsets Silhouettes Ltd*[79] (an action for breach of confidence). In that case the Court held that the defendants could not have manufactured the infringing articles in question without using confidential information obtained from the plaintiffs. Therefore the defendants were liable to account for all of their profits made on sales of infringing articles, not merely for excess profits made over and above those profits that they would have made had they used a non-infringing style.

It would appear from the above authorities that where a defendant could have used a non-infringing method for the production of a computer program and has merely obtained a small saving by an infringement, on an account of profits he would merely be liable for that small saving.

---

76   *Siddell v Vickers* (1892) 9 RPC 152.
77   (1838) 3 My. & Cr. 428.
78   Note 76 above.
79   [1964] 1 WLR 96.

Where, however, the program could not have been made without infringement, then he may be held liable for his entire profits, and the election of an account of profits may be considered.

It is to be noted however, that in *Potton Ltd v Yorkclose Ltd*[80] Millett J stated that the 'comparison' test between the cost of infringing and non-infringing products was only applicable where the infringement lay in the process by which the product was made, rather than the product itself.[81]

9.5 STATUTORY REMEDIES UNDER THE 1988 ACT

The 1988 Act contains certain sections which deal specifically with remedies for infringement of copyright. As with other parts of the Act, however, it is necessary to consider the transitional provisions to determine which statute governs particular acts.

Pursuant to paragraph 31(1) of Schedule 1, the remedies for infringement in sections 96 and 97 of the 1988 Act apply only in relation to infringements committed after 1 August 1989. Section 17 of the 1956 Act continues to apply in relation to infringements committed before commencement.

Importantly, conversion damages cannot be claimed after commencement of the new Act 'except for the purposes of proceedings begun before commencement'.[82] This removes the great injustice of conversion damages at least in respect of actions commenced after 1 August 1989.

9.5.1 Civil remedies under the 1988 Act

Pursuant to section 96(2), all such relief by way of damages, injunctions, account or otherwise is available to a plaintiff in an action for infringement of copyright as is available in respect of the infringement of any other property right.

It appears likely that additional damages will be easier to obtain under the 1988 than under the 1956 Act. Under section 17(3) of the 1956 Act the court was empowered to award additional damages, having regard to the flagrancy of the infringement; and to any benefit accruing to the defendant by reason of the infringement; if it was 'satisfied that effective relief would not otherwise be available to the plaintiff'. Under section 97(2) of the 1988 Act, this wording has been altered, and the court may award such additional damages as the justice of the case may require.

As a result of the abolition of section 18 of the 1956 Act, which deemed the plaintiff to be the owner of all infringing copies and thereby entitled him to delivery of infringing copies, the 1988 Act contains specific provisions which provide for delivery up.

---

80 [1990] FSR 11.
81 For a detailed consideration of accounts of profits, see Bentley, [1991] 1 EIPR 5.
82 Schedule 1 paragraph 31(2).

In particular, section 99 entitles a plaintiff to apply for an order for delivery up of infringing copies, but pursuant to section 113(1) such application may not be made after the end of a period of six years from the date on which the infringing copy was made. After delivery has taken place, section 114 enables a plaintiff to apply for an order that seized articles shall be forfeited to him or destroyed.

The 1988 Act also contains a right of 'self-help' enabling a copyright owner to seize and detain infringing copies of a work found exposed or immediately available for sale or hire. However, this right, embodied in section 100 of the Act, has emerged in a weakened form to that originally proposed; and has been made subject to specific safeguards.

In particular, persons are only entitled to enter premises to which the public have access, and may not seize anything in the possession, custody or control of a person at his permanent or regular place of business, and may not use any force.[83]

The intention is clearly to confine this form of seizure to clandestine traders, who frequently sell infringing copies from a suitcase.

Furthermore, section 100 is expressly made subject to section 114, which provides that on an application for the goods to be forfeited or destroyed, court rules shall provide for the service of notice on interested persons.[84]

9.6   CONVERSION DAMAGES

It is still necessary to consider the effect of conversion damages because of their continuing availability in actions commenced before 1 August 1989. Furthermore, in *Ransbury Gema AG v Electrostatic Plant Systems Ltd*[85] the Court of Appeal held that a plaintiff was entitled to amend a statement of claim in an action commenced before 1 August 1989 by the addition of further drawings, and to claim conversion damages in relation to those drawings after 1 August 1989. It was decided that since the drawings were modifications of drawings already in the action, and were alleged to be infringed by the defendant's articles already in the action, the plaintiff was not attempting to make out a new case but persisting in the old story.

This decision may enable a plaintiff in an action in respect of computer software to add additional versions of his program to an action commenced before August 1989 and to claim conversion damages in respect of infringements of these versions.

Section 18(1) of the Copyright Act 1956 entitles the owner of copyright to all rights and remedies for conversion or detention by any person of any infringing copy. For that purpose the owner of the copyright is deemed to

83   Section 100(3).
84   Section 114(3) to (5).
85   [1991] FSR 508. Cf. *Banks v CBS Songs Ltd*, *The Times*, 30 January 1992.

be the owner of every infringing copy of his work since the time when such infringement was made. A successful plaintiff is therefore entitled to claim damages for conversion of all infringing copies under the Torts (Interference with Goods) Act 1977.

The courts have made very high awards in copyright cases for damages for conversion. In particular, where articles have been disposed of for value, conversion damages have been assessed at the market value of such goods, frequently amounting to the defendant's entire turnover in infringing copies.[86] The unfairness of conversion damages is illustrated by the case of *Lewis Trusts v Bambers Stores Ltd.*[87] The defendants had manufactured and sold dresses in infringement of the plaintiff's copyright. Damages for infringement were assessed at a royalty rate of 50p per dress sold and amounted, with interest, to £6,337.53. The plaintiff also claimed conversion damages for the entire sale price of every dress sold. The quantum of damages under this head was affirmed by the Court of Appeal to amount to £171,166.08.

It is apparent that awards of conversion damages far exceed a reasonable royalty rate on each article sold. The difference between infringement and conversion damages was made clear by Lord Scarman in the case of *Infabrics Ltd v Jaytex Ltd*:

> In cases like the present, of industrial design, damages for infringement under section 17 are often small. Limited (in the absence of special circumstances) to the depreciation of the value of the copyright, they can be minimal. In the present case Infabrics paid only a few pounds for the design. But damages for conversion can be very great. If the industrial application of the infringing copies are a success damages are recoverable as if the owner of the copyright was the owner of every infringing copy sold.[88]

9.6.1 Conversion damages under the unamended Copyright Act 1956

Unauthorised copies of computer programs are generally in object form. Therefore the question which is likely to arise most frequently in relation to conversion damages is whether a copy program in object code is an 'infringing copy' within the meaning of section 18 of the Copyright Act 1956.

Section 18(3) of the Act defines 'infringing copy' in relation to a literary work as 'a reproduction of the work other than in the form of a cinematograph film'.

If object code is regarded as a reproduction in material form of source code, then object code made without consent would appear to amount of an 'infringing copy' within section 18.[89] However, this argument was not accepted in the Australian *Apple Computer* decision.[90] If, as in that case,

86   *John Lane, The Bodley Head Ltd v Associated Newspapers Ltd* [1936] 1 KB 715.
87   [1983] FSR 453.
88   [1982] AC 1 at 26.
89   See Chapter 5 above.
90   *Ibid.*

the conversion of source code to object code is held to be an adaptation of the source code, then such acts, even if done without consent, would not constitute infringing copies within the meaning of section 18. The section applies only to reproductions, not adaptations.

Nonetheless, where a copy in object code has been made from a program in object code, it may be that such acts constitute reproduction of an adaptation within section 2(5)(g) of the Copyright Act.[91] Such reproductions would arguably amount to infringing copies for the purpose of conversion damages.

The position would appear to be somewhat clearer in relation to the visual display generated by a computer program. If such display can be regarded as a cinematograph film within the meaning of section 13 of the Act, then an infringing copy is simply defined as 'a copy of the film'.[92]

9.6.2   Conversion damages under the Copyright (Computer Software) Amendment Act 1985

The 1985 Act appears to have done little to clarify the question of recovery of conversion damages in relation to computer software.

Section 1(2) states that a version of a program which is converted into or out of computer language or code, or into a different language or code, is an adaptation of the program.

As previously indicated, adaptations do not constitute infringing copies within the meaning of section 18. Conversion damages are only recoverable in relation to 'reproductions'.

Section 2 of the new Act specifies that reference in the Copyright Act 1956 to reproductions *in a material form* shall include references to the storage of that work in a computer.

The definition of 'infringing copy' in section 18 does not contain a reference to reproductions 'in a material form'. It refers instead to a reproduction 'otherwise than in the form of a cinematograph film'. It is arguable that a court is not entitled by virtue of section 2 of the new Act to include references to the storage of a work in a computer in any part of the Copyright Act 1956 which does not refer to reproduction in a material form. If this argument is accepted, then the recovery of conversion damages for unauthorised storage of a work in a computer is a matter of considerable doubt.

9.7   REMEDIES UNDER THE CRIMINAL LAW

Sections 107 to 110 of the 1988 Act deal with the criminal liability of persons who make or deal in articles which they know, or have reason to

---

91   *Ibid.*
92   Copyright Act 1956 section 18(3)(c).

believe, are infringing copies of a copyright work. It is noteworthy that sections 104 to 106, which set out presumptions as to title and subsistence of copyright, do not apply to proceedings for criminal offences specified in section 107; and therefore that these matters must be proved beyond reasonable doubt.[93]

Under section 108, the court is empowered to order delivery up of infringing copies in proceedings brought pursuant to section 107. Forfeiture or destruction of such articles is subject to the safeguards of section 114.

Section 109 empowers a justice of the peace to issue search warrants in respect of section 107 offences which have been or are about to be committed.

Transitional provisions in respect of section 107 and 109 are contained in Schedule 1 paragraph 33(1) to (2). Sections 107 and 109 apply only to acts done after commencement. Section 21 and 21A and B of the 1956 Act continue to apply in relation to acts done before commencement.

The powers of search and seizure under search warrants have proved useful in combating piracy of videotapes and sound recordings. They are likely to prove equally useful in relation to software piracy. However, it is clear that such powers must be exercised with caution. There is a potential conflict inherent in the grant of such powers between the liberty of a software user and the need to prevent software piracy. This conflict of policy in relation to search and seizure under the criminal law was expressed by Lord Denning MR in *Ghani v Jones*:

> We have to consider on the one hand the freedom of the individual. His privacy and possessions are not to be invaded except for the most compelling reasons. On the other hand we have to consider the interest of society at large in finding out wrongdoers and repressing crime.[94]

9.7.1   The contrast between civil and criminal remedies

The power of search and seizure under the criminal section may be likened in its effect to the grant and execution of an Anton Piller order under civil law.[95] However, many of the safeguards inherent in the grant of an Anton Piller order are absent in relation to the exercise of power under the criminal law. Specifically, a variety of undertakings are given by applicants for Anton Piller relief. These undertakings include:

(1) an undertaking to serve a Notice of Motion returnable within seven days to continue the injunction relief obtained by the application. This means that shortly after the search and seizure, the matter may be reviewed by the court in the light of evidence from both sides;

---

93   Section 107(6); cf. proceedings under section 108 where the presumptions do apply.
94   [1970] 1 QB 693 at 708.
95   For a consideration of Anton Piller relief, see above at paragraph 9.2.

(2) an undertaking to obey any order that the court may subsequently make as to damages sustained by the defendant which the plaintiff ought to pay.

(3) Specific liberty is given to the defendant to move the court to discharge or vary the order on 24 hours notice to the plaintiff's solicitors.

The combined effect of these safeguards is that shortly after execution of the order, a defendant has the opportunity to present his case, and to argue for return of articles and documents if they have been removed without good cause. A defendant is further entitled to claim compensation from the plaintiff in relation to loss sustained by reason of the order, if it subsequently appears that its grant was not justified.

Since these safeguards are not contained in the grant of a criminal search warrant, the remedies of the user of computer software whose goods are seized pursuant to such warrant are necessarily more limited. It may be observed that a considerable period may elapse before the defendant has the opportunity to present his case to the courts, by which time considerable loss may have been sustained for which there is no guarantee of compensation.

9.7.2 Remedies for wrongful seizure and detention

Where goods have been seized and are detained, their owner may bring an action claiming wrongful interference with goods. Section 4 of the Torts (Interference with Goods) Act 1977 specifically empowers a court to make an interlocutory order for delivery up of goods.[96]

In the case of *Patel v The Federation Against Copyright Theft Limited & Another*,[97] this Act formed the basis of a civil claim for wrongful interference with goods following seizure of videotapes under a criminal search warrant obtained pursuant to the provisions of section 21A of the 1956 Act.

Action was commenced for wrongful interference with goods, and a Notice of Motion served for delivery up of the goods. A quantity of videotapes were examined and returned by the defendants, who further gave undertakings to the court to return all further videotapes in their custody which had not been made the subject of a criminal charge by a specified date.

9.7.3 Wrongful interference with goods

The Torts (Interference with Goods) Act 1977 amalgamated the common law actions of trespass, replevin, detinue and conversion into one statutory tort – wrongful interference with goods. At common law, there was an overlap between trespass, detinue and conversion. Conversion, the broadest

---

96 The court also has a general power to make such an order under RSC Order 29 rule 2.
97 18 and 21 December 1984 (unreported).

category, was defined as:[98] 'Deliberate dealing with a chattel in a manner consistent with another's rights whereby that other is deprived of the use and possession of it.'

The scheme of the 1977 Act is as follows. Section 1 defines 'wrongful interference' which includes conversion, trespass to goods and 'any other tort so far as it results in damage to goods or to an interest in goods'.[99]

Section 2(1) of the Act abolished the former tort of detinue. The intention of the provisions appears to be to rationalise the categories of tort but not to exclude any act which would have been wrongful before the statute from the ambit of the new tort. However, it was argued in *Howard E. Perry & Co. Ltd v British Railways Board*[100] that wrongful detention of goods (as opposed to wrongful taking or disposal) was not conversion, and was therefore outside the scope of the new Act. This contention was rejected by Megarry VC who stated with reference to the scope of conversion under the new Act:

> There seems to me to be considerable force in the observation in Clerk & Lindsell on Torts page 682 that 'It is perhaps impossible to frame a definition which will cover every conceivable case' . . . There is a detention . . . which is consciously adverse to the plaintiffs' rights, and this seems to me to be the essence of at least one form of conversion.[101]

Principal acts of conversion include where property is wrongfully taken, where it is wrongfully parted with, and where it is wrongfully retained.

9.7.4 The meaning of 'wrongful' – seizure under warrant

'Wrongful interference' means interference without authority. If, therefore, goods are seized and retained under authority and in obedience to a search warrant, then no action would lie for wrongful interference. The interference would be lawful and 'justifiable'.[102]

9.7.5 Statutory authority – section 109 of the 1988 Act

The first question to be decided is whether a search has been executed in accordance with the powers given by the statute. If a search has been executed in a manner not authorised by statute, then the seizure becomes 'wrongful'. Section 109(1) empowers a justice of the peace to issue a warrant authorising a *constable* to enter and search premises. Section 109(3) permits authorisation in the warrant of *persons to accompany any constable who is executing it*. Section 109(4) empowers a *constable* (as opposed to the persons authorised to accompany him) to seize any article if *he reasonably believes* that it is evidence of an offence under the Copyright Act.

---

98   *Clerk & Lindsell on Torts*, Sweet & Maxwell, 1989 (16th edn), paragraph 22.10.
99   Section 1(d).
100   [1980] 1 WLR 1375.
101   *Ibid.* at 1380.
102   *Ibid. per* Megarry VC at 1381.

9.7.6　Conclusions on scope of copyright search warrants

In those circumstances, the following conclusions may be suggested in relation to section 109 of the 1988 Act:

(1) The warrant must be executed by the constable, not by the persons accompanying him.

(2) The reasonable belief that the goods are infringing must be formed by the constable, not the persons accompanying him.

(3) The persons accompanying him must sensibly be permitted to assist him in determination of his reasonable belief and even (arguably) in removal of the goods from the shelves.

(4) There is no statutory authority for the constable to delegate search for the goods, or formation of the reasonable belief that they are evidence of an offence, to the persons accompanying him.

9.7.7　Detention of goods for a reasonable period

Where articles are lawfully seized pursuant to a search warrant the police are obliged to retain those articles for no longer than is reasonably necessary in order to complete their investigations. This limitation was made clear by the Court of Appeal in *Ghani v Jones*.[103] The plaintiff applied for an interlocutory order for return of goods seized by the police under their common law powers. Talbot J at first instance made it clear that the burden was on the defendant to show that he was entitled to detain the articles:

> The first point which is clear is that the defendant detains these documents and passports from the plaintiff, and the burden is on him to show that he lawfully detains them. The second point is this: has the defendant shown that he has a right to retain these documents?[104]

Lord Denning MR considered a number of requisites to be satisfied in order for the police to continue to retain an article seized under their powers at common law. He stated that:

> The police must not keep the article, nor prevent its removal, for any longer than is reasonably necessary to complete their investigations or preserve it for evidence. If a copy will suffice, it should be made and the original returned. As soon as the case is over, or it is decided not to go on with it, the article should be returned.[105]

This limitation also applies to goods seized under a search warrant, which must be retained for no longer than is reasonably necessary.

103　Note 94 above.
104　*Ibid.* at 696.
105　*Ibid.* at 709.

Accordingly, in *Patel v The Federation Against Copyright Theft Limited & Another* Scott J held that unless the defendants were able to justify retention of videotapes seized, either on the basis of a reasonable suspicion that they were evidence of an offence under section 21 of the Copyright Act, or on the basis that they had not had a reasonable time to consider them, delivery up of the tapes would be ordered.[106]

9.7.8 Detention of goods seized pursuant to section 109

(1) Where a search warrant is lawfully obtained under the Copyright Act, and where in pursuance of such warrant the police search for and seize articles which they have reasonable grounds for believing to be material evidence of the crime for which they enter or of some other crime, they are entitled to detain the goods provided they act reasonably and to retain them no longer than is necessary.

(2) Where goods have been taken and no man has been arrested or charged, the burden is on the police to satisfy strict criteria of reasonable grounds for continuing to detain the goods.

In summary, it may be observed that criminal powers of search and seizure are likely to prove an effective deterrent against copying of computer software. However, the exercise of those powers must be in strict accordance with the words of the statute, and goods held must be examined and, if appropriate, returned, within as short a period as possible. If those powers are not so exercised, a person who has been subject to search and seizure of computer programs has the option to apply to the courts for return of those programs.

---

106 18 December 1984 (unreported).

10 Computer Misuse

10.0 INTRODUCTION

Most of the other chapters of this book are concerned with the protection of computer software against unauthorised use or copying. It is also important, however, to consider the protection available against damage to software (and data). This is an area of the law that has come under close scrutiny since the first edition of this book, with the result that the Computer Misuse Act 1990 has now been enacted. Although this is primarily concerned with 'hacking', the unauthorised obtaining of access to computer systems, it also provides protection against damage to software and data.

10.1 CRIMINAL DAMAGE ACT 1971

The Criminal Damage Act 1971 makes it an offence intentionally or recklessly to destroy or damage any property belonging to another without lawful excuse.[1] Since it is well established that information cannot be stolen,[2] it might be thought that it cannot be damaged either.[3] Thus one can see potential difficulties in the application of the Criminal Damage Act 1971 to damaging computer software or data. These may indeed have resulted in few prosecutions being brought. Where prosecutions have been brought, however, the courts have in the past strained to fit the facts within the statute.

In *Cox v Riley*,[4] the defendant deliberately erased the program from a printed circuit card which was used to operate a computerised machine. He was convicted under the Criminal Damage Act on the basis that the card had itself been damaged in the sense that it had been rendered useless.

---

1 Criminal Damage Act 1971 section 1(1).
2 *Oxford v Moss* (1979), 68 Cr App R 183. See 'Infringement of copyright is not theft' *per* Lord Wilberforce in *Rank Film Distributors Ltd v Video Information Centre* [1982] AC 380, 443 and *R v Lloyd* [1985] QB 829.
3 Particularly since property is defined for this purpose as property of a tangible nature: Criminal Damage Act 1971 section 10.
4 (1986) 83 Cr App R 54.

In *R v Whiteley*,[5] the defendant was a hacker who had gained access to the Joint Academic Network (JANET), obtaining the status of system manager. He deleted and added files, put on messages, made up users and changed passwords. He was acquitted of causing damage to the computers by bringing about temporary impairment, but convicted of criminal damage to the disks by altering the magnetic particles on them. The Court of Appeal said that if that if the disks had been empty, there would have been no damage, but since information was stored on them interference with that information amounted to an impairment of their value or usefulness and hence damage.

With due respect to the courts, it is submitted these decisions (particularly *Whiteley*) confuse the physical disk with the intangible information recorded on it. The whole point of computer disks (whether floppy or hard disks) is that they can be repeatedly erased and re-written over. This process in no sense damages the disk, for the disk remains the same disk and just as useful as when it was first bought. The only difference that rewriting to the disk makes is that the information is changed. Thus the disk is fulfilling its function. So far as the magnetic particles are concerned, they are expressly designed to be rearrangeable, and so it cannot be said that they have been damaged. Anyone who uses a word processor will appreciate this. If after writing this chapter on the word processor one of the authors had decided to delete the section on the Criminal Damage Act on the ground that it was not relevant, and had re-saved the file in that amended form, it would surely be nonsense to suggest that he had thereby 'damaged' the floppy disk. Nor would it make any difference if a third party had done this without the authors' consent. In both cases the disk would have remained as useful as before, and in both cases the information would have been lost. If, by contrast, one of the authors were to break the aerial off his own car, he would damage it just as much as if a vandal were to break it off.

In its Report on Computer Misuse[6] the Law Commission was of the view that 'damage' required some physical injury to a tangible thing.[7] It therefore recommended that neither an unauthorised modification of a computer's memory or computer storage medium, nor any resulting impairment of computer operations or data, should be capable of amounting to criminal damage under the 1971 Act, effectively reversing *Cox v Riley* and *Whiteley*.[8] This recommendation has been effected by section 3(6) of the Computer Misuse Act 1990. Thus the Criminal Damage Act is now reserved for cases of physical damage, which may of course be caused through the agency of a computer.

Instead, the Commission recommended the introduction of the specially-tailored offence of unauthorised modification of computer material that is

5   (1991) Crim.LR 436.
6   Law Com. No. 186 (Cm 819).
7   *Ibid.* at paragraph 2.29 to 30, 3.62.
8   *Ibid.* at paragraph 3.78.

now to be found in section 3 of the 1990 Act.[9] It is to be hoped that this will mean that the courts will no longer have to resort to such strained interpretations as in *Whiteley*.

10.2   COMPUTER MISUSE ACT 1990

10.2.1   The evolution of the Computer Misuse Act

The origin of the Computer Misuse Act lies in a request made in 1984 by the Law Society of Scotland to the Scottish Law Commission to consider 'the applicability and effectiveness of the criminal law of Scotland in relation to the use and abuse of computers, computer systems and other data storing, data processing and telecommunications systems'. The Scottish Law Commission produced a Consultative Memorandum in 1986 and a Report[10] in 1987. Also in 1987 the English Law Commission published a Working Paper[11] on Conspiracy to Defraud which raised a number of points connected with computer misuse. With this background the English Law Commission went on to investigate computer misuse. In September 1988 it published a Working Paper[12] in which it provisionally concluded that most forms of computer misuse were satisfactorily covered by existing English criminal law, but that 'hacking' and 'deception of a computer' were not. The latter was left to be considered during an examination of conspiracy offences, but during consultation on the working paper the Commission was persuaded that 'hacking' was a more urgent problem than it had previously been thought and published a Report recommending that anti-hacking legislation be enacted promptly.[13] This was despite the fact that the traditional approach to trespass in English law is that it is a civil wrong only and not a criminal offence, unless damage is caused: the Commission felt that trespass to a computer was more serious than other forms of trespass, for example to land. A possible explanation for this is that hacking usually involves at least an element of breach of confidence. At the end of 1989 the Government indicated that it would support a private member's bill on the subject and accordingly the Computer Misuse Bill was introduced by Michael Colvin MP on 20 December 1989. The Act received the Royal Assent on 29 June 1990 and came into force on 29 August 1990.[14]

---

9   *Ibid.* at paragraph 3.64 to 65.
10   Report on Computer Crime, Scot. Law. Com. No. 106 (Cm 174).
11   No. 104.
12   No. 110.
13   Report on Computer Misuse, Law Com. No. 186 (Cm 819).
14   Computer Misuse Act 1990 section 18(2).

10.2.2 Unauthorised access

Section 1 of the 1990 Act provides that:

(1) A person is guilty of an offence if –
(a) he causes a computer to perform any function with intent to secure access to any program or data held in any computer;
(b) the access he intends to secure is unauthorised;
(c) he knows at the time when he causes the computer to perform the function that this is the case.
(2) The intent a person has to have to commit an offence under this section need not be directed at:–
(a) any particular program or data;
(b) a program or data of any particular kind; or
(c) a program or data held in any particular computer.

10.2.2.1 *'Computer', 'program', 'data'*

Neither 'computer' nor 'program' is defined[15] although 'program' includes part of a program.[16] It seems likely that standard definitions will be applied. It should be remembered, however, that many machines are now microprocessor controlled, and so are potentially covered. In particular, the recent phenomenon of 'fax-hacking', in which the hacker instructs the fax machine either to send him documents stored in its memory or to copy him with documents being sent, may well be caught by this provision if 'computer' and 'program' are given a sufficiently wide interpretation.

'Data' is again undefined.[17] Although the word is potentially very wide, there is a limitation in that it must be held in a computer. This includes data held in a removable storage medium which is in the computer for the time being[18] (for example a floppy disk).

10.2.2.2 *'Access'*

'Access', on the other hand, is defined. By section 17(2) of the Act a person secures access to a program or data if he:

(a) alters or erases the program or data;
(b) copies or moves it to any storage medium other than that in which it is held or to a different location in the storage medium in which it is held;
(c) uses it; or
(d) has it output from the computer in which it is held (whether by having it displayed or in any other manner).

---

15   This is deliberate and in accordance with the Law Commission's recommendation: Cm 819 at paragraph 3.39. See Copyright, Designs and Patents Act 1988 section 3 discussed in Chapter 4 and Patents Act 1977 section 1(2)(c) discussed in Chapter 7.
16   Computer Misuse Act 1990 section 17(10).
17   Again this is deliberate: Cm 819 at paragraph 3.30(3). Contrast the Data Protection Act 1984 section 1(2).
18   Computer Misuse Act 1990 section 17(6).

A person 'uses' a program if the function he causes the computer to perform either causes the program to be executed or is itself a function of the program.[19] A program is output if the instructions of which it consists are output. The form in which the instructions or any data are output is immaterial; in particular it is immaterial whether or not they are capable of being executed or processed.[20]

These provisions cover almost all conceivable forms of hacking or attempts at hacking. They also appear to have the effect that many infringements of copyright in computer software will be offences under this section, in particular in the 'abuse of licence' situation where one person in an organisation buys a licence for a program but ten people copy it and use it. On the other hand, it would appear that eavesdropping (for example by deciphering electro-magnetic signatures of VDUs) is not to be covered because this would not involve causing the computer to perform any function.[21]

The effect of subsection (2) is that it is not a defence that the hacking was purely speculative in that the hacker either did not know or did not care what he was hacking into.

10.2.2.3 *'Unauthorised'*

Access is 'unauthorised', if the person is not himself entitled to control access of the kind in question to the program or data, and he does not have consent to such access to the program or data from a person who is so entitled.[22] This will therefore include the situation where an employee of a company who has limited access to the system exceeds his authorisation and obtains access to other levels of the system.[23]

10.2.3   Unauthorised access with intent to commit or facilitate a further offence

Section 2 of the 1990 Act provides that:

> (1) A person is guilty of an offence under this section if he commits an offence under section 1 above ('the unauthorised access offence') with intent —
>> (a) to commit an offence to which this section applies; or
>> (b) to facilitate the commission of such an offence (whether by himself or by any other person);
> and the offence he intends to commit or facilitate is referred to below in this section as the further offence.

---

19   *Ibid.*, section 17(3).
20   *Ibid.*, section 17(4).
21   This is in line with the Law Commission's recommendation: Cm 819 at paragraph 3.25.
22   Computer Misuse Act 1990 section 17(5).
23   This is in accordance with the Law Commission's recommendation: Cm 819 at paragraphs 3.35 to 37.

(2) This section applies to offences –
    (a) for which the sentence is fixed by law; or
    (b) for which a person of twenty-one years of age or over (not previously convicted) may be sentenced to imprisonment for a term of five years (or, in England and Wales, might be so sentenced but for the restrictions imposed by Section 33 of the Magistrates' Courts' Act 1980).

(3) It is immaterial for the purposes of this section whether the further offence is to be committed on the same occasion as the unauthorised access offence or on any future occasion.

(4) A person may be guilty of an offence under this section even though the facts are such that the commission of the further offence is impossible.

10.2.3.1 *'With intent'*

The enactment of this offence was recommended by the Law Commission to cover conduct falling short of commission of the further offence or an attempt to commit that offence. Section 1(1) of the Criminal Attempts Act 1981 requires there to be identified acts done by the accused which are immediately, and not just remotely, connected with the commission of an offence. The Commission considered that there were circumstances in which hacking for a particular criminal purpose might not amount to an attempt on this definition, yet ought to be susceptible of prosecution.[24] Accordingly this offence consists of the basic hacking offence under section 1 with the additional ingredient of an ulterior intention to commit or facilitate the commission of a further offence.

10.2.3.2 *'Further offence'*

The significance of the period of five years in the definition of 'further offence' in subsection (2) is that this is the same test as that which determines what is an arrestable offence under the Police and Criminal Evidence Act 1984.[25] In most cases the further offence will be one involving dishonesty, but others are possible.

10.2.4 Unauthorised modification

Section 3 of the 1990 Act provides that:

(1) A person is guilty of an offence if –
    (a) he does any act which causes an unauthorised modification of the contents of any computer; and
    (b) at the time when he does the act he has the requisite knowledge and the requisite intent.

(2) For the purposes of subsection (1)(b) above the requisite intent is an intent to cause a modification of the contents of any computer and by so doing –
    (a) to impair the operation of any computer;

---

24   Cm 819 at paragraphs 3.49 to 58.
25   Section 24(1).

(b) to prevent or hinder access to any program or data held in any computer; or

(c) to impair the operation of such program or the reliability of any such data.

(3) The intent need not be directed at –

(a) any particular computer;

(b) any particular program or data or a program or data of any particular kind; or

(c) any particular modification or a modification of any particular kind.

(4) For the purposes of subsection (1)(b) above the requisite knowledge is knowledge that any modification he intends to make is unauthorised.

(5) It is immaterial for the purposes of this Section whether an unauthorised modification or any intended effect of it of a kind mentioned in subsection (2) above is, or is intended to be, permanent or merely temporary.

10.2.4.1 'Modification'

'Modification' is defined as taking place if, by the operation of any function of the computer concerned or any other computer, any program or data held in the computer concerned is altered or erased, or any program or data is added to its contents.[26] It is also provided that any act which contributes towards causing such a modification shall be regarded as causing it. Thus this section should avoid the difficulties encountered with the application of the Criminal Damage Act to computers discussed above. The following activities would all appear to be within the scope of the section: erasing programs or data from memory or disk; planting viruses; worms or logic bombs in systems; circulating floppy disks containing viruses; putting a 'lock' on programs or data.

It is worth noting that this offence may be committed without 'hacking' as that term is commonly understood. For example, an employee who has just been given notice of redundancy but still has access to a system who maliciously erases important data would be caught by this section even if he was not caught by section 1.

10.2.4.2 'Unauthorised'

A modification is unauthorised if the person whose act causes it is not himself entitled to determine whether the modification should be made, and he does not have consent to the modification from a person who is so entitled.[27]

10.2.5 Alternative verdicts

A person prosecuted under section 2 or section 3 may be convicted in the alternative of the lesser offence under section 1.[28] This might be

26 Computer Misuse Act 1990 section 17(7).
27 *Ibid.*, section 17(8).
28 *Ibid.*, section 12(1).

important in a case similar to that of *R v Gold and Schifreen*,[29] where the defendants had succeeded in hacking into the Duke of Edinburgh's Prestel mail box. They were prosecuted with making a false instrument under the Forgery and Counterfeiting Act 1981 but the House of Lords held that a password could not be an instrument within the meaning of that Act. It is probable that on the facts of that case an offence under section 3 would now be committed, but in any event it is clear that an offence under section 1 would be committed.

10.2.6 *Mens rea*

All three offences under the Computer Misuse Act require intention on the part of the offender. It would therefore appear that recklessness is not sufficient (in contrast to, in particular, the Criminal Damage Act).

10.2.7 Jurisdiction

Given the potential for international hacking of computers, the Law Commission recommended in its Report that English courts should have jurisdiction over computer misuse that either originates from or is directed against computers located in the UK and that there should be provision for the trial of attempts and incitement to commit computer misuse offences abroad.[30] The latter was subject, however, to a recommendation of a requirement of 'double criminality', so that a conspiracy, attempt or incitement to commit a computer misuse offence abroad is only prosecutable if the acts contemplated would, if done, be an offence under the laws of the country where they were to take place.

These recommendations are given effect to by sections 4 to 9 of the Computer Misuse Act, which contain a complete code as to the territorial scope of the Act. These provide in essence that sections 1 and 3 of the Act have extraterritorial effect subject to a requirement for the existence of a 'significant link' with the jurisdiction.[31] A 'significant link' for the purposes of a section 1 offence may be constituted either by the defendant's presence in the jurisdiction when he did the act which caused the computer to perform the function or by the presence in the jurisdiction of the computer in question.[32] A 'significant link' for the purposes of section 3 may be constituted either by the defendant's presence in the jurisdiction when he did the act which caused the modification or by the fact that the modification occurred in the jurisdiction.[33]

29   [1988] AC 1063.
30   Cm 819 at paragraphs 4.1 to 3.
31   Computer Misuse Act 1990 section 4(1), (2).
32   *Ibid.*, section 5(2).
33   *Ibid.*, section 5(3).

10.2.8   Time limits

In relation to proceedings under section 1 of the Computer Misuse Act 1990, in place of the normal time limit for the laying of an information of six months from the commission of the offence,[34] there is a time limit of six months from the date on which evidence sufficient in the opinion of the prosecutor to warrant the proceedings came to his knowledge, subject to an overall time limit of three years from the commission of the offence.[35]

Proceedings for offences triable either way such as those under sections 2 and 3 of the 1990 Act are not subject to any statutory limitation period[36] and at common law there is no time limit on criminal prosecutions.[37] Nevertheless, delay in bringing a prosecution may give rise to prejudice and unfairness which by itself amounts to an abuse of process such that the tribunal may decline to entertain the proceedings.[38]

10.2.9   Search warrants

A search warrant can be issued by a circuit judge where he is satisfied by information on oath given by a constable that there are reasonable grounds for believing that an offence under section 1 of the 1990 Act has been or is about to be committed in any premises, and that evidence that such an offence has been or is about to be committed is in those premises.[39] Search warrants for offences under sections 2 and 3 can be obtained in the normal way under the Police and Criminal Evidence Act 1984.[40]

10.2.10   Penalties

The section 1 offence is only triable summarily. The penalty on conviction is imprisonment for up to six months or a fine up to level 5 on the standard scale[41] or both.[42] At the time of writing level 5 is £2,000.[43]

The section 2 and section 3 offences are each triable either way, and the penalties are the same in both cases. The penalty on summary conviction is imprisonment for up to six months or a fine up to the statutory

---

34   Magistrates' Courts Act 1980 section 127(1).
35   Computer Misuse Act 1990 section 11(2), (3).
36   See *Kemp v Liebherr-GB Ltd* [1987] 1 All ER 885.
37   *Halsbury's Laws*, 4th edn (reissue), Volume 11(1), paragraph 786.
38   *R v Clerk to the Medway Justices ex parte Department of Health and Social Security* [1986] Crim LR 686; *R v Bow Street Stipendiary Magistrate ex parte Cherry* (1990) 91 Cr. App. R. 283. Cf. *R v Central Criminal Court ex parte Randle* [1991] 1 WLR 1087.
39   Computer Misuse Act 1990 section 14(1).
40   Section 32(2)(b).
41   Defined by the Criminal Justice Act 1982 section 75 as the scale set out in the Criminal Justice Act 1982 section 37(2).
42   Computer Misuse Act 1990 section 1(3).
43   Criminal Penalties (Increase) Order 1984, SI 1984 No. 447, Article 3(4), Schedule 4.

maximum[44] or both.[45] At the time of writing the statutory maximum fine is £2,000.[46] The penalty on conviction on indictment is imprisonment for up to five years or a fine or both.[47] There is no limit on the fine that may be imposed, but it should be within the offender's capacity to pay.[48]

10.2.11   Civil remedies

On the face of it, the Computer Misuse Act is a purely criminal statute, and a victim of hacking has no civil right of action under it. Where an Act creates an obligation and enforces the performance in a specified manner, there is a presumption that the performance cannot be enforced in any other manner.[49] Where the only manner of enforcing performance provided by the statute is criminal prosecution, however, it is well established that there are two classes of exception to this principle:

> The first is where upon the true construction of the Act it is apparent that the obligation or prohibition was imposed for the benefit or protection of a particular class of individuals, as in the case of the Factories Acts and similar legislation . . .
>
> The second exception is where the statute creates a public right (that is, a right to be enjoyed by all of Her Majesty's subjects who wish to avail themselves of it) and a particular member of the public suffers . . . 'particular, direct and substantial' damage 'other and different from that which was common to all the rest of the public'.[50]

A recent example of the first class of exemption is *Rickless v United Artists Corp.*[51] where it was held by the Court of Appeal that the Performers' Protection Acts 1958 to 1972, although apparently enforceable by criminal prosecution only, conferred a civil right of action for breach of statutory duty as well.[52]

The question whether an action for breach of statutory duty under the Computer Misuse Act will lie remains to be tested in the courts. It is submitted, however, that it is unlikely that such action would succeed. As to the first exception, it is difficult to see that the statute protects a particular class of individuals, unless it can be said that computer users

---

44   Defined by the Criminal Justice Act 1982 section 74 as 'the prescribed sum' within the meaning of the Magistrates' Courts Act 1980 section 32.
45   Computer Misuse Act 1990 sections 2(5)(a), 3(7)(a).
46   Criminal Penalties (Increase) Order 1984, SI 1984 No. 447, Article 2(1) and Schedule 1.
47   Computer Misuse Act 1990 sections 2(5)(b), 3(7)(b).
48   *R v Churchill (No.2)* [1967] 1 QB 190 (reversed on other grounds *sub nom Churchill v Walton* [1967] 2 AC 224), *R v Garner* [1986] 1 WLR 73.
49   *Doe d. Murray v Bridges* (1831) 1 B & Ad 847 at 849 *per* Lord Tenterden CJ.
50   *Lonrho Ltd v Shell Petroleum Co. Ltd (No. 2)* [1982] AC 173 at 185 *per* Lord Diplock.
51   [1988] QB 40.
52   See Arnold, *Performers' Rights and Recording Rights*, ESC Publishing Ltd, 1990, Appendix 2.

generally are a particular class. As to the second exception, it does not appear that the statute creates a public right.

If this is correct, the only civil remedies that will generally be open to victims of hacking will be those for breach of confidence or infringement of copyright, depending on the circumstances.[53]

53 See Chapters 3 and 5.

Appendices

Copyright, Designs and Patents Act 1988

Chapter 48

ARRANGEMENT OF SECTIONS

PART I

COPYRIGHT

Chapter I

Subsistence, ownership and duration of copyright

Introductory

Section
1. Copyright and copyright works.
2. Rights subsisting in copyright works.

Descriptions of work and related provisions

3. Literary, dramatic and musical works.
4. Artistic works.
5. Sound recordings and films.
. . .

Authorship and ownership of copyright

9. Authorship of work.
10. Works of joint authorship.
11. First ownership of copyright.

Duration of copyright

12. Duration of copyright in literary, dramatic, musical or artistic works.
13. Duration of copyright in sound recordings and films.
. . .

Chapter II

Rights of copyright owner

Section
16. The acts restricted by copyright in a work.
17. Infringement of copyright by copying.
18. Infringement by issue of copies to the public.
19. Infringement by performance, showing or playing of work in public.
. . .
21. Infringement by making adaptation or act done in relation to adaptation.

Secondary infringement of copyright

22. Secondary infringement: importing infringing copy.
23. Secondary infringement: possessing or dealing with infringing copy.
24. Secondary infringement: providing means for making infringing copies.
. . .

Infringing copies

27. Meaning of 'infringing copy'.

Chapter III

Acts permitted in relation to copyright works

Introductory

28. Introductory provisions.

General

29. Research and private study.
. . .

Designs

51. Design documents and models.
52. Effect of exploitation of design derived from artistic work.
53. Things done in reliance on registration of design.
. . .

Works in electronic form

56. Transfers of copies of works in electronic form.
. . .

Miscellaneous: sound recordings, films and computer programs

66. Rental of sound recordings, films and computer programs.
. . .

Adaptations

76. Adaptations.
. . .

Chapter VII

Copyright licensing

. . .

Royalty or other sum payable for rental of certain works

142. Royalty or other sum payable for rental of sound recording, film or computer program.

. . .

Chapter IX

Qualification for and extent of copyright protection

Qualification for copyright protection

153. Qualification for copyright protection.
154. Qualification by reference to author.
155. Qualification by reference to country of first publication.

. . .

Extent and application of this Part

157. Countries to which this Part extends.
158. Countries ceasing to be colonies.
159. Application of this Part to countries to which it does not extend.
160. Denial of copyright protection to citizens of countries not giving adequate protection to British works.

Supplementary

161. Territorial waters and the continental shelf.
162. British ships, aircraft and hovercraft.

Chapter X

Miscellaneous and general

. . .

Transitional provisions and savings

170. Transitional provisions and savings.
171. Rights and privileges under other enactments or the common law.

Interpretation

172. General provisions as to construction.
173. Construction of references to copyright owner.

. . .

175. Meaning of publication and commercial publication.
176. Requirement of signature: application in relation to body corporate.
177. Adaptation of expressions for Scotland.
178. Minor definitions.

. . .

PART III
DESIGN RIGHT

Chapter I

Design right in original designs

Chapter II

Rights of design right owner and remedies

Chapter III

Exceptions to rights of design right owners

Copyright, Designs and Patents Act 1988

Chapter 48

An Act to restate the law of copyright, with amendments; to make fresh provision as to the rights of performers and others in performances; to confer a design right in original designs; to amend the Registered Designs Act 1949; to make provision with respect to patent agents and trade mark agents; to confer patents and designs jurisdiction on certain county courts; to amend the law of patents; to make provision with respect to devices designed to circumvent copy-protection of works in electronic form; to make fresh provision penalising the fraudulent reception of transmissions; to make the fraudulent application or use of a trade mark an offence; to make provision for the benefit of the Hospital for Sick Children, Great Ormond Street, London; to enable financial assistance to be given to certain international bodies; and for connected purposes.

[15th November 1988]

Be it enacted by the Queen's most Excellent Majesty, by and with the advice and consent of the Lords Spiritual and Temporal, and Commons, in this present Parliament assembled, and by the authority of the same, as follows:—

PART I

COPYRIGHT

Chapter I

Subsistence, ownership and duration of copyright

Introductory

1.—(1) Copyright is a property right which subsists in accordance with this Part in the following descriptions of work—

(a) original literary, dramatic, musical or artistic works,
(b) sound recordings, films, broadcasts or cable programmes, and
(c) the typographical arrangement of published editions.

(2) In this Part 'copyright work' means a work of any of those descriptions in which copyright subsists.

(3) Copyright does not subsist in a work unless the requirements of this Part with respect to qualification for copyright protection are met (see section 153 and the provisions referred to there).

   2.—(1) The owner of the copyright in a work of any description has the exclusive right to do the acts specified in Chapter II as the acts restricted by the copyright in a work of that description.

. . .

Descriptions of work and related provisions

   3.—(1) In this Part—

   'literary work' means any work, other than a dramatic or musical work, which is written, spoken or sung, and accordingly includes—

   (a) a table or compilation, and
   (b) a computer program;

   'dramatic work' includes a work of dance or mime; and
   'musical work' means a work consisting of music, exclusive of any words or action intended to be sung, spoken or performed with the music.

(2) Copyright does not subsist in a literary, dramatic or musical work unless and until it is recorded, in writing or otherwise; and references in this Part to the time at which such a work is made are to the time at which it is so recorded.

(3) It is immaterial for the purposes of subsection (2) whether the work is recorded by or with the permission of the author; and where it is not recorded by the author, nothing in that subsection affects the question whether copyright subsists in the record as distinct from the work recorded.

   4.—(1) In this Part 'artistic work' means—

   (a) a graphic work, photograph, sculpture or collage, irrespective of artistic quality,
   (b) a work of architecture being a building or a model for a building, or
   (c) a work of artistic craftsmanship.

(2) In this Part—

   'building' includes any fixed structure, and a part of a building or fixed structure;
   'graphic work' includes—

   (a) any painting, drawing, diagram, map, chart or plan, and
   (b) any engraving, etching, lithograph, woodcut or similar work;

   'photograph' means a recording of light or other radiation on any medium on which an image is produced or from which an image may by any means be produced, and which is not part of a film;
   'sculpture' includes a cast or model made for purposes of sculpture.

   5.—(1) In this Part—

   'sound recording' means—

   (a) a recording of sounds, from which the sounds may be reproduced, or

(b) a recording of the whole or any part of a literary, dramatic or musical work, from which sounds, reproducing the work or part may be produced,

regardless of the medium on which the recording is made or the method by which the sounds are reproduced or produced; and

'film' means a recording on any medium from which a moving image may by any means be produced.

(2) Copyright does not subsist in a sound recording or film which is, or to the extent that it is, a copy taken from a previous sound recording or film.

. . .

Authorship and ownership of copyright

9.—(1) In this Part 'author', in relation to a work, means the person who creates it.

(2) That person shall be taken to be—

(a) in the case of a sound recording or film, the person by whom the arrangements necessary for the making of the recording or film are undertaken;

. . .

(3) In the case of a literary, dramatic, musical or artistic work which is computer-generated, the author shall be taken to be the person by whom the arrangements necessary for the creation of the work are undertaken.

(4) For the purposes of this Part a work is of 'unknown authorship' if the identity of the author is unknown or, in the case of a work of joint authorship, if the identity of none of the authors is known.

(5) For the purposes of this Part the identity of an author shall be regarded as unknown if it is not possible for a person to ascertain his identity by reasonable inquiry; but if his identity is once known it shall not subsequently be regarded as unknown.

10.—(1) In this Part a 'work of joint authorship' means a work produced by the collaboration of two or more authors in which the contribution of each author is not distinct from that of the other author or authors.

. . .

(3) References in this Part to the author of a work shall, except as otherwise provided, be construed in relation to a work of joint authorship as references to all the authors of the work.

11.—(1) The author of a work is the first owner of any copyright in it, subject to the following provisions.

(2) Where a literary, dramatic, musical or artistic work is made by an employee in the course of his employment, his employer is the first owner of any copyright in the work subject to any agreement to the contrary.

. . .

Duration of copyright

12.—(1) Copyright in a literary, dramatic, musical or artistic work expires at the end of the period of 50 years from the end of the calendar year in which the author dies, subject to the following provisions of this section.

(2) If the work is of unknown authorship, copyright expires at the end of the period of 50 years from the end of the calendar year in which it is first made available to the public; and subsection (1) does not apply if the identity of the author becomes known after the end of that period.

For this purpose making available to the public includes—

    (a) in the case of literary, dramatic or musical work—
        (i) performance in public, or
        (ii) being broadcast or included in a cable programme service;

    (b) in the case of an artistic work—
        (i)   exhibition in public,
        (ii) a film including the work being shown in public, or
        (iii) being included in a broadcast or cable programme service;

but in determining generally for the purposes of this subsection whether a work has been made available to the public no account shall be taken of any unauthorised act.

(3) If the work is computer-generated neither of the above provisions applies and copyright expires at the end of the period of 50 years from the end of the calendar year in which the work was made.

(4) In relation to a work of joint authorship—

    (a) the reference in subsection (1) to the death of the author shall be construed—
        (i) if the identity of all the authors is known, as a reference to the death of the last of them to die, and
        (ii) if the identity of one or more of the authors is known and the identity of one or more others is not, as a reference to the death of the last of the authors whose identity is known; and
    (b) the reference in subsection (2) to the identity of the author becoming known shall be construed as a reference to the identity of any of the authors becoming known.

. . .

    13.—(1) Copyright in a sound recording or film expires—

    (a) at the end of the period of 50 years from the end of the calendar year in which it is made, or
    (b) if it is released before the end of that period, 50 years from the end of the calendar year in which it is released.

(2) A sound recording or film is 'released' when—

    (a) it is first published, broadcast or included in a cable programme service, or
    (b) in the case of a film or film sound-track, the film is first shown in public;

but in determining whether a work has been released no acount shall be taken of any unauthorised act.

. . .

Chapter II

Rights of copyright owner

The acts restricted by copyright

    16.—(1) The owner of the copyright in a work has, in accordance with the following provisions of this Chapter, the exclusive right to do the following acts in the United Kingdom—

    (a) to copy the work (see section 17);

(b) to issue copies of the work to the public (see section 18);
(c) to perform, show or play the work in public (see section 19);
(d) to broadcast the work or include it in a cable programme service (see section 20);
(e) to make an adaptation of the work or do any of the above in relation to an adaptation (see section 21);

and those acts are referred to in this Part as the 'acts restricted by the copyright'.

(2) Copyright in a work is infringed by a person who without the licence of the copyright owner does, or authorises another to do, any of the acts restricted by the copyright.

(3) References in this Part to the doing of an act restricted by the copyright in a work are to the doing of it—

(a) in relation to the work as a whole or any substantial part of it, and
(b) either directly or indirectly;

and it is immaterial whether any intervening acts themselves infringe copyright.

(4) This Chapter has effect subject to—

(a) the provisions of Chapter III (acts permitted in relation to copyright works), and
(b) the provisions of Chapter VII (provisions with respect to copyright licensing).

17.—(1) The copying of the work is an act restricted by the copyright in every description of copyright work; and references in this Part to copying and copies shall be construed as follows.

(2) Copying in relation to a literary, dramatic, musical or artistic work means reproducing the work in any material form.
  This includes storing the work in any medium by electronic means.

(3) In relation to an artistic work copying includes the making of a copy in three dimensions of a two-dimensional work and the making of a copy in two dimensions of a three-dimensional work.

(4) Copying in relation to a film, television broadcast or cable programme includes making a photograph of the whole or any substantial part of any image forming part of the film, broadcast or cable programme.
  . . .

(6) Copying in relation to any description of work includes the making of copies which are transient or are incidental to some other use of the work.

18.—(1) The issue to the public of copies of the work is an act restricted by the copyright in every description of copyright work.

(2) References in this Part to the issue to the public of copies of a work are to the act of putting in circulation copies not previously put into circulation, in the United Kingdom or elsewhere, and not to—

(a) any subsequent distribution, sale, hiring or loan of those copies, or
(b) any subsequent importation of those copies into the United Kingdom;

except that in relation to sound recordings, films and computer programs the restricted act of issuing copies to the public includes any rental of copies to the public.

19.—(1) The performance of the work in public is an act restricted by the copyright in a literary, dramatic or musical work.

(2) In this Part 'performance', in relation to a work—

    (a) includes delivery in the case of lectures, addresses, speeches and sermons, and
    (b) in general, includes any mode of visual or acoustic presentation, including presentation by means of a sound recording, film, broadcast or cable programme of the work.

(3) The playing or showing of the work in public is an act restricted by the copyright in a sound recording, film, broadcast or cable programme.

(4) Where copyright in a work is infringed by its being performed, played or shown in public by means of apparatus for receiving visual images or sounds conveyed by electronic means, the person by whom the visual images or sounds are sent, and in the case of a performance the performers, shall not be regarded as responsible for the infringement.
. . .

21.—(1) The making of an adaptation of the work is an act restricted by the copyright in a literary, dramatic or musical work.
For this purpose an adaptation is made when it is recorded, in writing or otherwise.

(2) The doing of any of the acts specified in sections 17 to 20, or subsection (1) above, in relation to an adaptation of the work is also an act restricted by the copyright in a literary, dramatic or musical work.
For this purpose it is immaterial whether the adaptation has been recorded, in writing or otherwise, at the time the act is done.

(3) In this Part 'adaptation'—

    (a) in relation to a literary or dramatic work, means—
        (i)   a translation of the work;
        (ii) a version of a dramatic work in which it is converted into a non-dramatic work or, as the case may be, of a non-dramatic work in which it is converted into a dramatic work;
        (iii) a version of the work in which the story or action is conveyed wholly or mainly by means of pictures in a form suitable for reproduction in a book, or in a newspaper, magazine or similar periodical;
    (b) in relation to a musical work, means an arrangement or transcription of the work.

(4) In relation to a computer program a 'translation' includes a version of the program in which it is converted into or out of a computer language or code or into a different computer language or code, otherwise than incidentally in the course of running the program.

(5) No inference shall be drawn from this section as to what does or does not amount to copying a work.

Secondary infringement of copyright

22. The copyright in a work is infringed by a person who, without the licence of the copyright owner, imports into the United Kingdom, otherwise than for his private and domestic use, an article which is, and which he knows or has reason to believe is, an infringing copy of the work.

23. The copyright in a work is infringed by a person who, without the licence of the copyright owner—

(a) possesses in the course of a business,
(b) sells or lets for hire, or offers or exposes for sale or hire,
(c) in the course of a business exhibits in public or distributes, or
(d) distributes otherwise than in the course of a business to such an extent as to affect prejudicially the owner of the copyright.

an article which is, and which he knows or has reason to believe is, an infringing copy of the work.

24.—(1) Copyright in a work is infringed by a person who, without the licence of the copyright owner—

(a) makes,
(b) imports into the United Kingdom,
(c) possesses in the course of a business, or
(d) sells or lets for hire, or offers or exposes for sale or hire,

an article specifically designed or adapted for making copies of that work, knowing or having reason to believe that it is to be used to make infringing copies.

(2) Copyright in a work is infringed by a person who without the licence of the copyright owner transmits the work by means of a telecommunications system (otherwise than by broadcasting or inclusion in a cable programme service), knowing or having reason to believe that infringing copies of the work will be made by means of the reception of the transmission in the United Kingdom or elsewhere.

. . .

Infringing copies

27.—(1) In this Part 'infringing copy', in relation to a copyright work, shall be construed in accordance with this section.

(2) An article is an infringing copy if its making constituted an infringement of the copyright in the work in question.

(3) An article is also an infringing copy if—

(a) it has been or is proposed to be imported into the United Kingdom, and
(b) its making in the United Kingdom would have constituted an infringement of the copyright in the work in question, or a breach of an exclusive licence agreement relating to that work.

(4) Where in any proceedings the question arises whether an article is an infringing copy and it is shown—

(a) that the article is a copy of the work, and
(b) that copyright subsists in the work or has subsisted at any time,

it shall be presumed until the contrary is proved that the article was made at a time when copyright subsisted in the work.

(5) Nothing in subsection (3) shall be construed as applying to an article which may lawfully be imported into the United Kingdom by virtue of any enforceable Community right within the meaning of section 2(1) of the European Communities Act 1972.

(6) In this Part 'infringing copy' includes a copy falling to be treated as an infringing copy by virtue of any of the following provisions —

. . .

section 56(2) (further copies, adaptations, etc. of work in electronic form retained on transfer of principal copy)

. . .

Chapter III

Acts permitted in relation to copyright works

Introductory

28.—(1) The provisions of this Chapter specify acts which may be done in relation to copyright works notwithstanding the subsistence of copyright; they relate only to the question of infringement of copyright and do not affect any other right or obligation restricting the doing of any of the specified acts.

(2) Where it is provided by this Chapter that an act does not infringe copyright, or may be done without infringing copyright, and no particular description of copyright work is mentioned, the act in question does not infringe the copyright in a work of any description.

(3) No inference shall be drawn from the description of any act which may by virtue of this Chapter be done without infringing copyright as to the scope of the acts restricted by the copyright in any description of work.

(4) The provisions of this Chapter are to be construed independently of each other, so that the fact that an act does not fall within one provision does not mean that it is not covered by another provision.

General

29.—(1) Fair dealing with a literary, dramatic, musical or artistic work for the purposes of research or private study does not infringe any copyright in the work or, in the case of a published edition, in the typographical arrangement.

. . .

(3) Copying by a person other than the researcher or student himself is not fair dealing if—

    (a) in the case of a librarian, or a person acting on behalf of a librarian, he does anything which regulations under section 40 would not permit to be done under section 38 or 39 (articles or parts of published works: restriction on multiple copies of same material), or

    (b) in any other case, the person doing the copying knows or has reason to believe that it will result in copies of substantially the same material being provided to more than one person at substantially the same time and for substantially the same purpose.

. . .

Designs

51.—(1) It is not an infringement of any copyright in a design document or model recording or embodying a design for anything other than an artistic work or a typeface to make an article to the design or to copy an article made to the design.

(2) Nor is it an infringement of the copyright to issue to the public, or include in a film, broadcast or cable programme service, anything the making of which was, by virtue of subsection (1), not an infringement of that copyright.

(3) In this section—
'design' means the design of any aspect of the shape or configuration (whether internal or external) of the whole or part of an article, other than surface decoration; and
'design document' means any record of a design, whether in the form of a drawing, a written description, a photograph, data stored in a computer or otherwise.

52.—(1) This section applies where an artistic work has been exploited, by or with the licence of the copyright owner, by—

(a) making by an industrial process articles falling to be treated for the purpose of this Part as copies of the work, and
(b) marketing such articles, in the United Kingdom or elsewhere.

(2) After the end of the period of 25 years from the end of the calendar year in which such articles are first marketed, the work may be copied by making articles of any description, or doing anything for the purpose of making articles of any description, and anything may be done in relation to articles so made, without infringing copyright in the work.

(3) Where only part of an artistic work is exploited as mentioned in subsection (1), subsection (2) applies only in relation to that part.

(4) The Secretary of State may by order make provision—

(a) as to the circumstances in which an article, or any description of article, is to be regarded for the purposes of this section as made by an industrial process;
(b) excluding from the operation of this section such articles of a primarily literary or artistic character as he thinks fit.

(5) An order shall be made by statutory instrument which shall be subject to annulment in pursuance of a resolution of either House of Parliament.

(6) In this section—

(a) references to articles do not include films; and
(b) references to the marketing of an article are to its being sold or let for hire or offered or exposed for sale or hire.

53.—(1) The copyright in an artistic work is not infringed by anything done—

(a) in pursuance of an assignment or licence made or granted by a person registered under the Registered Designs Act 1949 as the proprietor of a corresponding design, and
(b) in good faith in reliance on the registration and without notice of any proceedings for the cancellation of the registration or for rectifying the relevant entry in the register of designs;

and this is so notwithstanding that the person registered as the proprietor was not the proprietor of the design for the purposes of the 1949 Act.

(2) In subsection (1) a 'corresponding design', in relation to an artistic work, means a design within the meaning of the 1949 Act which if applied to an article would

produce something which would be treated for the purposes of this Part as a copy of the artistic work.

. . .

Works in electronic form

56.—(1) This section applies where a copy of a work in electronic form has been purchased on terms which, expressly or impliedly or by virtue of any rule of law, allow the purchaser to copy the work, or to adapt it or make copies of an adaptation, in connection with his use of it.

(2) If there are no express terms—

(a) prohibiting the transfer of the copy by the purchaser, imposing obligations which continue after a transfer, prohibiting the assignment of any licence or terminating any licence on a transfer, or
(b) providing for the terms on which a transferee may do the things which the purchaser was permitted to do,

anything which the purchaser was allowed to do may also be done without infringement of copyright by a transferee; but any copy, adaptation or copy of an adaptation made by the purchaser which is not also transferred shall be treated as an infringing copy for all purposes after the transfer.

(3) The same applies where the original purchased copy is no longer usable and what is transferred is a further copy used in its place.

(4) The above provisions also apply on a subsequent transfer, with the substitution for references in subsection (2) to the purchaser of references to the subsequent transferor.

. . .

Miscellaneous: sound recordings, films and computer programs

66.—(1) The Secretary of State may by order provide that in such cases as may be specified in the order the rental to the public of copies of sound recordings, films or computer programs shall be treated as licensed by the copyright owner subject only to the payment of such reasonable royalty or other payment as may be agreed or determined in default of agreement by the Copyright Tribunal.

(2) No such order shall apply if, or to the extent that, there is a licensing scheme certified for the purposes of this section under section 143 providing for the grant of licences.

(3) An order may make different provision for different cases and may specify cases by reference to any factor relating to the work, the copies rented, the renter or the circumstances of the rental.

(4) An order shall be made by statutory instrument; and no order shall be made unless a draft of it has been laid before and approved by a resolution of each House of Parliament.

(5) Copyright in a computer program is not infringed by the rental of copies to the public after the end of the period of 50 years from the end of the calender year in which copies of it were first issued to the public in electronic form.

(6) Nothing in this section affects any liability under section 23 (secondary infringement) in respect of the rental of infringing copies.
. . .

Adaptations

76.—An act which by virtue of this Chapter may be done without infringing copyright in a literary, dramatic or musical work does not, where that work is an adaptation, infringe any copyright in the work from which the adaptation was made.
. . .

Chapter V

Dealings with rights in copyright works

Copyright

90.—(1) Copyright is transmissible by assignment, by testamentary disposition or by operation of law, as personal or moveable property.

(2) An assignment or other transmission of copyright may be partial, that is, limited so as to apply—

(a) to one or more, but not all, of the things the copyright owner has the exclusive right to do;

(b) to part, but not the whole, of the period for which the copyright is to subsist.

(3) An assignment of copyright is not effective unless it is in writing signed by or on behalf of the assignor.

(4) A licence granted by a copyright owner is binding on every successor in title to his interest in the copyright, except a purchaser in good faith for valuable consideration and without notice (actual or constructive) of the licence or a person deriving title from such purchaser; and references in this Part to doing anything with, or without, the licence of the copyright owner shall be construed accordingly.

91.—(1) Where by an agreement made in relation to future copyright, and signed by or on behalf of the prospective owner of the copyright, the prospective owner purports to assign the future copyright (wholly or partially) to another person, then if, on the copyright coming into existence, the assignee or another person claiming under him would be entitled as against all other persons to require the copyright to be vested in him, the copyright shall vest in the assignee or his successor in title by virtue of this subsection.

(2) In this Part—

'future copyright' means copyright which will or may come into existence in respect of a future work or class of works or on the occurrence of a future event; and

'prospective owner' shall be construed accordingly, and includes a person who is prospectively entitled to copyright by virtue of such an agreement as is mentioned in subsection (1).

(3) A licence granted by a prospective owner of copyright is binding on every successor in title to his interest (or prospective interest) in the right, except a purchaser in good faith for valuable consideration and without notice (actual or constructive) of the

licence or a person deriving title from such a purchaser; and references in this Part to doing anything with, or without, the licence of the copyright owner shall be construed accordingly.

92.—(1) In this Part an 'exclusive licence' means a licence in writing signed by or on behalf of the copyright owner authorising the licensee to the exclusion of all other persons, including the person granting the licence, to exercise a right which would otherwise be exercisable exclusively by the copyright owner.

(2) The licensee under an exclusive licence has the same rights against a successor in title who is bound by the licence as he has against the person granting the licence.

93.—Where under a bequest (whether specific or general) a person is entitled, beneficially or otherwise, to—

(a) an original document or other material thing recording or embodying a literary, dramatic, musical or artistic work which was not published before the death of the testator, or
(b) an original material thing containing a sound recording or film which was not published before the death of the testator,

the bequest shall, unless a contrary intention is indicated in the testator's will or a codicil to it, be construed as including the copyright in the work in so far as the testator was the owner of the copyright immediately before his death.
. . .

Chapter VI

Remedies for infringement

Rights and remedies of copyright owner

96.—(1) An infringement of copyright is actionable by the copyright owner.

(2) In an action for infringement of copyright all such relief by way of damages, injunctions, accounts or otherwise is available to the plaintiff as is available in respect of the infringement of any other property right.

(3) This section has effect subject to the following provisions of this Chapter.

97.—(1) Where in an action for infringement of copyright it is shown that at the time of the infringement the defendant did not know, and had no reason to believe, that copyright subsisted in the work to which the action relates, the plaintiff is not entitled to damages against him, but without prejudice to any other remedy.

(2) The court may in an action for infringement of copyright having regard to all the circumstances, and in particular to—

(a) the flagrancy of the infringement, and
(b) any benefit accruing to the defendant by reason of the infringement,

award such additional damages as the justice of the case may require.

98.—(1) If in proceedings for infringement of copyright in respect of which a licence is available as of right under section 144 (powers exercisable in consequence of report of Monopolies and Mergers Commission) the defendant undertakes to take a licence on such terms as may be agreed or, in default of agreement, settled by the Copyright Tribunal under that section—

(a) no injunction shall be granted against him,

(b) no order for delivery up shall be made under section 99, and

(c) the amount recoverable against him by way of damages or on an account of profits shall not exceed double the amount which would have been payable by him as licensee if such a licence on those terms had been granted before the earliest infringement.

(2) An undertaking may be given at any time before final order in the proceedings, without any admission of liability.

(3) Nothing in this section affects the remedies available in respect of an infringement committed before licences of right were available.

99.—(1) Where a person—

(a) has an infringing copy of a work in his possession, custody or control in the course of a business, or

(b) has in his possession, custody or control an article specifically designed or adapted for making copies of a particular copyright work, knowing or having reason to believe that it has been or is to be used to make infringing copies,

the owner of the copyright in the work may apply to the court for an order that the infringing copy or article be delivered up to him or to such other person as the court may direct.

(2) An application shall not be made after the end of the period specified in section 113 (period after which remedy of delivery up not available); and no order shall be made unless the court also makes, or it appears to the court that there are grounds for making, an order under section 114 (order as to disposal of infringing copy or other article).

(3) A person to whom an infringing copy or other article is delivered up in pursuance of an order under this section shall, if an order under section 114 is not made, retain it pending the making of an order, or the decision not to make an order, under that section.

(4) Nothing in this section affects any other power of the court.

100.—(1) An infringing copy of a work which is found exposed or otherwise immediately available for sale or hire, and in respect of which the copyright owner would be entitled to apply for an order under section 99, may be seized and detained by him or a person authorised by him.

The right to seize and detain is exercisable subject to the following conditions and is subject to any decision of the court under section 114.

(2) Before anything is seized under this section notice of the time and place of the proposed seizure must be given to a local police station.

(3) A person may for the purpose of exercising the right conferred by this section enter premises to which the public have access but may not seize anything in the possession, custody or control of a person at a permanent or regular place of business of his, and may not use any force.

(4) At the time when anything is seized under this section there shall be left at the place where it was seized a notice in the prescribed form containing the prescribed particulars as to the person by whom or on whose authority the seizure is made and the grounds on which it is made.

(5) In this section—
> 'premises' includes land, buildings, moveable structures, vehicles, vessels, aircraft and hovercraft; and
> 'prescribed' means prescribed by order of the Secretary of State.

(6) An order of the Secretary of State under this section shall be made by statutory instrument which shall be subject to annulment in pursuance of a resolution of either House of Parliament.

Rights and remedies of exclusive licensee

101.—(1) An exclusive licensee has, except against the copyright owner, the same rights and remedies in respect of matters occurring after the grant of the licence as if the licence had been an assignment.

(2) His rights and remedies are concurrent with those of the copyright owner; and references in the relevant provisions of this Part to the copyright owner shall be construed accordingly.

(3) In an action brought by an exclusive licensee by virtue of this section a defendant may avail himself of any defence which would have been available to him if the action had been brought by the copyright owner.

102.—(1) Where an action for infringement of copyright brought by the copyright owner or an exclusive licensee relates (wholly or partly) to an infringement in respect of which they have concurrent rights of action, the copyright owner or, as the case may be, the exclusive licensee may not, without the leave of the court, proceed with the action unless the other is either joined as a plaintiff or added as a defendant.

(2) A copyright owner or exclusive licensee who is added as a defendant in pursuance of subsection (1) is not liable for any costs in the action unless he takes part in the proceedings.

(3) The above provisions do not affect the granting of interlocutory relief on an application by a copyright owner or exclusive licensee alone.

(4) Where an action for infringement of copyright is brought which relates (wholly or partly) to an infringement in respect of which the copyright owner and an exclusive licensee have or had concurrent rights of action—
> (a) the court shall in assessing damages take into account—
>> (i) the terms of the licence, and
>> (ii) any pecuniary remedy already awarded or available to either of them in respect of the infringement;
> (b) no account of profits shall be directed if an award of damages has been made, or an account of profits has been directed, in favour of the other of them in respect of the infringement; and
> (c) the court shall if an account of profits is directed apportion the profits between them as the court considers just, subject to any agreement between them;

and these provisions apply whether or not the copyright owner and the exclusive licensee are both parties to the action.

(5) The copyright owner shall notify any exclusive licensee having concurrent rights before applying for an order under section 99 (order for delivery up) or exercising the right conferred by section 100 (right of seizure); and the court may on the application of the licensee make such order under section 99 or, as the case may be, prohibiting or permitting the exercise by the copyright owner of the right conferred by section 100, as it thinks fit having regard to the terms of the licence.

. . .

Presumptions

104.—(1) The following presumptions apply in proceedings brought by virtue of this Chapter with respect to a literary, dramatic, musical or artistic work.

(2) Where a name purporting to be that of the author appeared on copies of the work as published or on the work when it was made, the person whose name appeared shall be presumed, until the contrary is proved —

(a) to be the author of the work;
(b) to have made it in circumstances not falling within section 11(2), 163, 165 or 168 (works produced in course of employment, Crown copyright, Parliamentary copyright or copyright of certain international organisations).

(3) In the case of a work alleged to be a work of joint authorship, subsection (2) applies in relation to each person alleged to be one of the authors.

(4) Where no name purporting to be that of the author appeared as mentioned in subsection (2) but —

(a) the work qualifies for copyright protection by virtue of section 155 (qualification by reference to country of first publication), and
(b) a name purporting to be that of the publisher appeared on copies of the work as first published,

the person whose name appeared shall be presumed, until the contrary is proved, to have been the owner of the copyright at the time of publication.

(5) If the author of the work is dead or the identity of the author cannot be ascertained by reasonable inquiry, it shall be presumed, in the absence of evidence to the contrary —

(a) that the work is an original work, and
(b) that the plaintiff's allegations as to what was the first publication of the work and as to the country of first publication are correct.

105.—(1) In proceedings brought by virtue of this Chapter with respect to a sound recording, where copies of the recording as issued to the public bear a label or other mark stating —

(a) that a named person was the owner of copyright in the recording at the date of issue of the copies, or
(b) that the recording was first published in a specified year or in a specified country,

the label or mark shall be admissible as evidence of the facts stated and shall be presumed to be correct until the contrary is proved.

(2) In proceedings brought by virtue of this Chapter with respect to a film, where copies of the film as issued to the public bear a statement—

(a) that a named person was the author or director of the film,
(b) that a named person was the owner of copyright in the film at the date of issue of the copies, or
(c) that the film was first published in a specified year or in a specified country,

the statement shall be admissible as evidence of the facts stated and shall be presumed to be correct until the contrary is proved.

(3) In proceedings brought by virtue of this Chapter with respect to a computer program, where copies of the program are issued to the public in electronic form bearing a statement—

(a) that a named person was the owner of copyright in the program at the date of issue of the copies, or
(b) that the program was first published in a specified country or that copies of it were first issued to the public in electronic form in a specified year,

the statement shall be admissible as evidence of the facts stated and shall be presumed to be correct until the contrary is proved.

(4) The above presumptions apply equally in proceedings relating to an infringement alleged to have occurred before the date on which the copies were issued to the public.

(5) In proceedings brought by virtue of this Chapter with respect to a film, where the film as shown in public, broadcast or included in a cable programme service bears a statement—

(a) that a named person was the author or director of the film, or
(b) that a named person was the owner of copyright in the film immediately after it was made,

the statement shall be admissible as evidence of the facts stated and shall be presumed to be correct until the contrary is proved.

This presumption applies equally in proceedings relating to an infringement alleged to have occurred before the date on which the film was shown in public, broadcast or included in a cable programme service.

. . .

Offences

107.—(1) A person commits an offence who, without the licence of the copyright owner—

(a) makes for sale or hire, or
(b) imports into the United Kingdom otherwise than for his private and domestic use, or
(c) possesses in the course of a business with a view to committing any act infringing the copyright, or
(d) in the course of a business—
(i)   sells or lets for hire, or
(ii) offers or exposes for sale or hire, or
(iii) exhibits in public, or
(iv) distributes, or
(e) distributes otherwise than in the course of a business to such an extent as to affect prejudicially the owner of the copyright,

an article which is, and which he knows or has reason to believe is, an infringing copy of a copyright work.

(2) A person commits an offence who—

(a) makes an article specifically designed or adapted for making copies of a particular copyright work, or
(b) has such an article in his possession,

knowing or having reason to believe that it is to be used to make infringing copies for sale or hire or for use in the course of a business.

(3) Where copyright is infringed (otherwise than by reception of a broadcast or cable programme)—

(a) by the public performance of a literary, dramatic or musical work, or
(b) by the playing or showing in public of a sound recording or film,

any person who caused the work to be so performed, played or shown is guilty of an offence if he knew or had reason to believe that copyright would be infringed.

(4) A person guilty of an offence under subsection (1)(a),(b),(d)(iv) or (e) is liable—

(a) on summary conviction to imprisonment for a term not exceeding six months or a fine not exceeding the statutory maximum, or both;
(b) on conviction on indictment to a fine or imprisonment for a term not exceeding two years, or both.

(5) A person guilty of any other offence under this section is liable on summary conviction to imprisonment for a term not exceeding six months or a fine not exceeding level 5 on the standard scale, or both.

(6) Sections 104 to 106 (presumptions as to various matters connected with copyright) do not apply to proceedings for an offence under this section; but without prejudice to their application in proceedings for an order under section 108 below.

108.—(1) The court before which proceedings are brought against a person for an offence under section 107 may, if satisfied that at the time of his arrest or charge—

(a) he had in his possession, custody or control in the course of a business an infringing copy of a copyright work, or
(b) he had in his possession, custody or control an article specifically designed or adapted for making copies of a particular copyright work, knowing or having reason to believe that it had been or was to be used to make infringing copies,

order that the infringing copy or article be delivered up to the copyright owner or to such other person as the court may direct.

(2) For this purpose a person shall be treated as charged with an offence—

(a) in England, Wales and Northern Ireland, when he is orally charged or is served with a summons or indictment;
(b) in Scotland, when he is cautioned, charged or served with a complaint or indictment.

(3) An order may be made by the court of its own motion or on the application of the prosecutor (or, in Scotland, the Lord Advocate or procurator-fiscal), and may

be made whether or not the person is convicted of the offence, but shall not be made—

(a) after the end of the period specified in section 113 (period after which remedy of delivery up not available), or

(b) if it appears to the court unlikely that any order will be made under section 114 (order as to disposal of infringing copy or other article).

(4) An appeal lies from an order made under this section by a magistrates' court—

(a) in England and Wales, to the Crown Court, and

(b) in Northern Ireland, to the county court;

and in Scotland, where an order has been made under this section, the person from whose possession, custody or control the infringing copy or article has been removed may, without prejudice to any other form of appeal under any rule of law, appeal against that order in the same manner as against sentence.

(5) A person to whom an infringing copy or other article is delivered up in pursuance of an order under this section shall retain it pending the making of an order, or the decision not to make an order, under section 114.

(6) Nothing in this section affects the powers of the court under section 43 of the Powers of Criminal Courts Act 1973, section 223 or 436 of the Criminal Procedure (Scotland) Act 1975 or Article 7 of the Criminal Justice (Northern Ireland) Order 1980 (general provisions as to forfeiture in criminal proceedings).

109.—(1) Where a justice of the peace (in Scotland, a sheriff or justice of the peace) is satisfied by information on oath given by a constable (in Scotland, by evidence on oath) that there are reasonable grounds for believing—

(a) that an offence under section 107(1)(a),(b),(d)(iv) or (e) has been or is about to be committed in any premises, and

(b) that evidence that such an offence has been or is about to be committed is in those premises,

he may issue a warrant authorising a constable to enter and search the premises, using such reasonable force as is necessary.

(2) The power conferred by subsection (1) does not, in England and Wales, extend to authorising a search for material of the kinds mentioned in section 9(2) of the Police and Criminal Evidence Act 1984 (certain classes of personal or confidential material).

(3) A warrant under this section—

(a) may authorise persons to accompany any constable executing the warrant, and

(b) remains in force for 28 days from the date of its issue.

(4) In executing a warrant issued under this section a constable may seize an article if he reasonably believes that it is evidence that any offence under section 107(1) has been or is about to be committed.

(5) In this section 'premises' includes land, buildings, moveable structures, vehicles, vessels, aircraft and hovercraft.

110.—(1) Where an offence under section 107 committed by a body corporate is proved to have been committed with the consent or connivance of a director, manager, secretary or other similar officer of the body, or a person purporting to act in any such capacity, he as well as the body corporate is guilty of the offence and liable to be proceeded against and punished accordingly.

(2) In relation to a body corporate whose affairs are managed by its members 'director' means a member of the body corporate.

Provision for preventing importation of infringing copies

111.—(1) The owner of the copyright in a published literary, dramatic or musical work may give notice in writing to the Commissioners of Customs and Excise—

(a) that he is the owner of the copyright in the work, and
(b) that he requests the Commissioners, for a period specified in the notice, to treat as prohibited goods printed copies of the work which are infringing copies.

(2) The period specified in a notice under subsection (1) shall not exceed five years and shall not extend beyond the period for which copyright is to subsist.

(3) The owner of the copyright in a sound recording or film may give notice in writing to the Commissioners of Customs and Excise—

(a) that he is the owner of the copyright in the work,
(b) that infringing copies of the work are expected to arrive in the United Kingdom at a time and a place specified in the notice, and
(c) that he requests the Commissioners to treat the copies as prohibited goods.

(4) When a notice is in force under this section the importation of goods to which the notice relates, otherwise than by a person for his private and domestic use, is prohibited; but a person is not by reason of the prohibition liable to any penalty other than forfeiture of the goods.

. . .

Supplementary

113.—(1) An application for an order under section 99 (order for delivery up in civil proceedings) may not be made after the end of the period of six years from the date on which the infringing copy or article in question was made, subject to the following provisions.

(2) If during the whole or any part of that period the copyright owner—

(a) is under a disability, or
(b) is prevented by fraud or concealment from discovering the facts entitling him to apply for an order,

an application may be made at any time before the end of the period of six years from the date on which he ceased to be under a disability or, as the case may be, could with reasonable diligence have discovered those facts.

(3) In subsection (2) 'disability'—

(a) in England and Wales, has the same meaning as in the Limitation Act 1980;
(b) in Scotland, means legal disability within the meaning of the Prescription and Limitation (Scotland) Act 1973;
(c) in Northern Ireland, has the same meaning as in the Statute of Limitations (Northern Ireland) 1958.

(4) An order under section 108 (order for delivery up in criminal proceedings) shall not, in any case, be made after the end of the period of six years from the date on which the infringing copy or article in question was made.

114.—(1) An application may be made to the court for an order that an infringing copy or other article delivered up in pursuance of an order under section 99 or 108, or seized and detained in pursuance of the right conferred by section 100, shall be—

(a) forfeited to the copyright owner, or
(b) destroyed or otherwise dealt with as the court may think fit,

or for a decision that no such order should be made.

(2) In considering what order (if any) should be made, the court shall consider whether other remedies available in an action for infringement of copyright would be adequate to compensate the copyright owner and to protect his interests.

(3) Provision shall be made by rules of court as to the service of notice on persons having an interest in the copy or other articles, and any such person is entitled—

(a) to appear in proceedings for an order under this section, whether or not he was served with notice, and
(b) to appeal against any order made, whether or not he appeared;

and an order shall not take effect until the end of the period within which notice of an appeal may be given or, if before the end of that period notice of appeal is duly given, until the final determination or abandonment of the proceedings on the appeal.

(4) Where there is more than one person interested in a copy or other article, the court shall make such order as it thinks just and may (in particular) direct that the article be sold, or otherwise dealt with, and the proceeds divided.

(5) If the court decides that no order should be made under this section, the person in whose possession, custody or control the copy or other article was before being delivered up or seized is entitled to its return.

(6) References in this section to a person having an interest in a copy or other article include any person in whose favour an order could be made in respect of it under this section or under section 204 or 231 of this Act or section 58C of the Trade Marks Act 1938 (which make similar provision in relation to infringement of rights in performances, design right and trade marks).

115.—(1) In England, Wales and Northern Ireland a county court may entertain proceedings under—

section 99 (order for delivery up of infringing copy or other article),
section 101(5) (order as to exercise of rights by copyright owner where exclusive licensee has concurrent rights), or
section 114 (order as to disposal of infringing copy or other article),

where the value of the infringing copies and other articles in question does not exceed the county court limit for actions in tort.

(2) In Scotland proceedings for an order under any of those provisions may be brought in the sheriff court.

(3) Nothing in this section shall be construed as affecting the jurisdiction of the High Court or, in Scotland, the Court of Session.

Chapter VII
Copyright licensing

Licensing schemes and licensing bodies

116.—(1) In this Part a "licensing scheme" means a scheme setting out—

(a) the classes of case in which the operator of the scheme, or the person on whose behalf he acts, is willing to grant copyright licences, and

(b) the terms on which licences would be granted in those classes of case;

and for this purpose a "scheme" includes anything in the nature of a scheme, whether described as a scheme or as a tariff or by any other name.

(2) In this Chapter a "licensing body" means a society or other organisation which has as its main object, or one of its main objects the negotiation or granting, either as owner or prospective owner of copyright or as agent for him, of copyright licences, and whose objects include the granting of licences covering works of more than one author.

(3) In this section "copyright licences" means licences to do, or authorise the doing of, any of the acts restricted by copyright.

(4) References in this Chapter to licences or licensing schemes covering works of more than one author do not include licences or schemes covering only—

(a) a single collective work or collective works of which the authors are the same, or

(b) works made by, or by employees of or commissioned by, a single individual, firm, company or group of companies.

For this purpose a group of companies means a holding company and its subsidiaries, within the meaning of section 736 of the Companies Act 1985.

Royalty or other sum payable for rental of certain works

142.—(1) An application to settle the royalty or other sum payable in pursuance of section 66 (rental of sound recordings, films and computer programs) may be made to the Copyright Tribunal by the copyright owner or the person claiming to be treated as licensed by him.

(2) The Tribunal shall consider the matter and make such order as it may determine to be reasonable in the circumstances.

(3) Either party may subsequently apply to the Tribunal to vary the order, and the Tribunal shall consider the matter and make such order confirming or varying the original order as it may determine to be reasonable in the circumstances.

(4) An application under subsection (3) shall not, except with the special leave of the Tribunal, be made within twelve months from the date of the original order or of the order on a previous application under that subsection.

(5) An order under subsection (3) has effect from the date on which it is made or such later date as may be specified by the Tribunal.

. . .

Chapter IX

Qualification for and extent of copyright protection

Qualification for copyright protection

153.—(1) Copyright does not subsist in a work unless the qualification requirements of this Chapter are satisfied as regards—

(a) the author (see section 154), or
(b) the country in which the work was first published (see section 155), or
(c) in the case of a broadcast or cable programme, the country from which the broadcast was made or the cable programme was sent (see section 156).

(2) Subsection (1) does not apply in relation to Crown copyright or Parliamentary copyright (see sections 163 to 166) or to copyright subsisting by virtue of section 168 (copyright of certain international organisations).

(3) If the qualification requirements of this Chapter, or section 163, 165 or 168, are once satisfied in respect of a work, copyright does not cease to subsist by reason of any subsequent event.

154.—(1) A work qualifies for copyright protection if the author was at the material time a qualifying person, that is—

(a) a British citizen, a British Dependent Territories citizen, a British National (Overseas), a British Overseas citizen, a British subject or a British protected person within the meaning of the British Nationality Act 1981, or
(b) an individual domiciled or resident in the United Kingdom or another country to which the relevant provisions of this Part extend, or
(c) a body incorporated under the law of a part of the United Kingdom or of another country to which the relevant provisions of this Part extend.

(2) Where, or so far as, provision is made by Order under section 159 (application of this Part to countries to which it does not extend), a work also qualifies for copyright protection if at the material time the author was a citizen or subject of, an individual domiciled or resident in, or a body incorporated under the law, of a country to which the Order relates.

(3) A work of joint authorship qualifies for copyright protection if at the material time any of the authors satisfies the requirements of subsection (1) or (2); but where a work qualifies for copyright protection only under this section, only those authors who satisfy those requirements shall be taken into account for the purposes of—

section 11(1) and (2) (first ownership of copyright; entitlement of author or author's employer),
section 12(1) and (2) (duration of copyright; dependent on life of author unless work of unknown authorship), and section 9(4) (meaning of 'unknown authorship') so far as it applies for the purposes of section 12(2), and
section 57 (anonymous or pseudonymous works: acts permitted on assumptions as to expiry of copyright or death of author).

(4) The material time in relation to a literary, dramatic, musical or artistic work is—

(a) in the case of an unpublished work, when the work was made or, if the making of the work extended over a period, a substantial part of that period;

(b) in the case of a published work, when the work was first published or, if the author had died before that time, immediately before his death.

(5) The material time in relation to other descriptions of work is as follows—

(a) in the case of a sound recording or film, when it was made;

(b) in the case of a broadcast, when the broadcast was made;

(c) in the case of a cable programme, when the programme was included in a cable programme service;

. . .

155.—(1) A literary, dramatic, musical or artistic work, a sound recording or film, or the typographical arrangement of a published edition, qualifies for copyright protection if it is first published—

(a) in the United Kingdom, or

(b) in another country to which the relevant provisions of this Part extend.

(2) Where, or so far as, provision is made by Order under section 159 (application of this Part to countries to which it does not extend), such a work also qualifies for copyright protection if it is first published in a country to which the Order relates.

(3) For the purposes of this section, publication in one country shall not be regarded as other than the first publication by reason of simultaneous publication elsewhere; and for this purpose publication elsewhere within the previous 30 days shall be treated as simultaneous.

. . .

Extent and application of this Part

157.—(1) This Part extends to England and Wales, Scotland and Northern Ireland.

(2) Her Majesty may by Order in Council direct that this Part shall extend, subject to such exceptions and modifications as may be specified in the Order, to—

(a) any of the Channel Islands,

(b) the Isle of Man, or

(c) any colony.

(3) That power includes power to extend, subject to such exceptions and modifications as may be specified in the Order, any Order in Council made under the following provisions of this Chapter.

(4) The legislature of a country to which this Part has been extended may modify or add to the provisions of this Part, in their operation as part of the law of that country, as the legislature may consider necessary to adapt the provisions to the circumstances of that country—

(a) as regards procedure and remedies, or

(b) as regards works qualifying for copyright protection by virtue of a connection with that country.

(5) Nothing in this section shall be construed as restricting the extent of paragraph 36 of Schedule 1 (transitional provisions: dependent territories where the Copyright Act 1956 or the Copyright Act 1911 remains in force) in relation to the law of a dependent territory to which this Part does not extend.

158.—(1) The following provisions apply where a country to which this Part has been extended ceases to be a colony of the United Kingdom.

(2) As from the date on which it ceases to be a colony it shall cease to be regarded as a country to which this Part extends for the purposes of—

(a) section 160(2)(a) (denial of copyright protection to citizens of countries not giving adequate protection to British works), and
(b) sections 163 and 165 (Crown and Parliamentary copyright).

(3) But it shall continue to be treated as a country to which this Part extends for the purposes of sections 154 to 156 (qualification for copyright protection) until—

(a) an Order in Council is made in respect of that country under section 159 (application of this Part to countries to which it does not extend), or
(b) an Order in Council is made declaring that it shall cease to be so treated by reason of the fact that the provisions of this Part as part of the law of that country have been repealed or amended.

(4) A statutory instrument containing an Order in Council under subsection (3)(b) shall be subject to annulment in pursuance of a resolution of either House of Parliament.

159.—(1) Her Majesty may by Order in Council make provision for applying in relation to a country to which this Part does not extend any of the provisions of this Part specified in the Order, so as to secure that those provisions—

(a) apply in relation to persons who are citizens or subjects of that country or are domiciled or resident there, as they apply to persons who are British citizens or are domiciled or resident in the United Kingdom, or
(b) apply in relation to bodies incorporated under the law of that country as they apply in relation to bodies incorporated under the law of a part of the United Kingdom, or
(c) apply in relation to works first published in that country as they apply in relation to works first published in the United Kingdom, or
(d) apply in relation to broadcasts made from or cable programmes sent from that country as they apply in relation to broadcasts made from or cable programmes sent from the United Kingdom.

(2) An Order may make provision for all or any of the matters mentioned in subsection (1) and may—

(a) apply any provisions of this Part subject to such exceptions and modifications as are specified in the Order; and
(b) direct that any provisions of this Part apply either generally or in relation to such classes of works, or other classes of case, as are specified in the Order.

(3) Except in the case of a Convention country or another member State of the European Economic Community, Her Majesty shall not make an Order in Council under this section in relation to a country unless satisfied that provision has been or will be made under the law of that country, in respect of the class of works to which the Order relates, giving adequate protection to the owners of copyright under this Part.

(4) In subsection (3) 'Convention country' means a country which is a party to a Convention relating to copyright to which the United Kingdom is also a party.

(5) A statutory instrument containing an Order in Council under this section shall be subject to annulment in pursuance of a resolution of either House of Parliament.

160.—(1) If it appears to Her Majesty that the law of a country fails to give adequate protection to British works to which this section applies, or to one or more classes of such works, Her Majesty may make provision by Order in Council in accordance with this section restricting the rights conferred by this Part in relation to works of authors connected with that country.

(2) An Order in Council under this section shall designate the country concerned and provide that, for the purposes specified in the Order, works first published after a date specified in the Order shall not be treated as qualifying for copyright protection by virtue of such publication if at that time the authors are—

(a) citizens or subjects of that country (not domiciled or resident in the United Kingdom or another country to which the relevant provisions of this Part extend), or
(b) bodies incorporated under the law of that country;

and the Order may make such provision for all the purposes of this Part or for such purposes as are specified in the Order, and either generally or in relation to such class of cases as are specified in the Order, having regard to the nature and extent of that failure referred to in subsection (1).

(3) This section applies to literary, dramatic, musical and artistic works, sound recordings and films; and 'British works' means works of which the author was a qualifying person at the material time within the meaning of section 154.

(4) A statutory instrument containing an Order in Council under this section shall be subject to annulment in pursuance of a resolution of either House of Parliament.

Supplementary

161.—(1) For the purposes of this Part the territorial waters of the United Kingdom shall be treated as part of the United Kingdom.

(2) This Part applies to things done in the United Kingdom sector of the continental shelf on a structure or vessel which is present there for purposes directly connected with the exploration of the sea bed or subsoil or the exploitation of their natural resources as it applies to things done in the United Kingdom.

(3) The United Kingdom sector of the continental shelf means the areas designated by order under section 1(7) of the Continental Shelf Act 1964.

162.—(1) This Part applies to things done on a British ship, aircraft or hovercraft as it applies to things done in the United Kingdom.

(2) In this section—

'British ship' means a ship which is a British ship for the purposes of the Merchant Shipping Acts (see section 2 of the Merchant Shipping Act 1988) otherwise than by virtue of registration in a country outside the United Kingdom; and 'British aircraft' and 'British hovercraft' mean an aircraft or hovercraft registered in the United Kingdom.

Chapter X

Miscellaneous and general

. . .

Transitional provisions and savings

170.—Schedule 1 contains transitional provisions and savings relating to works made, and acts or events occurring, before the commencement of this Part, and otherwise with respect to the operation of the provisions of this Part.

171.—(1) Nothing in this Part affects—

(a) any right or privilege of any person under any enactment (except where the enactment is expressly repealed, amended or modified by this Act);

(b) any right or privilege of the Crown subsisting otherwise than under an enactment;

(c) any right or privilege of either House of Parliament;

(d) the right of the Crown or any person deriving title from the Crown to sell, use or otherwise deal with articles forfeited under the laws relating to customs and excise;

(e) the operation of any rule of equity relating to breaches of trust or confidence.

(2) Subject to those savings, no copyright or right in the nature of copyright shall subsist otherwise than by virtue of this Part or some other enactment in that behalf.

(3) Nothing in this Part affects any rule of law preventing or restricting the enforcement of copyright, on grounds of public interest or otherwise.

(4) Nothing in this Part affects any right of action or other remedy, whether civil or criminal, available otherwise than under this Part in respect of acts infringing any of the rights conferred by Chapter IV (moral rights).

(5) The savings in subsection (1) have effect subject to section 164(4) and section 166(7) (copyright in Acts, Measures and Bills: exclusion of other rights in the nature of copyright).

Interpretation

172.—(1) This Part restates and amends the law of copyright, that is, the provisions of the Copyright Act 1956, as amended.

(2) A provision of this Part which corresponds to a provision of the previous law shall not be construed as departing from the previous law merely because of a change of expression.

(3) Decisions under the previous law may be referred to for the purpose of establishing whether a provision of this Part departs from the previous law, or otherwise for establishing the true construction of this Part.

173.—(1) Where different persons are (whether in consequence of a partial assignment or otherwise) entitled to different aspects of copyright in a work, the copyright owner for any purpose of this Part is the person who is entitled to the aspect of copyright relevant for that purpose.

(2) Where copyright (or any aspect of copyright) is owned by more than one person jointly, references in this Part to the copyright owner are to all the owners, so that, in particular, any requirement of the licence of the copyright owner requires the licence of all of them.

. . .

175.—(1) In this Part 'publication', in relation to a work—

(a) means the issue of copies to the public, and
(b) includes, in the case of a literary, dramatic, musical or artistic work, making it available to the public by means of an electronic retrieval system;

and related expressions shall be construed accordingly.

(2) In this Part 'commercial publication', in relation to a literary, dramatic, musical or artistic work means—

(a) issuing copies of the work to the public at a time when copies made in advance of the receipt of orders are generally available to the public, or
(b) making the work available to the public by means of an electronic retrieval system;

and related expressions shall be construed accordingly.

. . .

(4) The following do not constitute publication for the purposes of this Part and references to commercial publication shall be construed accordingly—

(a) in the case of a literary, dramatic or musical work—
  (i) the performance of the work, or
  (ii) the broadcasting of the work or its inclusion in a cable programme service (otherwise than for the purposes of an electronic retrieval system);
(b) in the case of an artistic work—
  (i) the exhibition of the work,
  (ii) the issue to the public of copies of a graphic work representing, or of photographs of, a work of architecture in the form of a building or a model for a building, a sculpture or a work of artistic craftsmanship,
  (iii) the issue to the public of copies of a film including the work, or
  (iv) the broadcasting of the work or its inclusion in a cable programme service (otherwise than for the purposes of an electronic retrieval system);
(c) in the case of a sound recording or film—
  (i) the work being played or shown in public, or
  (ii) the broadcasting of the work or its inclusion in a cable programme service.

(5) References in this Part to publication or commercial publication do not include publication which is merely colourable and not intended to satisfy the reasonable requirements of the public.

(6) No account shall be taken for the purposes of this section of any unauthorised act.

176.—(1) The requirement in the following provisions that an instrument be signed by or on behalf of a person is also satisfied in the case of a body corporate by the affixing of its seal—

section 78(3)(b) (assertion by licensor of right to identification of author in case of public exhibition of copy made in pursuance of the licence),
section 90(3) (assignment of copyright),
section 91(1) (assignment of future copyright),
section 92(1) (grant of exclusive licence).

(2) The requirement in the following provisions that an instrument be signed by a person is satisfied in the case of a body corporate by signature on behalf of the body or by the affixing of its seal—

> section 78(2)(b) (assertion by instrument in writing of right to have author identified),
> section 87(2) (waiver of moral rights).

177.—In the application of this Part to Scotland—

> 'account of profits' means accounting and payment of profits;
> 'accounts' means count, reckoning and payment;
> 'assignment' means assignation;
> 'costs' means expenses;
> 'defendant' means defender;
> 'delivery up' means delivery;
> 'estoppel' means personal bar;
> 'injunction' means interdict;
> 'interlocutory relief' means interim remedy; and
> 'plaintiff' means pursuer.

178.—In this Part—

> 'article', in the context of an article in a periodical, includes an item of any description;
> 'business' includes a trade or profession;
> 'collective work' means—
>> (a) a work of joint authorship, or
>> (b) a work in which there are distinct contributions by different authors or in which works or parts of works of different authors are incorporated;
> 'computer-generated', in relation to a work, means that the work is generated by computer in circumstances such that there is no human author of the work;
> 'country' includes any territory;
> 'the Crown' includes the Crown in right of Her Majesty's Government in Northern Ireland or in any country outside the United Kingdom to which this Part extends;
> 'electronic' means actuated by electric, magnetic, electro-magnetic, electro-chemical or electro-mechanical energy, and 'in electronic form' means in a form usable only by electronic means;
> 'employed', 'employee', 'employer' and 'employment' refer to employment under a contract of service or of apprenticeship;
> 'facsimile copy' includes a copy which is reduced or enlarged in scale;
> 'international organisation' means an organisation the members of which include one or more states;
> 'judicial proceedings' includes proceedings before any court, tribunal or person having authority to decide any matter affecting a person's legal rights or liabilities;
> 'parliamentary proceedings' includes proceedings of the Northern Ireland Assembly or of the European Parliament;
> 'rental' means any arrangement under which a copy of a work is made available—
>> (a) for payment (in money or money's worth), or
>> (b) in the course of a business, as part of services or amenities for which payment is made,
> on terms that it will or may be returned;
> 'reprographic copy' and 'reprographic copying' refer to copying by means of a reprographic process;

'reprographic process' means a process—
  (a) for making facsimile copies, or
  (b) involving the use of an appliance for making multiple copies,
and includes, in relation to a work held in electronic form, any copying by electronic means, but does not include the making of a film or sound recording;

'sufficient acknowledgement' means an acknowledgement identifying the work in question by its title or other description, and identifying the author unless—
  (a) in the case of a published work, it is published anonymously;
  (b) in the case of an unpublished work, it is not possible for a person to ascertain the identity of the author by reasonable inquiry;

'sufficient disclaimer', in relation to an act capable of infringing the right conferred by section 80 (right to object to derogatory treatment of work), means a clear and reasonably prominent indication—
  (a) given at the time of the act, and
  (b) if the author or director is then identified, appearing along with the identification that the work has been subject to treatment to which the author or director has not consented;

'telecommunications system' means a system for conveying visual images, sounds or other information by electronic means;

'typeface' includes an ornamental motif used in printing;

'unauthorised', as regards anything done in relation to a work, means done otherwise than—
  (a) by or with the licence of the copyright owner, or
  (b) if copyright does not subsist in the work, by or with the licence of the author or, in a case where section 11(2) would have applied, the author's employer or, in either case, persons lawfully claiming under him, or
  (c) in pursuance of section 48 (copying, &c. of certain material by the Crown);

'wireless telegraphy' means the sending of electro-magnetic energy over paths not provided by a material substance constructed or arranged for that purpose;

'writing' includes any form of notation or code, whether by hand or otherwise and regardless of the method by which, or medium in or on which, it is recorded, and 'written' shall be construed accordingly.

. . .

PART III
DESIGN RIGHT

Chapter I

Design right in original designs

Introductory

213.—(1) Design right is a property right which subsists in accordance with this Part in an original design.

(2) In this Part 'design' means the design of any aspect of the shape or configuration (whether internal or external) of the whole or part of an article.

(3) Design right does not subsist in—

    (a) a method or principle of construction,

    (b) features of shape or configuration of an article which—

        (i) enable the article to be connnected to, or placed in, around or against, another article so that either article may perform its function, or

        (ii) are dependent upon the appearance of another article of which the article is intended by the designer to form an integral part, or

    (c) surface decoration.

(4) A design is not 'original' for the purposes of this Part if it is commonplace in the design field in question at the time of its creation.

(5) Design right subsists in a design only if the design qualifies for design right protection by reference to—

    (a) the designer or the person by whom the design was commissioned or the designer employed (see sections 218 and 219), or

    (b) the person by whom and country in which articles made to the design were first marketed (see section 220),

or in accordance with any Order under section 221 (power to make further provision with respect to qualification).

(6) Design right does not subsist unless and until the design has been recorded in a design document or an article has been made to the design.

(7) Design right does not subsist in a design which was so recorded, or to which an article was made, before the commencement of this Part.

    214.—(1) In this Part the 'designer', in relation to a design, means the person who creates it.

(2) In the case of a computer-generated design the person by whom the arrangements necessary for the creation of the design are undertaken shall be taken to be the designer.

    215.—(1) The designer is the first owner of any design right in a design which is not created in pursuance of a commission or in the course of employment.

(2) Where a design is created in pursuance of a commission, the person commissioning the design is the first owner of any design right in it.

(3) Where, in a case not falling within subsection (2) a design is created by an employee in the course of his employment, his employer is the first owner of any design right in the design.

(4) If a design qualifies for design right protection by virtue of section 220 (qualification by reference to first marketing of articles made to the design), the above rules do not apply and the person by whom the articles in question are marketed is the first owner of the design right.

    216.—(1) Design right expires—

    (a) fifteen years from the end of the calendar year in which the design was first recorded in a design document or an article was first made to the design, whichever first occurred, or

(b) if articles made to the design are made available for sale or hire within five years from the end of that calendar year, ten years from the end of the calendar year in which that first occurred.

(2) The reference in subsection (1) to articles being made available for sale or hire is to their being made so available anywhere in the world by or with the licence of the design right owner.

Qualification for design right protection

217.—(1) In this Part—

'qualifying individual' means a citizen or subject of, or an individual habitually resident in, a qualifying country; and

'qualifying person' means a qualifying individual or a body corporate or other body having legal personality which—

(a) is formed under the law of a part of the United Kingdom or another qualifying country, and

(b) has in any qualifying country a place of business at which substantial business activity is carried on.

(2) References in this Part to a qualifying person include the Crown and the government of any other qualifying country.

(3) In this section 'qualifying country' means—

(a) the United Kingdom,

(b) a country to which this Part extends by virtue of an Order under section 255,

(c) another member State of the European Economic Community, or

(d) to the extent that an Order under section 256 so provides, a country designated under that section as enjoying reciprocal protection.

(4) The reference in the definition of 'qualifying individual' to a person's being a citizen or subject of a qualifying country shall be construed—

(a) in relation to the United Kingdom, as a reference to his being a British citizen, and

(b) in relation to a colony of the United Kingdom, as a reference to his being a British Dependent Territories' citizen by connection with that colony.

(5) In determining for the purpose of the definition of 'qualifying person' whether substantial business activity is carried on at a place of business in any country, no account shall be taken of dealings in goods which are at all material times outside that country.

218.—(1) This section applies to a design which is not created in pursuance of a commission or in the course of employment.

(2) A design to which this section applies qualifies for design right protection if the designer is a qualifying individual or, in the case of a computer-generated design, a qualifying person.

(3) A joint design to which this section applies qualifies for design right protection if any of the designers is a qualifying individual or, as the case may be, a qualifying person.

(4) Where a joint design qualifies for design right protection under this section, only those designers who are qualifying individuals or qualifying persons are entitled to

design right under section 215(1) (first ownership of design right: entitlement of designer).

219.—(1) A design qualifies for design right protection if it is created in pursuance of a commission from, or in the course of employment with, a qualifying person.

(2) In the case of a joint commission or joint employment a design qualifies for design right protection if any of the commissioners or employers is a qualifying person.

(3) Where a design which is jointly commissioned or created in the course of joint employment qualifies for design right protection under this section, only those commissioners or employers who are qualifying persons are entitled to design right under section 215(2) or (3) (first ownership of design right: entitlement of commissioner or employer).

220.—(1) A design which does not qualify for design right protection under section 218 or 219 (qualification by reference to designer, commissioner or employer) qualifies for design right protection if the first marketing of articles made to the design—

(a) is by a qualifying person who is exclusively authorised to put such articles on the market in the United Kingdom, and
(b) takes place in the United Kingdom, another country to which this Part extends by virtue of an Order under section 255, or another member State of the European Economic Community.

(2) If the first marketing of articles made to the design is done jointly by two or more persons, the design qualifies for design right protection if any of those persons meets the requirements specified in subsection (1)(a).

(3) In such a case only the persons who meet those requirements are entitled to design right under section 215(4) (first ownership of design right: entitlement of first marketer of articles made to the design).

(4) In subsection (1)(a) 'exclusively authorised' refers—

(a) to authorisation by the person who would have been first owner of design right as designer, commissioner of the design or employer of the designer if he had been a qualifying person, or by a person lawfully claiming under such a person, and
(b) to exclusivity capable of being enforced by legal proceedings in the United Kingdom.

221.—(1) Her Majesty may, with a view to fulfilling an international obligation of the United Kingdom, by Order in Council provide that a design qualifies for design right protection if such requirements as are specified in the Order are met.

(2) An Order may make different provision for different descriptions of design or article; and may make such consequential modifications of the operation of sections 215 (ownership of design right) and sections 218 to 220 (other means of qualification) as appear to Her Majesty to be appropriate.

(3) A statutory instrument containing an Order in Council under this section shall be subject to annulment in pursuance of a resolution of either House of Parliament.

Dealings with design right

222.—(1) Design right is transmissible by assignmment, by testamentary disposition or by operation of law, as personal or moveable property.

(2) An assignment or other transmission of design right may be partial, that is, limited so as to apply —

(a) to one or more, but not all, of the things the design right owner has the exclusive right to do;
(b) to part, but not the whole, of the period for which the right is to subsist.

(3) An assignment of design right is not effective unless it is in writing signed by or on behalf of the assignor.

(4) A licence granted by the owner of design right is binding on every successor in title to his interest in the right, except a purchaser in good faith for valuable consideration and without notice (actual or constructive) of the licence or a person deriving title from such a purchaser; and references in this Part to doing anything with, or without, the licence of the design right owner shall be construed accordingly.

223.—(1) Where by an agreement made in relation to future design right, and signed by or on behalf of the prospective owner of the design right, the prospective owner purports to assign the future design right (wholly or partially) to another person, then if, on the right coming into existence, the assignee or another person claiming under him would be entitled as against all other persons to require the right to be vested in him, the right shall vest in him by virtue of this section.

(2) In this section —

'future design right' means design right which will or may come into existence in respect of a future design or class of designs or on the occurrence of a future event; and
'prospective owner' shall be construed accordingly, and includes a person who is prospectively entitled to design right by virtue of such an agreement as is mentioned in subsection (1).

(3) A licence granted by a prospective owner of design right is binding on every successor in title to his interest (or prospective interest) in the right, except a purchaser in good faith for valuable consideration and without notice (actual or constructive) of the licence or a person deriving title from such a purchaser; and references in this Part to do anything with, or without, the licence of the design right owner shall be construed accordingly.

224.—Where a design consisting of a design in which design right subsists is registered under the Registered Designs Act 1949 and the proprietor of the registered design is also the design right owner, an assignment of the right in the registered design shall be taken to be also an assignment of the design right, unless a contrary intention appears.

225.—(1) In this Part an 'exclusive licence' means a licence in writing signed by or on behalf of the design right owner authorising the licensee to the exclusion of all other persons, including the person granting the licence, to exercise a right which would otherwise be exercisable exclusively by the design right owner.

(2) The licensee under an exclusive licence has the same rights against any successor in title who is bound by the licence as he has against the person granting the licence.

Chapter II

Rights of design right owner and remedies

Infringement of design right

226.—(1) The owner of design right in a design has the exclusive right to reproduce the design for commercial purposes—

(a) by making articles to that design, or
(b) by making a design document recording the design for the purpose of enabling such articles to be made.

(2) Reproduction of a design by making articles to the design means copying the design so as to produce articles exactly or substantially to that design, and references in this Part to making articles to a design shall be construed accordingly.

(3) Design right is infringed by a person who without the licence of the design right owner does, or authorises another to do, anything which by virtue of this section is the exclusive right of the design right owner.

(4) For the purposes of this section reproduction may be direct or indirect, and it is immaterial whether any intervening acts themselves infringe the design right.

(5) This section has effect subject to the provisions of Chapter III (exceptions to rights of design right owner).

227.—(1) Design right is infringed by a person who, without the licence of the design right owner—

(a) imports into the United Kingdom for commercial purposes, or
(b) has in his possession for commercial purposes, or
(c) sells, lets for hire, or offers or exposes for sale or hire, in the course of a business,

an article which is, and which he knows or has reason to believe is, an infringing article.

(2) This section has effect subject to the provisions of Chapter III (exceptions to rights of design right owner).

228.—(1) In this Part 'infringing article', in relation to a design, shall be construed in accordance with this section.

(2) An article is an infringing article if its making to that design was an infringement of design right in the design.

(3) An article is also an infringing article if—

(a) it has been or is proposed to be imported into the United Kingdom, and
(b) its making to that design in the United Kingdom would have been an infringement of design right in the design or a breach of an exclusive licence agreement relating to the design.

(4) Where it is shown that an article is made to a design in which design right subsists or has subsisted at any time, it shall be presumed until the contrary is proved that the article was made at a time when design right subsisted.

(5) Nothing in subsection (3) shall be construed as applying to an article which may lawfully be imported into the United Kingdom by virtue of any enforceable Community right within the meaning of section 2(1) of the European Communities Act 1972.

(6) The expression 'infringing article' does not include a design document, notwithstanding that its making was or would have been an infringement of design right.

Remedies for infringement

229.—(1) An infringement of design right is actionable by the design right owner.

(2) In an action for infringement of design right all such relief by way of damages, injunctions, accounts or otherwise is available to the plaintiff as is available in respect of the infringement of any other property right.

(3) The court may in an action for infringement of design right, having regard to all the circumstances and in particular to—

(a) the flagrancy of the infringement, and
(b) any benefit accruing to the defendant by reason of the infringement,

award such additional damages as the justice of the case may require.

(4) This section has effect subject to section 233 (innocent infringement).

230.—(1) Where a person—

(a) has in his possession, custody or control for commercial purposes an infringing article, or
(b) has in his possession, custody or control anything specifically designed or adapted for making articles to a particular design, knowing or having reason to believe that it has been or is to be used to make an infringing article,

the owner of the design right in the design in question may apply to the court for an order that the infringing article or other thing be delivered up to him or to such other person as the court may direct.

(2) An application shall not be made after the end of the period specified in the following provisions of this section; and no order shall be made unless the court also makes, or it appears to the court that there are grounds for making, an order under section 231 (order as to disposal of infringing article, &c.).

(3) An application for an order under this section may not be made after the end of the period of six years from the date on which the article or thing in question was made, subject to subsection (4).

(4) If during the whole or any part of that period the design right owner—

(a) is under a disability, or
(b) is prevented by fraud or concealment from discovering the facts entitling him to apply for an order,

an application may be made at any time before the end of the period of six years from the date on which he ceased to be under a disability or, as the case may be, could with reasonable diligence have discovered those facts.

(5) In subsection (4) 'disability'—

   (a) in England and Wales, has the same meaning as in the Limitation Act 1980;
   (b) in Scotland, means legal disability within the meaning of the Prescription and Limitation (Scotland) Act 1973;
   (c) in Northern Ireland, has the same meaning as in the Statute of Limitations (Northern Ireland) 1958.

(6) A person to whom an infringing article or other thing is delivered up in pursuance of an order under this section shall, if an order under section 231 is not made, retain it pending the making of an order, or the decision not to make an order, under that section.

(7) Nothing in this section affects any other power of the court.

   231.—(1) An application may be made to the court for an order that an infringing article or other thing delivered up in pursuance of an order under section 230 shall be—

   (a) forfeited to the design right owner, or
   (b) destroyed or otherwise dealt with as the court may think fit,

or for a decision that no such order should be made.

(2) In considering what order (if any) should be made, the court shall consider whether other remedies available in an action for infringement of design right would be adequate to compensate the design right owner and to protect his interests.

(3) Provision shall be made by rules of court as to the service of notice on persons having an interest in the article or other thing, and any such person is entitled—

   (a) to appear in proceedings for an order under this section, whether or not he was served with notice, and
   (b) to appeal against any order made, whether or not he appeared;

and an order shall not take effect until the end of the period within which notice of an appeal may be given or, if before the end of that period notice of appeal is duly given, until the final determination or abandonment of the proceedings on the appeal.

(4) Where there is more than one person interested in an article or other thing, the court shall make such order as it thinks just and may (in particular) direct that the thing be sold, or otherwise dealt with, and the proceeds divided.

(5) If the court decides that no order should be made under this section, the person in whose possession, custody or control the article or other thing was before being delivered up or seized is entitled to its return.

(6) References in this section to a person having an interest in an article or other thing include any person in whose favour an order could be made in respect of it under this section or under section 114 or 204 of this Act or section 58C of the Trade Marks Act 1938 (which make similar provision in relation to infringement of copyright, rights in performances and trade marks).

   232.—(1) In England, Wales and Northern Ireland a county court may entertain proceedings under—

   section 230 (order for delivery up of infringing article, &c),
   section 231 (order as to disposal of infringing article, &c.), or
   section 235(5) (application by exclusive licensee having concurrent rights),

where the value of the infringing articles and other things in question does not exceed the county court limit for actions in tort.

(2) In Scotland proceedings for an order under any of those provisions may be brought in the sheriff court.

(3) Nothing in this section shall be construed as affecting the jurisdiction of the High Court or, in Scotland, the Court of Session.

233.—(1) Where in an action for infringement of design right brought by virtue of section 226 (primary infringement) it is shown that at the time of the infringement the defendant did not know, and had no reason to believe, that design right subsisted in the design to which the action relates, the plaintiff is not entitled to damages against him, but without prejudice to any other remedy.

(2) Where in an action for infringement of design right brought by virtue of section 227 (secondary infringement) a defendant shows that the infringing article was innocently acquired by him or a predecessor in title of his, the only remedy available against him in respect of the infringement is damages not exceeding a reasonable royalty in respect of the act complained of.

(3) In subsection (2) 'innocently acquired' means that the person acquiring the article did not know and had no reason to believe that it was an infringing article.

234.—(1) An exclusive licensee has, except against the design right owner, the same rights and remedies in respect of matters occurring after the grant of the licence as if the licence had been an assignment.

(2) His rights and remedies are concurrent with those of the design right owner; and references in the relevant provisions of this Part to the design right owner shall be construed accordingly.

(3) In an action brought by an exclusive licensee by virtue of this section a defendant may avail himself of any defence which would have been available to him if the action had been brought by the design right owner.

235.—(1) Where an action for infringement of design right brought by the design right owner or an exclusive licensee relates (wholly or partly) to an infringement in respect of which they have concurrent rights of action, the design right owner or, as the case may be, the exclusive licensee may not, without the leave of the court, proceed with the action unless the other is either joined as a plaintiff or added as a defendant.

(2) A design right owner or exclusive licensee who is added as a defendant in pursuance of subsection (1) is not liable for any costs in the action unless he takes part in the proceedings.

(3) The above provisions do not affect the granting of interlocutory relief on the application of the design right owner or an exclusive licensee.

(4) Where an action for infringement of design right is brought which relates (wholly or partly) to an infringement in respect of which the design right owner and an exclusive licensee have concurrent rights of action—

    (a) the court shall, in assessing damages, take into account—
      (i) the terms of the licence, and
      (ii) any pecuniary remedy already awarded or available to either of them in respect of the infringement;

(b) no account of profits shall be directed if an award of damages has been made, or an account of profits has been directed, in favour of the other of them in respect of the infringement; and

(c) the court shall if an account of profits is directed apportion the profits between them as the court considers just, subject to any agreement between them;

and these provisions apply whether or not the design right owner and the exclusive licensee are both parties to the action.

(5) The design right owner shall notify any exclusive licensee having concurrent rights before applying for an order under section 230 (order for delivery up of infringing article, &c.); and the court may on the application of the licensee make such order under that section as it thinks fit having regard to the terms of the licence.

Chapter III

Exceptions to rights of design right owners

Infringement of copyright

236.—Where copyright subsists in a work which consists of or includes a design in which design right subsists, it is not an infringement of design right in the design to do anything which is an infringement of the copyright in that work.

Availability of licences of right

237.—(1) Any person is entitled as of right to a licence to do in the last five years of the design right term anything which would otherwise infringe the design right.

(2) The terms of the licence shall, in default of agreement, be settled by the comptroller.

(3) The Secretary of State may if it appears to him necessary in order to—

(a) comply with an international obligation of the United Kingdom, or
(b) secure or maintain reciprocal protection for British designs in other countries,

by order exclude from the operation of subsection (1) designs of a description specified in the order or designs applied to articles of a description so specified.

(4) An order shall be made by statutory instrument; and no order shall be made unless a draft of it has been laid before and approved by a resolution of each House of Parliament.

238.—(1) Where the matters specified in a report of the Monopolies and Mergers Commission as being those which in the Commission's opinion operate, may be expected to operate or have operated against the public interest include—

(a) conditions in licences granted by a design right owner restricting the use of the design by the licensee or the right of the design right owner to grant other licences, or
(b) a refusal of a design right owner to grant licences on reasonable terms,

the powers conferred by Part I of Schedule 8 to the Fair Trading Act 1973 (powers exercisable for purpose of remedying or preventing adverse effects specified in report of Commission) include power to cancel or modify those conditions and, instead or in addition, to provide that licences in respect of the design right shall be available as of right.

(2) The references in sections 56(2) and 73(2) of that Act, and sections 10(2)(b) and 12(5) of the Competition Act 1980, to the powers specified in that Part of that Schedule shall be construed accordingly.

(3) The terms of a licence available by virtue of this section shall, in default of agreement, be settled by the comptroller.

239.—(1) If in proceedings for infringement of design right in a design in respect of which a licence is available as of right under section 237 or 238 the defendant undertakes to take a licence on such terms as may be agreed or, in default of agreement, settled by the comptroller under that section—

(a) no injunction shall be granted against him,

(b) no order for delivery up shall be made under section 230, and

(c) the amount recoverable against him by way of damages or on an account of profits shall not exceed double the amount which would have been payable by him as licensee if such a licence on those terms had been granted before the earliest infringement.

(2) An undertaking may be given at any time before final order in the proceedings, without any admission of liability.

(3) Nothing in this section affects the remedies available in respect of an infringement committed before licences of right were available.

. . .

Chapter V

Miscellaneous and general

Miscellaneous

253.—(1) Where a person threatens another person with proceedings for infringement of design right, a person aggrieved by the threats may bring an action against him claiming—

(a) a declaration to the effect that the threats are unjustifiable;

(b) an injunction against the continuance of the threats;

(c) damages in respect of any loss which he has sustained by the threats.

(2) If the plaintiff proves that the threats were made and that he is a person aggrieved by them, he is entitled to the relief claimed unless the defendant shows that the acts in respect of which proceedings were threatened did constitute, or if done would have constituted, an infringement of the design right concerned.

(3) Proceedings may not be brought under this section in respect of a threat to bring proceedings for an infringement alleged to consist of making or importing anything.

(4) Mere notification that a design is protected by design right does not constitute a threat of proceedings for the purposes of this section.

254.—(1) A person who has a licence in respect of a design by virtue of section 237 or 238 (licences of right) shall not, without the consent of the design right owner—

(a) apply to goods which he is marketing, or proposes to market, in reliance on that licence a trade description indicating that he is the licensee of the design right owner, or

(b) use any such trade description in an advertisement in relation to such goods.

(2) A contravention of subsection (1) is actionable by the design right owner.

(3) In this section 'trade description', the reference to applying a trade description to goods and 'advertisement' have the same meaning as in the Trade Descriptions Act 1968.

Extent of operation of this Part

255.—(1) This Part extends to England and Wales, Scotland and Northern Ireland.

(2) Her Majesty may by Order in Council direct that this Part shall extend, subject to such exceptions and modifications as may be specified in the Order, to—

(a) any of the Channel Islands,
(b) the Isle of Man, or
(c) any colony.

(3) That power includes power to extend, subject to such exceptions and modifications as may be specified in the Order, any Order in Council made under section 221 (further provision as to qualification for design right protection) or section 256 (countries enjoying reciprocal protection).

(4) The legislature of a country to which this Part has been extended may modify or add to the provisions of this Part, in their operation as part of the law of that country, as the legislature may consider necessary to adapt the provisions to the circumstances of that country; but not so as to deny design right protection in a case where it would otherwise exist.

(5) Where a country to which this Part extends ceases to be a colony of the United Kingdom, it shall continue to be treated as such a country for the purposes of this Part until—

(a) an Order in Council is made under section 256 designating it as a country enjoying reciprocal protection, or
(b) an Order in Council is made declaring that it shall cease to be so treated by reason of the fact that the provisions of this Part as part of the law of that country have been amended or repealed.

(6) A statutory instrument containing an Order in Council under subsection (5)(b) shall be subject to annulment in pursuance of a resolution of either House of Parliament.

256.—(1) Her Majesty may, if it appears to Her that the law of a country provides adequate protection for British designs, by Order in Council designate that country as one enjoying reciprocal protection under this Part.

(2) If the law of a country provides adequate protection only for certain classes of British design, or only for designs applied to certain classes of article, any Order designating that country shall contain provision limiting, to a corresponding extent, the protection afforded by this Part in relation to designs connected with that country.

(3) An Order under this section shall be subject to annulment in pursuance of a resolution of either House of Parliament.

257.—(1) For the purposes of this Part the territorial waters of the United Kingdom shall be treated as part of the United Kingdom.

(2) This Part applies to things done in the United Kingdom sector of the continental shelf on a structure or vessel which is present there for purposes directly connected with the exploration of the sea bed or subsoil or the exploitation of their natural resources as it applies to things done in the United Kingdom.

(3) The United Kingdom sector of the continental shelf means the areas designated by order under section 1(7) of the Continental Shelf Act 1964.

Interpretation

258.—(1) Where different persons are (whether in consequence of a partial assignment or otherwise) entitled to different aspects of design right in a work, the design right owner for any purpose of this Part is the person who is entitled to the right in the respect relevant for that purpose.

(2) Where design right (or any aspect of design right) is owned by more than one person jointly, references in this Part to the design right owner are to all the owners, so that, in particular, any requirement of the licence of the design right owner requires the licence of all of them.

259.—(1) In this Part a 'joint design' means a design produced by the collaboration of two or more designers in which the contribution of each is not distinct from that of the other or others.

(2) References in this Part to the designer of a design shall, except as otherwise provided, be construed in relation to a joint design as references to all the designers of the design.

260.—(1) The provisions of this Part apply in relation to a kit, that is, a complete or substantially complete set of components intended to be assembled into an article, as they apply in relation to the assembled article.

(2) Subsection (1) does not affect the question whether design right subsists in any aspect of the design of the components of a kit as opposed to the design of the assembled article.

261. The requirement in the following provisions that an instrument be signed by or on behalf of a person is also satisfied in the case of a body corporate by the affixing of its seal—

    section 222(3) (assignment of design right),
    section 223(1) (assignment of future design right),
    section 225(1) (grant of exclusive licence).

262. In the application of this Part to Scotland—

    'account of profits' means accounting and payment of profits;
    'accounts' means count, reckoning and payment;
    'assignment' means assignation;
    'costs' means expenses;
    'defendant' means defender;

'delivery up' means delivery;
'injunction' means interdict;
'interlocutory relief' means interim remedy; and
'plaintiff' means pursuer.

263.—(1) In this Part—

'British design' means a design which qualifies for design right protection by reason
of a connection with the United Kingdom of the designer or the person by
whom the design is commissioned or the designer is employed;
'business' includes a trade or profession;
'commission' means a commission for money or money's worth;
'the comptroller' means the Comptroller-General of Patents, Designs and Trade
Marks;
'computer-generated', in relation to a design, means that the design is generated
by computer in circumstances such that there is no human designer;
'country' includes any territory;
'the Crown' includes the Crown in right of Her Majesty's Government in Northern
Ireland;
'design document' means any record of a design, whether in the form of a drawing,
a written description, a photograph, data stored in a computer or otherwise;
'employee', 'employment' and 'employer' refer to employment under a contract of
service or of apprenticeship;
'government department' includes a Northern Ireland department.

(2) References in this Part to 'marketing', in relation to an article, are to its being sold
or let for hire, or offered or exposed for sale or hire, in the course of a business, and
related expressions shall be construed accordingly; but no account shall be taken for
the purposes of this Part of marketing which is merely colourable and not intended to
satisfy the reasonable requirements of the public.

(3) References in this Part to an act being done in relation to an article for 'commercial
purposes' are to its being done with a view to the article in question being sold or hired
in the course of a business.
. . .

Schedule 1

Copyright: transitional provisions and savings

Introductory

1.—(1) In this Schedule—

'the 1911 Act' means the Copyright Act 1911,
'the 1956 Act' means the Copyright Act 1956, and
'the new copyright provisions' means the provisions of this Act relating to copyright, that is, Part I (including this Schedule) and Schedules 3, 7 and 8 so far
as they make amendments or repeals consequential on the provisions of Part I.

(2) References in this Schedule to 'commencement', without more, are to the date on
which the new copyright provisions come into force.

(3) References in this Schedule to 'existing works' are to works made before commencement; and for this purpose a work of which the making extended over a period
shall be taken to have been made when its making was completed.

2.—(1) In relation to the 1956 Act, references in this Schedule to a work include any work or other subject-matter within the meaning of that Act.

(2) In relation to the 1911 Act—

(a) references in this Schedule to copyright include the right conferred by section 24 of that Act in substitution for a right subsisting immediately before the commencement of that Act;

(b) references in this Schedule to copyright in a sound recording are to the copyright under that Act in records embodying the recording; and

(c) references in this Schedule to copyright in a film are to any copyright under that Act in the film (so far as it constituted a dramatic work for the purposes of that Act) or in photographs forming part of the film.

General principles: continuity of the law

3. The new copyright provisions apply in relation to things existing at commencement as they apply in relation to things coming into existence after commencement, subject to any express provision to the contrary.

4.—(1) The provisions of this paragraph have effect for securing the continuity of the law so far as the new copyright provisions re-enact (with or without modification) earlier provisions.

(2) A reference in an enactment, instrument or other document to copyright, or to a work or other subject-matter in which copyright subsists, which apart from this Act would be construed as referring to copyright under the 1956 Act shall be construed, so far as may be required for continuing its effect, as being, or as the case may require, including, a reference to copyright under this Act or to works in which copyright subsists under this Act.

(3) Anything done (including subordinate legislation made), or having effect as done, under or for the purposes of a provision repealed by this Act has effect as if done under or for the purposes of the corresponding provision of the new copyright provisions.

(4) References (expressed or implied) in this Act or any other enactment, instrument or document to any of the new copyright provisions shall, so far as the context permits, be construed as including, in relation to times, circumstances and purposes before commencement, a reference to corresponding earlier provisions.

(5) A reference (express or implied) in an enactment, instrument or other document to a provision repealed by this Act shall be construed, so far as may be required for continuing its effect, as a reference to the corresponding provision of this Act.

(6) The provisions of this paragraph have effect subject to any specific transitional provision or saving and to any express amendment made by this Act.

Subsistence of copyright

5.—(1) Copyright subsists in an existing work after commencement only if copyright subsisted in it immediately before commencement.

(2) Sub-paragraph (1) does not prevent an existing work qualifying for copyright protection after commencement—

(a) under section 155 (qualification by virtue of first publication), or

(b) by virtue of an Order under section 159 (application of Part I to countries to which it does not extend).

6.—(1) Copyright shall not subsist by virtue of this Act in an artistic work made before 1st June 1957 which at the time when the work was made constituted a design capable of registration under the Registered Designs Act 1949 or under the enactments repealed by that Act, and was used, or intended to be used, as a model or pattern to be multiplied by an industrial process.

(2) For this purpose a design shall be deemed to be used as a model or pattern to be multiplied by any industrial process—

> (a) when the design is reproduced or is intended to be reproduced on more than 50 single articles, unless all the articles in which the design is reproduced or is intended to be reproduced together form only a single set of articles as defined in section 44(1) of the Registered Designs Act 1949, or
> (b) when the design is to be applied to—
>> (i)   printed paper hangings,
>> (ii) carpets, floor cloths or oil cloths, manufactured or sold in lengths or pieces,
>> (iii) textile piece goods, or textile goods manufactured or sold in lengths or pieces, or
>> (iv) lace, not made by hand.

. . .

Authorship of work

10.—The question who was the author of an existing work shall be determined in accordance with the new copyright provisions for the purposes of the rights conferred by Chapter IV of Part I (moral rights), and for all other purposes shall be determined in accordance with the law in force at the time the work was made.

First ownership of copyright

11.—(1) The question who was first owner of copyright in an existing work shall be determined in accordance with the law in force at the time the work was made.

(2) Where before commencement a person commissioned the making of a work in circumstances falling within—

> (a) section 4(3) of the 1956 Act or paragraph (a) of the proviso to section 5(1) of the 1911 Act (photographs, portraits and engravings), or
> (b) the proviso to section 12(4) of the 1956 Act (sound recordings),

those provisions apply to determine first ownership of copyright in any work made in pursuance of the commission after commencement.

Duration of copyright in existing works

12.—(1) The following provisions have effect with respect to the duration of copyright in existing works.

The question which provision applies to a work shall be determined by reference to the facts immediately before commencement; and expressions used in this paragraph which were defined for the purposes of the 1956 Act have the same meaning as in that Act.

(2) Copyright in the following descriptions of work continues to subsist until the date on which it would have expired under the 1956 Act—

(a) literary, dramatic or musical works in relation to which the period of 50 years mentioned in the proviso to section 2(3) of the 1956 Act (duration of copyright in works made available to the public after the death of the author) has begun to run;

(b) engravings in relation to which the period of 50 years mentioned in the proviso to section 3(4) of the 1956 Act (duration of copyright in works published after the death of the author) has begun to run;

(c) published photographs and photographs taken before 1st June 1957;

(d) published sound recordings and sound recordings made before 1st June 1957;

(e) published films and films falling within section 13(3)(a) of the 1956 Act (films registered under former enactments relating to registration of films).

(3) Copyright in anonymous or pseudonymous literary, dramatic, musical or artistic works (other than photographs) continues to subsist—

(a) if the work is published, until the date on which it would have expired in accordance with the 1956 Act, and

(b) if the work is unpublished, until the end of the period of 50 years from the end of the calendar year in which the new copyright provisions come into force or, if during that period the work is first made available to the public within the meaning of section 12(2) (duration of copyright in works of unknown authorship), the date on which copyright expires in accordance with that provision;

unless, in any case, the identity of the author becomes known before that date, in which case section 12(1) applies (general rule: life of the author plus 50 years).

(4) Copyright in the following descriptions of work continues to subsist until the end of the period of 50 years from the end of the calendar year in which the new copyright provisions come into force—

(a) literary, dramatic and musical works of which the author has died and in relation to which none of the acts mentioned in paragraphs (a) to (e) of the proviso to section 2(3) of the 1956 Act has been done;

(b) unpublished engravings of which the author has died;

(c) unpublished photographs taken on or after 1st June 1957.

(5) Copyright in the following descriptions of work continues to subsist until the end of the period of 50 years from the end of the calendar year in which the new copyright provisions come into force—

(a) unpublished sound recordings made on or after 1st June 1957;

(b) films not falling within sub-paragraph (2)(e)above,

unless the recording or film is published before the end of that period in which case copyright in it shall continue until the end of the period of 50 years from the end of the calendar year in which the recording or film is published.

(6) Copyright in any other description of existing work continues to subsist until the date on which copyright in that description of work expires in accordance with sections 12 to 15 of this Act.

. . .

Acts infringing copyright

14.—(1) The provisions of Chapters II and III of Part I as to the acts constituting an infringement of copyright apply only in relation to acts done after commencement;

the provisions of the 1956 Act continue to apply in relation to acts done before commencement.

(2) So much of section 18(2) as extends the restricted act of issuing copies to the public to include the rental to the public of copies of sound recordings, films or computer programs does not apply in relation to a copy of a sound recording, film or computer program acquired by any person before commencement for the purpose of renting it to the public.

(3) For the purposes of section 27 (meaning of 'infringing copy') the question whether the making of an article constituted an infringement of copyright, or would have done if the article had been made in the United Kingdom, shall be determined—

    (a) in relation to an article made on or after 1st June 1957 and before commencement, by reference to the 1956 Act, and
    (b) in relation to an article made before 1st June 1957, by reference to the 1911 Act.

(4) For the purposes of the application of sections 31(2), 51(2) and 62(3) (subsequent exploitation of things whose making was, by virtue of an earlier provision of the section, not an infringement of copyright) to things made before commencement, it shall be assumed that the new copyright provisions were in force at all material times.

(5) Section 55 (articles for producing material in a particular typeface) applies where articles have been marketed as mentioned in subsection (1) before commencement with the substitution for the period mentioned in subsection (3) of the period of 25 years from the end of the calendar year in which the new copyright provisions come into force.

(6) Section 56 (transfer of copies, adaptations, &c. of work in electronic form) does not apply in relation to a copy purchased before commencement.

(7) In section 65 (reconstruction of buildings) the reference to the owner of the copyright in the drawings or plans is, in relation to buildings constructed before commencement, to the person who at the time of the construction was the owner of the copyright in the drawings or plans under the 1956 Act, the 1911 Act or any enactment repealed by the 1911 Act.
  . . .

Designs

    19.—(1) Section 51 (exclusion of copyright protection in relation to works recorded or embodied in design document or models) does not apply for ten years after commencement in relation to a design recorded or embodied in a design document or model before commencement.

(2) During those ten years the following provisions of Part III (design right) apply to any relevant copyright as in relation to design right—

    (a) sections 237 to 239 (availability of licences of right), and
    (b) sections 247 and 248 (application to comptroller to settle terms of licence of right).

(3) In section 237 as it applies by virtue of this paragraph, for the reference in sub-section (1) to the last five years of the design right term there shall be substituted a reference to the last five years of the period of ten years referred to in sub-paragraph (1) above, or to so much of those last five years during which copyright subsists.

(4) In section 239 as it applies by virtue of this paragraph, for the reference in sub-section (1)(b) to section 230 there shall be substituted a reference to section 99.

(5) Where a licence of right is available by virtue of this paragraph, a person to whom a licence was granted before commencement may apply to the comptroller for an order adjusting the terms of that licence.

(6) The provisions of sections 249 and 250 (appeals and rules) apply in relation to proceedings brought under or by virtue of this paragraph as to proceedings under Part III.

(7) A licence granted by virtue of this paragraph shall relate only to acts which would be permitted by section 51 if the design document or model had been made after commencement.

(8) Section 100 (right to seize infringing copies, &c.) does not apply during the period of ten years referred to in sub-paragraph (1) in relation to anything to which it would not apply if the design in question had been first recorded or embodied in a design document or model after commencement.

(9) Nothing in this paragraph affects the operation of any rule of law preventing or restricting the enforcement of copyright in relation to a design.

20.—(1) Where section 10 of the 1956 Act (effect of industrial application of design corresponding to artistic work) applied in relation to an artistic work at any time before commencement, section 52(2) of this Act applies with the substitution for the period of 25 years mentioned there of the relevant period of 15 years as defined in section 10(3) of the 1956 Act.

(2) Except as provided in sub-paragraph (1), section 52 applies only where articles are marketed as mentioned in subsection (1)(b) after commencement.

. . .

Assignments and licences

25.—(1) Any document made or event occurring before commencement which had any operation—

    (a) affecting the ownership of the copyright in an existing work, or
    (b) creating, transferring or terminating an interest, right or licence in respect of the copyright in an existing work,

has the corresponding operation in relation to copyright in the work under this Act.

(2) Expressions used in such a document shall be construed in accordance with their effect immediately before commencement.

26.—(1) Section 91(1) of this Act (assignment of future copyright: statutory vesting of legal interest on copyright coming into existence) does not apply in relation to an agreement made before 1st June 1957.

(2) The repeal by this Act of section 37(2) of the 1956 Act (assignment of future copyright: devolution of right where assignee dies before copyright comes into existence) does not affect the operation of that provision in relation to an agreement made before commencement.

. . .

Remedies for infringement

31.—(1) Sections 96 and 97 of this Act (remedies for infringement) apply only in relation to an infringement of copyright committed after commencement; section 17 of the 1956 Act continues to apply in relation to infringements committed before commencement.

(2) Sections 99 and 100 of this Act (delivery up or seizure of infringing copies, &c.) apply to infringing copies and other articles made before or after commencement; section 18 of the 1956 Act, and section 7 of the 1911 Act, (conversion damages, &c.), do not apply after commencement except for the purposes of proceedings begun before commencement.

(3) Sections 101 to 102 of this Act (rights and remedies of exclusive licensee) apply where sections 96 to 100 of this Act apply; section 19 of the 1956 Act continues to apply where section 17 or 18 of that Act applies.

(4) Sections 104 to 106 of this Act (presumptions) apply only in proceedings brought by virtue of this Act; section 20 of the 1956 Act continues to apply in proceedings brought by virtue of that Act.

32.—Sections 101 and 102 of this Act (rights and remedies of exclusive licensee) do not apply to a licence granted before 1st June 1957.

33.—(1) The provisions of section 107 of this Act (criminal liability for making or dealing with infringing articles, &c.) apply only in relation to acts done after commencement; section 21 of the 1956 Act (penalties and summary proceedings in respect of dealings which infringe copyright) continues to apply in relation to acts done before commencement.

(2) Section 109 of this Act (search warrants) applies in relation to offences committed before commencement in relation to which section 21A or 21B of the 1956 Act applied; sections 21A and 21B continue to apply in relation to warrants issued before commencement.

. . .

Qualifications for copyright protection

35.—Every work in which copyright subsisted under the 1956 Act immediately before commencement shall be deemed to satisfy the requirements of Part I of this Act as to qualification for copyright protection.

. . .

Copyright (Computer Software) Amendment Act 1985

An Act to amend the Copyright Act 1956 in its application to computer programs and computer storage.

[16th July 1985]

Be it enacted by the Queen's most Excellent Majesty, by and with the advice and consent of the Lords Spiritual and Temporal, and Commons, in this present Parliament assembled, and by the authority of the same, as follows: —

Copyright in computer programs

1.—(1) The Copyright Act 1956 shall apply in relation to a computer program including one made before the commencement of this Act) as it applies in relation to a literary work and shall so apply whether or not copyright would subsist in that program apart from this Act.

(2) For the purposes of the application of the said Act of 1956 in relation to a computer program, a version of the program in which it is converted into or out of a computer language or code, or into a different computer language or code, is an adaptation of the program.

Computer storage

2. References in the Copyright Act 1956 to the reduction of any work to a material form, or to the reproduction of any work in a material form, shall include references to the storage of that work in a computer.

Offences and search warrants

3. Where an infringing copy of a computer program consists of a disc, tape or chip or of any other device which embodies signals serving for the impartation of the program or part of it, sections 21 to 21B of the Copyright Act 1956 (offences and search warrants) shall apply in relation to that copy as they apply in relation to an infringing copy of a sound recording or cinematograph film.

Short title, interpretation, commencement and extent

4.—(1) This Act may be cited as the Copyright (Computer Software) Amendment Act 1985.

(2) This Act shall be construed as one with the Copyright Act 1956 and Part V of that Act (extension and restriction of operation of Act) shall apply in relation to the provisions of this Act as it applies in relation to the provisions of that Act.

(3) This Act shall come into force at the end of the period of two months beginning with the day on which it is passed.

(4) Nothing in this Act shall affect—

(a) the determination of any question as to whether anything done before the commencement of this Act was an infringement of copyright or an offence under section 21 of the said Act of 1956; or
(b) the penalty which may be imposed for any offence under that section committed before the commencement of this Act.

(5) This Act extends to Northern Ireland.

Computer Misuse Act 1990

Chapter 18

An Act to make provision for securing computer material against unauthorised access or modification; and for connected purposes.

[29th June 1990]

Be it enacted by the Queen's most Excellent Majesty, by and with the advice and consent of the Lords Spiritual and Temporal, and Commons, in this present Parliament assembled, and by the authority of the same, as follows:—

Computer misuse offences

1.—(1) A person is guilty of an offence if—

(a) he causes a computer to perform any function with intent to secure access to any program or data held in any computer;
(b) the access he intends to secure is unauthorised; and
(c) he knows at the time when he causes the computer to perform the function that that is the case.

(2) The intent a person has to have to commit an offence under this section need not be directed at—

(a) any particular program or data;
(b) a program or data of any particular kind; or
(c) a program or data held in any particular computer.

(3) A person guilty of an offence under this section shall be liable on summary conviction to imprisonment for a term not exceeding six months or to a fine not exceeding level 5 on the standard scale or to both.

2.—(1) A person is guilty of an offence under this section if he commits an offence under section 1 above ('the unauthorised access offence') with intent—

(a) to commit an offence to which this section applies; or
(b) to facilitate the commission of such an offence (whether by himself or by any other person);

and the offence he intends to commit or facilitate is referred to below in this section as the further offence.

(2) This section applies to offences—

(a) for which the sentence is fixed by law; or

(b) for which a person of twenty-one years of age or over (not previously convicted) may be sentenced to imprisonment for a term of five years (or, in England and Wales, might be so sentenced but for the restrictions imposed by section 33 of the Magistrates' Courts Act 1980).

(3) It is immaterial for the purposes of this section whether the further offence is to be committed on the same occasion as the unauthorised access offence or on any future occasion.

(4) A person may be guilty of an offence under this section even though the facts are such that the commission of the further offence is impossible.

(5) A person guilty of an offence under this section shall be liable—

(a) on summary conviction, to imprisonment for a term not exceeding six months or to a fine not exceeding the statutory maximum or to both; and

(b) on conviction on indictment, to imprisonment for a term not exceeding five years or to a fine or to both.

3.—(1) A person is guilty of an offence if—

(a) he does any act which causes an unauthorised modification of the contents of any computer; and

(b) at the time when he does the act he has the requisite intent and the requisite knowledge.

(2) For the purposes of subsection (1)(b) above the requisite intent is an intent to cause a modification of the contents of any computer and by so doing—

(a) to impair the operation of any computer;

(b) to prevent or hinder access to any program or data held in any computer; or

(c) to impair the operation of any such program or the reliability of any such data.

(3) The intent need not be directed at—

(a) any particular computer;

(b) any particular program or data or a program or data of any particular kind; or

(c) any particular modification or a modification of any particular kind.

(4) For the purposes of subsection (1)(b) above the requisite knowledge is knowledge that any modification he intends to cause is unauthorised.

(5) It is immaterial for the purpose of this section whether an unauthorised modification or any intended effect of it of a kind mentioned in subsection (2) above is, or is intended to be, permanent or merely temporary.

(6) For the purposes of the Criminal Damage Act 1971 a modification of the contents of a computer shall not be regarded as damaging any computer or computer storage medium unless its effect on that computer or computer storage medium impairs its physical condition.

(7) A person guilty of an offence under this section shall be liable—

(a) on summary conviction, to imprisonment for a term not exceeding six months or to a fine not exceednig the statutory maximum or to both; and

(b) on conviction on indictment, to imprisonment for a term not exceeding five years or to a fine or to both.

Jurisdiction

4.—(1) Except as provided below in this section, it is immaterial for the purposes of any offence under section 1 or 3 above—

(a) whether any act or other event proof of which is required for conviction of the offence occurred in the home country concerned; or
(b) whether the accused was in the home country concerned at the time of any such act or event.

(2) Subject to subsection (3) below, in the case of such an offence at least one significant link with domestic jurisdiction must exist in the circumstances of the case for the offence to be committed.

(3) There is no need for any such link to exist for the commission of an offence under section 1 above to be established in proof of an allegation to that effect in proceedings for an offence under section 2 above.

(4) Subject to section 8 below, where—

(a) any such link does in fact exist in the case of an offence under section 1 above; and
(b) commission of that offence is alleged in proceedings for an offence under section 2 above;

section 2 above shall apply as if anything the accused intended to do or facilitate in any place outside the home country concerned which would be an offence to which section 2 applies if it took place in the home country concerned were the offence in question.

(5) This section is without prejudice to any jurisdiction exercisable by a court in Scotland apart from this section.

(6) References in this Act to the home country concerned are references—

(a) in the application of this Act to England and Wales, to England and Wales;
(b) in the application of this Act to Scotland, to Scotland; and
(c) in the application of this Act to Northern Ireland, to Northern Ireland.

5.— (1) The following provisions of this section apply for the interpretation of section 4 above.

(2) In relation to an offence under section 1, either of the following is a significant link with domestic jurisdiction—

(a) that the accused was in the home country concerned at the time when he did the act which caused the computer to perform the function; or
(b) that any computer containing any program or data to which the accused secured or intended to secure unauthorised access by doing that act was in the home country concerned at that time.

(3) In relation to an offence under section 3, either of the following is a significant link with domestic jurisdiction—

(a) that the accused was in the home country concerned at the time when he did the act which caused the unauthorised modification; or
(b) that the unauthorised modification took place in the home country concerned.

6.—(1) On a charge of conspiracy to commit an offence under this Act the following questions are immaterial to the accused's guilt—

(a) the question where any person became a party to the conspiracy; and
(b) the question whether any act, omission or other event occurred in the home country concerned. .

(2) On a charge of attempting to commit an offence under section 3 above the following questions are immaterial to the accused's guilt—

(a) the question where the attempt was made; and
(b) the question whether it had an effect in the home country concerned.

(3) On a charge of incitement to commit an offence under this Act the question where the incitement took place is immaterial to the accused's guilt.

(4) This section does not extend to Scotland.

7.—(1) The following subsections shall be inserted after subsection (1) of section 1 of the Criminal Law Act 1977—

'(1A) Subject to section 8 of the Computer Misuse Act 1990 (relevance of external law), if this subsection applies to an agreement, this Part of this Act has effect in relation to it as it has effect in relation to an agreement falling within subsection (1) above.
(1B) Subsection (1A) above applies to an agreement if—
(a) a party to it, or a party's agent, did anything in England and Wales in relation to it before its formation; or
(b) a party to it became a party in England and Wales (by joining it either in person or through an agent); or
(c) a party to it, or a party's agent, did or omitted anything in England and Wales in pursuance of it;
and the agreement would fall within subsection (1) above as an agreement relating to the commission of a computer misuse offence but for the fact that the offence would not be an offence triable in England and Wales if committed in accordance with the parties' intentions.'

(2) The following subsections shall be inserted after subsection (4) of that section—

'(5) In the application of this Part of this Act to an agreement to which subsection (1A) above applies any reference to an offence shall be read as a reference to what would be the computer misuse offence in question but for the fact that it is not an offence triable in England and Wales.
(6) In this section "computer misuse offence" means an offence under the Computer Misuse Act 1990.'

(3) The following subsections shall be inserted after section 1(1) of the Criminal Attempts Act 1981—

'(1A) Subject to section 8 of the Computer Misuse Act 1990 (relevance of external law), if this subsection applies to an act, what the person doing it had in view shall be treated as an offence to which this section applies.
(1B) Subsection (1A) above applies to an act if—
(a) it is done in England and Wales; and
(b) it would fall within subsection (1) above as more than merely preparatory to the commission of an offence under section 3 of the Computer Misuse Act 1990 but for the fact that the offence, if completed, would not be an offence triable in England and Wales.'

(4) Subject to section 8 below, if any act done by a person in England and Wales would amount to the offence of incitement to commit an offence under this Act but for the fact that what he had in view would not be an offence triable in England and Wales—

(a) what he had in view shall be treated as an offence under this Act for the purposes of any charge of incitement brought in respect of that act; and
(b) any such charge shall accordingly be triable in England and Wales.

8.—(1) A person is guilty of an offence triable by virtue of section 4(4) above only if what he intended to do or facilitate would involve the commission of an offence under the law in force where the whole or any part of it was intended to take place.

(2) A person is guilty of an offence triable by virtue of section 1(1A) of the Criminal Law Act 1977 only if the pursuit of the agreed course of conduct would at some stage involve—

(a) an act or omission by one or more of the parties; or
(b) the happening of some other event;

constituting an offence under the law in force where the act, omission or other event was intended to take place.

(3) A person is guilty of an offence triable by virtue of section 1(1A) of the Criminal Attempts Act 1981 or by virtue of section 7(4) above only if what he had in view would involve the commission of an offence under the law in force where the whole or any part of it was intended to take place.

(4) Conduct punishable under the law in force in any place is an offence under that law for the purposes of this section, however it is described in that law.

(5) Subject to subsection (7) below, a condition specified in any of subsections (1) to (3) above shall be taken to be satisfied unless not later than rules of court may provide the defence serve on the prosecution a notice—

(a) stating that, on the facts as alleged with respect to the relevant conduct, the condition is not in their opinion satisfied;
(b) showing their grounds for that opinion; and
(c) requiring the prosecution to show that it is satisfied.

(6) In subsection (5) above 'the relevant conduct' means—

(a) where the condition in subsection (1) above is in question, what the accused intended to do or facilitate;
(b) where the condition in subsection (2) above is in question, the agreed course of conduct; and
(c) where the condition in subsection (3) above is in question, what the accused had in view.

(7) The court, if it thinks fit, may permit the defence to require the prosecution to show that the condition is satisfied without the prior service of a notice under subsection (5) above.

(8) If by virtue of subsection (7) above a court of solemn jurisdiction in Scotland permits the defence to require the prosecution to show that the condition is satisfied, it shall be competent for the prosecution for that purpose to examine any witness or put in evidence any production not included in the lists lodged by it.

(9) In the Crown Court the question whether the condition is satisfied shall be decided by the judge alone.

(10) In the High Court of Justiciary and in the sheriff court the question whether the condition is satisfied shall be decided by the judge or, as the case may be, the sheriff alone.

    9.—(1) In any proceedings brought in England and Wales in respect of any offence to which this section applies it is immaterial to guilt whether or not the accused was a British citizen at the time of any act, omission or other event proof of which is required for conviction of the offence.

(2) This section applies to the following offences—

    (a) any offence under this Act;
    (b) conspiracy to commit an offence under this Act;
    (c) any attempt to commit an offence under section 3 above; and
    (d) incitement to commit an offence under this Act.

Miscellaneous and general

    10.—Section 1(1) above has effect without prejudice to the operation—

    (a) in England and Wales of any enactment relating to powers of inspection, search or seizure; and
    (b) in Scotland of any enactment or rule of law relating to powers of examination, search or seizure.

    11.—(1) A magistrates' court shall have jurisdiction to try an offence under section 1 above if—

    (a) the accused was within its commission area at the time when he did the act which caused the computer to perform the function; or
    (b) any computer containing any program or data to which the accused secured or intended to secure unauthorised access by doing that act was in its commission area at that time.

(2) Subject to subsection (3) below, proceedings for an offence under section 1 above may be brought within a period of six months from the date on which evidence sufficient in the opinion of the prosecutor to warrant the proceedings came to his knowledge.

(3) No such proceedings shall be brought by virtue of this section more than three years after the commission of the offence.

(4) For the purposes of this section, a certificate signed by or on behalf of the prosecutor and stating the date on which evidence sufficient in his opinion to warrant the proceedings came to his knowledge shall be conclusive evidence of that fact.

(5) A certificate stating that matter and purporting to be so signed shall be deemed to be so signed unless the contrary is proved.

(6) In this section 'commission area' has the same meaning as in the Justice of the Peace Act 1970.

(7) This section does not extend to Scotland.

12.—(1) If on the trial on indictment of a person charged with—

(a) an offence under section 2 above; or
(b) an offence under section 3 above or any attempt to commit such an offence;

the jury find him not guilty of the offence charged, they may find him guilty of an offence under section 1 above if on the facts shown he could have been found guilty of that offence in proceedings for that offence brought before the expiry of any time limit under section 11 above applicable to such proceedings.

(2) The Crown Court shall have the same powers and duties in relation to a person who is by virtue of this section convicted before it of an offence under section 1 above as a magistrates' court would have on convicting him of the offence.

(3) This section is without prejudice to section 6(3) of the Criminal Law Act 1967 (conviction of alternative indictable offence on trial on indictment).

(4) This section does not extend to Scotland.

13.—(1) A sheriff shall have jurisdiction in respect of an offence under section 1 or 2 above if—

(a) the accused was in the sheriffdom at the time when he did the act which caused the computer to perform the function; or
(b) any computer containing any program or data to which the accused secured or intended to secure unauthorised access by doing that act was in the sheriffdom at that time.

(2) A sheriff shall have jurisdiction in respect of an offence under section 3 above if—

(a) the accused was in the sheriffdom at the time when he did the act which caused the unauthorised modification; or
(b) the unauthorised modification took place in the sheriffdom.

(3) Subject to subsection (4) below, summary proceedings for an offence under section 1, 2 or 3 above may be commenced within a period of six months from the date on which evidence sufficient in the opinion of the procurator fiscal to warrant proceedings came to his knowledge.

(4) No such proceedings shall be commenced by virtue of this section more than three years after the commission of the offence.

(5) For the purposes of this section, a certificate signed by or on behalf of the procurator fiscal and stating the date on which evidence sufficient in his opinion to warrant the proceedings came to his knowledge shall be conclusive evidence of that fact.

(6) A certificate stating that matter and purporting to be so signed shall be deemed to be so signed unless the contrary is proved.

(7) Subsection (3) of section 331 of the Criminal Procedure (Scotland) Act 1975 (date of commencement of proceedings) shall apply for the purposes of this section as it applies for the purposes of that section.

(8) In proceedings in which a person is charged with an offence under section 2 or 3 above and is found not guilty or is acquitted of that charge, he may be found guilty of an offence under section 1 above if on the facts shown he could have been found guilty of that offence in proceedings for that offence commenced before the expiry of any time limit under this section applicable to such proceedings.

(9) Subsection (8) above shall apply whether or not an offence under section 1 above has been libelled in the complaint or indictment.

(10) A person found guilty of an offence under section 1 above by virtue of subsection (8) above shall be liable, in respect of that offence, only to the penalties set out in section 1.

(11) This section extends to Scotland only.

14.—(1) Where a circuit judge is satisfied by information on oath given by a constable that there are reasonable grounds for believing—

(a) that an offence under section 1 above has been or is about to be committed in any premises; and
(b) that evidence that such an offence has been or is about to be committed is in those premises;

he may issue a warrant authorising a constable to enter and search the premises, using such reasonable force as is necessary.

(2) The power conferred by subsection (1) above does not extend to authorising a search for material of the kinds mentioned in section 9(2) of the Police and Criminal Evidence Act 1984 (privileged, excluded and special procedure material).

(3) A warrant under this section—

(a) may authorise persons to accompany any constable executing the warrant; and
(b) remains in force for twenty-eight days from the date of its issue.

(4) In executing a warrant issued under this section a constable may seize an article if he reasonably believes that it is evidence that an offence under section 1 above has been or is about to be committed.

(5) In this section 'premises' includes land, buildings, movable structures, vehicles, vessels, aircraft and hovercraft.

(6) This section does not extend to Scotland.

15.—The offences to which an Order in Council under section 2 of the Extradition Act 1870 can apply shall include—

(a) offences under section 2 or 3 above;
(b) any conspiracy to commit such an offence; and
(c) any attempt to commit an offence under section 3 above.

16.—(1) The following provisions of this section have effect for applying this Act in relation to Northern Ireland with the modifications there mentioned.

(2) In section 2(2)(b)—

(a) the reference to England and Wales shall be read as a reference to Northern Ireland; and
(b) the reference to section 33 of the Magistrates' Courts Act 1980 shall be read as a reference to Article 46(4) of the Magistrates' Courts (Northern Ireland) Order 1981.

(3) The reference in section 3(6) to the Criminal Damage Act 1971 shall be read as a reference to the Criminal Damage (Northern Ireland) Order 1977.

(4) Subsections (5) to (7) below apply in substitution for subsections (1) to (3) of section 7; and any reference in subsection (4) of that section to England and Wales shall be read as a reference to Northern Ireland.

(5) The following paragraphs shall be inserted after paragraph (1) of Article 9 of the Criminal Attempts and Conspiracy (Northern Ireland) Order 1983—

'(1A) Subject to section 8 of the Computer Misuse Act 1990 (relevance of external law), if this paragraph applies to an agreement, this Part has effect in relation to it as it has effect in relation to an agreement falling within paragraph (1).
(1B) Paragraph (1A) applies to an agreement if—
(a) a party to it, or a party's agent, did anything in Northern Ireland in relation to it before its formation;
(b) a party to it became a party in Northern Ireland (by joining it either in person or through an agent); or
(c) a party to it, or a party's agent, did or omitted anything in Northern Ireland in pursuance of it;

and the agreement would fall within paragraph (1) as an agreement relating to the commission of a computer misuse offence but for the fact that the offence would not be an offence triable in Northern Ireland if committed in accordance with the parties' intentions.'

(6) The following paragraph shall be inserted after paragraph (4) of that Article—

'(5) In the application of this Part to an agreement to which paragraph (1A) applies any reference to an offence shall be read as a reference to what would be the computer misuse offence in question but for the fact that it is not an offence triable in Northern Ireland.
(6) In this Article "computer misuse offence" means an offence under the Computer Misuse Act 1990.'

(7) The following paragraphs shall be inserted after Article 3(1) of that Order—

'(1A) Subject to section 8 of the Computer Misuse Act 1990 (relevance of external law), if this paragraph applies to an act, what the person doing it had in view shall be treated as an offence to which this Article applies.
(1B) Paragraph (1A) above applies to an act if—
(a) it is done in Northern Ireland; and
(b) it would fall within paragraph (1) as more than merely preparatory to the commission of an offence under section 3 of the Computer Misuse Act 1990 but for the fact that the offence, if completed, would not be an offence triable in Northern Ireland.'

(8) In section 8—

(a) the reference in subsection (2) to section 1(1A) of the Criminal Law Act 1977 shall be read as a reference to Article 9(1A) of that Order; and
(b) the reference in subsection (3) to section 1(1A) of the Criminal Attempts Act 1981 shall be read as a reference to Article 3(1A) of that Order.

(9) The references in sections 9(1) and 10 to England and Wales shall read as references to Northern Ireland.

(10) In section 11, for subsection (1) there shall be substituted—

'(1) A magistrates' court for a county division in Northern Ireland may hear and determine a complaint charging an offence under section 1 above or conduct a preliminary investigation or preliminary inquiry into an offence under that section if—
(a) the accused was in that division at the time when he did the act which caused the computer to perform the function; or
(b) any computer containing any program or data to which the accused secured or intended to secure unauthorised access by doing that act was in that division at that time.';

and subsection (6) shall be omitted.

(11) The reference in section 12(3) to section 6(3) of the Criminal Law Act 1967 shall be read as a reference to section 6(2) of the Criminal Law Act (Northern Ireland) 1967.

(12) In section 14—

(a) the reference in subsection (1) to a circuit judge shall be read as a reference to a county court judge; and
(b) the reference in subsection (2) to section 9(2) of the Police and Criminal Evidence Act 1984 shall be read as a reference to Article 11(2) of the Police and Criminal Evidence (Northern Ireland) Order 1989.

17.—(1) The following provisions of this section apply for the interpretation of this Act.

(2) A person secures access to any program or data held in a computer if by causing a computer to perform any function he—

(a) alters or erases the program or data;
(b) copies or moves it to any storage medium other than that in which it is held or to a different location in the storage medium in which it is held;
(c) uses it; or
(d) has it output from the computer in which it is held (whether by having it displayed or in any other manner);

and references to access to a program or data (and to an intent to secure such access) shall be read accordingly.

(3) For the purposes of subsection (2)(c) above a person uses a program if the function he causes the computer to perform—

(a) causes the program to be executed; or
(b) is itself a function of the program.

(4) For the purposes of subsection (2)(d) above —

(a) a program is output if the instructions of which it consists are output; and
(b) the form in which any such instructions or any other data is output (and in particular whether or not it represents a form in which, in the case of instructions, they are capable of being executed or, in the case of data, it is capable of being processed by a computer) is immaterial.

(5) Access of any kind by any person to any program or data held in a computer is unauthorised if —

(a) he is not himself entitled to control access of the kind in question to the program or data; and
(b) he does not have consent to access by him of the kind in question to the program or data from any person who is so entitled.

(6) References to any program or data held in a computer include references to any program or data held in any removable storage medium which is for the time being in the computer; and a computer is to be regarded as containing any program or data held in any such medium.

(7) A modification of the contents of any computer takes place if, by the operation of any function of the computer concerned or any other computer —

(a) any program or data held in the computer concerned is altered or erased; or
(b) any program or data is added to its contents;

and any act which contributes towards causing such a modification shall be regarded as causing it.

(8) Such a modification is unauthorised if —

(a) the person whose act causes it is not himself entitled to determine whether the modification should be made: and
(b) he does not have consent to the modification from any person who is so entitled.

(9) References to the home country concerned shall be read in accordance with section 4(6) above.

(10) References to a program include references to part of a program.

18.—(1) This Act may be cited as the Computer Misuse Act 1990.

(2) This Act shall come into force at the end of the period of two months beginning with the day on which it is passed.

(3) An offence is not committed under this Act unless every act or other event proof of which is required for conviction of the offence takes place after this Act comes into force.

Statutory Instrument
1989 No. 1100

DESIGNS

The Design Right (Semiconductor Topographies) Regulations 1989

Made	*29th June 1989*
Coming into force	*1st August 1989*

Whereas a draft of the following Regulations has been approved by resolution of each House of Parliament:

Now, therefore, the Secretary of State, being designated[1] for the purposes of section 2(2) of the European Communities Act 1972[2] in relation to the conferment and protection of exclusive rights in the topographies of semiconductor products, in exercise of the powers conferred on him by the said section 2(2) hereby makes the following Regulations:

Citation and commencement

1.—These regulations may be cited as the Design Right (Semiconductor Topographies) Regulations 1989 and shall come into force on 1st August 1989.

Interpretation

2.—(1) In these Regulations—

'the Act' means the Copyright, Designs and Patents Act 1988;[3]

'semiconductor product' means an article the purpose, or one of the purposes, of which is the performance of an electronic function and which consists of two or more layers, at least one of which is composed of semiconducting material and in or upon one or more of which is fixed a pattern appertaining to that or another function; and

1 S.I. 1987/448.
2 1972 c.68.
3 1988 c.48.

'semiconductor topography' means a design within the meaning of section 213(2) of the Act which is a design of either of the following:

    (a) the pattern fixed, or intended to be fixed, in or upon—

        (i) a layer of a semiconductor product, or

        (ii) a layer of material in the course of and for the purpose of the manufacture of a semiconductor product, or

    (b) the arrangement of the patterns fixed, or intended to be fixed, in or upon the layers of a semiconductor product in relation to one another.

(2) Except where the context otherwise requires, these Regulations shall be construed as one with Part III of the Act (design right).

Application of Copyright, Designs and Patents Act 1988, Part III

3. In its application to a design which is a semiconductor topography, Part III of the Act shall have effect subject to regulations 4 to 9 below.

Qualification

4.—(1) Section 213(5) of the Act has effect subject to paragraphs (2) to (4) below.

(2) Part III of the Act has effect as if for section 217 of the Act there was substituted the following:

'217.—(1) In this Part—

"qualifying individual" means a citizen or subject of, or an individual habitually resident in, a qualifying country; and

"qualifying person" means—

    (a) a qualifying individual,

    (b) a body corporate or other body having legal personality which has in any qualifying country or in Gibraltar a place of business at which substantial business activity is carried on, or

    (c) a person who falls within one of the additional classes set out in Part I of the Schedule to the Design Right (Semiconductor Topographies) Regulations 1989.

(2) References in this Part to a qualifying person include the Crown and the government of any other qualifying country.

(3) In this section "qualifying country" means—

    (a) the United Kingdom, or

    (b) another member State of the European Economic Community.

(4) The reference in the definition of "qualifying individual" to a person's being a citizen or subject of a qualifying country shall be construed in relation to the United Kingdom as a reference to his being a British citizen.

(5) In determining for the purpose of the definition of "qualifying person" whether substantial business activity is carried on at a place of business in any country, no account shall be taken of dealings in goods which are at all material times outside the country.'

(3) Where a semiconductor topography is created in pursuance of a commission or in the course of employment and the designer of the topography is, by virtue of section 215 of the Act (as substituted by regulation 5 below), the first owner of design right in that topography, section 219 of the Act does not apply and section 218(2) to (4) of the Act shall apply to the topography as if it had not been created in pursuance of a commission or in the course of employment.

(4) Section 220 of the Act has effect subject to regulation 7 below and as if for sub-section (1) there was substituted the following:

'220.—(1) A design which does not qualify for design right protection under section 218 or 219 (as modified by regulation 4(3) of the Design Right (Semiconductor Topographies) Regulations 1989) or under the said regulation 4(3) qualifies for design right protection if the first marketing of articles made to the design—
(a) is by a qualifying person who is exclusively authorised to put such articles on the market in every member State of the European Economic Community, and
(b) takes place within the territory of any member State.';

and subsection (4) of section 220 accordingly has effect as if the words 'in the United Kingdom' were omitted.

Ownership of design right

5.—Part III of the Act has effect as if for section 215 of the Act there was substituted the following:

'215.—(1) The designer is the first owner of any design right in a design which is not created in pursuance of a commission or in the course of employment.
(2) Where a design is created in pursuance of a commission, the person commissioning the design is the first owner of any design right in it subject to any agreement in writing to the contrary.
(3) Where, in a case not falling within subsection (2) a design is created by an employee in the course of his employment, his employer is the first owner of any design right in the design subject to any agreement in writing to the contrary.
(4) If a design qualifies for design right protection by virtue of section 220 (as modified by regulation 4(4) of the Design Right (Semiconductor Topographies) Regulations 1989), the above rules do not apply and, subject to regulation 7 of the said Regulations, the person by whom the articles in question are marketed is the first owner of the design right.'

Duration of design right

6.—(1) Part III of the Act has effect as if for section 216 of the Act there was substituted the following:

'216. The design right in a semiconductor topography expires—
(a) ten years from the end of the calendar year in which the topography or articles made to the topography were first made available for sale or hire anywhere in the world by or with the licence of the design right owner, or
(b) if neither the topography nor articles made to the topography are so made available within a period of fifteen years commencing with the earlier of the time when the topography was first recorded in a design document or the time when an article was first made to the topography, at the end of that period.'

(2) Subsection (2) of section 263 of the Act has effect as if the words 'or a semiconductor topography' were inserted after the words 'in relation to an article'.

(3) The substitute provision set out in paragraph (1) above has effect subject to regulation 7 below.

Confidential information

7. In determining, for the purposes of section 215(4), 216 or 220 of the Act (as modified by these Regulations), whether there has been any marketing, or anything has been made available for sale or hire, no account shall be taken of any sale or hire, or any offer or exposure for sale or hire, which is subject to an obligation of confidence in respect of information about the semiconductor topography in question unless either—

(a) the article or semiconductor topography sold or hired or offered or exposed for sale or hire has been sold or hired on a previous occasion (whether or not subject to an obligation of confidence), or

(b) the obligation is imposed at the behest of the Crown, or of the government of any country outside the United Kingdom, for the protection of security in connection with the production of arms, munitions or war material.

Infringement

8.—(1) Section 226 of the Act has effect as if for subsection (1) there was substituted the following:

'226.—(1) Subject to subsection (1A), the owner of design right has the exclusive right to reproduce the design—
(a) by making articles to that design, or
(b) by making a design document recording the design for the purpose of enabling such articles to be made.
(1A) Subsection (1) does not apply to—
(a) the reproduction of a design privately for non-commercial aims; or
(b) the reproduction of a design for the purpose of analysing or evaluating the design or analysing, evaluating or teaching the concepts, processes, systems or techniques embodied in it.'

(2) Section 227 of the Act does not apply if the article in question has previously been sold or hired within—

(a) the United Kingdom by or with the licence of the owner of design right in the semiconductor topography in question, or

(b) the territory of any other member State of the European Economic Community or the territory of Gibraltar by or with the consent of the person for the time being entitled to import it into or sell or hire it within that territory.

(3) Section 228(6) of the Act does not apply.

(4) It is not an infringement of design right in a semiconductor topography to—

(a) create another original semiconductor topography as a result of an analysis or evaluation of the first topography or of the concepts, processes, systems or techniques embodied in it, or

(b) reproduce that other topography.

(5) Anything which would be an infringement of the design right in a semiconductor topography if done in relation to the topography as a whole is an infringement of the design right in the topography if done in relation to a substantial part of the topography.

Licences of right

9.—Section 237 of the Act does not apply.

Revocation and transitional provisions

10.—(1) The Semiconductor Products (Protection of Topography) Regulations 1987[4] are hereby revoked.

(2) Sub-paragraph (1) of paragraph 19 of Schedule 1 to the Act shall not apply in respect of a semiconductor topography created between 7th November 1987 and 31st July 1989.

(3) In its application to copyright in a semiconductor topography created before 7th November 1987, sub-paragraph (2) of the said paragraph 19 shall have effect as if the reference to sections 237 to 239 were a reference to sections 238 and 239; and sub-paragraph (3) of that paragraph accordingly shall not apply to such copyright.

Eric Forth
Parliamentary Under Secretary of State,
29th June 1989   Department of Trade and Industry

SCHEDULE
ADDITIONAL CLASSES OF QUALIFYING PERSONS

Part I

Descriptions of additional classes

1. British Dependent Territory citizens.

2. Citizens and subjects of any country specified in Part II or III below.

3. Habitual residents of any country specified in Part II or III below, the Isle of Man, the Channel Islands or any colony.

4. Firms and bodies corporate formed under the law of, or of any part of, the United Kingdom, Gibraltar, another member State of the European Economic Community or any country specified in Part II below with a place of business within any country so specified at which substantial business activity is carried on.

Part II

Specified countries: citizens, subjects, habitual residents, bodies corporate and other bodies having legal personality

Japan
Switzerland
United States of America

4   S.I. 1987/1497.

Part III

Specified countries: citizens, subjects and habitual residents only

Austria
Finland
French overseas territories (French Polynesia; French Southern and Antarctic Territories; Mayotte; New Caledonia and dependencies; Saint-Pierre and Miquelon; Wallis and Futuna Islands)
Iceland
Norway
Sweden

Index